Top 40 Democracy

Top 40 Democracy

The Rival Mainstreams of American Music

ERIC WEISBARD

THE UNIVERSITY OF CHICAGO PRESS   CHICAGO AND LONDON

ERIC WEISBARD is assistant professor of American studies at the University of Alabama and the founder and longtime organizer of the acclaimed EMP Pop Conference.

The University of Chicago Press, Chicago 60637
The University of Chicago Press, Ltd., London
© 2014 by Eric Weisbard
All rights reserved. Published 2014.
Printed in the United States of America

23 22 21 20 19 18 17 16 15 14   1 2 3 4 5

ISBN-13: 978-0-226-89616-8 (cloth)
ISBN-13: 978-0-226-89618-2 (paper)
ISBN-13: 978-0-226-19437-0 (e-book)
DOI: 10.7208/chicago/9780226194370.001.0001

Library of Congress Cataloging-in-Publication Data

Weisbard, Eric, author.
    Top 40 democracy: the rival mainstreams of American music / Eric Weisbard.
        pages ; cm
    Includes bibliographical references and index.
    ISBN 978-0-226-89616-8 (cloth: alk. paper)—ISBN 978-0-226-89618-2 (pbk.: alk. paper)—
ISBN 978-0-226-19437-0 (e-book) 1. Radio programs, Musical—United States—History—
20th century. 2. Popular music radio stations—United States—History—20th century.
3. Popular music—United States—History—20th century. 4. Popular music genres—
United States—History—20th century. 5. Format radio broadcasting—United States—
History—20th century. I. Title. II. Title: Top forty democracy.
    ML68.W435 2014
    781.640973—dc23   2014017517

♾ This paper meets the requirements of ANSI/NISO Z39.48-1992 (Permanence of Paper).

Contents

Introduction

Let's begin with the radio in the 1979 Chevy Nova my grandma Cele gave me. A volume knob, a tuning knob, and five preset buttons for cementing a relationship with AM radio—that was it. At one point, driving, I came upon a venerable Top 40 DJ from Philadelphia who called himself the Geator with the Heater. Later, after hauling the indestructible green machine to the West Coast, I wondered at the Quiet Storm shows on KDIA that took Oakland soul listeners into sleep. In those same Bay Area years, circa 1989–92, Hot New Country was flourishing on my Nova. For an indie rocker who'd spun records on college radio by groups with names like Butthole Surfers, this country stuff beamed in from another planet. But as a captive to the Garth, Trisha, Clint, and Wynonna flow, I learned to hear another format on its own terms: the small rebellions and innovations that made sense when set against a constancy of sound and attitudes.

Keep those car buttons in mind for a bit longer. Each potentially represented a separate music format: Top 40, adult contemporary, rhythm and blues, country, or album-oriented rock. And each station played, consistently, proven hit records, whose basic qualities a regular listener could anticipate even before pushing the button. The identity of those listeners varied as much as the music did, to let advertisers target different consumer segments. In the 1950s, Top 40 had emerged as a programming style to help radio compensate for television's absconding with syndicated network shows. By the mid-1970s, the format system I will focus on offered different musical flavors of Top 40, rooted in divisions of age, gender, race, region, and economics but also blurring and crossing between those rival categories. The result was a particular model of commercialized cultural pluralism: a formatting of publics.

Radio formats created, I'll argue in this book, multiple mainstreams: distinct, if at times overlapping, cultural centers. While songs could not offend, and cause listeners to punch a different button, they were equally obliged to stir feeling, to strike a chord that would resonate more with repeat exposure—a process connecting listeners as a group. "Hound Dog," "Will You Love Me Tomorrow," "Dream On," "He Stopped Loving Her Today," "Say My Name": each of these hits from different decades, for those who had the radio on, still generate emotional allegiances. The objective of formats was to garner ads and sell records, but a flow of songs and banter had to be shaped and polished, an audience had to be defined. Formats did not just sell music—they normalized it. Formats did not just sell products—they touted categories of consumers.

Formats fascinate me as the opposite of everything that serious music fans value. I started this book with a particular goal: to understand the history not of rock and pop but of what has been called "rockism" and "poptimism"—the idea of commercial pop as a brain-dead wasteland that only the best and most authentic artists could resist, or, conversely, the rejoinder that pop offered pleasures that rock bigotry utterly missed. I'd hated rock orthodoxy of another kind in my days as a music critic, championing bands that sold few records but still mattered as much, cre- atively, as the Woodstock gang. The bigger story, it seemed as I began conceptualizing, was a mainstream one, how the range of hits produced by the supposedly stifling corporate structures of radio and records effortlessly—and without an ounce of idealism required—exceeded rock in its range of sounds, artists, audience, and creativity. Could one account for this, but also for the fact that so much eclecticism had been met with so much scorn?

Only, I have come to believe, by expanding how we hear music. DJs who rely on segues learn to notice how records begin and end; crate-digging hip-hop producers fixate on beats to sample. But one can also register songs as winners or losers in an endless recalibrating of formats—as on or off the soundtrack of their invented communities. "This song put me in the middle of the road," Neil Young famously wrote about "Heart of Gold," his 1972 Top 40 chart topper. "Traveling there soon became a bore so I headed for the ditch. A rougher ride but I met more interesting peo- ple there." In Young's rhetoric, it's better to burn out than to fade away, and rock and roll can never die. With formats steering the conversation, however, a reasonable question would be how *did* "Heart of Gold" put Young in MOR, the adult pop format? *Billboard*'s Easy Listening chart has the song cresting at number 8. "A Horse with No Name," by America, did better, hitting number 3 with a similar post-hippie mellowness. The middle had shifted: MOR, a format of Frank Sinatra types, now stretched to incorporate baby boom counterculture. MOR was becoming adult contemporary (AC): not the stuff of anthems like "Hey Hey, My My," but consequential for all that music informed—leisure choices and fashion; gender, sexuality, and manners; a notion of the good life turning from jazz's swinger urbanity to singer-songwriter rock's contemporary casual.

Formats let music occupy a niche in capitalism and—as with Johnny Carson's *Tonight Show*, with its monologue and interviews structure and MOR appeal—connect music to other show-business realms as well. Genres are different. Ordinary people don't proudly identify with formats, but some do identify with genres. One can have a hit song that goes "I was born country"; probably not "I was born adult contemporary." Music formats like MOR, AC, and Top 40 were crossover spaces, with no single dominant genre. A trickier category is music, like country, with both format and genre identity, making for something more porous in definition than honky-tonk, soul, or that Bruce Springsteen fans might prefer. Black-oriented pop divided between rhythm and blues (R&B), a format, and soul or hip-hop genres. Rock, in its 1970s form, was the Uncola of formats: a lucrative format posing as a rebel genre. Music genres, more inherently ideological, chafe at formats, with their centrist, commercial disposition.

Yet the very commercial tendencies that made radio formats, and the music they implanted in our consciousness, suspect aesthetically also made them trailblazers for the sounds, artists, and listeners left out by all that genre certainty. Formats, radio, and pop music deserve a much bigger place in the history of American culture than accounts rooted in genre and isolated records have afforded them. Their homogenizing tendencies popularized and routinized each eruption from the countercultural 1960s and 1970s and MTV 1980s to the grunge, gangsta, and new country 1990s. But equally important was this center's ability to redirect music as a social force: from "serious" fans who were often straight, white, male, and affluent to listeners less vocal and coherent but no less invested in what they heard. That tension structures this book. The safe radio pop that so many commentators have reviled for so many valid reasons opened as many doors as it closed.

My hope in what follows is to convince you that we can benefit from learning to think about music in the manner of the radio stations feeding sound into my old Chevy Nova and the record industry that generated the songs those stations needed for airplay: in terms of formats and the artists

and publics who embodied them. The payoff would be this: we'd redis-
cover the middle of American culture as a place at least as complicated,
diverse, and surprising as the margins.

The Logic of Formats

Nearly every history of Top 40 launches from an anecdote about how
radio station manager Todd Storz came up with the idea sometime between World War II and the early 1950s, watching with friends in a bar
in Omaha as customers repeatedly punched up the same few songs on
the jukebox. A waitress, after hearing the tunes for hours, paid for more
listens, though she was unable to explain herself. "When they asked why,
she replied, simply: 'I like 'em.'" As Storz said on another occasion, "Why
this should be, I don't know. But I saw waitresses do this time after time."
He resolved to program a radio station following the same principles: the
hits and nothing but the hits.[1]

Storz's *aha* moment has much to tell about Top 40's complicated relationship to musical diversity. He might be seen as an entrepreneur with his
ear to the ground, like the 1920s furniture salesman who insisted hillbilly
music be recorded or the 1970s Fire Island dancer who created remixes
to extend the beat. Or he could be viewed as a schlockmeister lowering
standards for an inarticulate public, especially women—so often conceived as mass-cultural dupes. Though sponsored broadcasting had been
part of radio in America, unlike much of the rest of the world, since its
beginnings, Top 40 raised hackles in a postwar era concerned about the
numbing effects of mass culture. "We become a jukebox without lights,"
the Radio Advertising Bureau's Kevin Sweeney complained. *Time* called
Storz the "King of the Giveaway" and complained of broadcasting "well
larded with commercials."[2]

Storz and those who followed answered demands that licensed stations serve a communal good by calling playlist catholicity a democracy
of sound: "If the public suddenly showed a preference for Chinese music,
we would play it . . . I do not believe there is any such thing as better or
inferior music." Top 40 programmer Chuck Blore, responding to charges
that formats stifled creative DJs, wrote, "He may not be as free to inflict
his musical taste on the public, but now, and rightfully, I think, the public
dictates the popular music of the day." Mike Joseph boasted, "When I
first go into a market, I go into every record store personally. I'll spend

up to three weeks doing interviews, with an average of forty-five minutes each. And I get every single thing I can get: the sales on every configuration, every demo for every single, the gender of every buyer, the race of every buyer. . . . I follow the audience flow of the market around the clock." Ascertaining public taste became a matter of extravagant claim for these professional intermediaries: broadcasting divided into "dayparts" to impact commuters, housewives, or students.[3]

Complicating the tension between seeing formats as pandering or as deferring to popular taste was a formal quality that Top 40 also shared with the jukebox: it could encompass many varieties of hits *or* group a subset for a defined public. This duality blurred categories we often keep separate. American show business grew from blackface minstrelsy and its performative rather than innate notion of identity—pop as striking a pose, animating a mask, putting on style or a musical. More folk and genre-derived notions of group identity, by contrast, led to the authenticity-based categories of rock, soul, hip-hop, and country.[4] Top 40 formats drew on both modes, in constantly recalibrated proportions. And in doing so, the logic of formats, especially the 1970s format system that assimilated genres, unsettled notions of real and fake music.

Go back to Storz's jukebox. In the late 1930s, jukeboxes revived a record business collapsed by free music on radio and the Great Depression. Jack Kapp in particular, working for the US branch of British-owned Decca, tailored the records he handled to boom from the pack: swing jazz dance beats, slangy vernacular from black urban culture, and significant sexual frankness. This capitalized on qualities inherent in recordings, which separated sound from its sources in place, time, and community, allowing both new artifice—one did not know where the music came from, exactly— and new realism: one might value, permanently, the warble of a certain voice, suggesting a certain origin. Ella Fitzgerald, eroticizing the nursery rhyme "A-Tisket, A-Tasket" in 1938 on Decca, with Chick Webb's band behind her, could bring more than a hint of Harlem's Savoy Ballroom to a place like Omaha, as jukeboxes helped instill a national youth culture. Other jukeboxes highlighted the cheating songs of honky-tonk country or partying R&B: urban electrifications of once-rural sounds. By World War II, pop was as much these brash cross-genre jukebox blends as it was the Broadway-Hollywood-network radio axis promoting Irving Berlin's genteel "White Christmas."[5]

Todd Storz's notion of Top 40 put the jukebox on the radio. Records had not always been a radio staple. Syndicated network stations avoided

"canned music"; record labels feared the loss of sales and often stamped
"Not Licensed for Radio Broadcast" on releases. So the shift that followed
television's taking original network programming was twofold: local radio
broadcasting that relied on a premade consumer product. Since there
were many more records to choose from than network shows, localized
Top 40 fed a broader trend that allowed an entrepreneurial capitalism—
independent record-label owners such as Sam Phillips of Sun Records,
synergists such as *American Bandstand* host Dick Clark, or station managers such as Storz—to compete with corporations like William Paley's
Columbia Broadcasting System, the so-called Tiffany Network, which
included Columbia Records. The result, in part, was rock and roll, which
had emerged sonically by the late 1940s but needed the Top 40 system to
become dominant with young 45 RPM–singles buyers by the end of the
1950s.[6]

An objection immediately presents itself, one that will recur throughout this study: Was Top 40 rock and roll at all, or a betrayal of the rockabilly wildness that Sam Phillips's roster embodied for the fashioning of
safe teen idols by Dick Clark? Did the format destroy the genre? The best
answer interrogates the question: Didn't the commerce-first pragmatism
of formatting, with its weak boundaries, free performers and fans inhibited
by tighter genre codes? For Susan Douglas, the girl group records of the
early 1960s made possible by Top 40 defy critics who claim that rock died
between Elvis Presley's army induction and the arrival of the Beatles. Yes,
hits like "Leader of the Pack" were created by others, often men, and were
thoroughly commercial. Yes, they pulled punches on gender roles even as
they encouraged girls to identify with young male rebels. But they "gave
voice to all the warring selves inside us struggling." White girls admired
black girls, just as falsetto harmonizers like the Beach Boys allowed girls
singing along to assume male roles in "nothing less than musical cross-
dressing." Top 40's "euphoria of commercialism," Douglas argues, did
more than push product; "tens of millions of young girls started feeling, at
the same time, that they, as a generation, would not be trapped." Top 40,
like the jukebox before it and MTV afterward, channeled cultural democracy: spread it but contained it within a regulated, commercialized path.[7]

We can go back further than jukebox juries becoming American Band-
stands. Ambiguities between democratic culture and commodification
are familiar within cultural history. As Jean-Christophe Agnew points out
in his study *Worlds Apart*, the theater and the marketplace have been
inextricable for centuries, caught up as capitalism developed in "the fundamental problematic of a placeless market: the problems of identity,

intentionality, accountability, transparency, and reciprocity that the pursuit of commensurability invariably introduces into that universe of par-
ticulate human meanings we call culture." Agnew's history ranges from
Shakespeare to Melville's *Confidence Man*, published in 1857. At that
point in American popular culture, white entertainers often performed
in blackface, jumping Jim Crow and then singing a plaintive "Ethiopian"
melody by Stephen Foster. Eric Lott's book on minstrelsy gives this racial
mimicry a handy catchphrase: *Love and Theft*. Tarred-up actors, giddy
with the new freedoms of a white man's democracy but threatened by
industrial "wage slavery," embodied cartoonish blacks for social comment
and anti-bourgeois rudeness. Amid vicious racial stereotyping could be
found performances that respectable theater disavowed. Referring to
a popular song of the era, typically performed in drag, the *New York
Tribune* wrote in 1853, " 'Lucy Long' was sung by a white negro as a
male female danced." And because of minstrelsy's fixation on blackness,
African Americans after the Civil War found an entry of sorts into entertainment: as songwriter W. C. Handy unceremoniously put it, "The best
talent of that generation came down the same drain. The composers, the
singers, the musicians, the speakers, the stage performers—the minstrel
shows got them all." If girl groups showcase liberating possibility in commercial constraints, minstrelsy challenges unreflective celebration.[8]

Entertainment, as it grew into the brashest industry of modernizing
America, fused selling and singing as a matter of orthodoxy. The three-act
minstrel show stamped formats on show business early on, with its song-
and-dance opening, variety-act olio, and dramatic afterpiece, its interlocu-
tors and end men. Such structures later migrated to variety, vaudeville,
and Broadway. After the 1890s, tunes were supplied by Tin Pan Alley
sheet-music publishers, who professionalized formula songwriting and
invented "payola"—ethically dubious song plugging. These were song
factories, unsentimental about creativity, yet the evocation of cheap tin-
niness in the name was deliberately outrageous, announcing the arrival
of new populations—Siberian-born Irving Berlin, for example, the Jew
who wrote "White Christmas." Tin Pan Alley's strictures of form but multiplicity of identity paved the way for the Brill Building teams who wrote
the girl group songs, the Motown Records approach to mainstreaming
African American hits, and even millennial hitmakers from Korean "K-
Pop" to Sweden's Cheiron Studios. Advertisers, Timothy Taylor's history
demonstrates, used popular music attitude as early as they could—sheet-
music parodies, jingles, and the showmanship of radio hosts like crooner
Rudy Vallee designed to give products "ginger, pep, sparkle, and snap."

The Lucky Strike Hit Parade, a Top 40 forerunner with in-house vocalists performing the leading tunes, was "music for advertising's sake," its conductor said in 1941.[9]

Radio, which arrived in the 1920s, was pushed away from a BBC model and toward what Thomas Streeter calls "corporate liberalism" by leaders like Herbert Hoover, who declared as commerce secretary, "We should not imitate some of our foreign colleagues with governmentally controlled broadcasting supported by a tax upon the listener." In the years after the 1927 Radio Act, the medium consolidated around sponsor-supported syndicated network shows, successfully making radio present by 1940 in 86 percent of American homes and some 6.5 million cars, with average listening of four hours a day. The programming, initially local, now fused the topsy-turvy theatrics of vaudeville and minstrelsy—*Amos 'n' Andy* ranked for years with the most popular programs—with love songs and soap operas aimed at the feminized intimacy of the bourgeois parlor. Radio's mass orientation meant immigrants used it to embrace a mainstream American identity; women confessed sexual feelings for the likes of Vallee as part of the bushels of letters sent to favored broadcasters; and *Vox Pop* invented the "man on the street" interview, connecting radio's commercialized public with more traditional political discourse and the Depression era's documentary impulse. While radio scholars have rejected the view of an authoritarian, manipulative "culture industry," classically associated with writers such as the Frankfurt School's Theodor Adorno, historian Elena Razlogova offers an important qualification: "by the 1940s both commercial broadcasters and empirical social scientists . . . shared Adorno's belief in expert authority and passive emotional listening." Those most skeptical of mass culture often worked inside the beast.[10]

Each network radio program had a format. So, for example, Kate Smith, returning for a thirteenth radio season in 1942, offered a three-act structure within each broadcast: a song and comedy slot, ad, drama, ad, and finally a segment devoted to patriotism—fitting for the singer of "God Bless America." She was said by *Billboard,* writing with the slangy prose that characterized knowing and not fully genteel entertainment professionals, to have a show that "retains the format which, tho often heavy handed and obvious, is glovefit to keep the tremendous number of listeners it has acquired and do a terrific selling job for the sponsor"—General Foods. The trade journal insisted, "Next to a vocal personality, a band on the air needs a format—an idea, a framework of showmanship."[11]

Top 40 formats addressed the same need to fit broadcast, advertiser, and public, but through a different paradigm: what one branded with an on-air jukebox approach was now the radio station itself, to multiple sponsors. Early on, Top 40s competed with nonformat stations, the "full service" AM's that relied on avuncular announcers with years of experience, in-house news, community bulletins, and songs used as filler. As formats came to dominate, with even news and talk stations formatted for consistent sound, competing sonic configurations hailed different demographics. But no format was pure: to secure audience share in a crowded market, a programmer might emphasize a portion of a format (Quiet Storm R&B) or blur formats (country crossed with easy listening). Subcategories proliferated, creating what a 1978 how-to book called "the radio format conundrum." The authors, listing biz slang along the lines of *MOR*, *Good Music*, and *Chicken Rock*, explained, "Words are coined, distorted and mutilated, as the programmer looks for ways to label or tag a format, a piece of music, a frame of mind."[12]

A framework of showmanship in 1944 had become a frame of mind in 1978. Formats began as theatrical structures but evolved into marketing devices—efforts to convince sponsors of the link between a mediated product and its never fully quantifiable audience. Formats did not idealize culture; they sold it. They structured eclecticism rather than imposing aesthetic values. It was the customer's money—a democracy of whatever moved people.

The Counterlogic of Genres

At about the same time Todd Storz watched the action at a jukebox in Omaha, sociologist David Riesman was conducting in-depth interviews with young music listeners. Most, he found, were fans of what was popular—uncritical. But a minority of interviewees disliked "name bands, most vocalists (except Negro blues singers), and radio commercials." They felt "a profound resentment of the commercialization of radio and musicians." They were also, Riesman reported, overwhelmingly male.[13]

American music in the twentieth century was vital to the creation of what Grace Hale's account calls "a nation of outsiders." "Hot jazz" adherents raved about Louis Armstrong's solos in the 1920s, while everybody else thought it impressive enough that Paul Whiteman's orchestra could syncopate the Charleston and introduce "Rhapsody in Blue." By the 1930s, the in-crowd were Popular Front aligned, riveted at the pointedly misnamed cabaret Café Society, where doormen had holes in their gloves and Billie Holiday made the anti-lynching, anti-minstrelsy "Strange Fruit" stop all breathing. Circa Riesman's study, the hipsters Norman Mailer and Jack Kerouac would celebrate redefined hot as cool, seeding a 1960s San Francisco scene that turned hipsters into hippie counterculture.[14]

But the urge to value music as an authentic expression of identity appealed well beyond outsider scenes and subcultures. Hank Williams testified, "When a hillbilly sings a crazy song, he feels crazy. When he sings, 'I Laid My Mother Away,' he sees her a-laying right there in the coffin. He sings more sincere than most entertainers because the hillbilly was raised rougher than most entertainers. You got to know a lot about hard work. You got to have smelt a lot of mule manure before you can sing like a hillbilly. The people who has been raised something like the way the hillbilly has knows what he is singing about and appreciates it." Loretta Lynn reduced this to a chorus: "If you're looking at me, you're looking at country." Soul, rock, and hip-hop offered similar sentiments. An inherently folkloric valuation of popular music, Karl Miller has written, "so thoroughly trounced minstrelsy that historians rarely discuss the process of its ascendance. The folkloric paradigm is the air that we breathe."[15]

For this study, I want to combine subcultural outsiders and identity-group notions of folkloric authenticity into a single opposition to formats: genres. If entertainment formats are an undertheorized category of analysis, though a widely used term, genres have been highly theorized. By sticking with popular music, however, we can identify a few accepted notions. Music genres have rules: socially constructed and accepted codes of form, meaning, and behavior. Those who recognize and are shaped by these rules belong to what pioneering pop scholar Simon Frith calls "genre worlds": configurations of musicians, listeners, and figures mediating between them who collectively create a sense of inclusivity and exclusivity. Genres range from highly specific avant-gardes to scenes, industry categories, and revivals, with large genre "streams" to feed subgenres. If music genres cannot be viewed—as their adherents might prefer—as existing outside of commerce and media, they do share a common aversion: to pop shapelessness.[16]

Deconstructing genre ideology within music can be as touchy as insisting on minstrelsy's centrality: from validating Theft to spitting in the face of Love. Producer and critic John Hammond, progressive in music and politics, gets rewritten as the man who told Duke Ellington that one of his most ambitious compositions featured "slick, un-negroid musicians," guilty of "aping Tin Pan Alley composers for commercial reasons." A Hammond obsession, 1930s Mississippi blues guitarist Robert Johnson has his credentials to be called "King of the Delta Blues" and revered by the likes of Bob Dylan, Eric Clapton, and the Rolling Stones questioned by those who want to know why Delta blues, as a category, was invented and sanctified after the fact and how that undercut more urban and vaudeville-inflected, not to mention female, "classic" blues singers such as Ma Rainey, Mamie Smith, and Bessie Smith.[17]

The tug-of-war between format and genre, performative theatrics and folkloric authenticity, came to a head with rock, the commercially and critically dominant form of American music from the late 1960s to the early 1990s. Fifties rock and roll had been the music of black as much as white Americans, southern as much as northern, working class far more than middle class. Rock was both less inclusive and more ideological: what Robert Christgau, aware of the politics of the shift from his first writing as a founding rock critic, called "all music deriving primarily from the energy and influence of the Beatles—and maybe Bob Dylan, and maybe you should stick pretensions in there someplace." Ellen Willis, another pivotal early critic, centered her analysis of the change on the rock audience's artistic affiliations: "I loved rock and roll, but I felt no emotional identification with the performers. Elvis Presley was my favorite singer, and I bought all his records; just the same, he was a stupid, slicked-up hillbilly, a bit too fat and soft to be really good-looking, and I was a middle-class adolescent snob." Listening to Mick Jagger of the Rolling Stones was a far different process: "I couldn't condescend to him—his 'vulgarity' represented a set of social and aesthetic attitudes as sophisticated as mine."[18]

The hippies gathered at Woodstock were Riesman's minority segment turned majority, but with a difference. They no longer esteemed contemporary versions of "Negro blues singers": only three black artists played Woodstock. Motown-style format pop was dismissed as fluff in contrast to English blues-rock and other music with an overt genre lineage. Top 40 met disdain, as new underground radio centered on "freeform"—meaning free of format. Music critics like Christgau, Willis, and Frith challenged these assumptions at the time, with Frith's *Sound Effects* the strongest account of rock's hypocritical "intimations of sincerity, authenticity, art—noncommercial concerns," even as "rock became the record industry." In a nation of outsiders, rock ruled, or as a leftist history, *Rock 'n' Roll Is Here to Pay*, snarked, "Music for Music's Sake Means More Money." Keir Keightley elaborates, "One of the great ironies of the second half of the twentieth century is that while rock has involved millions of people buying a mass-marketed, standardized commodity (CD, cassette, LP) that is available virtually everywhere, these purchases have produced intense feelings of freedom, rebellion, marginality, oppositionality, uniqueness and authenticity." In 1979, rock fans led by a rock radio DJ blew up disco records; as late as 2004, Kelefa Sanneh felt the need to deconstruct rockism in the *New York Times*.[19]

Yet it would be simplistic to reduce rockism to its disproportions of race, gender, class, and sexuality. What fueled and fuels such attitudes toward popular music, ones hardly limited to rock alone, is the dream of music as democratic in a way opposite to how champions of radio formats justified their playlists. Michael Kramer, in an account of rock far more sympathetic than most others of late, argues that the countercultural era refashioned the bourgeois public sphere for a mass bohemia: writers and fans debated in music publications, gathered with civic commitment at music festivals, and shaped freeform radio into a community instrument. From the beginning, "hip capitalism" battled movement concerns, but the notion of music embodying anti-commercial beliefs, of rock as revolutionary or at least progressive, was genuine.[20] The unity of the rock audience gave it more commercial clout: not just record sales, but arena-sized concerts, the most enduring music publication in *Rolling Stone*, and ultimately a Rock and Roll Hall of Fame to debate rock against rock and roll or pop forever. Discursively, if not always in commercial reality, this truly was the Rock Era.

The mostly female listeners of the Top 40 pop formats bequeathed by Storz's jukebox thus confronted, on multiple levels, the mostly male listeners of a rock genre that traced back to the anti-commercial contingent of Riesman's interviewees. A democracy of hit songs, limited by its capitalist nature, was challenged by a democracy of genre identity, limited by its demographic narrowness. The multi-category Top 40 strands I will be examining were shaped by this enduring tension.

Pop Music in the Rock Era

Jim Ladd, a DJ at the Los Angeles freeform station KASH-FM, received a rude awakening in 1969 when a new program director laid down some rules. "We would not be playing any Top 40 bullshit, but real rock 'n' roll; and there was no dress code. There would, however, be something known as 'the format.'" Ladd was now told what to play. He writes bitterly about those advising stations. "The radio consultant imposed a statistical grid over the psychedelic counterculture, and reduced it to demographic research. Do you want men 18–24, adults 18–49, women 35–49, or is your target audience teens? Whatever it may be, the radio consultant had a formula." Nonetheless, the staff was elated when, in 1975, KASH beat Top 40 KHJ, "because to us, it represented everything that we were trying to change in radio. Top 40 was slick, mindless pop pap, without one second of social involvement in its format." Soon however, KAOS topped KASH with a still tighter format: "balls-out rock 'n' roll."[21]

Ladd's memoir, for all its biases, demonstrates despite itself why it would be misleading to view rock/pop or genre/format dichotomies as absolute divisions. By the mid-1970s, album-oriented rock (AOR) stations, like soul and country channels, pursued a format strategy as much as Top 40 or AC, guided by consultants and quarterly ratings. Rock programmers who used genre rhetoric of masculine rebellion ("balls-out rock 'n' roll") still honored Storz's precept that most fans wanted the same songs repeated. Stations divided listeners explicitly by age and gender and tacitly by race and class. The division might be more inclusive: adults, 18–49; or less so: men, 18–34. The "psychedelic counterculture" ideal of dropping out from the mass had faded, but so had some of the mass: crossover appeal was one, not always desirable, demographic. And genre longings remained, with Ladd's rockist disparagement of Top 40 symptomatic: many, including those in the business, quested for "social involvement" and disdained format tyranny. If AOR was formatted à la pop, pop became more like rock and soul, as seen in the power ballad, which merged rock's amplification of sound and self with churchy and therapeutic exhortation.[22]

Pop music in the rock era encompassed two strongly appealing, sometimes connected, but more often opposed impulses. The logic of formats celebrated the skillful matching of a set of songs with a set of people: its proponents idealized generating audiences, particularly new audiences, and prided themselves on figuring out what people wanted to hear. To believe in formats could mean playing it safe, with the reliance on experts and contempt for audiences that Razlogova describes in an earlier radio era: one cliché in radio was that stations were never switched off for the songs they didn't play, only the ones they did. But there were strong business reasons to experiment with untapped consumer segments, to accentuate the "maturation" of a buying group with "contemporary"—a buzzword of the times—music to match. To successfully develop a new format, like the urban contemporary approach to black middle-class listeners, marked a great program director or consultant, and market-to-market experimentation in playlist emphasis was constant. Record companies, too, argued that a song like "Help Me Make It through the Night," Kris Kristofferson's explicit 1971 hit for Sammi Smith, could attract classier listeners for the country stations that played it.

By contrast, the logic of genres—accentuated by an era of countercul- ture, black power, feminism, and even conservative backlash—celebrated the creative matching of a set of songs and a set of ideals: music as artistic expression, communal statement, and coherent heritage. These were not necessarily anti-commercial impulses. Songwriters had long since learned the financial reasons to craft a lasting Broadway standard, rather than cash in overnight with a disposable Tin Pan Alley ditty. As Keightley shows, the career artist, steering his or her own path, was adult pop's gift to the rock superstars. Frank Sinatra, Chairman of the Board, did not only symboli- cally transform into Neil Young, driving into the ditch if he chose. Young actually recorded for Reprise Records, the label that Sinatra had founded in 1960, whose president, Mo Ostin, went on to merge it with, and run, the artist-friendly and rock-dominated major label Warner Bros. Records.[23]

Contrast Ladd's or Young's sour view of formatting with Clive Davis, who took over as president of Columbia Records during the rise of the counterculture. Writing just after the regularizing of multiple Top 40 strands, Davis found the mixture of old-school entertainment and new- school pop categories he confronted, the tensions between format and genre, endlessly fascinating. He was happy to discourse on the reasons why an MOR release by Ray Conniff might outsell an attention-hogging album by Bob Dylan, then turn around and explain why playing Las Vegas had tainted the rock group Blood, Sweat & Tears by rebranding them as MOR. Targeting black albums, rather than singles, to music buy- ers intrigued him, and here he itemized how he accepted racial divisions as market realities, positioning funk's Earth, Wind & Fire as "progres- sive" to white rockers while courting soul nationalists too. "Black radio was also becoming increasingly militant; black program directors were refusing to *see* white promotion men. . . . If a record is ripe to be added to the black station's play list, but is not quite a sure thing, it is ridiculous to have a white man trying to convince the program director to put it on."[24]

The incorporation of genre by formats proved hugely successful from the 1970s to the 1990s. Categories of mainstream music multiplied, major record labels learned boutique approaches to rival indies in what Timo- thy Dowd calls "decentralized" music selling, and the global sounds that Israeli sociologist Motti Regev sums up as "pop-rock" fused national genres with a common international structure of hitmaking, fueled by the widespread licensing in the 1980s of commercial radio channels in countries formerly limited to government broadcasting. In 2000, I was given the opportunity, for a *New York Times* feature, to survey a list of the top 1,000 selling albums and top 200 artists by total US sales, as registered by SoundScan's barcode-scanning process since the service's introduction in 1991. The range was startling: twelve albums on the list by Nashville's Garth Brooks, but also twelve by the Beatles and more than twenty linked to the gangsta rappers in N.W.A. Female rocker Alanis Morissette topped the album list, with country and AC singer Shania Twain not far behind. Reggae's Bob Marley had the most popular back-catalogue album, with mammoth total sales for pre-rock vocalist Barbra Streisand and jazz's Miles Davis. Even "A Horse with No Name" still had fans: *America's Greatest Hits* made a top 1,000 list that was 30 percent artists over forty years old in 2000 and one-quarter 1990s teen pop like Backstreet Boys. Pop meant power ballads (Mariah Carey, Celine Dion), rock (Pink Floyd, Metallica, Pearl Jam), and Latin voices (Selena, Marc Anthony), five mellow new age Enya albums, and four noisy *Jock Jams* compilations.[25]

Yet nearly all this spectrum of sound was owned by a shrinking number of multinationals, joined as the 1990s ended by a new set of vast radio chains like Clear Channel, allowed by a 1996 Telecommunications Act in the corporate liberal spirit of the 1927 policies. The role of music in sparking countercultural liberation movements had matured into a well-understood range of scenes feeding into mainstreams, or train-wreck moments by tabloid pop stars appreciated with camp irony by omnivorous tastemakers. The tightly formatted world that Jim Ladd feared and Clive Davis coveted had come to pass. Was this true diversity, or a simulation? As Keith Negus found when he spoke with those participating in the global pop order, genre convictions still pressed against format pragmatism. Rock was overrepresented at record labels. Genre codes shaped the corporate cultures that framed the selling of country music, gangsta rap, and Latin pop. "The struggle is not *between* commerce and creativity," Negus concluded, "but about what is *to be* commercial and creative." The friction between competing notions of how to make and sell music had resulted in a staggering range of product, but also intractable disagreements over that product's value within cultural hierarchies.[26]

Top 40 Democracy in a Consumers' Republic

Clive Davis's invocation, above, of black power ideology impacting soul music merchandising is a reminder of the epochal history that formatting both reflected and skewed. The rise of Top 40, with its ties to black music, paralleled not only civil rights but also the companion notion of "selling the race." *Ebony*, a lifestyle magazine, launched in Chicago in 1945; Memphis's WDIA became a black-oriented radio station in 1948; *Billboard* renamed its race records section "Rhythm & Blues" in 1949. "Black radio made the 'Negro market' into a national reality," one study concludes, and Detroit's Motown Records, with innumerable Top 40 hits, defined black pop entrepreneurship exceeding the Negro market. Soul and funk rendered "Black Is Beautiful" something to show not tell, hitting on both black-oriented and Top 40 stations in a late sixties moment that saw dramatically expanded advertising aimed at African Americans.[27]

Still, the independently black-owned Motown, which signed the Jackson 5 in 1969, would not enjoy the greatest of jackpots: Michael Jackson's 1982 *Thriller*, the best-selling album of all time. That was Davis's CBS, whose black-music division had come to dominate R&B by offering ambitious performers the corporate heft to cross over on levels Motown had only dreamt about. Racially packaged music that no longer symbolized black enterprise had far different connotations: a ghetto, or in crossover a whitewashing. The 1987 NAACP Report "The Discordant Sound of Music" argued, "No other industry in America so openly classifies its operations on a racial basis. . . . The structure of the industry allows for total white control and domination."[28] Motown was sold to a multinational rival of CBS in 1988. Given this history, did formatting disperse black cultural nationalism or steal its most covetable qualities?

Chronology matters here, because the use of Top 40 for both identity and crossover categories, which began in earnest in the late 1960s and solidified by the mid-1970s, intersects two pivotal stories: the rise of new social movements (black power, hippie counterculture, feminism, gay liberation, the religious right), but also what Jefferson Cowie calls "the last days of the working class" as beneficiaries of industrial America's postwar prosperity. The multiple-formats system succeeded because spreading affluence justified accommodating different *collective* identities. Yet postindustrial trends after the early 1970s worked to widen wealth gaps. Neoliberalism, the notion that privatization unleashed productivity, favored yuppie and New Economy ideals of personalized consumption.[29] Here, one shopped to become different, not to validate a mass or group identity. Already divided against itself by genre/format and rock/pop dualities, the system of radio and records that peaked in the 1970s came under siege from these trends—advertiser insistence on reaching affluent buyers in the 25–54 category clashed with much of the pop music core audience. Top 40 itself, the mass-appeal approach of playing the widest variety of hits, was especially challenged, with stations abandoning the format at the onset of the 1980s and even more decisively in the early 1990s, but similar concerns faced black-oriented stations leery of playing hip-hop and rock stations whose heavy metal offerings were seen as blue collar in appeal.

Historians have debated the democratic legacy of consumerism for generations, with an initial, quite countercultural skepticism about advertising's "captains of consciousness" manipulating American values giving way to accounts that viewed ad makers as "apostles of modernity" or asserted agency on behalf of workers and women's leisure and spending choices. The revisionists then found their own revisionists, with Thomas Frank's *Conquest of Cool* viewing consumer "choice" as a capitalist strategy unto itself, and Taylor's history of music and advertising ending with the irony that what had been jingles written by the likes of Barry Manilow became, by the 1990s, the ad realm as hipster forum for Nick Drake revivalism and Moby licensing. Charles McGovern bemoans how "the conflation of democracy with spending" created "a consensual nation in which the quest for good became the pursuit of goods." Lizabeth Cohen's *Consumers' Republic*, the most influential account of market segmentation in the era I am focused on, reaches pessimistic conclusions, finding a "tendency toward hierarchy and exclusion." Cohen sees the entwining of consumer and citizen identities "accentuating what divided Americans and undermining common concerns." Her chapter on "culture," however, revolves entirely around the ways in which ads interpellated new subjectivities: the Pepsi Generation and youth culture, for example. Writing of marketing aimed at African Americans, she critiques it for diverting spending on black-owned businesses and making blacks not just "a more legitimate and lucrative market, but increasingly over the postwar era, a separate one."[30]

But commercial music was more than its marketing—the recurring anthems, cherished by listeners, which filled even tightly constructed formats demonstrated that. Culture itself deserves a stronger position in the study of consumer culture. An understanding of formats can help that process. This consumerism did not always follow divisive pathways: formats grouped audiences as much as it splintered them, with the sometimes faltering Top 40 hits approach rebounding decisively in the mid-1980s, the late 1990s, and most recently in an era of Portable People Meter technologies. The Top 40 system, as it multiplied, rigged commercial tallies of popularity to recognize demographic differences—to have many formats was to have many pop charts, so different groups achieved the illusion of majority status within formats that favored them. Yet success in a more differentiated chart often boosted crossover between categories. An R&B song that did well enough might earn Top 40 play, then airtime on AC. A fair accounting of Top 40 within the Consumers' Republic and unchecked neoliberal capitalism must come back to particular music, particular formats, and the ways these aggregated as much as segregated publics.

Radio had led in the move away from mass broadcasting, as Michele Hilmes argues: "Radio became the place where those culturally excluded from television's address could regroup and find a new identity."[31] But the segmentation of formatting was not limitless. Despite the plethora of subcategories, a few major music formats emerged by the 1970s and— with the important later addition of Latino-oriented programming— they still all remain dominant. Formats needed to convince advertisers that the public being addressed separately was commercially worthy. As Diane Pecknold has chronicled, the Country Music Association, founded in 1958, created the Country Music Hall of Fame and televised CMA Awards to demonstrate that a style originating with white working-class southerners now held national appeal. To fragment country any further would have hampered these efforts, and it has remained largely intact.[32]

Because of this collective quality, formats produced not only parallel mainstreams but parallel modernization, meeting changing circumstances of American life with at times identical, at times contrasting, responses that owed much to their audience orientation and invented traditions. There was long history here, the tidal "hidden histories" that George Lipsitz evokes poetically in his argument for music as "a vitally important repository for collective memory." The music that extended that history was textured more than programmatic—the grain of certain kinds of voices, emotions more than lyrics, instrument sounds as homology for group style. Lauren Berlant, writing about "intimate publics" in a manner that Jason Loviglio has connected to radio, notes that in this realm "consumers of its particular stuff *already* share a worldview and emotional knowledge that they have derived from a broadly common historical experience[;] . . . it is a place of recognition and reflection." Yet what does this amount to politically? Berlant coins the term "juxtapolitical" for the resultant confusion: "People attached to each other by a *sense* that there is a common emotional world available to those individuals who have been marked by the historical burden of being harshly treated in a generic way and who have more than survived social negativity by making an aesthetic and spiritual scene that generates *relief from the political*."[33] Top 40 formats rarely challenged political or economic structures. But their multiplicity and centrism aligned to ratify quite different answers to what it was normal to feel and be.

Consider a musical example that moves us from rockism and poptimism back to race and a broader sense of the messy ambiguities of Top 40 democracy. Aretha Franklin singing "Respect," a number 1 R&B and number 1 Top 40 song in 1967, emblemizes that moment's connecting of women's, black, and youthful liberation. Aretha Franklin singing "Break It to Me Gently" ten years later, again a number 1 R&B song but only reaching 85 on the Hot 100 chart that measured Top 40 success, might indicate growing racial division. Or it might reflect two formats answering different needs. For R&B, the domesticated "vibe" of romantic ballads, now given the subformat designation Quiet Storm, extended soul's imperative to normalize black communal identity. Disco, featuring many black singers, used crossover Top 40 to parade alternative identities, exchanging the genre and gender certainties of Franklin hits like "(You Make Me Feel Like) A Natural Woman" for the softness of a Barry White or drag performer Sylvester's identity-questioning "You Make Me Feel (Mighty Real)." Franklin, like fellow titan James Brown, complained bitterly about disco, contrasting its ephemeral impact with "the permanent value and staying power of soul music." She blamed the pop system: "Radio stations were shoving rhythm & blues back in the corner." Franklin's prose attacked marketplace racism. But her artistic values enacted rockism from a soul perspective, using genre ideals to disparage disco's short-lived format appeal. While opposing entrenched power, she on another level represented it.[34]

Given these intersecting claims, the impact of the radio format system, within a segmenting consumer culture, on issues of cultural and political democracy cannot be reduced to a rockist, poptimist, Consumers' Republic, or racial paradigm. One discovers crossover channels that closeted identity: gay performers and immigrants putting sonically airbrushed versions of their lives on top of the pops; MOR performers whose quick rises and spectacular falls reflected a powerlessness to define who they were. And one finds genre channels that flaunted uninhibited identity, but in a "balls-out" or "natural woman" fashion that drew boundaries. In a format system that deployed genre, pop's affect-driven, juxtapolitical, commodified crossover publics acted as counterpublics to the sanctioned normativity of genre publics. Every format, every station on the 1970s radio dial, offered a choice not between mainstream and underground but between rival mainstreams, operating in a way much as cultural studies has long described subcultures: refashioning the center to serve their needs.

When highly commercial formats operate like street subcultures, and citizens of genre worlds like Franklin complain as if reading from an Adorno screed, something is going on worth chronicling rather than assuming. Those details are where this history lives, but I'll end this section with what seems to me a paradox, a bait and switch that Top 40 democracy sets for its critics. Every attempt to oppose a format mainstream, by renouncing capitalism or compromise, registers entitlement and privilege: middle-class, male, white, heterosexual, northern, hipster, genre, or some other form.

The Long Histories of Formats

White baby boomers who attended rock festivals were hardly the only people transformed by music in the postwar era. The chapters that follow set a range of stories against one another to sketch and assess America's multiple mainstreams. Each tracks a performer, record label, or radio station rooted in the format system but battling the conflicting imperatives it generated. The examples play out over decades—"long history," akin to studies of civil rights that go beyond bus boycotts and voting acts to showcase enduring structural issues.[35] Radio lived quarter to quarter, performers album to album or hit to hit, but taking the long view lets us see as a whole what formatting registered: freedom movements confronting niche marketing; rock, soul, hip-hop, and country ideals tempted by pop possibilities. Formats imperfectly met lasting needs, for performers, sellers, and listeners alike. They were centering guides as Americans moved through history, differentiated to the extent that not everybody was on quite the same journey.

My first chapter looks at the Isley Brothers, whose hits connect to dramatically different cultural arcs: the contrast of the manic testifying of "Shout" (1959) that white fraternity brothers danced to in togas in *Animal House* (1978, set in 1962) and the slow jam "Footsteps in the Dark" (1977) sampled by rapper Ice Cube on "It Was a Good Day" (1993). Raised in an African American enclave generated by Cincinnati's restrictive housing policies, the siblings relocated when successful to Teaneck, New Jersey, one of the few suburbs to vote for integration, and for which they named their record label, T-Neck. But their appeal took an opposite course: it began as Top 40 ("Twist and Shout"), then became black-oriented R&B ("For the Love in You"). Their career went from MOR talent competitions to rock and roll primitivism, from Motown to soul nationalism, from corporate R&B on CBS to an iconic position in the hip-hop generation. The Isley family could shift in such Zelig-like fashion because they pursued, as ambitious entertainers, what Guthrie Ramsey has codified as Afromodernism: the ideal of black expression uniting uplift and pleasure, rural and urban, race and pop.[36] When African American experience bifurcated on class lines and rock turned away, R&B compensated with a holistic vision of blackness—formatted Afromodernism.

Chapter 2 revolves around Dolly Parton, whose enduring connections to the impoverished but folkloric mountains of Tennessee, country's wellsprings, were always mediated by television: childhood appearances on a program aimed at farmers from the state capital; syndication as the female singer on Porter Wagoner's "barn dance" broadcasts to old-fashioned fans; and superstardom as a regular guest on Johnny Carson's *Tonight Show*, where her southern folksiness charmed an MOR demographic. A similar balancing act, making traditionalism contemporary, informed the surge of country as a whole: to over a thousand radio stations featuring the music in the 1970s and more than two thousand in the 1980s. Many commentators have bemoaned the abandonment of "true" country by commercial radio, or assumed that the music endorsed reactionary politics. My reading stresses centrism. Parton and the Country Music Association participated in "the Southernization of America" and "Americanization of the South" by stretching definitions of "country": an invented term, ripe with implications for white southerners in a period of civil rights and shifts from rural to suburban living. Country was a genre of authenticity and anti-hippie anthems like "Okie from Muskogee." But it also named a format, respected in the perpetually New South as a thriving industry and defined by "I Will Always Love You": Parton's statement of aspiration and version of a power ballad.

Chapter 3 uses a record label, A&M, founded by musician Herb Alpert and businessman Jerry Moss, to highlight both the record industry and MOR/AC, the format of older suburban listeners. AC listeners and record execs shared a desire to embrace but manage the changes as rock and counterculture took hold. Record sellers found their place in a less centralized pop system of genres and formats, just as married adults experimented with the less rigid middle-class notion of leisure and the good life mythically located in California, A&M's home. MOR in the 1960s was Alpert's fictionally international Tijuana Brass, selling sexy exotica with *Whipped Cream and Other Delights*. AC emerged in the electric guitar attached to "Goodbye to Love" by suburban siblings the Carpenters and in the Laurel Canyon feminism of Carole King on *Tapestry*. But a pattern emerged: from Alpert to the Carpenters and teen idol Peter Frampton, the center did not hold, with A&M performers disparaged and dropped from playlists and the record industry becoming a cultural symbol of greed and manipulation. Centrism fostered diversity and maximized profit, but its aversion to musical definition, which is to say genre, led to constant fads and backlashes. Within all this vicissitude was a gender story. The shift from MOR to AC reflected a turn from radio's addressing housewives to its giving women office music. Yet the record industry, overvaluing genre, had trouble valorizing female consumers.

Top 40, the other umbrella format category, did have a mandate that worked for the record business: to represent arriving sounds and styles of pop modernity. Chapter 4 is about England's Elton John, who had US Top 40 hits for thirty straight years, from 1970 to 1999. John idolized American music, particularly African American music, and he self-consciously chose to be less rock than Top 40. A first closeted, then openly gay man, he maneuvered fantastic consumerism to position himself outside demography and convention. The identification he felt for Top 40 reflected the format's gateway role for non-countercultural social change secured through commodification. Top 40 meant youth in America, but it meant America itself in John's postwar England, and to follow his career is to see how it evolved to represent Americanization, British Invasion, and ultimately globalization. Top 40 needs to be understood as a format of outsiders opting in, where rock prized opting out.

Chapter 5 explores a radio station, WMMS, aka "The Buzzard," which dominated Cleveland radio in the 1970s and 1980s by pitching "balls-out rock 'n' roll" to a city struggling with deindustrialization. Rock on radio was transformed from underground freeform aimed at college students to an AOR approach whose Joe Sixpack ethos was symbolized by Bruce Springsteen. Yet in the early 1980s the station experienced its greatest ratings success and crisis of definition when it played Michael Jackson, a push against segregated formatting but also a nod to a sales staff that believed it needed yuppie listeners rather than working-class "earthdogs" who preferred metal. (Reversing the MOR/AC story, here the record industry was succeeding, but struggling to find a place in radio's format continuum.) Ultimately, WMMS was defeated in the ratings by syndicated jock Howard Stern, a voice for those earthdogs, and the diminished station was bought by the megachain Clear Channel. Clear Channel made any notion of WMMS as Cleveland's special station absurd, but it had the corporate power to devote a format to earthdog listeners—struggling white men, 18–34, united by belligerence.

My final chapter moves the story to the first decade of the 2000s, showing that even in a time of enormous technological change that diminished radio, formats remained a powerful structuring force in music and culture, with Top 40 resurgent, blockbusters eclipsing the margins' "long tail," and *American Idol* the biggest TV program. R&B and country once again struggled with their format positions, rising in parts of the decade and falling in others, as issues that were constant in their long histories recurred—the ever-questioned nature of their mainstream consumer reach, resistance to hip-hop as a crossover element in Top 40, and women as a genre element in country music. New rock had it still worse: the genre's historical antipathy to its format role left a class- and age-splintered array of white male–oriented radio stations, more attuned to past than present, though rock sounds flourished where the need to *be* rock was less in question, as within the subformat Hot AC. Spanish-language radio demonstrated how each effort to subsume genre within format took a different shape; the most constant tension was between the working-class and nationalized address of regional Mexican music, the most popular US approach in radio ratings and record sales, and the superstar internationalism of a Ricky Martin or Jennifer Lopez that drew upon salsa, pop, and hip-hop.

As I hope these chapter briefs suggest, telling popular music history as a tale of multiple formats up-ends conceptions bequeathed by focused genres. Fragmentation or commodification by one group's standards becomes the occupation of the center by other actors. Hit songs rely on "hooks" to create familiarity through repeated airplay, fostering album purchases and the star branding of musicians.[37] Enduring hitmakers knew that the best hooks inscribed identity as much as music: songs such as Parton's "Coat of Many Colors" or "Fight the Power" by the Isleys reconciled genre and format to perform a persona that resonated with a public.

That identity was subject to poaching—"Fight the Power," a black power anthem, was claimed by a white working-class group rioting over busing, for whom rock was too middle class to feel congenial. And that identity could be vague: the indeterminacy of the Top 40 lyrics Bernie Taupin wrote for Elton John to sing concealed his sexuality. But the result was that even in a "rock era" of unprecedented commercial and cultural clout, pop multiplicity was the more lasting story.

Reclaiming the Center

Why defend a system like Top 40, which everybody knows is suspect? My answer joins the aesthetic and the political: I have learned to love listening to a mainstream extending itself even more than to an underground emerging. Among many documents in the A&M Records archives at UCLA I found a simple telegram, sent from the London office to Jerry Moss in 1979. It reads, "The Incredible Shrinking Dickies Album enters industry chart here next week at no. 22. Number [sic] of retail accounts tells me that it is out-selling the Bee Gees new album. Obviously we are all delighted here, but what a strange world we live in." In that note I recognize a fellow traveler, fascinated by motions in the middle. The sentiment is not that different from Dolly Parton, the same year, performing "Johnny's Song" to the man who let her leap formats.

But 1979 also saw the electoral triumph of neoliberalism in England with Margaret Thatcher's election, followed by Reagan's in the United States in 1980. Against victories of privatization and deregulation, claims of transgression for commercial culture feel suspect. "Candle in the Wind" was a song about Marilyn Monroe on the 1970s Elton John album *Goodbye Yellow Brick Road*; in retrospect, we can hear a coded statement by a still closeted "friend of Dorothy." This meaning changed in 1997, when a fully out John sang it at Princess Diana's funeral just weeks after mourning murdered fashion designer Gianni Versace alongside not only the princess but John's life partner and eventual husband, David Furnish. Did "Candle in the Wind '97" symbolize new openness in public life, aided by Top 40's crossover pluralism? The globally televised funeral of a "people's princess" owed much to new Labor prime minister Tony Blair, who like his friend Bill Clinton broke with Thatcher-Reagan in governing style and affiliations, yet remained neoliberal in policy. A skeptic might call John's performance and the resulting single, which finally broke the sales record of "White Christmas," ruling-class reconfiguration.

So we are left with a force too vital to ignore and too constrained to fully celebrate. Music formats can't be accused of corrupt commodification, since it is only through commercial processes that they achieve viability. The mean they revert to involves an entertainer from a somehow emergent group using the star-making machinery afforded by a prevailing technological and economic paradigm to reach a larger audience whose composition is never completely clear. While the component pieces are evanescent, the format system has provided a stable means for groups on the margins of public discourse, *including oppositional discourse*, to sing and feel things together. We should argue about what gets communicated—we almost can't stay quiet about it—but the importance of the channel is evident. It is, by nature, central.

I have not attempted to explore pop formatting outside the United States or to compare music with other cultural forms. Yet radio's move to format group identity proved critical for American and global media. Many general-interest magazines halted publication as radio formats were solidifying (the *Saturday Evening Post* in 1969, *Look* in 1971, *Life* in 1972), superseded by targeted publications. Television was for a time the last gasp of mass media, but David Letterman joked, "TV is becoming like radio," in 1989, as he confronted the proliferation of cable. Internationally, the fragmenting effects of cable coincided with the allowing of commercially formatted radio stations to supplement government stations. In France, for example, the number of commercial radio stations went from none in 1981 to 1,200 in 1991. While television seemed the key media story of the 1950s, radio's method of scaling mass publics proved more influential over time, and pointed the way to the networked communications of the Internet era.[38]

While my focus here is primarily on performers and businesspeople, on putting a framework around those shifty, tantalizing songs, there is much evidence that formatting has affected not only the creation of American culture but its reception. Writing in 1994, Joshua Gamson described "production awareness," arguing that while some audiences for the celebrity system remained mystified believers, or aimed to discover the "real lives" of stars, more postmodern audiences practiced "an engaged disbelief, and the revelation of technique feeds rather than damages their interest." If debates about postmodernism have faded since then, public demand for the staging of "reality television" has only increased. Audiences for *American Idol*, rooting for a contestant to resonate with millions and then find the right pop niche, are practicing a fan version of format thinking. In *Idol,* precursors like karaoke singing and the MTV show for teen girl viewers *Total Request Live* and concurrent phenomena like the screen games *Rock Band* and *Guitar Hero*, which Henry Jenkins calls "convergence culture," Top 40 democracy lives on.[39]

Historians have worked to trace the birth of modern conservatism, somehow overlooked during what Rick Perlstein calls the "feedback loop" that made each initial media recounting of the counterculture an exaggeration of the last. But if we now know more about the Right, we still have far to go in coming to terms with what Christopher Waterman once dubbed "the excluded middle." As I completed this book, I was happy to see other work looking to reclaim the musical center as a place of analysis. Regev's global pop-rock sociology finds "'autonomy' and 'commercialism' are two sides on an axis of creativity that infuse each other in a dynamic of expansion." Mitchell Morris brings a musicological focus to the sentimental songs of Cher, Dolly, and Karen Carpenter, esteeming commercial "slipperiness" for giving communities "unsuitable for inclusion in the rock myth" hits that "shattered the illusion of a common taste." Pouring over trade publications, Kim Simpson delineates the format shift within radio at the turn of the 1970s, while sociologist Gabriel Rossman challenges conventional wisdom about buying the charts in the first part of the 2000s. David Hesmondhalgh applies British cultural studies acuity to pop/rock and countercultural versus neoliberal divides, seeking to pinpoint "why music matters" despite the mainstream's limits.[40]

Top 40, and the music formats that it fostered, should prove no less important for the work left to follow. Formatting impelled a push and pull between reinforcing group identities in one mode, such as rock and soul, and complicating them in another, such as AC or hot new country. It operated in dueling directions, separatism and crossover, creating what sociologist Richard Peterson once termed, speaking of country music, "the dialectic of hard-core and soft-shell."[41] This may explain why country's best sellers have been more regularly the likes of Garth Brooks, Johnny Cash, and Taylor Swift than the musical equivalents of talk-radio conservatives such as Rush Limbaugh and Glenn Beck. But the larger truth is that a similar dialectic has structured a range of musical areas, producing what Amiri Baraka, for example, called R&B's "changing same." My chapters draw on the feminist gender analysis that has impelled much terrific revisionist country-music scholarship, the long overdue takeover of black-music scholarship by black scholars concerned to complicate rather than essentialize identity, the insistence of recent newspaper, magazine, and online writers on replacing rock and rap criticism with pop criticism, and the mix of history and cultural studies work that has fleshed out what we understand about popular music as a whole. I hope the results show how often-separated realms of academic and journalistic writing cohere.

Committed to consumerism and self-transformation, Top 40 and its associated formats has remained the province of social outsiders looking to become symbolic insiders, whether gay Englishmen, midwestern African Americans, or blondes from the hills of Tennessee. Formatting has mediated economic shifts and social attitudes, resting on intangibles: sentimental ballads about lost movie stars and princesses; drug dealers from Brooklyn invoking Rat Packers from Hoboken. Rock and roll imagined a teen notion of rebellion uniting star and audience, capitalism and subculture, races, classes, and nations. Top 40 pop formats bore the responsibility of making the sale. No wonder the results can both awe and demoralize us. We need to learn to hear this history, to hear format invading genre, mainstreams swapping codes, a center that sang better than it politicked.

It is suggestive to notice how the anecdote that launches the next chapter functions in a different context. The story is one of a prom weekend in Chicago, during which white students held their school's official prom and black students held a counterprom to guarantee hearing music they wanted to dance to—and draw upon for a hallowed life ritual. For Lani Guinier, Bill Clinton's controversial and quickly withdrawn nominee to lead the Civil Rights Division of the Justice Department, the prom story is an opportunity to reflect on her political passion: finding ways for democracies to better include minority populations constantly outvoted in head-to-head balloting. She suggests strategies that might have produced a prom playlist that all students could have embraced. "As a solution that permits voters to self-select their identities, cumulative voting also encourages cross-racial coalition building. No one is locked into a minority identity. Nor is anyone necessarily isolated by the identity they choose."[42] Arguably, though, the best illustration of her goals would have been the Chicago radio dial, where stations playing R&B, rock, and other formats coexisted in a manner allowing for different majority perspectives to prevail, and for cross-racial hits as well. In the democracy of the Top 40, there were many ways to reach the charts.

CHAPTER ONE

It's *Whose* Thing?

The Isley Brothers and Rhythm and Blues

In 1991, reporter Isabel Wilkerson filed a front-page tale of two proms. The planning committee at Chicago's Brother Rice High School had hired the kind of band that many black students detested. "They want that hard-rocking, bang-your-head-against-the-wall kind of stuff," one senior complained, but he and other African Americans, only 12 percent of the school, were outvoted. A rival prom was soon organized. "And so," Wilkerson wrote, "while about 200 white couples and six black couples danced to rock music in two adjoining ballrooms at the Marriott Hotel, about 30 black couples listened to [records by] the Isley Brothers and Roy Ayers, danced the Electric Slide and crowned their own prom king and queen." Integration, Wilkerson concluded, had failed. An inability to even celebrate a prom in one place was more than a symbolic conflict. It reflected fundamental, unresolved differences over how to fashion a nation that could be collectively American.[1]

Too bad no one asked the Isley Brothers for an opinion. Their first hit, 1959's "Shout," epitomized what would become soul music, the sound of black liberation, yet it was revived in the blockbuster 1978 comedy *Animal House* as the ultimate white fraternity anthem. Their second hit, "Twist and Shout," cowritten and produced by Bert Berns, the Jewish son of Russian immigrants, featured a Mexican version of an Afro-Cuban dance rhythm and would be covered and virtually trademarked by England's Beatles. Guitarist Jimi Hendrix, one of rock's few black legends after the late sixties, toured and made his initial recording with the Isleys. Their early seventies albums often contained cover versions of rock material, and their concerts in the later seventies were modeled on rock spectacle, with flash pots and guitar solos galore.[2]

FIGURE 1.1 June 23, 1973, *Billboard* advertisement for the Isley Brothers' signing with Columbia Records. To black performers, the label represented what a period writer called "the indefinable, CBS-trademarked aura of power, mystery and devastating sophistication." For Columbia head Clive Davis, racial nationalism presented a business challenge. Davis wrote of the Isleys: "They were self-contained, producing themselves, and were right in the forefront of black music's excitement." A corporate soul synthesis defined R&B as a format. Author's collection.

Despite this crossover history, the Isley Brothers did not remain favorites of the white rock audience. If anything, they crossed back. Funk songs
like 1975's "Fight the Power," a late black power anthem, and romantic
ballads like "Between the Sheets" earned them a permanent place in the
hearts of African Americans. The Isleys' songs would be sampled by rappers such as Salt 'n' Pepa, Notorious B.I.G., and Ice Cube. A younger artist, R. Kelly, refashioned singer Ronald Isley in music videos as a gangster
character named Mr. Biggs. In 2003, with Kelly's help and a black public whose buying power could now be measured in bar-code scans rather
than the rock-biased record-store estimates, the Isley Brothers album
Body Kiss debuted in *Billboard* at number 1, more than forty years after
their first hit.

The Isley Brothers' journey from a cross-racial following to a mostly
black one challenges a still too commonplace assumption: that countercultural rock music, after it emerged proclaiming "Born to Be Wild" and
"Sympathy for the Devil," pursued within its quest for freedom ideals of
integration and civil rights.[3] Instead, rock's commercial development, into
a genre formatted through FM radio's album-oriented rock (AOR) stations, segregated sonic rebellion. But this is only part of the story of the
Isleys—and of black pop music in the rock era. As rock radio evolved in the
1970s, so too did black-oriented radio, which though rarely black-owned
and increasingly corporate in its "urban contemporary" presentation—
with strong ties to black-music divisions of major record labels—became
an institutional bastion of overtly African American expression. Between
these two genre formats could be found crossover formats, Top 40 and
adult contemporary (AC), which played black performers but rarely
songs with ideological messages or a racialized address. Chronicling the
Isley Brothers from the 1950s to 2000s positions rock and roll, rhythm and
blues (R&B), and Top 40 as three sometimes joined, sometimes clash-
ing long histories. The relationship of race, rock, and radio was unstable
and contradictory long before a Chicago prom appeared in the *New York
Times*.

Accounts of how this played out have varied significantly. Those who
print the legend correlate Elvis Presley and Martin Luther King Jr. and
conclude that "the new 'crossover' music of rock 'n' roll challenged the
color line," that "white people and black people came together to celebrate music powerful enough to break down ancient walls." Others
wonder why, then, by 1985 a Black Rock Coalition needed to insist that
African Americans had a place within rock: "In the post–civil rights era

United States," Maureen Mahon tells us, "an interest in rock music marks an African American as someone who has either misunderstood which music is appropriate for his or her consumption or has abandoned black culture by investing in what is perceived as a white music form." Peter Guralnick's classic history of soul makes pivotal King's 1968 murder, shattering the integrationist spirit of "sweet soul music" and replacing it with James Brown's "Say It Loud (I'm Black and I'm Proud)." But Paul Gilroy, Nelson George, and Mark Anthony Neal, key theorists of soul culture, believe the real letdown was corporate commodification—Gilroy says television's *Soul Train* "belongs to your American apartheid," George blames urban contemporary broadcasting in the 1970s and 1980s, and Neal calls "Rhythm & Bullshit" on the effects of radio mergers in the 1990s.[4]

My intent is to let the experience of the Isley Brothers tell a story in line with historians who now speak of a "long civil rights movement," to recognize that the 1950s' and 1960s' overturning of southern Jim Crow laws was only one aspect of a contestation that began earlier, lasted longer, and was equally northern.[5] From this perspective, the bifurcation of R&B and rock is not primarily a story about a shattered civil rights dream. And the growth of R&B as its own category is at least as important. African Americans, well before and long after the movement peaked, sought culturally unifying but commercially viable music against ever mutating barriers, including white appropriation. Research on the Decatur Street scene in 1910s Atlanta finds black domestic workers ballin' the jack to sounds that might have been ragtime or blues—musicology mattered less than that these working-class leisure spots were a "Negro playland" that, while open to all, had an "African majority." The biggest Atlanta club, the Eighty One Theater, helped anchor a black-oriented vaudeville entertainment circuit, the Theater Owners Booking Association. The TOBA's nickname was "Tough on Black Asses," and theater owners were white. Still, this "chitlin' circuit" created networks where professional music existed on primarily nonwhite terms. From the Eighty One alone came blues singer Bessie Smith, gospel pioneer Thomas Dorsey, and Perry Bradford, who'd write and produce the first blues recorded by an African American, Mamie Smith's "Crazy Blues."[6]

It is hardly a stretch to see continuities between the world Bradford evokes in his "Original Black Bottom Dance" ("started in Georgia and it went to France / It's got everybody in a trance") and Jermaine Dupri and Ludacris, some ninety years later, singing "Welcome to Atlanta" ("big

beats, hit streets"). R&B as a format operated much like the chitlin' circuit. It was always underfunded, high ratings not translating into high ad
sales and station owners said to turn to it as a last resort. Indianapolis
assistant station manager Amos Brown told *Radio & Records* in 1979,
"One thing Black stations should understand is that their advertisers
don't want to be there. If an advertiser could, he'd want to be on the number one, two or three radio stations in the market. They don't trust it, they
don't understand it, they still don't believe that black people in this day
and age control billions of dollars in the country." Radio analyst Sean
Ross complained that owners tried to "run a successful Black/Urban station for next to nothing."[7]

Nonetheless, within the R&B format, black music was defined by
majority black audiences, in particular female audiences, in a manner
that Top 40 and certainly rock radio did not allow for. "In black culture,"
African American studies scholar James Snead wrote in an influential
essay, "the thing (the ritual, the dance, the beat)" has to be "there for
you to pick it up when you come back to get it." It's striking how well
this describes the presumptions of formatted radio listening: the sound,
and sense of being personally addressed, must be there each time the
channel comes on. Despite its relative weakness in radio generally, black-
oriented radio institutionalized R&B in just such a fashion. History recast
black music in other ways: the civil rights pinnacle celebrated in soul, the
depoliticized sounds of disco, the postindustrial critique of racial uplift
delivered by hip-hop. "Radio stations, I question their blackness," Public
Enemy rapper Chuck D thundered in 1987. "They call themselves black
but we'll see if they play this." But R&B remained underneath it all, the
"changing same" that Amiri Baraka described. Its historic role was to
mediate the process that Adam Green calls "selling the race" and Guthrie
Ramsey terms "Afromodernism": an attempt to reconcile commerce and
community, folk roots and pop spectacle, secular and sacred.[8]

The advantage of the Isley Brothers' elongated career is that it con-
denses into a single case study of R&B's position within a multigenera-
tional narrative and interweave of music formats. Though the Isleys were
inducted into the Rock and Roll Hall of Fame in 1992, few rank them as
great innovators. They were a savvy act, changing with the times. But as
George Lipsitz appreciates, "As entertainers whose livelihood depended
on purchases by the public, the Isley Brothers (and many other musicians
like them) mined the memories, experiences, and aspirations of their audiences to build engagement and investment in the music they made." Their
hits proved iconic, sealing pivotal social moments into popular memory.[9]

"Shout": R&B and Afromodernism

The great hit song that launched the Isley Brothers, "Shout," was recorded in New York in 1959 for the major label RCA. Ronald Isley begins a cappella, bending out *well* in the preacherly fashion his early idol Clyde McPhatter had taught him, then saying, "you know you make me want to"—and here his brothers join up and the band kicks in—"shout!" He continues to call out phrases, which they echo, and then reaches for a high falsetto. A minute in, there is a full downshift and wiggling in tempo, his brothers fall out, and a keyboard emerges, played not by a studio musician but by Herman Stephens, from the family's Baptist church in Cincinnati. The song's second half on 45 (joined in most album versions) becomes a virtual religious service, with claps in response to sermonizing and audience participation sections that lower and raise the volume. The song is a clamorous participatory ritual, uncannily distilled into a recording. "Soul music" as a phrase existed only in jazz in 1959, but by fusing sanctified and secular, African American inheritances and commercial pop, the Isleys delivered a key prototype.

How did "Shout" happen? The emergence of "rhythm and blues," a coinage of *Billboard* in 1949, and the equally new concept of black-oriented commercial radio reflected a fundamental shift in African American identity: the presence, as of World War II, of a majority urban population, often migrated from rural southern backgrounds, self-consciously modern in wanting the culture they could purchase to express freedoms unavailable in daily life. The result, defined as Afromodernism in Guthrie Ramsey's important study *Race Music*, was heard in the electrified jump blues party music of Louis Jordan, which led to the soul crews of James Brown. But it also extended to the rhetorically classy *Ebony* magazine (launched in 1945), gospel music as an autonomous professional circuit, and the strategic style eclecticism of performers such as Dinah Washington, Sam Cooke, Ray Charles, and Aretha Franklin. As Ramsey writes, "If one of the legacies of nineteenth-century minstrelsy involved the public degradation of the black body in the American entertainment sphere, African Americans used this same signifier to upset a racist social order and to affirm in the public entertainment and the private sphere their culture and humanity." "Shout" was a defining statement of Afromodernism.[10]

This is not, of course, how "Shout" was heard by rock and roll fans. No one has better expressed the biases of young white 1950s listeners than

Jeff Greenfield, the future TV commentator, who as a teen attended inter-racial concerts staged by Alan Freed in Brooklyn: "Brewed in the hidden corners of black American cities, its rhythms infected white Americans, seducing them out of the kind of temperate bobby-sox passions out of which Andy Hardy films are spun. Rock and roll was elemental, savage, dripping with sex; it was just as our parents feared."[11] That, we shall see, is the view of "Shout" seen in *Animal House*, where it is performed for white fraternity brothers. But "Shout" as Afromodernism is different. Its rawness is skillful, rooted in church practices and professional enter-tainment, in an urbanity that accepts no contradiction between respect-able and uninhibited, the vernacular of the South and the slickness of the North. Confronting R&B's long history as a format puts "Shout" and the Isleys in this context.

"My father told my mother he wanted a group like The Mills Brothers," Ronald Isley remembered, "and right away she had four boys!" O'Kelly Isley was a North Carolina native and vaudeville veteran who had sung with a touring stage revue, the Brown Skin Models, before finding God and spiritual music; he married Sallye Bernice of Georgia, a church pia-nist and choir singer. In short succession, four sons were born: O'Kelly (1937), Rudolph (1939), Ronald (1941), and Vernon (1942). Two younger brothers would follow, with Ernie (1952) and Marvin (1953) destined to join their siblings in the 1970s, and Vernon died young, but for now O'Kelly had his quartet.[12]

As for his role models, the Mills Brothers, hailing from near Cincinnati, where the Isleys came to live during World War II, had used their close-knit harmonies to simulate madcap jazz ensembles, croon smooth bal-lads, and cross every racial boundary marker in American entertainment. They appeared on Rudy Vallee's radio program, recorded duets with Bing Crosby, and were filmed for *The Big Broadcast*. Their biggest hit, "Paper Doll," promoted with a Soundie (an early jukebox-type music video), topped the pop charts and sold millions from 1943 to 1944. Deriving from barbershop quartets, influencing jubilee gospel quartets, and anticipat-ing the street-corner vocal groups of R&B, the Mills Brothers exempli-fied African American "middle of the road," or MOR, with hits into the 1960s.[13]

If the Mills Brothers were O'Kelly's paradigm, Sallye Bernice steered her sons toward the "gospel highway" of church choirs, talent competi-tions, and sheet-music publishing that Thomas Dorsey and his partner Sallie Martin had created in Chicago and spread through black urban

America. It was the sacred version of the chitlin' circuit, but with more room for women as performers and entrepreneurs. Gospel acts dealt with "notoriously crooked" promoters and united audiences spanning generations and denominations, seeking uplift but also entertainment. As Mahalia Jackson's 1947 "I Will Move on up a Little Higher" demonstrated, gospel connected economic mobility with Christian striving.[14] Family legend has three-year-old Ronald Isley winning a war bond in a spirituals contest at Union Baptist Church in Cincinnati. Soon, he and his brothers became regulars in a network that incubated performers in a blend of the old Methodist hymns ("Amazing Grace," for example) with foot-stamping, hand-clapping beats, and call-and-response vocals that burst into vowel-stretching melismas.

This was the music of the ring shout, the ritual played for fun and sheer intensity in "Shout," living proof of a subject still under active debate in 1959: that African culture had survived slavery and diaspora. The ring, as Samuel Floyd attests, was a space where worshippers could move communally in a rare instance of freedom. The ring shout never expressed "natural" blackness: rather, as in urban gospel and the Isleys' recording, it provided a form open to adaptation. Western Africans from numerous tribes "altered to their new circumstances the apart-playing, polyrhythms, cross-rhythms, time line, elisions, hockets, ululations, tremolos, vocables, grunts, hums, shouts, and melismatic phrasings of their homeland." Through such blendings, African Americans became a nation within a nation.[15]

Isley family legend continues with a more secular but no less syncretic story: Ronald, at age seven, singing at Chicago's Regal Theater with the iconic Dinah Washington. Born Ruth Jones in Tuscaloosa, Washington reinvented herself in Chicago. "I sing everything," she said when called "Queen of the Blues." "Blues, pops, and if I have to, I can even *go to church* on the people." That savvy, the church used in the theater, the South used in the North, lay at the core of Afromodernism—a merging of working-class leisure with middle-class consumerism. The fashion spreads in *Ebony* matched Washington's risqué but elegant "Long John Blues." If gospel had become entrepreneurial, sinful tunes had moved on up in status.[16]

When Ronald Isley grew older, however, his role model became Clyde McPhatter, a one-time gospel singer, originally from North Carolina, who recorded with the R&B group the Dominoes. McPhatter's bodacious tenor broke into gospel shouts on hits like "Have Mercy Baby," teaching singers like Isley to testify in secular realms. His group's "Sixty Minute

Man," a barely disguised sex romp, became the first R&B hit to break pop, putting the Dominoes on the bill of original rock and roll DJ Alan Freed's Moondog Coronation Ball, the 1952 Cleveland concert that announced a cross-racial youth audience. Less remembered is the Dominoes' place as new Mills Brothers: part of middle-of-the-road show business. Leader Billy Ward, a Juilliard graduate and gospel coach, secured them time on Arthur Godfrey's national radio show, *Talent Scouts*, singing the folk song "Goodnight Irene." Later, the Dominoes played Ed Sullivan's televised *Toast of the Town* and spent months in Las Vegas's Hotel Sahara.[17]

Sullivan, Godfrey, and Ted Mack, of *The Ted Mack Original Amateur Hour*, took pride in using television and radio to feature black performers. When Georgia governor Herman Talmadge complained because *Arthur Godfrey and His Friends,* on CBS-TV, featured the Mariners, a black and white quartet formed in the navy, Sullivan called him "stupid and vicious." Mack, whose show debuted both Gladys Knight and Louis Farrakhan (then Walcott), said in the *Chicago Defender*, "We of the Original Amateur Hour have always felt our program is democracy at work." Singer Cab Calloway agreed. "Such top television stars as Arthur Godfrey, Milton Berle, Ed Sullivan, Jack Carter and a host of others have insisted upon presenting the Negro entertainers on their shows as the complete social equals of other entertainers."[18]

The Isley family's new home, Cincinnati, was far less accommodating. A "borderland city," just up from the segregated South, it pushed its expanding black population into restricted ghettos. Poet and black arts activist Nikki Giovanni, a childhood neighbor of the Isleys, remembers de facto segregation in restaurants and a teacher commenting that Emmet Till, lynched in Mississippi in 1955, got what he deserved. The Isleys lived in Lincoln Heights, a separately incorporated suburb of sorts: "the ugliest collections of shacks I have ever seen," a Better Housing League representative declared.[19] Still, scale alone generated urban culture. Sallye Bernice Isley became choir director at the First Baptist Church, encouraging her family's musical aspirations. The Dominoes were a regular presence in the city because they were on King Records, among the most important independent R&B labels. And WCIN became a black-oriented radio station in 1953.

Black-oriented radio had emerged before Top 40 itself did, with the success of WDIA in Memphis after 1948 leading to some six hundred stations and more than one thousand black DJs aiming programs at African American listeners by 1957. Chicago's Al Benson—formerly Arthur

Leaner of Jackson, Mississippi—represented Afromodernism on the airwaves. Older DJs, such as Jack Cooper, removed any overtly black or working-class qualities from their on-air presentation. Benson stressed what he called "native talk," bridging southernisms and urban slang. "Everybody had to see Al if they wanted to sell to the black market in Chicago, whether it was beer or rugs or Nu Nile hair cream," a DJ disciple reported. "He wasn't pretending to be white. He sounded black."[20] Benson used his prominence to agitate against discrimination that, in the North, was uncodified but no less rigid. And he played the new R&B music of performers like the Dominoes, rather than Cooper's preferred big band jazz.

Even in the confines of Cincinnati, the Isleys sensed they had options: connected to growing gospel and R&B worlds but dreaming of crossover as well. Ronald recalled, "My mother taught us in order to survive in this business, 'You've got to sing everything, learn everything.' From gospel, which was our starting point, country and western, R&B, pop, fast songs, slow songs. . . . I can do all of Frank Sinatra's stuff, all of Johnny Mathis' stuff. I was raised on that." From the late 1940s on, the brothers performed regularly. Nikki Giovanni remembers "the itch," the signature dance move of Vernon Isley. "Vernon would stand on stage and reach around and swizzle his hips and the amateur night audience would be on their feet." Though Vernon died young after being hit by a car, his older siblings persevered and in 1955 were showcased on *The Original Amateur Hour*. "The next week, watching at home, Ted announced that we received the most write-in votes ever! We won a watch with diamonds and red rubies, and took turns wearing it," Rudolph later remembered.[21]

Emboldened, and prodded by their father's death from a heart attack, the Isley Brothers relocated to New York in spring 1956: Ronald, still not fifteen; slightly older brothers O'Kelly Jr. and Rudolph; and Rudolph's young wife, Elaine Jasper (whose brother Chris Jasper would much later join the group along with Ernie and Marvin Isley). Almost immediately, the trio's vocal prowess and zany routines generated attention. *Ebony* ran a captioned photo of them in the November 1956 issue. Ronald waved his hands preacher style over his brothers. "[They] take pride in versatility and disclaim Rock 'n' Roll classification," the item read.

Why would the Isley Brothers disclaim rock and roll in 1956, the year of Elvis Presley's national breakthrough, when that classification meant 25 out of the year's 125 pop singles were R&B crossovers? To a family whose vaudeville patriarch aspired to be the new Mills Brothers, whose matriarch led it through nine years in the "sacred songs" world, as *Ebony* still called it, and who studied every pop genre, Afromodernist "versatility" meant more than rock and roll. Youth music was a medium of singles, not more lucrative albums, indie labels rather than major labels, and one-nighters or package tours rather than weeklong theater engagements. *Ebony* preferred black performers at home in adult pop, blurring racial lines through smoothness rather than wildness, like the ballad singer Ronald Isley studied. Johnny Mathis, whose *Greatest Hits* album would spend a staggering 490 weeks on the *Billboard* charts, was twenty-two when *Ebony* profiled him in 1957. In the feature, a "young white girl . . . stammered, 'What are you? I know you're not colored.' Johnny looked and smiled. 'Yes I am,' he said." Well into the 1960s, Motown's Supremes recorded albums of pop standards and became Ed Sullivan regulars. Stax acts, viewed as less pop conscious than Motown's, pursued similar goals. Manager Phil Walden explained why Otis Redding sang the standard "Try a Little Tenderness": "That was when we were talking about *career* songs where he could be on the Ed Sullivan Show or playing the Copa. These things were terribly, terribly important." "Before there was a color thing there was an age thing," Kelly Isley said a generation later, after rock and soul had forged distinct publics. "People would tell you, you appeal to the teenagers or you appeal to the 27–30 age group." Harry Belafonte, with his matinee looks and calypso routines disguising radical politics, sold a million albums on RCA, followed there by the Isleys and gospel-turned-secular star Sam Cooke.[22]

Three scrappy years in New York preceded the recording of "Shout." The group stole its contract back from a shady label owner who had neglected to make a copy. But the Isleys' vocal and choreographic skills, honed in the gospel circuit, allowed success even without a hit, as an act known, *Ebony* wrote, for "splits, cartwheels and heart attacks for the easily shocked," as well as outlandish stage attire. They played Alan Freed rock and roll concerts at the Brooklyn Paramount and a bar mitzvah at Temple Gates of Zion in New Jersey. During a show at the Howard Theatre, one of the linchpins of the old TOBA circuit, an RCA Records executive saw their mesmerizing routine for "Shout" and urged recording.[23]

Something of Vernon's swizzle was in the weave of bodies and voices. So too was the McPhatter idolization; "Shout" had been created as an ad-lib on a hit by Jackie Wilson, McPhatter's replacement in the Dominoes and a similar singer. The man from RCA might not have thought Mills

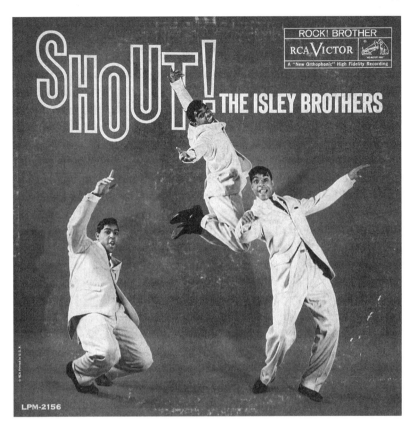

FIGURE 1.2 Cover of the Isley Brothers, *Shout* LP (RCA, 1959). The image of zany siblings in supper-club attire suggests the balance being struck between the title single, aimed at Top 40 dancers, and the W. C. Handy and Irving Berlin standards, aimed at traditional adult album listeners. Collection of John Beeler.

Brothers, but the links were there in the *Shout* album, with its W. C. Handy and Irving Berlin covers. For "Shout" itself, the group was given producers Hugo Peretti and Luigi Creatore, who would soon record Cooke as well. The Italian cousins, originally noticed for white singer Georgia Gibbs's R&B covers, made blended products for Top 40 consumption. Their first RCA chart topper was white doo-wop quartet the Tokens singing the South African–derived "Lion Sleeps Tonight." Their final hit, Van McCoy's "The Hustle," paired a veteran black-music figure with dance steps from Latin clubs. RCA hired them as independent producers—a new category at majors trying to appropriate the indie mentality. When they presented "Shout" to executives, Creatore recalled, it met skepticism. "So I said, 'with all due respect, if you were sixteen years old and black, you would understand.' "[24]

The two great stories of black culture emerging in the 1950s, as preserved in American memory, are the civil rights movement, enacted by what Evelyn Brooks Higginbotham has called "the politics of respectability," and rock and roll's exact opposite: an exaggerated wildness. R&B, as a radio category and the founding black-oriented format (rather than a defined genre like electric blues), was caught somewhere between. Yet that also gave it versatility, within an increasingly urban, nationalized, consumerist, and assertive African American culture. Performers such as Cooke and the Isley Brothers drew from the gospel and secular black theater circuits, sowing what would soon be soul music. Teen-oriented rock and roll, adult-oriented pop, and black-oriented R&B coexisted, giving performers a range of options at a time when Cincinnati spent a decade trying to integrate one public pool.[25]

Twists: R&B, Top 40, and Civil Rights in the Early 1960s

In 1962, the Isley Brothers hit a fork in the road. They were recording Burt Bacharach and Hal David's orchestral and romantic "Make It Easy on Yourself." Bacharach came in, found they had changed the lyrics to "Are You Lonely by Yourself," and furiously insisted they quit. Jerry Butler, on Chicago's black-owned Vee-Jay Records, had the first released version (a top 20 R&B and pop hit), and the Walker Brothers topped Britain's charts with it in 1965. Dionne Warwick, who sang the demo, part of her long connection to Bacharach and David, enjoyed Easy Listening chart success with a 1970 version. The Isleys' tape saw daylight on collector labels in 1990 and remains tough to find. Ronald Isley used his clout forty years later to record an entire album with Bacharach. At a supperclub date with the composer, he told the story from stage. The punch line was that, with a few minutes left in the 1962 session, the Isleys recorded a bigger hit—"Twist and Shout."[26]

This anecdote of the haphazard qualities of show business can, with coaxing, tell us a few things about an era dominated by crossover formats: Top 40 and adult pop. First, it was a moment of unprecedented identity exchange—racial boundaries blur alongside gender boundaries when we contemplate who wrote, recorded, sold, danced to, and fantasized the music. Second, that confusion of sounds and sources within songs served a purpose: it kept mainstream pop fascinating, but removed from the more pointed messages of folk and free jazz. And third, the blurriness, like the liberal consensus that marked the era's politics, was fated not to last. Meaning would be fixed to these songs—different meanings by different groups. A rock fan like Bruce Springsteen (who calls the Beatles cover "the first record I ever learned" and still performs the song) might hear liberation in the tossed-off "Twist and Shout."[27] For Ronald Isley, however, making sophisticated music on one's own terms was paramount, even if it took decades. Cultural crossover, in the high-water era of civil rights, worked in a range of directions.

The public reception of "Shout," after its 1959 release by RCA, suggests some of these complexities. "When we went to RCA the people we dealt with were old men of 50 or 60 or even 70," Kelly Isley remembered later. "They couldn't understand any of the acts." Nonetheless, RCA had coined money with Elvis Presley and wanted other Top 40 youth acts.

"Shout" met a strange fate, becoming a Top 40 standard without high chart success. "It was an instant smash with all the major jocks—like George Woods in Philadelphia and Alan Freed in New York," Ronald Isley recalled. Woods was a prominent R&B DJ, but the song never became an R&B hit; perhaps RCA never courted that *Billboard* format. Nor was the label good at building up the single's crossover momentum—it crested at number 47 on the Hot 100, and the Isleys' one-year RCA contract expired. Yet "Shout" persisted: reissued by RCA in 1962, it ultimately topped a million. A song that secularized church ritual, referencing the ring shout's use of music and motion to join a diasporic population, now welcomed others into the fold.[28]

Joey Dee and the Starliters, known for their "Peppermint Twist," charted with a version in 1962, followed that year by Bronx doo-wop singer Dion. California surf band the Sentinals put it out on a 1963 album. Queens girl group the Shangri-Las released it as a single in 1964, the same year British pop singer Lulu had her first top 10 UK hit with it. The Kingsmen, the quintessential Northwest garage band, covered it in 1965. In 1966, another set of garage rockers, ? and the Mysterians, made up of Latinos from Michigan, released a version. Louisiana swamp rocker Dale Hawkins reports, "Back then if you didn't play 'Shout' you might just as well stay home."[29] Men and women, from different races, places, and musical categories, all sang "Shout," with different levels of churchiness and call and response. But every version I have encountered switched tempos, indicating a common goal: to build excitement on the dance floor.

If the early 1960s witnessed both civil rights milestones and, to quote careful chronicler Brian Ward, "the most racially integrated popular music scene in American history," musical integration came through dancing more than folk protest songs. "The Twist," above all, an R&B number with a black following, was covered by Chubby Checker (also African American), saturated by all-important Top 40 booster *American Bandstand,* then charted a second time when it became popular with adults attending early discotheques. Black Panther Eldridge Cleaver famously called the dance "a guided missile, launched from the ghetto into the very heart of suburbia. The Twist succeeded, as politics, religion, and law could never do, in writing in the heart and soul what the Supreme Court could only write on the books." Sustained crossover led *Billboard* to suspend its R&B chart from November 1963 to January 1965, when Beatlemania reinstated the listing.[30]

Beyond dancing, the early 1960s were a triumph for Afromodernism, with its strategically varied expression and canny use of consumer culture. Ray Charles's *Modern Sounds in Country and Western Music* topped the pop album chart, with the single "I Can't Stop Loving You" number 1 in Top 40, R&B, and Easy Listening (though not country). Detroit's Motown was black-owned but concentrated on northern whites; Memphis's Stax was white-owned but concentrated on southern blacks. James Brown bankrolled King to release a rare kind of R&B album, the sensation *Live at the Apollo.* Black consumer spending rose from $15 billion in 1953 to $27 billion in 1963, and R&B was now heard on more than eight hundred radio stations. In 1964, 71 percent of blacks reported that they listened regularly to the radio, compared to 57 percent of whites. Smooth and jive talkers alike, heirs to both Al Benson and Jack Cooper, appeared on the black-oriented stations in Birmingham, marking class-inflected divisions over vernacular speech. Yet during the worst movement confrontations, DJs from both camps defied white owners, coding messages to "reinforce a powerful sense of solidarity."[31]

"Twist and Shout," the unexpected hit that replaced Ronald Isley crooning a Bacharach ballad, showed how even an innocuous song could encase strikingly multicultural processes. Bert Berns, the child of Russian immigrants who cowrote and produced it (moving on to the Isleys after a failed version by the Top Notes), was from a breed of largely Jewish songwriter-producers adapting Tin Pan Alley methods to make Top 40 rock and roll—the Brill Building scene. If "Shout" evoked a particular place, the Isleys' church, "Twist and Shout" began where the earlier song ended up, in the multiracial dance-floor democracy of the twist, placing the brothers' falsetto wails and massed harmonies (including the famous *ah-ah-ah-ah-AH!* bridge) against a Latin dance groove: the *son jarocho*, a Vera Cruz version of the Afro-Cuban *son*, rhythmic anchor for styles like the mambo. Such *clavé* beats were common in hits from the Brill Building; the writers frequently walked along Broadway to the Palladium, where Machito and Tito Puente brought proto-salsa to interracial audiences.[32]

Where the rooted "Shout" required that the Isleys bring their pianist in from Cincinnati, the musicians on "Twist and Shout" were urbane black professionals playing through trends. Paul Griffin, session pianist, went from Harlem church music and the Apollo Theater to later Bob Dylan and Steely Dan albums. Trumpeter Dud Bascomb had ties to Duke Ellington but would work the session for "Say It Loud (I'm Black and I'm Proud)." For that matter, the indie label Scepter/Wand, which released "Twist and Shout," as well as the first girl group smash "Will You Love Me Tomorrow," had been founded by Florence Greenberg, previously an accountant's wife from New Jersey, in professional and personal partnership with African American artists and repertoire (A&R) man Luther Dixon.[33]

The sense of racial inclusiveness that the Isleys experienced within the Brill Building scene extended to everyday life. The brothers bought homes for themselves and for their mother and younger siblings in the New York City suburbs of Englewood and Teaneck, New Jersey, a far cry from Lincoln Heights. The "Englewood Movement" was a two-year, successful, battle to desegregate schools, including civil disobedience. Teaneck had been known nationally for its racial attitudes since 1955, when national media attended the first public meeting of the Teaneck Civic Conference, formed to oppose realtor blockbusting. In April 1957, the conference had staged a musical, called *It's a Small World*, with an interracial cast of fifty and an appearance by the African performer Olatunji. In 1964, overcoming a campaign by the John Birch Society, Teaneck voted to desegregate its school system.[34]

That same year, the Isley Brothers decided to use the business experience they had gathered within the Brill Building milieu and release a single on their own record label (though distributed by Atlantic). They named that label for one of their new towns, T-Neck. This was very much a claim on suburban Americanism. The Isley clan had never lost their faith in family, religion, free enterprise, and, when it came to cultural expression, willing assimilation. The family of Motown's Berry Gordy, with their

Booker T. Washington Grocery Store and the family real estate co-op that
funded the label's start-up costs, operated with virtually identical principles.[35] It was hardly black power—but still race conscious and proud.
Another version of "Twist and Shout" had appeared in 1964, not one of
many, as with "Shout," but a mammoth smash. The Beatles cover reached
number 2 on the US pop charts (where the Isley version, a number 2 R&B
hit, had halted at 17), in an April 1964 week when all five top singles were
by the Fab Four. "Twist and Shout" kept much of the earlier hit, from the
Latin rhythm to the gospel (and Little Richard) falsetto, but the Liverpool
singers played up the *ah-ah-ah-ah-AH!* part to suggest rock-and-roll rawness. Future law professor Randall Kennedy, a child at the time, says, "We
laughed at all the white people going crazy, though there was also a little
resentment. We'd hear the Beatles do 'Twist and Shout' and we'd think
'what about the Isley Brothers version of "Twist and Shout"?' It was yet
another instance of white people finding they could only identify with
other white people." Kennedy adds, "It wasn't soul music."[36]

The Isley Brothers were more generous. As the Beatles appeared on
Ed Sullivan in February 1964, performing "Twist and Shout," the whole
family watched. "My brothers called a meeting," Ernie remembered. "It
was like the Security Council at the U.N. They were saying, 'Everything's
gonna change now.' "[37] The response came on "Testify," the debut T-Neck
recording in June. The song deployed one of the group's hallmarks, vocal
imitations—in this case, James Brown, Ray Charles, Jackie Wilson . . .
and the Beatles. "Now *they've* got some soul," the Isleys sang, in what
sounded like homage far more than accusation. A young Jimi Hendrix,
soon to go with the group to England, stay, and become rock's foremost
instrumentalist, accompanied on guitar.

Was the group's optimism justified? "Testify" flopped commercially, and
the brothers signed with Motown, flourishing on Top 40 despite Beatlemania. The label made its primary audience clear. The cover of the Isleys
1966 album *This Old Heart of Mine* set the band aside to feature a young
white couple on the sand, adoring each other over a beach ball. Berry
Gordy wrote in his memoir, "When selling to the mainstream market I
had learned long before that you had to deal with people's prejudices." He
was rueful that Beatles management tricked him into a reduced royalty on
"Money," of all songs, but conceded he'd have made the deal knowingly:
"A part of something is always better than all of nothing." That was his
gambit, illustrated by how southern distributors were persuaded to accept
black salesmen: "How much money do you make a year off Motown?"[38]

FIGURE 1.3 Cover of the Isley Brothers, *This Old Heart of Mine* LP (Motown, 1966). The Afromodern crossover ambitions of the pioneering black-owned label, which called itself "The Sound of Young America," led to an album cover that chose the white fans Motown hoped to reach rather than the group itself. Collection of John Beeler.

Martin Luther King Jr., addressing black DJs in 1967, embraced the crossover goal with weightier language. "In a real sense, you have paved the way for social and political change by creating a powerful bridge between black and white. School integration is much easier now that they share a common music, a common language, and enjoy the same dances. You introduced youth to that music and created a language of soul and promoted the dances which now sweep across race, class and nation." Rudolph Isley echoed the sentiment. "I remember being in Selma, Alabama, around the time of Dr. King's Freedom March, and we were asked about cancelling our appearance at a white college. Of course not! That was our own march toward equality."[39]

But how equal were they? The Beatles went from "Twist and Shout' to the adult "Yesterday" and *Sgt. Pepper's Lonely Hearts Club Band*—the rock album as art statement. The Isley Brothers of "Twist and Shout" were less mobile. Appearing in 1961 as part of a multi-artist revue formed by Top 40 DJ Murray the K (who in 1964 would proclaim himself the Fifth Beatle), they were billed with Stax's Carla Thomas, teen idol Bobby Vee, Chubby Checker, surf duo Jan & Dean, Johnny Mathis, R&B singer Ben E. King, and many others. They remained associated with this fun-loving, cross-genre, cross-racial Top 40 eclecticism. Yet they still relied on a wild stage act. James Brown recalled, "We saw the Isley Brothers coming from the back of the theater, swinging on ropes, like Tarzan, onto the stage. They hardly had to sing at all. They'd *already* killed 'em."[40]

The pop-culture work that best captures the essentially cartoonish role the Isleys played for rock and roll and Top 40 listeners, despite insisting on a sophisticated versatility, is *Animal House,* the blockbuster 1978 comedy. The film is set at a white college in Pennsylvania in 1962, where the lovable losers of the Delta House fraternity have been dealt a blow by Dean Wormer and his ROTC henchmen's uptight, ramrod straight, rock and roll–hating forces of evil. There is only one thing to do: hold a toga party. A room full of men in white sheets shake and shimmy to a fictitious R&B band called Otis Day & the Knights—performing "Shout." Raising and lowering their arms, bowing to the beat, the frat boys of "Shout" both revere and deprecate the baptismal liberation of R&B, converted by white appreciation into rock and roll.

There is more than a hint here of a new kind of blackface minstrelsy, stereotypes that African Americans were compelled to enact. *Animal House* director John Landis later said that the Knights were modeled on two actual groups playing Pacific Northwest fraternities in the early sixties, the Hot Nuts and Five Screaming Niggers, suggesting how long the minstrel model persisted. Writer John Edgar Wideman felt this past rise up as he watched a Detroit Pistons crowd in the Michael Jordan era, raucously responding to "Shout" played with clips from *Animal House* on the big video screens.

> White college kids in togas twist and shout and knock themselves out. A riot of
> sloppy boozing, making out, sophomoric antics to the beat of a jackleg, black
> rhythm-and-blues band that features a frenzied, conk-haired singer, sweating,
> eyes rolling, gate-mouthed, screaming, "Hey-ay, hey-ay, Hey-ay, hey-ay, shout!
> C'mon now, shout." Minstrel auctioneer steering the action higher, higher.

Musicians on the screen performing for their audience of hopped-up, pampered students fuse with the present excitement, black gladiators on the hardwood floor of the Palace revving up their whooping fans. Nothing is an accident. Or is it? Do race relations progress, or are we doomed to a series of reruns?

In the self-aware *Animal House*, besotted Delta House kids follow Otis Day to a black nightclub, where the Knights are less exaggerated in performance. "Otis! My man!" the white student in Ray Charles shades calls out. The singer is horrified to see them, and a fight breaks out. The movie insists we recognize the exoticism in cross-racial appreciation. During the nightclub scene, one white student asks another what she's majoring in. "Primitive cultures" is the response.[41]

The reception of the Isley Brothers in the Top 40 era demonstrates the thorniness of apparent musical integration. It was a period of optimism about race relations that dreamed of, and at times strove for, an America integrated by consumer modernity. Yet this required very particular paths of crossover: anti-ideological notions of entertainment in the land of a thousand dances. The lack of clear definition was brought home when "Shout" was claimed, with ideological fervor, by young white rock and roll fans as a marker of *their* identity, replicating the participatory culture of African America while remaining racially separated in lived experience. In whiteness historian David Roediger's analysis, this stance symbolized "a new 'postminstrel' claim, one based on sharing not simply the craft of African American musicians but also the soul."[42] These differences, less bothersome in the hopeful early 1960s, widened over time.

Soul and Black Nationalism

In a remarkable 1969 theme issue of *Ebony*, "The Black Revolution," Larry Neal's "Black Art and Black Liberation" declared the black arts movement a cultural counterpart to Stokely Carmichael's political demand for black power. Both, Neal asserted, wanted "Self-Definition and Self-Determination," blackness being "essentially a nationalistic concept" built by struggle. Art must join in "along lines that are rooted in an Afro-American and Third World sensibility." W. E. B. Du Bois, in *The Souls of Black Folk*, had called American blackness a "Double Consciousness . . . two warring ideals." It was time, Neal wrote, to end that ambiguity. "Can you dig it?" Black music was key, "the highest achievement of the race."

The revolution needed "the *feeling* of a James Brown or an Aretha Franklin." However, "a change of reference is needed in black popular music also. Like: We can't go into the future singing: *Who's Making Love to Your Old Lady* or *It's Your Thang, Do With It What You Wanna Do.*"[43]

Neal's distinctions made more sense rhetorically than musically. Former gospel singer Johnnie Taylor's "Who's Making Love" was the biggest hit to date for Stax, the Memphis label, by 1969 black-run, whose vision of black and white musicians grooving together helped produce the "feeling" behind Franklin's arrival as Queen of Soul. "It's Your Thing," the title and lyric of which Neal distorted, had revived the T-Neck label and the Isley Brothers' career, topping the soul charts, reaching number 2 pop, and winning them their only Grammy. Appropriately, Aretha Franklin later covered "It's Your Thing." When Ronald Isley sang, "It's your thing, do what you wanna do, I can't tell you who to sock it to," he evoked Franklin's "Respect," with its shouts of "sock it to me" and "freedom!" Pop culture's late 1960s "spectacular blackness" could no more be purified than Neal's article could run in *Ebony* without full-page ads for Bacardi and Shell nearby. As Amy Ongiri writes, "The black arts and black power movements' investment in a utopian world outside the Babylon of commodification occurred, ironically, precisely at the moment when African American vernacular culture experienced a massive crossover commodification through popular film, music, and visual culture."[44]

From the late 1960s to early 1970s, black power ideology was at its height, and soul music achieved unprecedented success, both as a separate format of at times striking militancy and a crossover music that blended black affirmation into a groovier Top 40. If America was more racially polarized, as typified by *Ebony*'s "Black Revolution" issue or Richard Nixon replacing Lyndon Johnson, many whites now accepted the imperative of acknowledging black culture. *Ebony* saw its ad revenues triple, to nearly $10 million, and the June 1969 issue of *Sales Management* contained an article, "Communicating Soul Style," that defined words like *boss*, *down*, and *jive*. "What resulted," historian Lizabeth Cohen asserts, "was a new commercial culture that reified—at times even exaggerated—social differences in the pursuit of profits, often reincorporating disaffected groups into the commercial marketplace."[45]

The process of appropriating difference produced strange affiliations. Loosening his image, Nixon appeared on *Laugh-In* during the 1968 campaign to deliver the hip TV comedy's black-culture-derived, but no longer black-culture-identified, catchphrase: "Sock it to me." Later, he won the 1972 endorsement of James Brown, one of the black arts movement's heroes, appealing to Brown's belief in commercial enterprise. In black-oriented pop music generally, a visual Afrocentricity played out on album covers, reflecting a sonic blackness emphasized in the elongated LP tracks of such enduring statements as *What's Going On*, *Talking Book*, and *Spirit in the Dark*. But the period also saw a system of genre and crossover main-streams lock into place—its chronicler, Kim Simpson, japes that "soul, like every other commercial music radio format, underwent a period of identity agony in the early seventies crisis that settled down into a care-fully controlled, apolitical-sounding entertainment machine before the decade was over." Larry Neal was not the only worried listener. Corporate America did not reify or exaggerate differences, but it did format them: growing black-oriented expression into a parallel mainstream. Artists like the Isleys were central to the process.[46]

The instant funk groove of "It's Your Thing"—passed across speaker channels between bass riff, guitar scratch, summoning piano chords, and ride cymbal; horns and full drums surging in after Ronald Isley—gave the song a different affect than the group's earlier iconic songs. Rather than a church rite or urbane Latin dance beat, this evoked a big soul revue—instrument parts interlocked in a demonstration of group prowess. James Brown, who trademarked the approach, defined sonic black power—aggressively modern and masculine, stressing funkiness as an innately black quality. "It's Your Thing" positioned itself between Brown and his key successor, Sly and the Family Stone, a biracial, male-female band dancing to a looser notion of freedom. "It's Your Thing," with Ronald Isley's tenor weaving where Brown's rasp imposed itself, left funk open to other liberation: hippie, women's, and gay.

None of this flexibility was coincidental. "It took us a year and a half to find a formula for a sound," Ronald Isley declared. If Neal idealized soul as a racially nationalist genre, this was format thinking: concerned to stretch categories and unite music with publics. "Not a formula for one catchy hit, but a way of doing things that will work for other artists and sounds as well."[47] On the pop charts of the May 3, 1969, *Billboard*, number 2 hit "It's Your Thing" was sandwiched between songs derived from the hippie musical *Hair*. First came the 5th Dimension, black sing-ers from Los Angeles who had bigger pop hits than R&B ones. The Cowsills, number 3, were clean-cut white models for television's *Partridge Family*, mocking hippies with a sarcastic "Hair." In this context, "It's Your Thing," with its open-ended lyric ("do what you wanna do"), did not come

off as a particularly racial statement. On soul radio, however, its senti-
ments fit just as well with Brown's strident "I Don't Want Nobody to Give
Me Nothing (Open Up the Door I'll Get It Myself)," scarcely played on
Top 40.

The Isleys, like Brown, presented themselves as black power entrepreneurs, a reconciliation of Afromodernism with a new age of cultural
nationalism. For "It's Your Thing" they had rejuvenated their T-Neck
label. On the back of their album *It's Our Thing*, an article reprinted from
R'n'B World announced that the Isleys were no longer dancing off the
stage (a trademark) and through life; "we're businessmen now," Rudolph
Isley said. *Soul*, a black-owned and politically minded Los Angeles music
magazine, noted that T-Neck's success gave executive positions to African
American employees, concluding, "The Isleys are pleased with what they
have been able to achieve as men." Rockers in 1969, like black arts activists, disavowed corporate ambitions. The Isleys stressed bringing their
younger brothers into what Ronald called "the business. . . . But first they
have to finish school." Here, nationalism encompassed older notions of
uplift.[48]

The group also put on an ambitious festival concert at Yankee Stadium,
billed as the "First Soul Brothers Summer Music Festival." Actor and
Malcolm X associate Ossie Davis spoke, and Muhammad Ali watched
from the stands. In the film version, gospel legend Clara Ward appeared
first, performing spiritual "Swing Low Sweet Chariot" as a tambourine-
clapping ring shout with her singers. Venerable chitlin' circuit comedienne
Moms Mabley joked from the stage, "Did you see whitey bringing me
up here?" and then eulogized Lincoln, King, and Kennedy with her version of "Abraham, Martin and John." Ike and Tina Turner brought soul-
revue energy to Beatles, Creedence Clearwater Revival, Rolling Stones,
and Sly Stone songs, culminating aptly with "Land of 1000 Dances." The
Edwin Hawkins Singers returned the show to gospel with their crossover
hit "Oh Happy Day." A white soul group, the Brooklyn Bridge, offered a
medley of Curtis Mayfield covers. Judy White, daughter of Café Society–
era folksinger Josh White and a T-Neck signing, sang "Somebody's Been
Messin' with My Thang" in sequins. Then the Isleys took a victory lap.
The results became a double LP and feature film: "One Night In June The
Isley Brothers Brought Soul To The City," trumpeted the poster.[49]

But the film did poorly, no T-Neck signing achieved significant commercial success, and the Isleys themselves would struggle for equivalent success until 1973. The group published a notable advertisement in

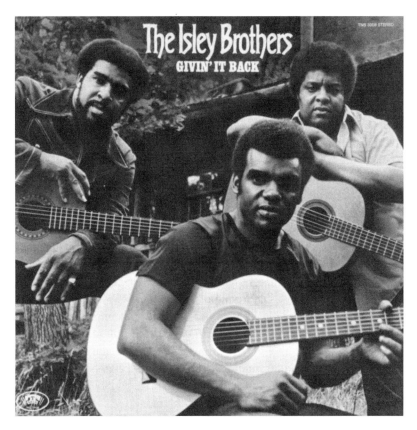

FIGURE 1.4 Cover of the Isley Brothers, *Givin' It Back* LP (T-Neck, 1971). Covering songs by the likes of Crosby, Stills, Nash, and Young; War; and their former sideman Jimi Hendrix, the Isleys here modeled themselves to suggest a multicultural counterculture that sales results proved more fantasy than reality. Collection of John Beeler.

Billboard. "We're taking 'Black Berries' off the market!" it proclaimed. "Although you made us number 43 bullet, Cashbox 79 bullet, Billboard, and 56 bullet, Record World we found that for a lot of people this record wasn't their thing, and our thing is to make your thing easier."[50] The song, an ode to the sexiness of black skin, was the strongest race-pride statement the group would make. The LP it was part of, *The Brothers: Isley*, whose cover image nodded to cultural radicalism by putting the trio in monklike robes, scraped the album charts at number 180.

So the Isleys experimented, drawing on their training in versatility. *Givin' It Back* was "reverse crossover" music à la Dinah Washington, soulfully revamping singer-songwriter rock. The three Isley front men held acoustic guitars they didn't play and wore the least flashy clothing of their careers on the cover. One song combined Neil Young's "Ohio," about the Kent State shootings in their home state, with former sideman Jimi Hendrix's Vietnam number and electric guitar workout "Machine Gun." A gospel-inflected rendition of the Crosby, Stills, and Nash rock smash "Love the One You're With" proved a good-size R&B hit. *Brother, Brother, Brother* addressed working-class black concerns with "Work to Do" and applied the new freedoms of the LP medium to an extended, slow-groove bedroom version of Carole King's "It's Too Late."

The group finalized its synthesis of black power, counterculture, and the LP's adult possibilities by signing a distribution deal for T-Neck with the biggest major label. Columbia Records had commissioned a 1972 Harvard Business School report that recognized separate, but linked, pop targets. "Soul radio is of strategic importance to the record companies for two principle reasons: first, it provides access to a large and growing record buying public, namely, the Black consumer. Second, and for some of the record companies more important, it is perhaps the most effective way of getting a record to a Top 40 playlist." Columbia subsequently created a black-music division with African American executives, signed Earth, Wind & Fire away from Warner Music, and made a distribution deal with Philadelphia International, the label that defined upscale R&B. CBS's leadership in black pop would culminate in Michael Jackson's record-busting 1982 release *Thriller*. To black performers, the rewards were what a period writer called "the indefinable, CBS-trademarked aura of power, mystery and devastating sophistication. CBS artists are given expensive and deferential receptions, and receive favorable exposure in the media." For Columbia head Clive Davis, racial nationalism simply presented a business challenge. He hired black promotions people. Artist repertoire was more of a barrier, as Aretha Franklin's early 1960s struggles on Columbia had proven. For this the Isleys' collective talents proved critical. Davis wrote, "Who would the producer be? What kind of material would be used? I used this sort of thinking in signing the Isley Brothers in 1973. They were self-contained, producing themselves, and were right in the forefront of black music's excitement. They hit the top of the charts with a gold single and a gold album almost as soon as the contract ink was dry."[51]

The Isleys' first Columbia album marked a major redefinition of the group. The title, *3+3*, signified the formal addition of three new band members: younger siblings Ernie Isley (guitar, and drums while recording) and Marvin Isley (bass), and brother-in-law Chris Jasper (keyboards). The new bandmates were versed in contemporary sounds: on the album's breakout hit, "That Lady," Ernie played a "phase shifted" guitar engineered by early synthesizer pioneers and Stevie Wonder collaborators Malcolm Cecil and Robert Margouleff. In 1964, when written and first recorded by the trio, the song had been another failed ballad: a smoky number playing an exotically orchestrated groove off Isley's unearthly high crooning to describe a mysterious beauty. Almost a decade later, its futuristic guitar, Afro-Latin percussion, and production gloss amounted to adult pop of a different kind: a teaser for *3+3* as a soul *album*, now as much a commodity as the soul single earlier. If "Shout" exhorted listeners to church, "Twist and Shout" to the dance floor, and "It's Your Thing" to let loose, "That Lady" said fire up the stereo and bask. The album was marketed in a *New York Times* music store advertisement that also promoted "New York's First Exclusive Quadrophonic Showroom."[52]

But when heard on black-oriented radio, particularly the stereo FM R&B stations that paralleled LPs in their rise, the polished "That Lady" heralded a second arrival: R&B radio as a self-consciously executed *format*, rather than a cast of DJ personalities or unstructured effort to reach black consumers. New York's Frankie Crocker was pivotal, an AM soul DJ hired in the late 1960s' "sock it to me" crossover by leading Top 40 WMCA, who found 1970s success steering WBLS-FM, black-owned by Inner City Broadcasting. There, he turned "The Total Black Experience in Sound" into "urban contemporary": programming that kept its tone "mellow, deep, and sexy," as he wrote—"we took off the screaming and shouting on the air." Crocker, avid in disco, relished crossover: he played whites on WBLS, sought white listeners, and was accused of betraying radio's blackness. Yet WBLS remained black-oriented. Harry Allen, "media assassin" for Public Enemy, wrote in *Vibe* after Crocker's death in 2000, "In his hands, radio became the locus for urbane, worldly, African Americans with disposable income and nuanced musical palates." *Vibe*, a magazine of similar goals, hailed his "drawing listeners of all races to black stations."[53]

Attempts to deploy black power on radio failed for reasons that Larry Neal might have predicted. William Barlow's study concludes, "Virtually all the progressive black FM radio ventures in the late 1960s and early 1970s faced the same conflict. In almost every instance, the original Black Power political agenda . . . yielded to the station's profit-making mission." This was not simply white control: Inner City Broadcasting's owners included Percy Sutton, a powerful black politician. In Washington, WHUR, operated by the black college Howard University, canceled after eighteen months the approach "360 Degrees: The Black Experience in Sound," whose unofficial theme song was Gil Scott Heron's "The Revolution Will Not Be Televised." Its new format, "Ebony Lifestyle," was musically conservative—and more popular with black listeners.[54]

Just as Marvin Gaye's protest song "What's Going On" gave way to his no less soulful sex song "Let's Get It On," most commercially ambitious black artists reconfigured to consistently reach the expanded black mainstream market. Motown abandoned Detroit for Los Angeles after 1971, emphasizing its superstar album artists rather than hit records produced communally. The Isleys abandoned any pretext of developing T-Neck into a multi-artist label and concentrated on themselves. They were now reliant on an increasingly corporate model of soul. R&B thrived, its reach extended to the majority African American population that supported it as a separate format and pop listeners of all kinds who embraced its crossover stars. But a sense of compromise and curtailment lingered. "Black music has always been confined in some corner," Ronald Isley would repeatedly complain in subsequent years.[55]

The Heat Is On: Major-Label R&B

It is useful, measuring the corporate path taken by black pop music, to contrast African American experience in film. In 1971, Melvin Van Peebles's independent production *Sweet Sweetback's Baadasssss Song* and then the MGM studio's *Shaft* proved the potency of the black moviegoing public. By late 1972, 25 percent of Hollywood films in production were black oriented, as opposed to just 3 percent in 1970. Where Sidney Poitier, a "respectable Negro," earlier defined the black male on film, the new stars were "superstuds": violent, sexual, and hip ghetto figures. But when the "blaxploitation" fad ended, so did black-oriented films. Black music continued: 114 soul albums reached the pop top 10 between 1971 and 1981.[56]

Much attests to the success of the balance the Isley Brothers struck on Columbia. To DJ and music historian Rickey Vincent, they were "the epitome of funky black manhood." Critic Scott Poulson-Bryant calls them "self-assured black folks' music at its best." As Carol Cooper sees it, "Our vernacular, our accent, if you will, is all over the Isley family's putatively 'pop' material." Cooper's notion of pop with a vernacular accent is telling: for the Isleys, the one extended the reach of the other. In 1974, with CBS's help, the brothers performed a vibrant "Live It Up" on Dinah Shore's morning TV show, realizing the MOR promise of their early Ted Mack appearance. "I really felt that!" she exclaimed as they wrapped. They also promoted the album with a show not at Harlem's Apollo but midtown's Felt Forum, where they stressed Ernie's showboating guitar work. The encore was a version of "Listen to the Music" by the Doobie Brothers, a California rock band gone steadily soulful. Uptown in the Bronx, pioneering hip-hop DJ Kool Herc began connecting records by the Isley and Doobie Brothers in his live sets.[57]

In the summer of 1975, to quote Vincent, "the Isleys ruled." *The Heat Is On* had topped both the soul and, for the first time in the Isleys' career, pop album charts, on the strength of "Fight the Power." When the group played New York this time, they headlined Madison Square Garden, with Mayor Beame sending an emissary to declare "Fight the Power Day." Opening with the grunts of a James Brown track and the clavinet of a Stevie Wonder one, the funk song went, "I try to play my music / They say my music's too loud / I tried talkin' about it, / I got the big runaround / And when I rolled with the punches / I got knocked on the ground / By all this bullshit goin' down." For black listeners the rebellion registered as what historian Robin Kelley calls "loud talking," where "the voices themselves, especially the loud and profane, literally penetrated and occupied white spaces." The key word was *bullshit*, bleeped by some stations but not all. Comedian Cedric the Entertainer recalls, "We'd wait on Ron Isley to get to the part where he'd say 'bullshit,' and then we'd sing it strong. Every kid in the hood sang it at the same time. It'd be nighttime, all the kids would be doing their homework, the radio on in the background, and then all of a sudden you'd hear the word bullshit from every home and apartment with a kid. It was like an epidemic of Tourette's, but you knew it was just the Isley Brothers on the radio." After "Fight the Power" and two more extended funk jams with guitar solos, the second half of *The Heat Is On* switched gears. The album's second hit, "For the Love of You"— driven by Chris Jasper's keyboards, Ronald Isley's falsetto, and backing percussion—was followed by "Sensuality" and "Make Me Say It Again Girl" in a side-long vinyl seduction.[58]

The corporate soul formula worked. Where their previous albums had varied widely, the Isleys' Columbia-distributed releases, virtually all of which hit gold or platinum between 1973 and 1984, maintained an

FIGURES 1.5 AND 1.6 Covers of the Isley Brothers, *Showdown* LP (T-Neck/Columbia, 1978) and *The Heat Is On* LP (T-Neck/Columbia, 1975). After almost fifteen years of relentless stylistic shifting, the Isley Brothers' Columbia albums maintained an almost brutally consistent image: soul fashion underlined with major label gloss. Collection of John Beeler.

almost brutally consistent image. Sales strategies were coordinated by H. LeBaron Taylor, CBS's first vice president of black marketing, who had earlier brought Philadelphia's WDAS into the format era and by 1979 had a staff of sixty-one, almost exclusively African American. The LP covers showcased upscale "street" fashions selected by theater-world costume designer Bernard Johnson; vinyl sides alternated between funk on side A and side B for the bedroom. "We became known as the 'summer group,'" Marvin Isley later noted. "Every summer we were going to have a hot album out, and everybody's going to be makin' love, and it was like 'Look forward to the summer as the Isley Brothers time of year.'"[59]

Isley Brothers albums were not masterpieces, but listening to them was a ritual to depend on—a formatted experience. If the Great Migration's synthesis of southern rural rawness and northern urban cosmopolitanism produced Afromodernism, the corporate Isleys connected two generations of the concept in their funk. Kelly Isley puts it simply: "We can be real heavy, we can be sweet, we can be down home and soulful." The younger Isleys emphasized other qualities. They were said to "smirk" at "Shout." "Our music is about so much more now," Ernie Isley explained. "We've got a lot more to say musically and lyrically. I-IV-V chord changes and three guys jumping up and down, screaming and shouting 'wooo' just isn't where we're at." Chris Jasper noted his training at the Cincinnati Conservatory of Music: "Most people didn't know they were getting a taste of Ravel and Debussy in their funk!"[60]

While complex chordings were part of the boutique CBS-era mix, so was a stronger connection to rock culture than the older brothers had managed. Ernie Isley claimed, "I guess you could say that we have gone further into Hard Rock than ever before," and an author at the time called the new members "some of the first black heavy metal kids."[61] Like rockers, the expanded Isleys were, in the lingo of the day, a "self-contained" unit: able to write and perform without external help. "All musical and vocal performances by The Isley Brothers: 3+3 Only," many of the Columbia releases proclaimed in a rhetoric of authenticity. The special effects at concerts by the Isleys, like Earth, Wind & Fire or Parliament-Funkadelic, connected funk to arena rock.

For all their glitzy success and classical and rock music flourishes, the Isley Brothers still represented the family-rooted racial uplift they had projected in 1969. Another consistent note to each Columbia album was a conspicuous thanks to mother Sallye. It was well publicized that the younger siblings had studied music at C. W. Post College at the older brothers' expense. The Isleys in 1967 were, to a patronizing commentator, an "extremely exciting stage act in which the three large gentlemen literally lose pounds of weight per show." The Isleys of 1975 in the *Ebony* spin-off *Black Stars* were business executives, self-contained not only musically but in "control over their destiny." Kelly Isley said, "We're just like any other black corporation that is staffed and owned by blacks that just happen to be us. We had a black promoter do our 28-day tour. And they were all sell outs."[62]

On albums like *Live It Up, The Heat Is On, Harvest for the World, Go for Your Guns,* and *Showdown,* a streak of five number 1 R&B albums between 1974 and 1978, the Isley Brothers managed, with a blending of aggressiveness, tenderness, and political messages like "Harvest for the World," to reconcile contradictions pulling African Americans apart. The 1970s saw the gap between blacks and whites widen for the first time since World War II, with 30.6 percent of black families in 1978 below the poverty line in contrast to 8.7 percent of whites. Urban ghettos replaced southern Jim Crow as the image of African American misery. Still, the middle class continued expanding. Between 1970 and 1986, the black suburban population grew from 3.6 million to 7.1 million; 1.1 million blacks attended college in 1977, a 500 percent increase over 1960. Sociologist William Julius Wilson's 1978 study, *The Declining Significance of Race,* argued that the black middle-class exodus kept those left behind trapped in poverty.[63]

Dynamics were quite different in the black-music division of Columbia, a ghetto of a different kind perhaps, but the earlier cross-class one. "Our music deals with the street," Kelly Isley questionably argued in 1974, but the suburb-based group worked to symbolize racial wholeness. Amiri Baraka was impressed by how the black arts movement's ambitions for a popular avant-garde had endured. "You've got people in rhythm and blues like the Isley Brothers talking about 'The Powers that Be,'" he said, stressing that the sound was as powerful as the words: "Now, you can also perceive these concerns in what they are actually playing; for them to actually sing it will let you in on it, but that's what they are playing anyway."[64]

Where the white reception of "Shout" had been fervent to the point of racial caricature, 1970s and early 1980s Isleys recordings would be preserved in African American memory as totems of peacefulness and healing. In middle-class circles, the songs became material for black weddings and BAP (Black American Princess) guidebooks; they provide the sonic wallpaper of African American romance literature and have been a favorite of best-selling author E. Lynn Harris. "You knew what time it was when an Isley beat came on the stereo," a character in a Trisha Thomas novel rhapsodizes. "Time to just kick back, let the groove steal you away." Another protagonist sketched by playwright Ntozake Shange hears the Isleys' "Love the One You're With." "I feel my survivor kick in and take a deep breath."[65]

African Americans associated with the ghetto felt the Isleys' appeal too. When rapper Ice Cube suggests how it feels to catch a break, on "It Was a Good Day," he samples "Footsteps in the Dark" from *Go for Your Guns*. Author John Edgar Wideman, pained by the white reception of "Shout," identified the later Isleys with the emotions of his brother cruising with a drug dealer friend: "Sweet, slow stuff and everybody's happy. Everybody's feeling good. Talking up dreams. What we gon spend our riches on. Passing round a jug of Thunderbird." For John Fountain, a *New York Times* reporter from Chicago's projects, "There was nothing like the Isley Brothers pouring from speakers on a hot August day at the block club party on Komensky. As the Isleys played, time stood still, the melody and the smell of barbecue smoke drifting on a summer breeze."[66]

The Isley Brothers and major-label soul had become a staple commodity. Yet this formatted consumer experience produced cultural transposition, much as "Shout" had surfaced out of traditions that few within the pop world of 1959 would have recognized. Gerald Early usefully distinguishes between a black public, connected through consumption, and black community; this black public outlasted the demise of the "second ghetto" neighborhoods that, as Suzanne Smith documents for Motown and Detroit, originally nurtured Afromodernist R&B. "In black culture," to quote James Snead again, "the thing (the ritual, the dance, the beat) is 'there for you to pick it up when you come back to get it.'" Southern migrants had brought those "things" North. Now, even as African American identity fragmented along class lines, R&B offered symbolic racial unity as an ongoing commercial product.[67]

"Fight the Power," Part 2: White Backlash against R&B

As a pop hit with lyrics about unspecified "powers that be," "Fight the Power" was as ripe for appropriation as "Shout." The Isleys intended it to be demographically vague: "I was just trying to make a universal statement that people could agree with regardless of their background," Ernie

Isley told *Black Stars*. But it's doubtful he would have expected the song
to resound during a white working-class riot in Boston:

> Everyone sang along to "Fight the Power." The teenagers in Southie still lis-
> tened only to black music. . . . One time an outsider walked through Old Colony
> wearing a dungaree vest with a big red tongue and THE ROLLING STONES printed
> on the back. . . . He got a bottle thrown at his head and was called a pussy. Rock
> and roll was for rich suburban people with long hair and dirty clothes. . . . Of
> course no one called it black music—we couldn't see what color anyone was
> from the radio—but I knew the Isley Brothers were black because I'd seen
> them on "Soul Train." But that didn't bother anyone in the crowd; what mat-
> tered was that the Isley Brothers were singing about everything we were watch-
> ing in our streets right now, the battle between us and the law.[68]

Here, "Fight the Power" blasts out of a speaker at police in the midst of a
summer 1975 protest by white Irish Catholics inflamed at court-mandated
public school busing.

In a pop music universe of parallel formats, white uses of black-
produced but not always black-oriented music could take conflicting
courses. For Michael Patrick MacDonald and his friends, the class divisions that rivaled racial divisions played out in gendered language, as rock
became associated with moneyed, aloof, and sexually suspect hippies.
Working-class white boys felt instead a class and male kinship with black
music, as the Isleys gave them a sense of the "streets." Yet their experience of the music was mediated, learned through radio or *Soul Train*,
not socializing. And there was no compunction about using "Fight the
Power" for political ends opposite of a group who named their label after
an integrated suburb. Ralph Ellison captured the disconnect: "What, by
the way, is one to make of a white youngster who, with a transistor radio,
screaming a Stevie Wonder tune, glued to his ear, shouts racial epithets at
black youngsters trying to swim at a public beach?"[69]

The white rock and roller, dancing at the altar of "Shout," had always
been a problematic figure—loving an abstraction of black culture but
living separately. Within countercultural rock, a related dynamic arose:
whites who no longer shared the present with black culture, revering older
variants of African American music, from jazz to blues, but castigating
contemporary material. White critic Richard Corliss contrasted the "pop
r&b exemplified by the Shirelles and the Isley Brothers" with "the vis-
ceral, dirt-pure stuff of John Lee Hooker and Bo Diddley." Taking Larry

Neal in a decidedly new direction, a writer in *Sounds*, a progressive rock magazine, claimed, "Today's soul, the REAL music, not the 'sock-it-to-me' or 'is everybody happy' corn, is being sung by whites." "Sock-it-to-me" blacks, such as the Isleys, were replaced as figures of rebellion by the likes of Janis Joplin or Van Morrison. Keir Keightley concludes, "Raised on Top 40 and unafraid of popular success for select, *authentic* rock perform-ers, the newborn rock culture featured a massive youth audience which saw itself, nonetheless, as opposed to the mass mainstream and all that stood for."[70]

In attacking Top 40, rockers undercut the primary channel that let black music reach a white audience. For example, Buddah Records, which distributed T-Neck releases from "It's Your Thing" to the Isleys' signing with Columbia, was run by Neal Bogart. Bogart had begun his career with Philadelphia's Cameo-Parkway label, home of Chubby Checker during the twist era, then established Buddah as the leading force behind face-less "bubblegum pop": the 1910 Fruitgum Company, Ohio Express, and Archies, whose song "Sugar, Sugar" was the biggest single of 1969. No admirer of protest songs, Bogart wrote, "Music was meant to be happy, free, unashamed, relaxed, natural and easy, easy, easy." Still, the label was a lifeline for ambitious black artists, distributing not only T-Neck but Curtis Mayfield's Curtom Records, and giving Gladys Knight and the Pips more freedom than Motown. Bubblegum irreverence sustained soul ide-alism, from Mayfield's blaxploitation hit "Superfly" to Knight's "Midnight Train to Georgia."[71]

Rockers saw only calculation. College journalist Howard Wuelfing admitted in 1973, "For a long time, like most white kids, I had very little use for black music; I liked Hendrix, of course I dug the blues, and later on I got to know and love Miles Davis and other jazzmen, but the bulk of black music made me turn a paler shade of white. It seemed so slick, con-trived, and phoney, not 'real' music at all, just commercial confection of about the same aesthetic level as the Archies." Evidence supported such views. Motown obscured black faces. Black arts advocates like Larry Neal separated crossover soul from the movement. Even Hendrix affirmed rock identity by saying of his time with the Isleys, "I had to conform" and "I always wanted more than that," and refusing the call-and-response tropes that passed from the black church into pop culture. "Top-40 stuff is all out of gospel, so they try to get everybody up and clapping, shouting 'yeah, yeah.' We don't want to get everybody up. They should just sit there and dig it."[72]

Rock, as it turned into a format, segregated itself racially as Top 40
never had. Milwaukee program director George Wilson confirmed, "The
college kids a few months ago used to dig soul because they thought it
was hip. But I think the growth in popularity of progressive rock on the
campuses has hurt soul." By 1975, Ronald Isley rued, "The FM progressive stations don't play us because they have us classified as R&B." Kelly
Isley agreed: "We're glad they play our records in the discos. But we *hope*
they'll play our records everywhere." In a *Rolling Stone* with John Belushi
on the cover for *Animal House,* the brothers' complaints reflected their
long-standing willingness to adapt. "If a person says, 'We cannot play a
particular artist because they have a particular sound,' that's cool," said
Ernie Isley. "But then you cut a song like 'Summer Breeze' and they say,
'I can't play that.' You cut a song like 'Fight the Power'—'I can't play that.'
You cut 'Livin' in the Life/Go for Your Guns'—'I can't play that!' Now
you're sayin', 'Okay, what is it that I have to put in the grooves for you to
be able to play?'" Kelly added, "I don't think we would have any problem
crossing over if the color of the skin was different. It's not the color of the
music."[73]

Bob Gooding, one of the few African Americans to program an AOR
station, Columbus, Ohio's WCOL, talked about his battles against "the
kind of programming in which we say, 'OK, we don't play any Black music
other than Stevie Wonder." But he admitted that his white, male 18–34-year-
old listeners, "when they get together with their peers, they'll sit around
and say, 'I like Ted Nugent." Nugent, midwestern veteran of 1960s Top 40
garage rock, had reformatted himself as a hard rock maniac. Songwriter
Willie Dixon, masterful at Afromodernist combinations of primitive and
sophisticated, gave "Wang Dang Doodle" to Howlin' Wolf in 1960: an
electric blues boogie set in a mythic southern juke joint where Automatic
Slim partied with Razor Totin' Jim. Nugent's rewrite was blunter and
more leering: "Wang Dang Sweet Poontang." Fans, not required by newer
formats to listen beyond their own, downed a six-pack and hit the arena.
Max Floyd, of Kansas City AOR station KYYS, was asked if he played
black music. "It depends on what you consider. Stevie Wonder of course is
not Black. And that's the kind of stuff we play and consider it Black. But
we really don't, no."[74]

The alternative, in reaching beyond black audiences, as Kelly Isley had
noted, was disco, like a twist craze or bubblegum single in being open to
black music—but only within tight, deracinated parameters. Neal Bogart,
who'd gone from Chubby Checker at Cameo-Parkway to the Isleys at

Buddah, now had Casablanca and Donna Summer, an African American diva voicing productions of Europe's Giorgio Moroder. An Isleys hit that sent one message in a black working-class neighborhood, and another in a white one, registered as interracial transgression in a discotheque: "The Chinese guy in a vest, no shirt, Levi's bellbottoms and his dancing partner, a white girl with a pert steno permanent and a red hot pants suit . . . he's arched backwards on his hands and feet and she is straddling him, pumping down and up to the beat of 'Fight the Power.'" Rockers burned disco records at a Chicago baseball game. But disco also offended blacks, for decontextualizing soul into what one programmer called "jukebox radio."[75]

Exactly while "Shout," a dance song, was exoticized in *Animal House*, the Isleys found themselves written off by rock fans, much like disco, as formulaic, hackneyed, and repetitive. Powerhouse guitarist Ernie Isley responded in frustration, "Rock & roll in its basic sense is repetitive. . . . There are groups right now playing the same, identical licks as Chuck Berry and Little Richard! The same phrases! And everybody says how great they are!" An unrepentant pop act, the Isley Brothers *were* repetitive: "Surf and Shout" chased "Twist and Shout" in the charts, as "Pop That Thang" did "It's Your Thing." Albums like *The Heat Is On* divided into slow sides and fast sides. But the deeper problem was the purpose of the repetition. As theorists of African American music insist, repetition and "sameness" root black sounds communally, providing equilibrium. James Snead underlines black music being ritualistically available, rather than "new" in a modernist sense. Tricia Rose notes of hip-hop sampling that mass-culture critiques that equate repetition with commodification slight black aesthetics. This extends back to 1970s R&B, later the key source of hip-hop samples. Rockers might love particular black music, but not a black-oriented pop format.[76]

The disco backlash swept aside nearly all black commercial music apart from R&B radio. Songs by blacks had occupied one-third of pop hits since 1968, but that ended for a time, with black Top 40 falling to one-fifth in 1980, then one-twentieth in 1981 and one-tenth in 1982. *Los Angeles Times* critic Robert Hilburn observed, "'Death to Disco became a rallying cry. In its enthusiasm, a large percentage of [the] white audience equated anything black with a dance floor trend." In Portland, nine hundred people parked at a drive-in to see *Animal House* smashed records and chanted "disco sucks." Despite two dozen subsequent black radio hits over the next three decades, the Isleys never again received significant airplay outside R&B. "Take Me to the Next Phase," a soul top 10 in 1978, was not in the pop 100. Programmers said bluntly, "We feel that by generally sticking to a 'vanilla' sound the audience knows what to expect" and claimed black pop was not "as relatable as it used to be" to suburbanites.[77]

The backlash against black music coincided with Ronald Reagan's election; affirmative action and social welfare were under siege, and African Americans by two to one reported feeling closer to blacks in Africa than whites in America. Rock critic Lester Bangs wrote of the new "White Noise Supremacists," lamenting, "Most white people think the whole subject of racism is boring."[78] Early MTV VJ (video jockey) Mark Goodman, whose station played virtually no black artists, said to David Bowie in 1983, "We grew up in an era where the Isley Brothers meant something to me. But what does it mean to a seventeen-year-old?" To which Bowie responded, "I'll tell you what the Isley Brothers or Marvin Gaye means to a *black* seventeen-year-old and surely he's part of America."[79]

Aka Mr. Biggs: The Hip-Hop Era

Spike Lee captured the frustrations of postindustrial soul culture in his 1989 film *Do the Right Thing*. For its main song, "Fight the Power," rappers Public Enemy took the Isleys' title and refrain, "fight the powers that be." As in 1975 ("I try to play my music / They say my music's too loud"), character Radio Raheem blasts the song, from his ever-present boom box. This "loud talking" blackness infuriates the owner of Sal's Pizzeria, where photos of Italian American celebrities abound but no blacks are represented. An altercation over both matters leads to police choking Raheem to death and patrons burning the restaurant. Lee is sardonic about crossover effecting positive racial change: Sal's son in the movie argues that because of their celebrity, "Magic [Johnson], Eddie [Murphy], and Prince are not niggers. I mean they're not black."

A couple of years before the film, critic Nelson George published *The Death of Rhythm and Blues*, charging that black music had dissolved. Compared commercially to Top 40, country, or rock as a format, R&B and black-oriented radio was small-time: 8 percent of radio stations in 1985. The stations suffered a bad "power ratio," meaning disproportions between listener numbers and ad dollars, due to persistent sponsor skepticism about black purchasing power. Owners often sought a Top 40 mix of listeners across race lines or claimed class appeal by eliminating slangy "neckbone" DJs. Hip-hop was resisted as a "ghetto" sound. Performers were required by the majors, who kept them in black-music divisions, to court black radio. This gave those whose styles did not match prevailing radio norms few options. Crossover stars like Michael Jackson and Prince, who had conquered MTV and the post-disco backlash, favored bigger Top 40 stations and nonblack media outlets, seeming to relinquish racial identification.

The unequal treatment given the R&B format, and its primarily commercial orientation, had long rankled. Kelly Isley complained, "The black radio stations—where are they at? The right-hand side of the dial, way down. The signals are screwed up." Two African American media critics wrote, "What is black, has an affinity with some twenty million people, and has abdicated its responsibilities for a fast dollar? The answer is black radio." *Billboard*'s Leonard Pitts said of crossover stars, "Black is no longer good enough. They prettify it up with high-sounding euphemisms like 'I don't see color' and 'I make universal music,' but the net results remain the same." A 1987 NAACP Report called popular music, with its racial classifications, a field of "white domination."[80]

Had the commercial formatting of black pop into black-oriented and crossover channels perpetuated inequality? Hip-hop, the musical genre of the collapsing inner city and mass black imprisonment, largely developed outside R&B and commercial formatting. Rap rhetoric, especially as gangsta rappers following N.W.A codified what had been a more eclectic style, rejected uplift and collective struggle. Nelson George complained, "I came up on the we-shall-overcome tradition of noble struggle, soul and gospel music, positive images, and the conventional wisdom that Civil Rights would translate into racial salvation. Today I live in a time of goin'-for-mine materialism, secular beat consciousness, and a more diverse, fragmented, even postmodern black community."[81]

But R&B did not die in the 1980s. The overlapping dynamic of black-oriented and crossover channels continued to foster new sounds and preserve cultural continuity. Consider "Between the Sheets," a number 3 R&B hit (no pop crossover) in 1983 for the Isley Brothers. It begins with meshed synthesizer bass and keyboard lines, luxurious against slow claps and programmed beats. With the era of funk arena ritual ended, the group winnowed to a different functionality—bedroom ballads, the kind Isleys had fought to croon, then placed on the second sides of their albums. Top 40 stations that played black music discounted African American romantic ballads. Not black radio, saved by a "Quiet Storm" subformat of

R&B aimed at 25–49, primarily female listeners with incomes upward of $30,000—African American adult contemporary, the "buppie" version of yuppie. Neither as political nor aggressive as "Fight the Power" in either version, the secular-spiritual vibe of Quiet Storm instead romanticized and continued to solidify black communalism.[82]

A decade later, "Between the Sheets" came back to different effect, sampled in rapper Notorious B.I.G.'s 1995 "Big Poppa," an urban hit that then did cross over to pop. Some whites, younger versions of Boston's Michael Patrick MacDonald, again identified with black music: the bravado of rappers like B.I.G., former drug dealer Christopher Wallace. MTV had a major hit with *Yo! MTV Raps* and regularly featured black artists. Los Angeles station Power 106 and New York station Hot 97, owned by the Ennis chain, courted a multiracial youth market and taught radio to integrate and normalize hip-hop. Top 40 was less white than ever. Yet critic Charles Aaron found "double unconsciousness," Du Bois's opposite, when he examined white appreciation for hip-hop: "failing to look at oneself through the eyes of others, and living under a delusion of 'oneness.'" Crossover success continued to elude meaningful racial engagement.[83]

But "Big Poppa" was part of a second, less obvious crossover process. As hip-hop business historian Dan Charnas points out, while some "sold street culture to suburban White audiences," others, like Andre Harrell of Uptown Records, mentor to Notorious B.I.G. producer Sean "Puff Daddy" Combs, "sold a smooth, upscale take on hip-hop to Black America." Harrell called the approach "ghetto fabulous," but the links back to Afromodernist ideals of navigating between Louis Jordan and *Ebony* should be clear. Those selling black music recognized both forms of crossover, negotiating "between the street and the executive suite." The format system's need to expand and intertwine different mainstreams worked to keep hip-hop and R&B realms where new moguls like Combs experimented with how far black pop could stretch. And the vibe of R&B, particularly that least rock and roll side of it used commercially to seduce black women, provided a sonic resource, connecting even gangsta rappers to the black family.[84]

In the same period, Ronald Isley was reborn as Mr. Biggs, a character he portrayed first in the video for his duet with R. Kelly, "Down Low (Nobody Has to Know)." Kelly, a Chicagoan with roots in gospel and talent competitions similar to Isley's, had emerged as "King of R&B," reviving the style in relationship to hip-hop. In the video, Biggs was a murderous gangster—but also resonant enough, in his combination of riches and insecurity, to earn multiple sequels. Much as black radio had been required by format position to absorb hip-hop (as it earlier had black power), R&B reworked itself to register post-soul disillusionment and neoliberal materialism.

If R&B had been threatened in the 1980s, by 1999, when it came time to release a retrospective Isleys collection, the group could count on an overall African American consumer marketplace approaching $500 billion, supporting within music multiple niches and subformats. "We are servicing the boxed set to jammin' oldies and urban adult and specific mainstream urban and crossover stations that have these flashback shows, like WKTU in New York or [KPWR] Power 106 in L.A.," an industry figure reported. A Chicago program director noted, "As a format, we've been playing Isley Brothers for 30 years. I don't think their popularity ever went away. Every time they release an album, their core audience goes to the store and buys it." As the twenty-first century dawned, John McClain, musical director for 1970s soul outfit the Sylvers at age sixteen, was now an executive at DreamWorks, excited to take Isley material platinum again. *Essence* spotlighted them at a music festival for black middle-class women. BET, the Black Entertainment Television channel, presented a lifetime achievement award. Ronald Isley had a recurring role on a Steve Harvey sitcom aimed at blacks, teaming at times with rapper Lil' Bow Wow. "Our people have stuck with us through thick and thin," Isley said.[85]

Mr. I: Formats and Freedom

When Elizabeth Isley Barkley—child of Rudolph Isley and Elaine Jasper, the teenage couple who left Cincinnati for New York in 1956—reflects on life as "one Isley Brother's daughter," she recalls the party the older brothers threw when the younger ones finished college, hiring Duke Ellington and his band. She remembers her mother attending Rhema Bible School, bringing her husband into the fold, and the two recording *Shouting for Jesus*. But often her memories turn to money. The white Rolls Royce purchased from Debbie Reynolds. Diamond initial rings and pearl necklaces given to her and her sisters. Most vividly, the ritual at the end of the group's tours. "The Isley Brothers would finally sit, now understandably tired, quietly counting their briefcase full of money. It was a part of their routine to be gathered together, passing out stacks of money wrapped neatly in bank bands to one another. We would sit and watch as we had a million times before."[86]

In *R&B Rhythm and Business: The Political Economy of Black Music*, novelist and radio producer Norman Kelley argues that "black music operates within a 'structure of stealing,'" dating to slavery, then blackface minstrelsy, and continuing music-industry exploitation of black talent. It isn't hard to find a similar moral in the long history of the Isley Brothers. Early, they stole a contract back from a label owner. On tour, they learned to guarantee good treatment: "Rudy Isley had a .357 magnum that he had a license to carry around. I think the Isleys always got paid," said one of their engineers, Malcolm Cecil. A picture of Ronald's unfinished New Jersey mansion, seized for back taxes in 1979, ran in *Jet*. Rudolph Isley's home, the largest in Teaneck, was sold at auction to Bill Murray. There are hints online of lawsuits over royalties between the younger and older brothers. Most recently, Ronald Isley served three years in prison, from 2007 to 2010, for tax evasion. Barkley writes, "My father did not want any of us involved in show business. He would tell us in many of his lectures that show business is a cutthroat industry and that he wanted us to stay away."[87]

The Isley Brothers, "3+3" in their most heralded years, were down to 1+1 by the early 2000s: Ronald with Ernie on the still-iconic guitar. Kelly Isley died of a heart attack in 1986. The three younger Isleys briefly formed Isley-Jasper-Isley, with "Caravan of Love" winning huge R&B but no pop attention. Subsequently, Rudolph Isley entered the ministry, Chris Jasper went solo, and Marvin Isley developed diabetes, retired, and passed away in 2010. After Ronald Isley left prison, his first solo album was released. The title, *Mr. I*, might be read as the end step in a process: family reduced to individual egotism. It could be a verdict, too, on formats, which created an African American mainstream but on materialistic and precarious terms. Cultural studies theorist Paul Gilroy has been heated along these lines, writing, "I mourn the disappearance of the pursuit of Freedom as an element in black vernacular culture." As Gilroy judges history, "I have watched their oppositional imaginings first colonized and then vanquished by the leveling values of the market that was once, but is no longer, stimulated by commerce in live human beings. Any lingering countervalues are seen today as a pseudo-transgressive adjunct to the official business of selling."[88]

But maybe it says something of the continuities that bind black pop against all fate that a father from the Brown Skin Models begat a child who sang with Dinah Washington; aspired to the Mills Brothers and Clyde McPhatter; became a peer of the Beatles, Berry Gordy, Aretha Franklin, and Earth, Wind & Fire; then a patriarchal figure to the likes of Public Enemy, Notorious B.I.G., and even Lil' Bow Wow. R&B, born out of the shift in African American life from a predominantly southern and rural existence to a predominantly northern and urban one, ultimately evolved into a black-oriented segment of mainstream commercial culture. Neither pure crossover nor purely separatist, neither as culturally integrated as rock and roll's mythologizers might have hoped nor as transgressively nationalist as advocates of black power might have dreamed, R&B in its most mainstream guise still offered African American culture a format where black identity, no matter how it diversified and permeated, was always a dominant concern.

The soul acts who flourished in the 1970s—figures such as James Brown, the Staple Singers, the O'Jays, Harold Melvin, the Dells, Johnnie Taylor, Bobby Womack, the Meters, and Labelle—were often R&B veterans like the Isleys, with roots going back decades. They represented a combination of entrepreneurship, musicality, race pride, and the confident sexuality embedded in the grooves of the "Ebony Lifestyle." It's arguable whether a more integrated or less commercial music sphere would have asserted and maintained such continuities—a cherished value in R&B. For the Isleys and many others, what Amiri Baraka called "the changing same of R&B," and rockers castigated as a bland sameness, survived well beyond the election of Ronald Reagan and the black-music backlash. That might be something to shout about.

CHAPTER TWO

Duets with Modernity

Dolly Parton and Country

On January 19, 1977, the eve of Jimmy Carter's presidential inauguration, Dolly Parton made her first solo guest appearance on *The Tonight Show*. Only four weeks later, she was invited to return again. The singer later credited these appearances, along with a prime-time Barbara Walters interview, with transforming a musician "very big in the country-western field," as Johnny Carson first introduced her, into what she told Walters she intended to become: a "superstar." To say thanks, she wrote "Johnny's Song," never recorded to my knowledge, but unveiled on the show in 1979 and again, with modifications, in 1989.[1]

Parton, as she often did, sang conversationally sitting next to her host, long nails tapping as she accompanied herself on guitar. The natural, spare performance belied her blatantly constructed appearance. "I have come a long way from the hills of Tennessee," she began, evoking origins as always. Then she stuck it to Nashville. "But I never really made it 'til the Johnny Carson show." She compared before—"polyester paradise," "hillbilly heaven," "moonshine," "a forty-eight-foot mobile home"—and after: a country-speak "mansion on the hill" that in the 1989 rewrite had become "a mansion in Bev Hills," even as her "penthouse on the coast" grew to an "empire on the coast." Parton's 1979 song exulted, "From here no telling where." The global celebrity, movie star, and mogul of 1989 knew where. In 1979, she was Hollywood. By 1989, she was Dollywood.

We might call the topic of Parton's tossed-off ditty a format leap: from country to middle of the road/adult contemporary (MOR/AC). I want to present her in such terms, as a pop musician navigating intersections of entertainment and identity with a political acuity akin to her exact

FIGURE 2.1 Dolly Parton in performance, 1978. Parton aggressively applied country's mix of commercial styling and homey authenticity, taking both to extremes that at times chafed against Nashville codes. But like Nashville, she struggled to balance ambition and origin, pop and country, format and genre. © Lynn Goldsmith/Corbis. Used by permission.

contemporary, Bill Clinton. And as a representative figure in the story
of how country music the genre and country music the format, two very
different beasts, have rubbed each other the wrong way, if to sometimes
profitable ends. The 1970s and 1980s, the decades of Parton's greatest
fluctuation, were the period in which, through formatting, country established itself as a blockbuster-level pop music category. In 1979, country
aspired to Dolly Parton. In 1989, country was becoming Garth Brooks.

Country the genre, especially so-called hard country and its patron
saint Hank Williams, located its soul in honky-tonk: the music as working
class, rowdy, publicly performed, and male. Women could survive in this
conception, but mostly as voices from the mountains, representing roots,
as epitomized by the Carter Family and Loretta Lynn. In recent years,
feminist historians have challenged the music's gendering. Women uncomfortable playing honky-tonks needed other avenues. Some became radio
barn-dance singers, like Linda Parker. Some featured on TV barn shows,
like Parton with Porter Wagoner. Some used talent shows, like Patsy Cline
on the Arthur Godfrey show in the 1950s or Carrie Underwood on *American Idol* in the early 2000s. Women, marginal to country as a genre, were
central to its growth as a format. As artists and fans, they found a perch
in the very media settings that a "real country" partisan often viewed as
most problematic.[2]

For the authors of a voluminous study of the subject, "Dolly Parton
is the most famous, most universally beloved, and most widely respected
woman who has ever emerged from country music."[3] But she is also the
best example, male or female, of how country—the genre of working-
class and rural white southerners—reinvented itself. Too often viewed
as conservative or betraying rural tradition, country became pop with a
different accent, as determined a claiming of consumer America as anything in the rock and R&B-driven Top 40. Because it served commercial
imperatives, the music confronted changing times with confidence and
humor more than "lost cause" intransigence.

Country music has long been seen in quite different ways. In national
politics, it was "the ballad of the Silent Majority," of segregationist presidential candidate George Wallace and his victorious opponent Richard
Nixon. In feminist terms, it was the music of Tammy Wynette's "Stand
by Your Man." Historian James Gregory calls it a genre of "rock-ribbed,
patriotic, patriarchal, plain-folk traditionalism." Writing in 1973, critic
Richard Goldstein spoke for many when he concluded, "Country music
comes equipped with a very specific set of values, which include . . .

political conservatism, strongly differentiated male and female roles, a heavily punitive morality, racism, and the entire constellation of values around which is centered the phrase 'rugged individualism.' To me, it is, truly, the perfect musical extension of the Nixon administration."[4]

But country as represented by Dolly Parton is more complicated: not reactionary so much as social transformation by a different path. Born, like Clinton, in 1946, Parton was very much a baby boomer, influenced by television, Elvis Presley, and other 1950s youth culture, then by the altering mores of the 1960s and 1970s. She placed career ahead of her unconventional marriage or children; embraced drag queens, plastic surgery, and disco's Studio 54. All the while, she insisted on her religious faith, pride in southern heritage, and continuing connection to the country audience. This was a Nashville insider, before and after her pop breakthrough: she earned the music's highest honor, Entertainer of the Year, in 1978, even while pursuing crossover so avidly as to appear on a *Playboy* cover.

If putting Dolly Parton at country's center resists assumptions of conservatism, it also challenges the view that commodification destroyed country's essence. Historian James Cobb once marveled, "Years ago sensitive liberal commentators were warning that they could detect the ominous overtones of the South's conquest of the national mindset— 'the Southernization of America'—in the defiant and gritty lyrics of Merle Haggard. Paradoxically enough, they now seem equally distressed that they can hear in the bouncy and slickly produced stylings of Garth Brooks the loss of regional character and identity that has come with the 'Southernization of America.'" From the onset, country was a blend, its "folk" ballads often minstrel creations of northern songwriters, its rhythms shared with African American music. Centering in Nashville by the 1940s, country as a format responded to rock and roll by draping itself in a newly codified tradition while modernizing its production processes. Artists talked about their "industry" with pride, not apologies. Dolly Parton may have crossed over from country to pop, but country already was pop. Asked to define "the Nashville Sound," Chet Atkins jingled change, saying "that is the Nashville Sound."[5] Like country, Parton achieved her identity *through* commodification. Born into a stereotyped and commercialized region—the hills of Tennessee and their hillbillies— she had a knack: she could evoke tradition while appearing modern. Her format leap only extended this to a new audience.

As with rhythm and blues (R&B), country was smaller as a market than rock or the middle that Carson represented. And as with R&B, country ultimately found the rock audience less receptive than it appeared, instead expanding into its own mainstream category—too big to ignore and too commercial for some whose identities it built upon. In many ways they are bookends. Yet country has been felt to look backward, while R&B dreamed forward. James Gregory's history dispels stereotypes of backwoods white southerners foundering in the North, but finds they elected to remain apart, building areas of "discrete influence," including a nationalized country music.[6] From Dollywood to Grand Ole Opry, country has claimed the past, while R&B seized the present. If R&B flirted with Top 40, country was frequently cast as a version of MOR/AC—adult pop.

In the late 1970s and early 1980s, no performer more spectacularly merged country and pop culture than Dolly Parton. She was, her slogan went, "taking country with me." Yet her manufactured appearance, from wigs to surgically altered breasts, raised equal comment. Barbara Walters asked her, "Dolly, where I come from, would I have called you a hillbilly?" She also asked, "Is it all you?" No one would identify Parton, a friend to Jane Fonda, with Wallace or Nixon. Still, she had a welcome place in country music. Parton, like Nashville, struggled to balance ambition and origin, pop and country, format and genre. She harmonized or made bantering dialogue out of these oppositions, much like the form that nurtured her: the duet.

TV Barn Dances and Music Row: Inventing the Country Format

Among Dolly Parton's many signature quotations is the line "I was on TV before my family even owned one." Her mountain community, Sevierville, Tennessee, was about thirty-five miles from the capital in Knoxville, where a grocery store magnate who bragged he had not worn shoes before age eight sponsored radio and TV programs. Parton began appearing on *The Cas Walker Farm and Home Hour* when she was ten, in 1956; recorded and cajoled herself onto the Grand Ole Opry before high school; released a single on Mercury Records and signed a songwriting deal while in high school; then left for Nashville upon graduation in 1964. None of this discounts growing up in a large, poor farming family, or the influence of mother Avie Lee, wed at fifteen, who sang her children old ballads. But in a region that often saw televisions installed before plumbing and relatives going north and back, what folklorists might deem cultural impurity came naturally. Parton's grandfather was a fiery Church of Christ preacher. He also wrote a song that country queen Kitty Wells recorded. Sister Willadeene said of Sevier County in the 1980s, "It is a strange combination of computers and cornfields, atomic plants and outside toilets, tourism and tent revivals."[7]

Parton had two modes of existence: a rural, religious, arguably archaic upbringing in the mountains, and urban, secular, and contemporary channels that provided distance from origins. This was not atypical. The South had long been mythologized in minstrel and Tin Pan Alley plantation songs. To be southern meant confronting notions of hillbilly Dixie as backward, if nobly anti-industrial. The Appalachians epitomized natural America for the local-color movement of the 1870s and 1880s. Tourism catered to the myths, with the Great Smoky Mountains National Park removing modern buildings and Gatlinburg billed as "Americans the Twentieth Century Forgot." In 1950 Gatlinburg's business elite went to Florida in shabby clothes and "talked just as hillbilly as we could" to drum up vacationers. The Partons watched bemusedly. "Only the rich folk went to Gatlinburg," another sister, Stella, attested. "Folks like us just worked there."[8]

Feeding the allure was the persistence of English ballads in mountain culture, gathered in Cecil Sharp's 1919 collection *Folksongs of the Southern Appalachians*. Women were crucial to the process: southern mothers who passed on songs as part of domestic ritual and northern settlement-house workers who ratified tradition—what Olive Dean Campbell called "the recognition and preservation of all that is native and fine." In the 1930s, folklorists John and Alan Lomax came to the mountains, documenting with recording devices the lore that serviced a mostly northern folk revival.[9]

Commercial recordings of rural favorites had been available earlier than that, however, since Fiddlin' John Carson's 1923 version of Will Hays's 1871 sheet-music smash, "Little Old Log Cabin in the Lane." In 1925, the revue soon called the Grand Ole Opry began on Nashville's WSM. In 1927, Ralph Peer set up in Bristol, Tennessee, recording the traditional Carter Family and drifter Jimmie Rodgers for shared royalties. Peer's song mining bordered on colonialism: southern heritage profiting northern companies. Little regional pride accrued to the music: in 1943, Tennessee governor Prentice Cooper declined to attend the first national Opry broadcast, accusing star Roy Acuff of making Nashville, "the Athens of the South" for its Parthenon re-creation, a "hillbilly capital." Yet Acuff, older than Parton but also first heard on Knoxville radio, soon defined New South professionalism, creating publisher Acuff-Rose. As publishers and studios joined the Opry as city staples, perceptions changed. Acuff ran for governor himself (unsuccessfully) in 1948, and after Hank Williams died, in 1953, a new Tennessee governor traveled out of state to the memorial.[10]

By the time a young Parton aired on *Cas Walker*, country had been recast as a key southern industry—only to be nearly swept away by rock and roll. *Newsweek* titled a 1952 overview "Country Music Is Big Business, and Nashville Is Its Detroit," where Acuff said, "I'm a seller and not a singer." The new image pursued dignity. As *Newsweek* noted, the term *country* was "preferred by its practicioners instead of hillbilly music." Songs like "The Tennessee Waltz" and Tony Bennett's covers of Hank Williams became pop crossovers. Yet as Memphis rockabilly (meaning rock and hillbilly) Elvis Presley charted nationally in 1956, many stations converted to Top 40 hits programming. This removed country shows. Formats were the new standard, and in 1960 only eighty-one stations specialized in country as a format. "Rock music almost smothered out country music," recalled Porter Wagoner, who topped country charts with his 1956 "A Satisfied Mind." "Even though I had the number one song . . . about the only thing we could work was the little clubs, the skull orchards, the dives." A teacher of Parton's recalled, "If you were going to try to be upper middle class, whether you liked country music or not, you didn't admit it." A fellow student agreed. "You had the town class and the country class."[11]

Country rebounded, using what Diane Pecknold has traced as a combination of trade association sponsorship and invented tradition to transform a threatened genre into a polished format. The Country Music Association, founded in 1958 out of an earlier Country Music Disc Jockey Association, created advertiser presentations called "The Selling Sound of Country Music." As *Broadcasting* reported, this effort showed the audience for country was "no longer limited to hayseeds, Okies, rubes or Jed Clampetts." A highly produced Nashville Sound of "countrypolitans" like Eddy Arnold took hold, with a CMA consultant proclaiming, "*Modern* country music has no relationship to rural or mountain life. . . . You find no screech fiddles, no twangy guitars, no mournful nasal twangs in the *modern* Nashville sound of country music." But the strategy also stressed heritage: in 1961 the CMA began using Opry broadcasts to induct members into a still-unbuilt Country Music Hall of Fame. Codifying tradition boosted the music's aura. Parton's "Down on Music Row" mythologized her arrival in Nashville. "In the fountain at the Hall of Fame / I washed my face and read the names / In the walkway of the stars."[12]

In 1960, Vanderbilt economist William Nicholls demanded, "The South must choose between tradition and progress." Country music sought not to make that choice. In Joli Jensen's analysis, the rhetoric of not just playing but *being* country, mythologizing both working-class honky-tonks and the Grand Ole Opry, was compensatory: "Industry had to find a way to link back up with the imaginary authentic homes of country music—the green hills, back porch, barn dance, dim lit bar. If this link could be made symbolically, the new style—the Nashville Sound—could still be 'country,' in spite of its pop-styled sound and origins." Hominess let country remain "identifiable as a genre, different from and more 'real' than pop or rock music."[13]

Dolly Parton applied the country format's mix of pop styling and homey authenticity aggressively, taking both to extremes that chafed against Nashville codes. From the start she balanced her repertoire. On Cas Walker broadcasts, where she danced the twist in a bouffant hairdo, she most frequently covered Rose Maddox, whose rhythms anticipated rock and roll, and George Jones, who defined honky-tonk. Her first single paired the innocuous "Puppy Love," sung over a Top 40 beat, with an original, "Girl Left Alone," about the consequences of sex. In 1963, six Parton recordings purporting to be Kitty Wells remakes were released on a cheaply made album: *Million Seller Hits Made Famous by Country Queens*. In fact, two were older, a folk ballad and a temperance tract, with a third a Parton original, "Letter to Heaven," about a child killed trying to mail her dead mother. All three highlighted young people at risk. Parton melded teen pop drama with such nineteenth-century weepers as "The Baggage Coach Ahead."[14]

Parton sought a course between the racism, sexism, and acceptance of fate she rejected around her and downplaying rural southern identity altogether. In Nashville, she exchanged the high school boyfriend who'd said "I'm glad they shot the niggerlovin' son of a bitch" when they heard Kennedy was assassinated for Carl Dean, son of a paving contractor, who listened to soul singer Otis Redding on the radio. They married in 1966, after Parton made clear that career came before home life or children. Parton bluntly critiqued her upbringing: "I used to see relatives marrying one ol' shitty guy after another and their teeth would rot out and I'd think, 'That is not what I'm-a-gonna do with my life.'" Yet she also resisted the crossover avenue open to southerners in the Top 40 era. Fred

Foster signed her to his label Monument, whose biggest act, Roy Orbison, recorded with Nashville session men but had pop hits. Foster thought Parton should do the same and control her twangy vibrato. Parton ultimately insisted on country material.[15]

That a young professional as determined as Parton chose to actively pursue country music, rather than Top 40, said much about Nashville's resurgence. Music Row exuded commercial ambition. And format-conscious country was open to women's ambition. Parton's first solo hits, "Dumb Blonde" ("this dumb blonde ain't nobody's fool") and a humorous cheating song, "Something Fishy," showcased the teasing vernacular of a modern woman with an unmitigated southern accent. In May 1967, Parton was invited to guest on *The Wilburn Brothers Show*, a syndicated half-hour program three years into a decade-long run. Loretta Lynn was the show's regular "girl singer." That week, she did "Get What'cha Got and Go," an up-tempo song—part of her number 1 country music album, *Don't Come Home a-Drinkin' (With Lovin' on Your Mind)*—dismissing a man prone to go "downtown where the go-gos go." Parton performed "Dumb Blonde" sitting on part of the farmhouse set. The Wilburns offered "You Win Again," noting their steel guitarist, Don Helms, had recorded it with the great Hank Williams. There were comedy sketches as corny as old vaudeville, and a spiritual number the banjo-playing clown comedian joined in on. The audience was asked to patronize the sponsors. Everyone danced over the final credits.[16]

Television rivaled the CMA and Nashville as an underpinning of country, particularly aiding female performers. "When country music started getting on TV, people realized that we are not just hillbillies and hicks," Parton has said. In 1956, *Billboard* listed eighty-nine locally aired country TV broadcasts, originating in thirty-one states, and there were multiple network series: *Ozark Jubilee, Midwestern Hayride*, and shows hosted by Pee Wee King, Eddy Arnold, Jimmy Dean, and Tennessee Ernie Ford. These low-budget affairs took their barn-dance set-up from radio. As the Nashville sound made country radio less traditional, TV programs visually supplied a sense of "home." They were musically diverse, with room for older and newer material. Hosted by men, they gave costarring positions to women artists, an elevation: the Opry had four female members as of 1955 and only 10 percent of recordings featured women. The alternative was honky-tonks, difficult places for women. Parton admitted, "I was always scared in honky-tonks and dives and chicken-wire places when I played them."[17]

Later in 1967, Parton was invited to join the biggest syndicated country TV program, *The Porter Wagoner Show*. Wagoner had been born in 1927 to farmers in the Ozarks; dropping out of elementary school to help his family working as a meat cutter was in his legend. Red Foley invited him to appear on the *Ozark Jubilee*, which aired on ABC after 1954 and also introduced the pop and country prodigy Brenda Lee. Unlike Lee, Wagoner had no chance of Top 40 success. Yet he was not a throwback. He idolized Roy Acuff and bluegrass inventor Bill Monroe, pivotal figures in modernizing tradition. He hired a Russian Jew from Hollywood, Nudie Cohn, and his assistant, Manuel Cuevas, to design elaborate rhinestone suits that made him, in Cuevas's words, "the status quo of flash." His band's key musician, Buck Trent, played a hybrid "electric banjo." His first hit, "Company's Coming," featured a black vocal group. In 1979, Wagoner stirred waters at the Opry by inviting James Brown to perform, a slot rarely offered to non-country acts and certainly not soul singers. "I wish I could go out there and speak my mind, but I won't," Wagoner's hero, Acuff, was said to mutter backstage.[18]

The program Wagoner had started hosting in 1961 was a medicine show: since 1879, the sponsor, Chattanooga Medicine Company, had sold products like the laxative Black Draught. A prominent cast member, comedian and bassist Speck Rhodes, used a blacked-out front tooth to add to the hillbilly look. Wagoner's audience was fanatically loyal: at his urging, 86 percent of them returned a Chattanooga questionnaire. But the music could be adventurous. "Green, Green Grass of Home," written by Curly Putman, who authored "Dumb Blonde" for Parton, went from Wagoner's rendition to an international hit for Tom Jones. Wagoner made concept albums like those of Frank Sinatra and the Beatles, such as the down-and-out *Confessions of a Broken Man*. He was succeeding in 1967 with an old-school entertainer's credo that he passed along to Parton: "Make 'em laugh, make 'em cry . . . and *scare hell out of 'em*."[19]

For a twenty-one-year-old Dolly Parton, ten years of entertaining behind her, the dictate made perfect sense. The folklorists whose impact could still be felt in the Smoky Mountains had depended, Jane Becker notes, on "the invisibility of the Southern Appalachian people in the present."[20] Country musicians recognized no distinction between commercial music and authentic southern expression—only the challenge to be as visible as possible in the present, lit up like a forty-pound rhinestone suit if need be. Between the Nashville sound, the marketing of country

FIGURE 2.2 Porter Wagoner & The Wagon Masters, KRNT-TV (Des Moines, Iowa) studio art card, used in late 1960s to advertise syndicated broadcasts. With Speck Rhodes's blacked-out teeth and sponsorship from dubious medical products, *The Porter Wagoner Show* struck some southerners as "everything we wanted to leave behind." Author's collection.

tradition, and the visualization of the synthesis on television, a genre had been stretched into a pop format.

As Pecknold points out, the secret of country's renewed commercial success was that its old audience was newly valuable, having seen its income swell. In 1940, southerners earned roughly 60 percent of typical American income; by 1960, the figure was 75 percent and climbing, hitting 85 percent by the early 1970s. Only 7 percent of southerners in 1970 engaged in agricultural work; the census stopped counting sharecroppers as a category. Country made this transition with the region. A white-collar metropolis like Nashville epitomized how the selling South challenged the fortress South, even during the civil rights era.[21]

In 1967, the year Dolly Parton began selling Black Draught laxatives on a medicine show, the Beatles released *Sgt. Pepper's Lonely Hearts Club Band* and San Franciscans proclaimed the summer of love. Country seemed to issue from a different century. But Loretta Lynn and Dolly

Parton were part of a new cultural flowering as well: at home in the go-gos and poised in front of a camera, nobody's fools.

A Coat of Many Colors: Country Music under Fire

The CMA Awards first aired on television in 1968. Hosts Roy Rogers and Dale Evans made cowboy films—the western side of country and western. But the first presenter was Chet Atkins, introduced as "Mr. Nashville" and dressed, like all male guests, in a tuxedo. "This is kinda easy, but I'd rather be playing guitar," said the famed session musician, producer, and label executive. Then he handed the award for vocal group to his RCA Records charges Porter Wagoner and Dolly Parton. Nashville had gone uptown, to invoke the dichotomy with down home. But young Jeannie C. Riley, whose "Harper Valley P.T.A." was as much Top 40 as country, came out in boots and a gown that had been retailored at the last minute to end high above the knees.[22]

By 1974, the CMA could pat itself on the back. From the new Opryland complex, host Johnny Cash proclaimed, "In 1961, 80 radio stations throughout the nation were called country music stations. Well, today, the number is over 1000, and the simple fact is that country is today's contemporary music." The critical word was *contemporary*. But what did "country" still mean? Tuxedos were out, and a looser counterculture look was in. When Atkins appeared this time, with the venerable Acuff, to present best female vocalist, he likely expected to hand Parton another trophy: she was on a streak of number 1 singles. As the envelope opened, Acuff looked puzzled. "Oliver Newton-John," he said. Australian Olivia Newton-John's acceptance speech, taped in Europe, talked of "fulfilling an ambition of mine" to record in Nashville. Disgruntled performers, including Parton, formed an association for country traditionalism. It was unsuccessful. The next year, John Denver, also foreign to Music City, was named Entertainer of the Year. Denver was displayed via satellite from Australia. Presenter Charlie Rich lit the results card on fire.

Dolly Parton had not yet set off for Hollywood. But differences over how country should present itself and whom it might include were already deeply felt in Nashville. In the heated politics of the late 1960s and early 1970s, a southern strategy became central to what strategist Kevin Phillips termed "the emerging Republican majority." Country in particular was thought to represent patriotism, religiosity, and patriarchal whiteness.

Wallace and Nixon enlisted country acts and ran ads on country programs. Yet the branding of country as die-hard right wing was as simplistic
a projection as the branding of hillbillies had been. It neither explained
the tuxedoes of 1968 nor Olivia Newton-John in 1974. From a Music Row
perspective, the most heated issues were commercial ones: contesting a
genre and format. Country balanced contradictory premises—rusticity
and New South sophistication, working-class masculinity and white-collar
femininity, self-expression and corporate production. Parton captured the
politics of a loaded euphemism: "People now are acting embarrassed to
say I'm country. Or to say they love the Porter Wagoners and the Hank
Snows and the Ernest Tubbs and the Roy Acuffs and the mountain music.
Why that's like being ashamed of your mama and daddy and your family.
A person that denies their heritage is a person that was never happy."[23]

As a newcomer, Parton emphasized country ties. She told fan publication *Country Song Roundup*, "I never lived in a city at all," discounting
her summers in Knoxville, and emphasized isolation: "We had an old battery radio—every now and then, when it didn't fade out." Everett Corbin,
a defender of traditionalism, wrote, "The Dolly Parton story, although an
interesting one, is not unusual in the sense of hardships suffered by the
artist in rising above the miseries of farm life. The majority of our Country
singers have had similar backgrounds." Parton's resistance to crossover
earned plaudits. "Although recording five 'pop' records, Dolly's heart was
set on recording Country music," Corbin's paper reported, while Parton
assured *Country Song Roundup*, "A lot of people ask me if I have a desire
to be in the movies but I really don't."[24]

Nonetheless, Parton the fashionable working woman registered as
modern. Her booking agency's one-sheet stressed her songwriting first.
While mentioning her "country parents" and "furniture which could have
come out of a history book," Moeller Talent noted that Parton's "professional career" dated to age ten and that "she enjoys the people in the
business." A photo captured her wearing headphones, listening like a session veteran to a playback in the studio. Parton "turned heads" in 1969,
a Nashville paper reported, wearing a pink jumpsuit on the Grand Ole
Opry; her "Dior originals" were mentioned in a 1970 RCA press bio.
The single and title track of her first solo album for RCA in 1968, "Just
Because I'm a Women," made clear Parton's sense of feminine equality. A
woman confesses her sexual experience, the chorus blunt: "My mistakes
are no worse than yours / Just because I'm a woman."[25]

Dolly Parton could be both backwoods and modern in this era's country music. The documentary *The Nashville Sound*, filmed during a 1969

industry convention, captured a breakout format swelling the center. Veterans Bill Monroe and Roy Acuff were still in vogue. Loretta Lynn, Skeeter Davis, and other newer performers courted fan clubs and country radio. Shelby Singleton, producer of "Harper Valley P.T.A.," flaunted chic clothes, shades, and sideburns. Tracy Nelson of country-rock band Mother Earth testified for the underground. Charley Pride was celebrated as country's first black star, winning over the Opry by saying, "It's my music, and I love it better than anything else in the world." The same year, *The Johnny Cash Show*'s mix of rock, country, and pop acts, *Hee Haw*'s combination of a barn-dance show and hip comedy *Laugh-In*, and *Glenn Campbell's Goodtime Hour* all became network hits. Pop embraced every flavor, country included, as the 1960s ended. "Tuesday I'm producing a country-pop novelty, Wednesday an R&B novelty, Thursday a bubble-gum, Friday it's folk-rock with Connie Francis," Singleton told reporter Paul Hemphill.[26]

Wagoner, seen folksily welcoming viewers to "Music City, U.S.A.," at the start of *Nashville Sound*, represented what founding country music historian Bill Malone called "the hillbilly singer in a time of stylistic cloudiness." To Hemphill, who said Wagoner had "the pure hard-country fans by the throat," he was "a hollow-chested, big-nosed, toothy, rough-handed, lanky good old boy who wears a diamond-studded saddle-shaped ring and peroxided-ducktailed-sideburned hair and garishly sequined cowboy suits that defy description. He addresses everybody as 'hoss' and his language is sprinkled with things like 'her and me is goin'' and 'soon's we git th' thang drawed up.' "[27] But Wagoner's "y'all come" vernacular pivoted on consumerism. He was shown in the film advertising (with Parton's help) Goo Goo Candy Clusters during an Opry broadcast.

Despite having said, "I don't try to do anything for the uptown people," Wagoner fit the boosterish New South. Contrast Hemphill's tone with producer Bob Ferguson in an industry how-to book: "Those artists who survive and grow, like Porter Wagoner, prepare themselves in depth for every possible contingency before a session. Porter and his staff confer creatively with the record producer and reach a definite decision about the compositions to be recorded. The musicians to be used are decided upon (they always include Porter's own band, the Wagon Masters). The design of the LP jacket is planned; the writer for the liner notes is selected. Nothing is hit-or-miss about a Porter Wagoner album." In *Nashville Sound* Wagoner was seen at a golf tournament, saying, "I don't think they expect the country figures to play too good," before taking a practiced swing.[28]

Wagoner, the rhinestone hillbilly with his 4 to 6 million weekly viewers, was a polished, forward-thinking embodiment of a style many found hopelessly archaic. Southern historian Edward Ayers confesses, "We liked it when the Byrds or Dylan did country, but the real stuff we saw on Saturday afternoon TV—Porter Wagoner with Dolly Parton in shiny outfits and bouffant hair—struck us as everything we wanted to leave behind." The make 'em cry and scare 'em Wagoner and Parton favored songs that country radio was dropping from its playlists and *Hee Haw* recurrently mocked as "gloom, despair, and agony on me, deep dark depression, excessive misery," material literary scholar Teresa Goddu calls the "repressed in mainstream country music" and an "old South" counterpart to the New South. "I like ballads—real strong, pitiful, sad, crying ballads," Parton said before Wagoner hired her. The duet "Jeannie's Afraid of the Dark," a Parton original about an ill-fated little girl, was the team's most requested in concert. Yet it scarcely received radio airplay.[29]

In response, Parton and Wagoner made 'em laugh, taking a more contemporary approach: comic duets, starting with "The Last Thing on My Mind" by Greenwich Village folk artist Tom Paxton. As part of the "girl singer" trend, *Music City News* noted, male-female duets had become an even bigger country-music staple than before. Each of the three pivotal female singers of the time had a partner: Loretta Lynn and Conway Twitty, Tammy Wynette and George Jones, Parton and Wagoner, as well as Johnny Cash and June Carter Cash. Homey but upbeat, testing gender limits in a manner more bantering than confrontational, the era's duets captured country's pairing of contemporary pop and southern values. Parton's solo success began with equally jovial material. "Muleskinner Blues" dated back to Jimmie Rodgers. But with the sound effect of a whip cracking used in campy fashion, a rock rhythm, and electrified picking where a bluegrass banjo had been, the song's discotheque feminization of male material tweaked tradition. Similarly, "Joshua," a 1971 Parton original and her first country number 1, highlighted a drum pattern and dance beat as it cozied up to a bearded hermit in a run-down shack.[30]

Songs as arch and urbane as "Joshua" and "Muleskinner Blues" wink at standard characterizations of country in this era. For example, Dan Carter writes, "The lyrics, derided by sophisticates for their sentimentality, captured the intensely personal preoccupations of a traditional culture; love unfulfilled or gone wrong, faithless women, bad whiskey, and the ultimate triumph of traditional morality." When Parton did record such themes, as with "My Blue Ridge Mountain Boy" about a woman gone to sin in New Orleans, radio was unreceptive—it peaked at number 45. Carter sees Merle Haggard as symbolic of "men who drank hard, worked harder, loved their country, and had little use for welfare cheats or unpatriotic hippies. More and more, country music was becoming the conservative voice of young white working-class Americans across America." Yet Haggard, far from this stereotype in his catalogue of work, unreservedly rebuked George Wallace. "Any time I represent George Wallace, man, I'm liable to lose a lot of my fans. Wallace is unrefined and uncontemporary. He's strictly against the black man. He wants to keep 'em niggers."[31]

Haggard had reason to be self-conscious about his contemporary appeal despite the hippie-baiting "Okie from Muskogee" and sequel "Fighting Side of Me." Most right-wing country acts were outdated, like Ernest Tubb singing "It's America (Love It or Leave It)," or marginal to the format, like Anita Bryant and Sergeant Barry Sadler. Country radio pursued what *Look* called a "hip face-lift." Kris Kristofferson, the "first superstar of the new country music," opened playlists to candor about sex and drugs with "Help Me Make It through the Night" and "Sunday Morning Coming Down." "In the rock business they used to say 'talk dirty and play the hits' and it seems like in the country business 'you talk clean and play the dirty hits,'" said Indianapolis country station general manager (GM) Don Nelson. Radio's goal was relevance, not prurience: Nelson contentedly noted that Stouffer, maker of frozen TV dinners, had dropped its opposition to the country format.[32]

Bill Malone argues that country politics were "eclectic and contradictory," not straightforwardly reactionary. Commercial imperatives, linked to the role of women in expanding country's reach as a format, guaranteed that. Tammy Wynette, a staunch Republican whose "Stand by Your Man" was heard by some as submissive, pointedly noted her multiple husbands: "I guess I've proven that I don't believe in staying with a man you no longer love." She was adamant: "I absolutely will not let *anyone* make me feel guilty about being a working mother." Long after the controversy her hit inspired, she wrote, "In those years, there weren't more than a half-dozen women headlining their own shows in country music, and every time one of us stood up for our rights she made a point for us all. We had our own 'liberation movement' going, but I don't think any of us were aware of it. I know I wasn't. All I wanted was the right to work in my chosen field and be treated with as much respect as the men who did the same job." Rebuking country's purported obeisance to farm life, Wynette snorted,

"I don't *ever* want to walk through a cotton field again. Every time we pass one in the bus I get a backache."[33]

Still, as Nixon invited country singers to the White House, centrist channels that had included country pushed away. CBS canceled shows it deemed "too rural" for advertisers, including *Hee Haw* (afterward syndicated), Cash's show, and sitcoms *Green Acres* and *Beverly Hillbillies*. While country music and R&B were assumed to take opposite stances on social transformation, their parallels are instructive. Both moved from mainstream appeal to an image of radical intransigence at the turn of the 1970s. Each, as genres fragmenting Top 40 formatting, targeted listeners whose particularity was encouraged rather than suppressed. This fed statements of identity pride. Soul had James Brown's "Say It Loud (I'm Black and I'm Proud)." Merle Haggard, proud to be an "Okie from Muskogee," recorded "I Take a Lot of Pride in What I Am." Loretta Lynn was proud to be a coal miner's daughter.[34]

And Dolly Parton had "Coat of Many Colors," a defining statement cementing her as a major country figure. Even when it was known only through concert and TV versions, *Country Song Roundup* made it the focus of a profile, which ended, "Dolly Parton is a complex, totally feminine woman, whose values lie in the importance of things like the story behind the coat of many colors." Parton's mother, the song relayed, fashioned her coat out of scraps, enchanting her with the biblical tale of Joseph. But when Dolly wore the coat to school, she was ridiculed. There the verses ended, but this was no old-fashioned weeper. The tone was victorious, musically with the "rich" production and lyrically: "I was rich as I could be, in my coat of many colors that my mama made for me, made just for me." *Just for me.* The meaning was double: Christian parable of solace in family; motivational message of a star who wore special clothing routinely. Country origins were hard, but the ordinary could transform. A photo of young Parton in the coat appeared in *Country Song Roundup* in 1969 and on 1971's *Coat of Many Colors*.[35]

Despite its eventual importance, "Coat of Many Colors" was not a number 1 country song, and a subsequent album of similar themes, *My Tennessee Mountain Home*, reached no higher than 19 on the country charts. Wagoner eventually told Parton that "all this Smoky Mountain squalor no longer captivated the housewives or the disc jockeys." Parton took him at his word. "Jolene," despite its tune's Appalachian modalities, was a frustrated love song with a modern beat that earned a *Billboard* profile: "Songs Go Pop, She Stays Country." Her next three singles mentioned "Love" in their title. All, like "Jolene," hit number 1. The greatest, "I Will Always Love You," was covered by Whitney Houston in 1992's *The Bodyguard,* driving soundtrack sales of 17 million.[36]

The original country smash, however, sold about 200,000 copies. As Ferguson explained in his how-to book, country and R&B hits meant 100,000 sold; pop, 500,000; and rock, 750,000. Here, too, country and R&B resembled each other. Yet their potential was different. Recall James Gregory's argument. Racist housing policies concentrated migrating blacks in ghettoes close to the urban center. White southern migration was suburban and dispersed. In part as a result, black music registered as urban and modern. White southern vernacular registered as reactionary. The implications for radio were important. The music industry saw R&B as a vanguard genre and country as a backward one. R&B was ripe for crossover *into* Top 40 if it succeeded with blacks. A country hit, like Parton's "I Will Always Love You," was presumed of no pop interest. Country-pop crossover, whether by an unaccented Arkansan such as Glen Campbell or Olivia Newton-John, meant crossover *out of* adult pop (MOR/AC) to country listeners. A consultant explained, "Most pop stations are reluctant to play country artists, while the opposite is true of country stations. They're always looking to get wider demographics."[37]

Concerned to seem contemporary to advertisers, country radio played adult pop: the easy listening of Newton-John and Denver. Country labels fashioned music with a similar sound. Paul Hemphill charged, "Suddenly country wasn't country anymore. Artistic, yes. Soulful, no." The new Association of Country Entertainers stated as its purpose "to preserve the identity of country music as a separate and distinct form of entertainment." Wagoner turned to the fan magazine *Country Song Roundup* to complain, "The MOR, the country pop, so to speak, has carved a big hole in the true Country music." He noted sardonically, "The trade papers and the CMA must feel a lot different." Wagoner had resisted singing songs that attacked hippies after "Okie from Muskogee" made Merle Haggard's fortune. He encouraged Parton to reshape her material to please modern housewives and country radio; by 1979 he'd invite Brown to the Opry. Still, in the face of MOR blurring with country, he turned ugly. "It's kind of like mixing all the races. I feel like each race should have equal rights in every phase of life, but they shouldn't all mix together—intermarriage, and so forth. I feel all music should be the same way. It should have equal opportunity, but there should be a separation."[38]

The CMA, by contrast, promoted country as racially inclusive. Pride, the most popular black performer Nashville had produced, hosted the 1975 CMA Awards where Denver's victory card went up in flames. Introducing Freddy Fender, Pride said, "He calls himself the Tex-Mex singer, and is very proud of it." Next to stage came Johnny Rodriguez, another of country's great Latino hopes. Presenting best female vocalist, pop-country singer Mac Davis teased pop-country singer Bobby Goldsboro about his outfit: "You look like Gladys Knight and the Pips [an R&B group] blew up on you."

The most listened-to country station in America in the mid-1970s was not southern, but Chicago's WMAQ. Its program director (PD), Mississippi native Bob Pittman, was only twenty-two when *Radio & Records* interviewed him in 1976. Like Clive Davis, his closest counterpart in the record industry, Pittman was fascinated by formats positioning sound to sell audiences. "WMAQ plays Country music with the tightness of Top 40 radio, but with the class and warmth of Pop/Adult radio," he told *Radio & Records*. A short playlist of songs and adult orientation in address were two keys. Another was caution with MOR/AC acts. "We've found some great discrepancies between record sales and our call-out research. For example, an Olivia Newton-John record or a Glen Campbell tends to appeal to these very passive people that don't buy records and don't call request lines." Pittman, soon to found MTV and much later to become CEO of radio chain Clear Channel, saw the country format as a flame to tend, not a musical ideal. Asked if he realized his success made him one of the most talked-about program directors in the nation, Pittman replied, "Most hated . . ."[39]

Overall, *Radio & Records* concluded, country had changed dramatically. "Country music has progressed tremendously over the last five to ten years. The lyrics of today's Country recordings are more explicit and leave less to the imagination than they once did. Artists' styles and appearances as well as product, have all become modernized to a great degree. Long hair and funky clothing are in." Yet the challenges that prompted formatting remained. CMA executive director Jo Walker acknowledged, "It is still the contention of some advertisers that the Country music fan doesn't buy expensively packaged foods or they don't take airline trips." To reach, or appear to reach, more upscale listeners was a constant priority that contradicted a populist genre.[40]

Ultimately, the CMA found a way to reinforce country's identity in the midst of a hip facelift. "I'm not sure where the idea for Fan Fair originated, but I know that Porter was involved right at the beginning," said

Walker about a new Nashville institution. Beginning in 1972 with five thousand participants, doubling the next year, Fan Fair offered a week of star showcases and autograph signings. Like TV barn dances, it supplied cultural ballast. Where the CMA had canonized the tradition of country, now it singled out the loyalty of country fans, who as Pittman noted were active, rewarding favorites with decades of support.[41]

Where was Dolly Parton in all this? Her look and manner challenged the class implications of country's mandated contemporaneity. Carole-Anne Tyler has shrewdly pointed out, "It is only from a middle-class point of view that Dolly Parton looks like a female impersonator." This contextualizes Parton's caustic comments about a CMA inclusive to all but the music appearing downscale: "Every year I've been on the CMA awards show, even when I was just presenting, they have always asked me to wear less hair and make-up. Then I would be like everybody else and I don't want to be like everybody else." Yet, when Parton did finally win best female vocalist, in 1975, it was for "Love Is Like a Butterfly," an MOR-type recording that made no class assertions. Parton was executing her own crossover campaign. In 1974, she quit Wagoner's TV show; in 1976, she stopped having him oversee her albums—seventeen solo and thirteen duet LPs since 1967. Significantly, given the links between musical and racial crossover, Parton's first self-produced album included two covers of R&B songs that had become Top 40 hits: "My Girl" and "Higher and Higher." Wagoner said that Parton "wanted to be more like Aretha Franklin and scream on songs."[42]

"I Will Always Love You" encapsulated Parton's ambitions: to leave Wagoner and the structural isolation of country. If its counterpart as Parton's defining statement, "Coat of Many Colors," was a genre anthem hinting at pop stardom, "I Will Always Love You" was a format anthem aware of which roots it was yanking out. It seemed, on the surface, a saccharine MOR/AC ballad—the title line drawn out for maximum impact in the chorus. Later, Parton revealed it a farewell note to Wagoner. "Bittersweet memories, that's all I have and I'm taking with me," she sang, moving forward while looking back. The most traditionally country element in the song, its closing recitation—sung instead by Whitney Houston in her blockbuster power-ballad version—celebrated the least country subject, romantic love. Parton spends more time analyzing the topic in her memoir than her years with Wagoner. Country people, she explains, her father included, struggled to express love. It belonged to a pop culture—urban, middle-class—fairy tale.[43]

Country Song Roundup ran two profiles of Parton in 1974, as she prepared to transform herself. In one, she was told, "You may be the nearest
thing we have in Nashville to being glamorous," and hinted at the wise-
cracking icon to come. Asked, "You're a very happily married housewife,
Dolly, is that right?" she responded, "I don't know about the housewife
too much, but I am married. 'Course I don't spend too awful much time
at home . . ." In the other she recounted her mother's mountain songs, her
great-grandma's autoharp, and her cooking the poor family's salvation:
"polk salat," a mountain weed. Hobbies? "I love to spend my time with
my cows," Parton said. A streak of defensiveness rose up briefly. "I'm as
good as gold when people are good to me, but when people start cutting
me because I'm country and cut country people, I can cut back. I'm not
going to be embarrassed by those kind of people. I'm not ashamed of
what I am."[44]

From Hillbilly Heaven to Beverly Hills: Crossing Over

In the cynical depths of the 1970s, between Nixon's resignation and Carter's
election, Robert Altman directed *Nashville*, a corrosive satire of country
music, American politics, and their shared intoxication with celebrity and
manipulation. The female lead, played by Ronee Blakley, was modeled
on Lynn, but "My Idaho Home," performed at Nashville's Parthenon
copy, imitated Parton's "My Tennessee Mountain Home." Karen Black,
another of the actresses, appeared on *Dolly*. She was pressed to share
warm feelings about Music City—anecdotes of Nashville fawning over
Hollywood celebrities. The program cut to footage of Parton, at the faux
Parthenon, in a Greek outfit, singing the MOR ballad "First Time Ever
I Saw Your Face." *Dolly*, the first country TV series hosted by a woman,
lasted one season, a stylistic mess.[45]

Parton transformed from Nashville to global icon, but it helps to retain
how preposterous the quest could appear. To many, country remained
a corny joke. One pop style claimed to resist formula: the rock underground. But Parton found it impossible for a woman to embody the outlaw status rock bestowed on Willie Nelson and Waylon Jennings, or for
a rural southerner to be elevated to singer-songwriter artiste. Her crossover required the most rootless option: MOR/AC, which left her making
disco records and headlining a Vegas revue. Parton the personality—
movie star, "queen of the tabloids," and motivational speaker—replaced

Parton the musician. Country followed Parton's course. The "urban cowboy" craze swelled stations from 1,400 to 2,300 between 1979 and 1983.
Country retooled to place its songs in MOR/AC. Benefiting were women,
whose tally of number 1 country hits rose from twelve in the 1960s to
eighty in the 1970s.[46]

Parton had reason to think, as she separated from Porter Wagoner,
that the rock world would embrace her. Wagoner did too. In 1976, he
hand typed a memo to RCA executives:

> Concerning Dolly's records, there must be something, I mean must be some-
> thing, done about Dolly's records in the underground markets. This is the area
> where we can sell more Dolly Parton albums than all the other fields combined.
> The kids of the underground nature are really into Dolly in a big way. They
> love her records. They attend her concerts. But her albums are not at their
> stores. . . . They're up the street at the nice big record shop with the clear glass
> window and a beautiful display inside where you'll find the Best of Floyd
> Cramer, the Best of Perry Como, etc. But back in those little psychedelic places
> are where people like Linda Ronstadt, Emmylou Harris, Papa John [Creach]
> and so forth sells millions and millions of albums. . . . Rolling Stone, People, and
> the Village [Voice] magazine from New York and approximately 7 other lead-
> ing underground papers have done in-depth articles on Dolly, so the promotion
> is already done for us.

Wagoner's sense of rock as "psychedelic" and *People* as an underground
publication might have been off, but his point was accurate: what passed
for mainstream did not outsell what passed for underground, particularly
with albums—the key challenge for country acts in the 1970s.[47]

As Billy Sherrill, head of country artists and repertoire (A&R) for
CBS, put it, "Blue Oyster Cult can sell double platinum without a hit
single. Country music to the average country buyer is more of a background type music than the kind of music that kids get into and memo-
rize every lyric and drum and guitar lick." R&B, with its ties to Top 40
pop, had crossed this divide more quickly than country, with its ties to an
audience perceived as passive about album purchases. Norrow Wilson,
branch manager of Warner Music in Nashville, said, "The pop people
allocate all kinds of money to spend on albums, but they don't seem to
see country ever selling that much—but they didn't see it for r&b either
and look what's happening there." A 1976 study found that in country,
singles still outnumbered albums in sales. In pop as a whole, most bought

LPs at record stores first, then discount stores, then department stores. It reversed for country. Joe Galante, Parton's executive at RCA, understood: "Consumers are also often intimidated by the strong rock orientation of record stores' displays, designs and the clerks themselves, leading to an uncomfortable feeling in general."[48]

The exception was country acts with rock attitude. RCA in 1976 released *Wanted! The Outlaws*, the first country album to get the new certification platinum—a million seller. Interest in crossing country and rock had brewed for years. *Country Music,* modeled on *Rolling Stone* and featuring some of its writers, was founded in 1972 to nurture underground country. The first record review praised Kristofferson for combining "appeal to both rock and country markets with an almost uncanny blend of personal sex appeal, hip lifestyle, shades of country roots, simple but catchy melodies, and updated versions of the Lonesome Cowboy/ Ruthless Gunfighter lyrical theme." Registered Democrat Tom T. Hall, who'd written "Harper Valley P.T.A." and the antiwar "Hello Vietnam," assured the magazine that Haggard's politics were fluid: "One day he's probably liberal and another day something else." Conway Twitty professed love for rockers Creedence Clearwater Revival. *Country Music* differed from *Country Song Roundup* in applying rock's anti-commercial aesthetics to the country industry. In his "In Defense of the Telecaster Cowboy Outlaws," critic-provocateur Dave Hickey saluted Waylon Jennings and Willie Nelson as "just about the only folks in Nashville who will walk into a room where there's a guitar and a *Wall Street Journal* and pick up the guitar." Using Hickey's title, Nelson, Jennings, Jennings's wife Jessi Coulter, and Tompall Glaser became "the Outlaws," RCA-sanctioned genre rebels against format mainstreaming.[49]

By 1976, with Carter running as a religious southerner but New South pragmatist who quoted Bob Dylan and talked to *Playboy*, country music declared itself progressive Americana. Tanya Tucker, Nashville's teen idol, hit with "I Believe the South Is Gonna Rise Again," rebel spirit for an integrationist punch line: "but not the same as it was back then." In *Country Music*, whose bicentennial issue dressed Parton on the cover as the Statue of Liberty, one letter writer complained, "It seems if you aren't for Jimmy Carter, you aren't for country music." *Country Rambler* called Carter "The Outlaw's Choice" in its launch issue. Charlie Daniels said, "This is the first time there's been an alternative candidate from the South: Jimmy Carter. It's always been George Wallace or nobody." The publisher wrote, "New country music is NOT an exercise in plastic what's

July 1976, One Dollar
COUNTRY MUSIC
SPECIAL ISSUE
The Country Bicentennial
The History Of Country Music, Part One
Country's Russian Birthday Party: Roy Clark In The USSR
The All-Time All-Star Hit Parade
Waylon/Jessi Centerfold

FIGURE 2.3 Parton as the Statue of Liberty on cover of the July 1976 bicentennial issue of *Country Music* magazine. Remembered as a bastion of conservatism, country in the year of Jimmy Carter's election flirted with rock counterculture. Author's collection.

right with America flag-waving. It is simple music that reflects the needs of people who need one another within a framework of individual independence." He concluded, "Just ain't no Generation Gap among true Country Ramblers."[50]

Yet a gap remained between underground country and Nashville. Even as the Sun Belt became an economic force, rockers looked to country for countercultural disaffection from a suburban mainstream. Marc Landy, director of the Appalachian Oral History Project, wrote, "The qualities of protest, cynicism, moralism and plaintiveness which have long characterized southern music have, at this chaotic juncture in our history, transformed it into the popular music of contemporary America." Those against CMA gloss discovered commonalities with hippies. *Music City News* proclaimed, "Stand up, lovers of tradition; the longhairs, hippies, and youngsters have stepped in to save us!" The writer insisted, "Country music is going pop BECAUSE too many radio station program directors won't play so-called underground country music."[51]

Parton had fans in the rock underground, where dead-baby songs like "Jeannie's Afraid of the Dark," backward to country radio, were prized as unvarnished expression. The Grateful Dead's Jerry Garcia was known to be a major fan. Hickey advocated as passionately for her as he had for the Outlaws. Hunter S. Thompson touted her in *Fear and Loathing: On the Campaign Trail*. In *Country Style*, singer-songwriter Maria Muldaur said Parton "goes beyond that canned syrup out of Nashville." Told her "show of independence" from Wagoner had attracted "'underground' country fans, the younger set," Parton responded, "That's all I hear lately. People keep asking me if I'm aware of how popular I'm becoming in those areas. I had to look and live like the hippies are looking and living now. . . . The faded denim and stringy hair and scrubbed faces . . . I know what it feels like to live down to earthy—to be earth people. I still am inside."[52]

One of the few variety-program episodes Parton cherished connected her with two female rock singer-songwriters. Linda Ronstadt covered "I Will Always Love You." Emmylou Harris, who had partnered with country rocker Gram Parsons, remade "Coat of Many Colors." When they appeared on *Dolly*, the tone became folkloric, the three harmonizing the old favorite, "Silver Threads and Golden Needles."

Yet when Parton tested her underground credentials, the results disappointed. She opened for Willie Nelson on a tour dubbed "The Outlaw and the Lady" and found his fans were not hers. *Country Music* reported, "If the guys have long hair and wear dungarees and flannel shirts—that progressive country look—then they've come to see Willie. If they're

rednecks with flattops who bring women with teased hair wearing short
skirts or tight pants, then they've come to see Dolly." The early 1977
album *New Harvest . . . First Gathering*, the first without Wagoner's input,
topped country charts, helped by "Applejack," a song in the upbeat yet
down-home style of "Joshua." But the album stalled at number 71 pop.
Rock single "Light of a Clear Blue Morning" did even worse. "You know
how rock audiences are," Parton said. "They like certain songs, but now if
the image doesn't fit, if the personality is not fitting, they feel, 'Oh, that's
hokey,' or 'that person's corny.'" She fumed to RCA, "When you son-of-a-
bitches learn how to sell a female Elton John with long hair and big boobs
that dresses like a freak, then we'll make some money."[53]

Where rock failed her, MOR/AC provided a platform. In particular,
television once again gave Parton a route to the public. Her early *Tonight
Show* appearances followed a pattern: perform a pop song, joke with
Carson, end with a country number. It was a balance, like Parton's duets
with Wagoner or the CMA fusing progress and tradition. Similarly, two
story lines about Parton fascinated Carson. One was essentially country
and southern: her upbringing in a poor family of twelve children. But the
other was essentially pop and female: her unconventional marriage to Carl
Dean, who never saw her perform and rarely saw her. TV appearances
became the most complete way to experience Parton's multiplicity. Was it
all a pose? As Parton became a superstar, in 1977–78, Studio 54 opened
and disco crested. Earlier, black power, the Bicentennial, and southern
pride had favored what the popular TV miniseries dubbed *Roots*. Now
the dominant note was artifice and image. Parton fit the mood: she was
feted by Andy Warhol, Mick Jagger, John Belushi, and Jack Nicholson;
teased a gay audience in San Francisco, "Well, 'tis the season to be jolly";
acknowledged the "gimmick" of her appearance. Celebrity culture loved
both sides of Parton's duet with modernity: impudence toward tradition
and incorporation of heritage. Photographer Annie Leibovitz shot her in
unnatural poses with an equally unreal physique, Arnold Schwarzenegger,
yet the accompanying feature called her a "purifier." Parton responded,
"City people, I think they get caught up with a southern, a country person
who has a contentment and a peacefulness. I am certainly not *pure*, but
I guess that depends on how you look at things." If her breasts were the
joke—"here they are, Dolly Parton"—her progress in life was the sentimental payoff.[54]

Parton finally secured a Top 40 and AC hit, as well as country, with
"Here You Come Again," written by two Brill Building veterans, Cynthia
Mann and Barry Weill. The song, an adult flirtation, was light in tone

FIGURE 2.4 Parton with Johnny Carson on *The Tonight Show*, 1977. Carson has just said, "I would give about a year's pay to peek under there." Parson's ability to flourish in such charged moments allowed her format leap. Still from *Tonight Show Memories* (DVD, Respond2 Entertainment, 2002).

but aggressively marketed. "We called every station in the country," said Tony Scotti of the Scotti Brothers. "We have more than a dozen people on our staff who do nothing but phone work." A program director said, "I don't think the song was strong enough to become a million-seller. The promotion behind it sold it." Producer Gary Klein had worked with Barbra Streisand, Glen Campbell, and Gladys Knight. One label executive charged, "He's a lousy producer. He's hired to take people from one field to another and make them more acceptable to middle-of-the-road radio. He represents the middlebrow middleground in our business."[55]

Parton had severed remaining connections with Porter Wagoner, ended her Nashville-produced TV program, found West Coast booking agents, and hired as management Olivia Newton-John's company. *Esquire,* asking an interview for a feature on Parton, Lynn, and Wynette, was told, "We don't want her lumped in with those country singers." Promoters were informed, "Dolly's management is expecting this show

to be promoted basically as a top 40 presentation; not country. We do not
want to find, once the tour is on the road, that a country station has its call
letters on a show or is a presenting station. We do not object to radio time
buys on country stations as long as the top 40 stations are purchased as
well."[56]

Discarded, apparently, was the artist who said in 1975, "I don't think
commercial. I write from my heart." Who, asked about feminism, de-
murred, "I know a lot less about woman's liberation than you think.
Remember I was brought up in a household of men and taught men were
head of the household. I still believe this." She had told Nashville the
greatest thing was "being born and *then* being born again," elaborating,
"We used to enjoy the revival meetings and wouldn't have missed any of
them for the world, even if we did have to walk to them." Now, Parton
confessed that in her grandfather's hellfire rendition, "We thought God
was a monster in the sky." Her sex quips earned Mae West comparisons.
Her gay following, "on hand to celebrate Dolly's tacky fashion and newfound disco success," adulated the diva who called her twenty-three-room
Nashville mansion Tara. When tabloids exposed her sharing a Central
Park apartment with her manager, she retorted, "He's not interested in
any woman." Embracing disco, she made "Baby I'm Burnin'." "Dolly
Parton Is Hot! Dolly Parton Is for All Formats . . . All Demographics!"
shouted an ad in the music trades.[57]

"I am Dolly Parton from the mountains, and that's what I'll remain,"
she had pledged. And *Cosmopolitan* quoted her as if she really were still
a hillbilly. "They come in when I was eight. Yes, I've had titties since I
was eight. Got mah period when I was nine. I jest grew up rul quick. Took
after mah father's people more than mah mamma's. I looked grown-up
when I was eleven." Asked on *Mike Douglas* if her family had owned a
television, she said, "If we had, it would have had to run on kerosene."
Joking about a subject that would later inspire her literacy campaigns, she
told a radio host her dad "couldn't even read John Deere." Parton might
have been the only superstar of the 1970s who *Playboy* asked, "When did
you first use a flush toilet?" Her mainstream pop brought regular howls
from admirers. In *Rolling Stone* Tom Carson wrote, "In the year since
Dolly Parton's widely publicized crossover from the country genre to the
MOR mainstream, the quality of her music has gone dramatically down-
hill while her fame vaults toward the tinsel regions of instant media celebrity," calling her album *Heartbreaker* "flat-out commercial shmaltz aimed
straight at the *Johnny Carson Show*." Told by a writer that he hadn't liked

FIGURE 2.5 Parton on the cover of *People* magazine, April 4, 1977. As Parton moved from country to MOR/AC appeal, the institutions that could popularize and recontextualize a performer—magazines, television, everything represented by Hollywood—mattered as much as radio. Author's collection.

her recent recordings, Parton replied with a twist Bill Clinton might have learned from: "To be even franker, neither did I!"[58]

But then, records were no longer her main platform. "I've used my time in a wiser way than if I had totally thrown myself into just my music and my songs," she informed *Parade*. "Then I wouldn't have done the movies. And I wouldn't have done Vegas. I wouldn't have progressed to this point. I am not particularly fond of some of the pop music I recorded, but I needed it to be really appreciated." As the *Saturday Night Fever* soundtrack became the biggest-selling album in history, Parton applied her own multimedia synergy. She went from crossover to cross-promotion: weeks at Vegas casinos that paid up to $400,000, more than any other performer; a starring role and Oscar nomination in the film *Nine to Five*; a poster to rival actress Farrah Fawcett-Majors. Appearing with Cher on a TV special, dressing up like a Bunny on the cover of *Playboy*, or serving as exposé of the minute in *Photoplay*, the *Enquirer*, and *Us Weekly*, became as central to her status as any hit record. Looking back in 1991, she saluted her tabloid-magazine base: "I think they've done more for my career than my record sales just by stirring up stuff and keeping you hot."[59]

For traditionalist critics, Parton had offended all norms of the country genre. A critic in Charleston called her disco-era song "Two Doors Down," about casual sex, "absolutely sickening," saying, "What she wants to be is a teen-age idol, playing in front of pot-smoking crowds at rock concerts." Porter Wagoner charged, "Her family, her own blood—she would turn her back on them. . . . I don't believe a country girl singer would do things in the manner of she's done them. Like the *Playboy* thing. Do you think Kitty Wells would do that?" Everett Corbin, first to cover her in *Music City News*, made her a villain of his book *Storm over Nashville*.[60]

Yet as country critic Patrick Carr nails it, "Music Row, as always, accepted success." "I'm not leaving country, I'm taking country with me," Parton said repeatedly. Courting Nashville, she sang "Here You Come Again" on the 1977 CMA Awards and joshed with longtime Opry comedienne Minnie Pearl. The next year she became Entertainer of the Year. Now she was the artist from outside the country field, in format terms, whose pop breakout had gone from MOR to country. "Some of us have known Dolly Parton since she was just a youngster, starting out in country music, and now we realize that we have to share her with the rest of the country, whether we want to or not," said return host Johnny Cash, no stranger to crossover. "As a matter of fact, she's on the cover of

Playboy magazine, and she's not a centerfold. I sneaked a peek, didn't you?" Country remained a southern industry; sales arbitrated legitimacy. Hank Snow—an RCA artist since 1936 who'd complained, "If it keeps on the way it's going, I'd say country music, as we know it, will be gone in two years"—resigned in 1977 as president of the Association of Country Entertainers. He admitted, "These stations are successful with their top-forty. And as long as they are successful, you can't argue with them." When *Country Music* accused Parton of having "an inferiority complex" about the music, a reader commented, "Country Music Magazine, long before Dolly slicked up her image, slicked up its image. . . . Ms. Parton's goals are much the same as yours—to bring country music to the city."[61]

"To bring country music to the city": Parton fulfilled what the CMA sought. Updating tradition, she became a crossover superstar who could only be country. Her promotions for Breeze soap powder on the Wagoner show were still fondly recalled. "You got to look at anything like a business," she said to the trade magazine *Hits*, matter-of-fact that "Here You Come Again" was "not the kind of song I sing well" but made sense strategically. She recited sales figures for different singles, one-nighter guarantees, the cost of her tour bus. She told Walters during their first interview, in pop "you can make millions compared to thousands." To a Tennessee writer, she added, "I love the traditional ways. But the traditional records aren't selling very much." Parton called her Las Vegas revue "a bigger show—more uptown—than I would do in concert. And there's no denying the money is really great."[62]

The notion of taking country "uptown" had driven format growth. Parton made that quest about expanding, not eradicating, identity, deploying class and gender. Dolly Parton, woman or worker, loomed larger, when necessary, than Dolly Parton, southerner. The 1980 movie *Nine to Five* was an example. If Jane Fonda, according to Parton, said, "Dolly'll get us the South" in pushing for her hire, the film's working women lived in the North.[63] The secretary Parton played, warding off her boss's advances, was hardly uptown. Parton's self-composed theme, her first to reach number 1 Top 40, was not country sounding with its caffeinated typing pool rhythm—but far from a love song: "You spend your life putting money in his wallet." The even bigger 1983 hit, "Islands in the Stream," a duet with Kenny Rogers written by the Bee Gees, was romantic fantasy. But the karaoke chestnut-to-be retained the needy energy of her duets with Wagoner.

Could Nashville follow her lead? "Country's Hot," *Billboard* declared in 1979; more than two thousand stations now aired the format, number 1 in eighty-four radio markets. Jim Fogelson, president of MCA Nashville, uttered an increasingly common sentiment: "Modern country music is more and more becoming the MOR music of the U.S." As disco faded, a new John Travolta movie, *Urban Cowboy*, promoted a country-pop boom. *Coal Miner's Daughter*, about the life of Loretta Lynn, emphasized the singer as a proto-feminist. *Radio & Record*'s publisher wrote, "Country is going through a national phenomenon, and the demographics are proven and salable. Country stations all across that nation are making money—it seems it's been the avoided area for some reason, and all of a sudden it's the center of attention. It differs from disco in that disco was a brand new fad that didn't have any track record, no one knew where the listeners were. Country makes perfect sense for radio, and I'm surprised it took as long as it did." New York's WHN won high ratings going country, and three Los Angeles stations started in 1980 alone.[64]

Women, so often the antidote to country's backward image, remained central to format expansion; they occupied an unprecedented eight of the top eleven slots on the country singles charts one week in 1980. Barbara Mandrell, country music's new leading lady, hosted a successful variety show on NBC, reached the AC charts and some Top 40 stations with "(If Loving You Is Wrong) I Don't Want to Be Right," then celebrated with "I Was Country When Country Wasn't Cool." As one consultant put it, "People who a year or two ago would never admit that they listened to a Country station because of the stigma attached, now feel it's okay because of the mass media, television and, of course, the music industry. After all, Barbara Mandrell is a very nice-looking lady, and I'm sure she doesn't drive a pickup truck with a gun rack."[65]

Hungry Again: 1980s Neotraditionalism

Even during an adamant crossover campaign, Dolly Parton kept faith with her own version of country traditionalism, as exemplified by "Me and Little Andy." The country-themed second performance on her debut Carson appearance, it became her standout composition on the crossover *Here You Come Again*. Many found it mawkish. Pete Axthelm wrote in *Newsweek*, "It is about a little girl and a faithful dog, a drunken daddy and a broken home. In the last verse, everybody dies." Parton had countless songs like this early on, the weepers a modernizing country radio spurned, *Porter Wagoner Show* fans revered, and her small rock cult cherished as extreme. A musician on Parton's 1977 supper-club tour with Mac Davis, part of her MOR move, recalled her fighting management to keep it in the set list. "You and I may be very jaded and sophisticated and think that song transcends the boundaries of good taste, but that's Dolly's song. And the average person out there will cry when she sings it." For Axthelm, the song was proof that "Dolly is crossing over with her country soul intact." For Mitchell Morris most recently, who ends his study of mainstream 1970s pop (including Parton) with "Me and Little Andy," the "over the top" sentimentality of its performance draws upon deeply rooted histories of suffering that negate the camp potential of a crossover performance: "The music that Parton sings is the best proof of her contention that she is a simple country woman—her bid to claim something that looks very like an essential identity." Parton used related rhetoric: true country luxuriated in the abject. In 1983's *Dolly in Concert* performance from London for HBO, she introduced "Me and Little Andy": "This one is absolutely *pitiful*." Later, she added, "Well, I can see you love them old sad songs, just like I do. I love country music, it's my favorite of all."[66]

Nashville writer Jack Hurst smartly observed, "Parton's music didn't abruptly leave the country mainstream, as is often charged; it had never been in it. Part of her music, the innocent Appalachian part, had always been far behind country music's times, whereas her fascination with combining the innocent part with rebellious rock and pop techniques was far ahead of them. Musically, she was Daisy Mae in overdrive." Format country inherently balanced tradition and pop. But Hurst's last comment, a play on Alan Lomax calling bluegrass "folk music in overdrive," is worth savoring. Bluegrass transformed comic and old-timey southern music into a revered invented tradition. Parton worked similar magic. Walters had asked, "Do you ever feel that you're a joke?" Superstar Dolly used humor, femininity, and lore to traditionalize the New South. Nashville tourism ads featuring her in *Better Homes and Gardens*, *Southern Living*, and *Reader's Digest* garnered twenty-three thousand information requests and eighteen leads on major conventions. In the 1980s, she created her own theme park, Dollywood, profitably steeped in regional crafts, family entertainment, and splashy rides. Again she harmonized with the format ambitions of country, which now commercialized "neotraditionalism."[67]

It would be deceptive to present Parton's crossover as untroubled. When Walters returned for a second interview in 1982, Parton performed at a casino rather than the rodeo of five years back, and spoke in her mansion, not her tour bus. She was excited about a new cosmetics line: "I am your all-American girl, so to speak." But she also spoke of "female problems" and collapsing onstage. Part of her anguish came from star-ring in *Best Little Whorehouse in Texas*, "the moral issue of whether to do it, being from a religious family." Parton sang a Jesus song written in her down spell, "Calm on the Waters." And she announced Dollywood, her "Smoky Mountain fairyland." Parton increasingly projected confu-sion in her work. A second hosted TV program, this time on ABC in 1987, ended as quickly as the first: Parton singing Hank Williams with campy children's TV star Pee-wee Herman was unsuccessful hybridity. Longing for home became her most frequent theme. The powerful "Appalachian Memories" captured southern migrants adrift; "Tennessee Homesick Blues" adorned a movie about turning Sylvester Stallone into a country singer that led *Billboard* to ask "Dolly, How Could You?" The TV spe-cial *A Smoky Mountain Christmas* offered a parable of a down-home per-former fleeing Hollywood.[68]

Country's fall had been as quick as its 1979–82 rise, with album sales returning to 9 percent of the industry total, their preboom percentage. *Radio & Records* editor Ken Barnes found, crunching the numbers in 1985, that the percentage of country hits reaching the Top 40 was down from 5 to 6 percent during the boom, back to nothing—MTV never played country videos. AC stations that had been parsimonious with country songs, playing 4–7 percent of country hits before the boom, then 12–15 percent during it, were again dismissive—now playing 7–9 percent of Nashville hits. Was country *too* country? With Reagan replacing Carter in the White House, Moral Majority replacing Silent Majority, country's outlaw gestures became more explicitly right wing and separatist than in the early 1970s; Hank Williams Jr. recorded "A Country Boy Can Survive," with lyrics about shooting muggers in New York City. Though 31 million Americans were said to listen to country each day, the format still struggled, particularly in non-southern big city markets, where Drew Horowitz, GM of Chicago station WUSN, said there remained the per-ception that "all Country listeners are ignorant, blue-collar shitkickers." Radio ad buyers, usually college-educated women in their twenties, could not relate. Complaints were heard from Nashville of "format bigotry." The "Southernization of America" could, it was now demonstrated (and not for the last time), be rethought. Or was country not country enough? Bill Malone ended his revised *Country Music, U.S.A.*, in 1984 unsure if country would lose its "heritage and history." He quoted a DJ: "Let us remember what happens when you kill the roots of a tree—it dies." The *New York Times* in 1985 declared country a "Music in Decline," with the

Nashville sound generation fading off. "Nashville's production-line country music is too slick and pop oriented to appeal to frontier nostalgia,"
Robert Palmer concluded.[69]

Whichever claim applied, Nashville soon had an answer: "neotraditionalism." Less than two years later, the *Times* found the opposite story:
"a new sound." Or, perhaps, an old one. Country the genre was saving
country the format. "Record companies here in Nashville are franti-
cally competing to sign young singers and songwriters who look back to
the great honky-tonk tradition of the 1940's and 50's," Stephen Holden
declared. "The movement's biggest new stars—Randy Travis, George
Strait, the Judds, Dwight Yoakam, Reba McIntire, Steve Earle and the
O'Kanes—eschew the canned sentimentality of performers like Kenny
Rogers and Barbara Mandrell." Bill Malone, revising his book yet again
in 2002, called the theme of country after its mid-1980s crisis "Tradition
and Change." Neotraditionalism was another balancing act. Technology
was critical, MCA Nashville head Jimmy Bowen told Holden. Updated
studio equipment imparted contemporary qualities to records with retro
elements. Nashville was not becoming less dominant or less polished:
performers like Earle and Yoakam, who resisted format consistency, had
shorter mainstream country careers than Strait, McIntire, and the Judds,
who defined country radio for decades. There had been a ruthless changing of the guard: as "classic rock" calcified and R&B resisted hip-hop,
country broke more new acts than at any time since tempestuous 1974.
As KMPS/Seattle PD Jay Albright, said, "The key is that these so-called
traditional artists are singing songs which are relatable to today's audience, which ultimately means more than any 'traditional' or 'modern'
label. . . . These acts work so well because they sound traditional to the
upper demos while also being acceptable to the younger demos. This is
due to the sound and production values they embody."[70]

The other underpinnings of country as a format also stayed current.
The CMA kept advocating; its report "A New Look at Building Country
Music Radio Audiences" insisted that the average fan was essentially AC:
"34 years old, female, has one or two children, some college education,
a full-time or part-time job and earns $27,800 a year." The results were
effective: a comprehensive survey found that equal audience size earned
an AC station 137–38 percent of advertising dollars; R&B stations a
paltry 70 percent; Top 40, 97–107 percent, depending on the audience's
whiteness; and rock, 108 percent. Country was below AC and news/talk,
but still 114 percent. And television, working with the Opry, again reinforced "home." The Nashville Network (TNN), operated by Opryland

owner Ed Gaylord, provided a cable channel whose lead figure, Ralph Emery, was a throwback to personality rather than format radio. Country Music Television (CMT) aired videos MTV would not play; Gaylord purchased it in 1991. The Opryland USA complex, by 1989, was Tennessee's largest employer: 3,200 workers and 2 million annual visitors.[71]

Rivaling Opryland was Dollywood, opened in 1986. Parton was now a co-owner of a venture managed by Herschend Family Entertainment, which also turned Branson, Missouri, into a tourist destination showcasing older country acts. Dollywood, located in Pigeon Forge, next to Sevierville, built upon a failed old-timey amusement park. As Dollywood, it became CMA-style traditionalism. Dollywood brought Hollywood— videos, special effects, themes of self-transformation—to Parton's Tennessee mountain origins: a replica of the sharecropper shack Parton's family lived in, the coat of many colors displayed. The mission statement, "Create Memories Worth Repeating," evoked format programming. Dollywood celebrated place, but also a fantasy of place. The Smoky Mountains had been a tourist destination aimed at outsiders. Now, most drove from the South. Dollywood, like country, was a southerner-pitched southern strategy.[72]

As Dollywood opened, Parton left—or was dropped by—RCA, part of the major-label purge of Nashville Sound–era artists. One year later, her long-awaited collaboration with Emmylou Harris and Linda Ronstadt, *Trio*, came out. "There's no pop on it. I'm real happy with it," Parton said.[73] Yet the album was a neotraditionalist commercial product soon certified platinum. The three women, harmonizing on the opening Parton/Wagoner song, "The Pain of Loving You," reworked Parton's staple as a duets singer, actress with Fonda and Lily Tomlin on *Nine to Five*, and guest on Johnny Carson: the creation of a lively conversation between modernity and tradition. Parton, the most rural and Nashville but also the most pop leaning, balanced Harris's and Ronstadt's folk-derived notions of authenticity, for results as close to rock crossover as Parton ever managed.

Oh, Romeo: Returning to Country

In 1993, on television of course, the CMA gave Dolly Parton an award show created just for her. Career highlights were presented by Kenny Rogers, the pop-country fixture who'd co-sung her biggest 1980s hit— the AC transubstantiation of her Wagoner duets. But there had been so

Memories with my family always come to mind when I think about the Great Smoky Mountains. This is where I nourish my soul and replenish my heart. I'd like to welcome you to my Smoky Mountain home. While you're here, let God's beauty nestle you and your family real close. I promise you'll make some special memories of your very own that are sure to last a lifetime. From my home to your heart, I'm glad you're here.

The Applause Award is the most prestigious award for theme parks. Dollywood is one of only 15 parks recognized worldwide for its operations, creative accomplishments, originality and sound business development. The award is presented by Liseberg in Gothenburg, Sweden.

FIGURE 2.6 Brochure for Dollywood, 2011. In the era of minstrelsy and vaudeville, songwriters pitched fantasies of a plantation South to northerners; later, the Smoky Mountains were a symbol of folk anti-modernity. Now, Dollywood offered those in the region control of such mediated notions of fun and restoration. Author's collection.

many triumphs. "Coat of Many Colors," "Jolene," and the undying "I Will Always Love You," number 1 country again when reprised for *Best Little Whorehouse in Texas*, then Whitney Houston's smash. The films *Nine to Five*, *Steel Magnolias* (a sentimental chronicle of white southern women), and a production company, Sandollar, with manager Sandy Gallin, whose credits ranged from MOR *Father of the Bride* to powerful AIDS quilt documentary *Common Threads*. Dollywood, benefiting her

Smoky Mountains. Parton thanked all who'd aided her storied career. She joked that she had "kind of stepped in it a little when I wanted to cross over." Then she performed "White Limozeen," a song written with Mac Davis.[74]

Like her song about Carson, "White Limozeen" celebrated "Daisy Mae in Hollywood," traveling from "the breadlines to the headlines." But this was a format leap in the other direction. Its message, aimed at Nashville rather than middle America, was "she's the same old down-home girl." The 1989 *White Limozeen* album, produced by neotraditionalist Rickey Skaggs, returned to the country format. "He's Alive," by Christian-music singer Don Francisco, courted those who found *Best Little Whorehouse* and the *Playboy* cover offensive. Again, Parton demonstrated instincts for occupying the center. In the 1990s, country performers and labels were cautious of pop crossover. They sought to make country, on its own autonomous terms, as big as any other pop genre.

An ad for *White Limozeen* ran in *Radio & Records* in 1989, next to a short article on "New Artist" Garth Brooks, described as having a "neo-traditional style." By 1993, when Parton was feted, Brooks was American music's biggest-selling album artist. A "hat act" in his Oklahoma rodeo garb, Brooks mixed the formatted honky-tonk pioneered by performers like Strait ("Friends in Low Places") with the striver's sentimentality and countrified power ballads that Parton helped introduce ("If Tomorrow Never Comes," "Shameless"). He broke sales records without cross-ing commercial categories—easier since 1991, as SoundScan measured album sales based on bar-code scans, revealing how much earlier store estimates devalued Nashville. Tradition still counted: Brooks was a Grand Ole Opry member and one year signed autographs at Fan Fair for twenty-four hours. But Brooks, whose "We Shall Be Free" risked diminished radio play to advocate racial and sexual tolerance, was clearly no sharecropper's son. His suburban cohort of "hot" acts incorporated arena rock, making the country audience more youthful. Brooks regularly visited Carson's replacement, Jay Leno, who knew country listeners were a core part of his demographic.[75]

Once again, a country boom reflected the changing place of the South. From 1970 to 1990, the eleven states of the original Confederacy and Kentucky had grown by 20 million people, 40 percent, twice the national rate. The first southern-born president since Jimmy Carter had taken office. Bill Clinton was no country devotee: not with Secret Service nick-name "Elvis," a daughter named after a Joni Mitchell song, a campaign appearance on MTV, and a cameo playing sax on *Arsenio Hall*. Hillary

Clinton said she was not going to be "some little woman standing by my man like Tammy Wynette." Still, Clinton, born the same year as Parton, had another nickname—Bubba. Like Parton, his humble background, folksiness, and undisguised ambition made him an icon. Clinton, as much new southerner as Parton, grasped the mix, from evangelicalism to NASCAR and Walmart, modernizing the region. When the National Endowment for the Arts came under attack, Clinton shrewdly nominated CMA director Bill Ivey to head the agency.[76]

Parton in 1993 was on CMT performing her video "Romeo": four giggling female country artists dissecting the body of a guy played by Nashville "hunk" Billy Ray Cyrus, whose line-dancing megahit "Achy Breaky Heart" had succeeded on Top 40 and country. "I may not be in love, but let me tell you I'm in heat," Parton squealed, a line some country radio stations objected to. For a performer who'd called herself a "vanilla sinner," country did not mean rock notions of abandonment, but could be pushed to allow for working women on a girls' night out, ogling a younger man. Had women in country come a long way since Kitty Wells's victimized "It Wasn't God Who Made Honky Tonk Angels?" That same year, Parton, Lynn, and Wynette collaborated on an album, singing Wells's anthem. In country, present and past were never far apart.

There were still other Parton personae in 1993. *Vogue* pictured her in a Betsey Johnson dress and Jill Sander evening coat, touting the Revlon cosmetics line Dolly Parton's Beauty Confidence. She taped an infomercial and wrote "Confidence," which commodified the turn of the seventies pride anthems: "It ain't what you wear, it ain't what you drive, everybody needs a sense of pride. It only comes from a place inside they call confidence." Parton saluted her Beverly Hills neighbors. "Mostly it's all gay up and down this street, and you know, they're just gentle, sweet, sensitive people. They never bother me. They want to protect me. They're honored that I'm here, and I am honored that they're here. It's a sweet feeling." Then she provoked in a different direction, saying she'd wanted to do a TV series about a country singer who became a gospel singer. "But everybody's afraid to touch anything that's religious because most of the people out here are Jewish, and it's a frightening thing for them to promote Christianity."[77]

It is easy to become intoxicated by Parton's many guises. Pamela Wilson argues that she cannily manipulated southernness, femininity, and class to exploit the contradictions in these ideologies: "In today's cosmopolitan, rapidly globalizing society, the construction of cultural identities is increasingly becoming a symbolic process rather than a result of geographic positioning. . . . Country music contributes to it by constructing notions of 'Southernness' or 'country-ness' to which consumers can subscribe." But Parton's choices were not limitless—she could not cancel her subscription to "country-ness." And Wilson, like many focused on Parton the celebrity, gives little attention to Parton the musician. Curtis Ellison, by contrast, sketching a Parton concert from about the moment she received her CMA lifetime honor, shows how fluctuations distilled into repertoire: a set of up-tempo dance numbers, dating to the disco era; ballads set in the Tennessee mountains; a medley of pop hits showcasing Parton the Vegas entertainer and duets artist; a sequence of recent material aimed explicitly at women; and as an encore, "He's Alive." Ellison writes that fans "had seen her professional, autobiographical, and spiritual personas come together in a charismatic presentation preaching faith and personal action as a means to both spiritual and material reward." In other words, Parton stressed uplift narratives over "pitiful" scenarios, MOR smashes over rock moves, and celebrity wisdom over the chronicler of sexual struggle. Some identities fit the format she'd built for herself better than others.[78]

But there is no reason to emphasize failure in a chronicling of Dolly Parton. In 1993, *People* claimed she was worth $70 million; a decade later, *Rolling Stone* revised that estimate to $300 million. When major labels stopped releasing her, she allied with an independent bluegrass label and released three critically acclaimed albums that harkened back to mountain ballads. She joked that "she had to get rich to sing like she was poor again."[79] Lest anyone call her a purist, she also remade Led Zeppelin's "Stairway to Heaven" and the southern grunge rocker "Shine." Recent recordings include *For God and Country*'s patriotic numbers, including Lee Greenwood's Reagan-Bush rally song "God Bless the USA"; *Those Were the Days*, a peace theme (Bob Dylan's "Blowin' in the Wind," for example) including a collaboration with Yusuf Islam, the former Cat Stevens, banned from America after September 11; and the Oscar-nominated "Travelin' Thru," written for *Transamerica*, a film about a pre-operative transsexual. Ultimately, she does as she likes.

Still, when Parton wants to ascend the charts, her first thought is of country: "I have had a half-assed so-called crossover-pop career," she said in 1995. Most recently, she was heard in a 2006 duet with singer—and subsequent CMA Awards host—Brad Paisley. The CMA approach Parton had helped solidify had proven enduring. "These days, of course, country music is the most successful part of the recording industry. Hopefully, in some way, I can take credit for some of that change," she wrote in her 1994 memoir. Then she ruefully struck an old-timer's note of her own: "The 'nationalization' of country music and the Top 40 kind of thinking that goes with it have made it hard for an over-forty hillbilly to get radio airplay anymore."[80]

For even Parton to complain shows that formatting country still sat uneasily with idealizations of the music as a genre. Visiting Nashville in 1996, cultural sociologist Keith Negus found a company town riven with insecurities in a dissipating boom. Commercial radio was too powerful, Walt Wilson, GM of Capitol Nashville, told Negus, "If you cut the album for mainstream radio and radio says, 'No thanks,' then you've got to go back in and recut the album, or else you've got to let the artist go." Outsiders had difficulty understanding Nashville as a community; Joe Galante, Parton's former boss at RCA, said, "People in New York still don't understand country music. . . . The people that are here, that are in this town, care about the music and they're proud of what they do and don't like people to look down upon their country format."[81] Echoing the Association of Country Entertainers, George Strait and Alan Jackson in 2001 recorded "Murder on Music Row," accusing Nashville of dishonoring country's legacy.

Yet between them, and without ever stepping out of the country format, Strait and Jackson had sold more than 100 million albums. Country, the invented vision of an industry and consensus voice of the modernizing South and transplanted white southerners, stayed primarily upbeat and confident during civil rights, the mass entry of women into the workforce, and the transformation of farmland to suburbs. The example of another, angrier radio format—talk radio—provides a useful contrast. This is not to call progressive the format that essentially banned the Dixie Chicks after Natalie Maines criticized George Bush. Moreover, and as Porter Wagoner demanded in 1975, country prospered by segregating itself, not only racially but by keeping a wary distance from crossover spaces of Top 40 and AC. Walls were erected in the opposite direction too: New York City did not have a country station between 2003 and 2012, and the CMA still releases reports like the 1992 "America's Sold on Country" and 2009 "Consumer Segmentation Study." But country's commercialization, need to thrive apart, format bottom line conquering genre ideals, has had a centrist effect. Country remains pop.[82]

And women remain central to country as pop—if unstably so. Shania Twain in the 1990s emphasized her model-like glamour and producer-husband Mutt Lange's pop-rock sound, scoring a massive AC hit with "You're Still the One." The Dixie Chicks were anti–Shania Twain traditionalists—playing their own instruments, releasing a single ("Long Time Gone") blasting country radio for not playing Haggard and Cash. After Maines not only criticized Bush but favored Bruce Springsteen over outlaw country star Toby Keith, an anti–Dixie Chicks figure briefly ascended. Gretchen Wilson's "Redneck Woman" asserted a working-class trailer-park persona and the video featured Hank Williams Jr. Carrie Underwood won *American Idol,* where country was allowed to compete for pop prominence with R&B and rock. Most recently, Taylor Swift received an MTV Video Music Award over Beyoncé (to Kanye West's consternation) and has seen her hits regularly chart Top 40, AC, and country. Honky-tonk feminist Miranda Lambert, groomed by a televised country talent show, splits Wilson and Swift.

Trying to capture the back-and-forth of country over the years, Richard Peterson wrote of "a dialectic of hard-core and soft shell." Thinking about the particular place of gender within these swings, Pamela Fox argued that the competing claims of masculinity and femininity in relationship to race and class produced "shifting modes of authenticity."[83] As I see it, the perennial, lucrative tension between genre and format proved decisive. Despite the "Southernization of America" proclaimed in the 1970s, country remains the one geographically separate wing of the format system. The Opry and Hall of Fame codify the past and provide continuity. Commercial radio maintains contemporary talent. Blue-collar men find primary voice in honky-tonk; office-worker women in what Lynn, Wynette, and Parton launched. Country singers can be Australian, like Keith Urban (succeeding Olivia Newton-John), or Canadian, like Shania Twain (succeeding Hank Snow). But within the format, a southern notion of America remains dominant. Everyone in country is a traditionalist now—and contemporary too.

CHAPTER THREE

Contemporary Adults

A&M Records and Middle of the Road

Song promoter Jerry Moss wrote a short history in 1970 of A&M Records, the label he'd founded with trumpeter Herb Alpert in a merger of talents and last initials. Begun in a garage in 1962, A&M initially reflected what Moss called the "frontier" status of California's music industry. But after Alpert's Tijuana Brass sold 13 million albums in 1966, A&M purchased the Charlie Chaplin film lot. Power in records had shifted west, and power in Hollywood had shifted to music. A&M was "self-contained" and "agile" as a company, Moss claimed, able to operate as "hopefully, the cleanest machine around!" It had survived a transition to rock and away from the jazzier Alpert and Sergio Mendes. But its biggest act now was the Carpenters, a brother-sister duo still living at home in an Orange County suburb, whose smooth love songs were hardly counterculture. Moss claimed record labels should "span all music forms." He certainly did not want to revolutionize music. "A&M has never tried to be a full step ahead of everybody," he told his colleagues. "We've always tried to be a half-step, so that it was easily understood what we were trying to do. We believe that this is how change should occur—a yard at a time— rather than going for the long pass."[1]

A&M Records exemplifies two related and undervalued vantage points for pop music in the rock era: business leaders who produced hits and the middle of the road (MOR) or by 1980 adult contemporary (AC) radio success of many big sellers. MOR/AC, like Top 40, was a crossover format, drawing from multiple genres. Where Top 40 allied with rock and roll and youth culture, MOR/AC profitably catered to older suburban listeners. MOR listeners and record sellers, in the cultural tumult of the

FIGURE 3.1 Herb Alpert and Jerry Moss at the gates of the A&M Records lot. Alpert and Moss, artist and record executive, were older than the counterculture, but shared—like many adult listeners and industry leaders—a desire to take part in cultural and social change, just on their own terms. The result: a pop center of hits, backlashes, and future guilty pleasures. © Bettmann/Corbis. Used by permission.

1960s and 1970s, were not the baby boom children of Top 40 and rock—
Alpert and Moss were each born in 1935. Still, they craved youthfulness,
California, and consumer fun. A yard at a time, opting for hits designed
to be "easily understood," middle of the roaders validated music's restruc-
turing of American mores. They sometimes even led the way.

If the soft center of American music was often its most diverse province,
this was a tolerance without honor. Those in the middle were maligned by
rock, soul, country, and hip-hop partisans as debased sellers and mindless
consumers. The adult mainstream, often women moving—as the format
did—from housewives to office workers, had no structure or language to
legitimize preferences. Record-label staffers conceived MOR/AC listeners as too passive to purchase albums. Radio station owners, catering to
the most lucrative segment in advertising, never needed the rhetoric used
to elevate other formats. Centrist tastes were in constant upheaval: from
easy listening to disco, one season's blockbuster was the next one's embar-
rassment and a future guilty pleasure. Those selling hits were even less
respected. "Industry rule number four thousand eighty," A Tribe Called
Quest's Q-Tip rapped. "Record company people are shady."

Our understanding of record companies is still anemic, skewed by
knee-jerk hostility toward commodification and romantic ideologies of
particular genres. The title of an important early study, *Rock 'n' Roll Is
Here to Pay*, reflected a New Left politics that fought for rock rebellion
over pop blandness. Sometimes, this pitted heroic independent labels
against corrupt major labels: Andre Millard takes it as axiomatic that
"independent companies were the vehicles to bring a new popular music
to Americans." The founders of A&M might well share this view. But
revisionists see indie values as a form of cultural elitism. Keith Negus's
treatment of the 1980s British music industry found an irrational priority
given to guitar-based rock bands, not what all publics preferred. Simon
Frith observes that while "the standard line of rock 'n' roll history is that
an authentic (that is, folk) sound is continually corrupted by commerce,
it could equally well be argued that what the history actually reveals is a
commercial musical form continually being recuperated in the name of
art and subculture." In other words, major labels may have been *too* influenced by anti-commercial impulses.[2]

One can see evidence for both interpretations in the history of A&M.
While celebrated as an innovative indie, its company culture disparaged
some of its most successful groups, such as the Carpenters. To disc sellers,
it represented an ideal: independently owned but competitive with major
conglomerates; patient about developing talents into stars; changing to

fit the times. Still, A&M never escaped what the Tijuana Brass had made it: a label specializing in MOR acts whose popularity could vanish under rock scorn, as Alpert's did in 1969 and as happened later to the Carpenters, Captain & Tennille, and Peter Frampton. These tensions were both generational and gendered. Moss emphasized young male rock fans. "His taste made us all a bit more honest," he said, speaking in 1972, of the "serious record buyer," a *Rolling Stone* reader. But most A&M best sellers appealed to women across age lines.[3]

A third way of viewing major labels bursts out of almost every scrap of paper deposited by Alpert and Moss in UCLA's A&M Records Collection. That is the idea of the "record man," comfortable at translating popular taste across any demographic divide. In the same 1972 speech, Moss said, "I'm simply not a 'numbers' man. But I am a 'Record Man.'" Alpert elaborated, "The record business is still the most exciting place to be 'cause you just never know who's going to walk in through that door." Industry leaders best at selling pop in the rock era, such as Mo Ostin at Warner Bros., Clive Davis at Columbia and later Arista, Ahmet Ertegun at Atlantic, and David Geffen at Elektra-Asylum and later Geffen, pursued every tributary. Ertegun explained, "You have to develop a second ear. The first ear is your private taste, which is what moves you personally. The second ear is one that, when you listen to a piece of music and you personally think it's terrible but it's a hit commercially—the second ear has to say, 'This is great!'" The quotation comes from a *New Yorker* profile of Ertegun, titled "Eclectic, Reminiscent, Amused, Fickle, Perverse." The five words are a manifesto unto themselves for popular-music studies: can one write about industry figures and MOR/AC listeners in a manner that encompasses that complex mind-set? Ertegun was said to have "an infatuation not only with the artifacts but with the processes of American culture, and this infatuation has often brought him into places unexplored by the cultivated enthusiast. Ahmet has come to have an interest in whatever works."[4]

From this perspective, the transformation of mainstream entertainment that A&M participated in produced a pop sphere characterized less by an oppositional tone, or inherent conformity, so much as a dizzying ability to institutionalize newness. For Motti Regev, the intersection of rock and MOR/AC drove an "inner logic of eclecticism." Others have noted the increased omnivorousness of elite American taste, the rising tendency of celebrity culture to focus on "backstage" aspects (process over product), a shift to post-ethnic, cosmopolitan affiliations, and the "long tail" of consumer choice.[5]

MOR/AC was central to these processes. Radio consultant E. Alvin Davis said that for advertisers, "A/C is all prime rib. The core audience is the highly desirable 25–34 demo, skewing strongly on both sides of that core. . . . If milk is nature's most nearly perfect food, A/C must surely be radio's most nearly perfect format."[6] MOR and AC stations played music pitched as unthreatening: Frank Sinatra and Herb Alpert in the 1960s, the Carpenters and Barry Manilow in the 1970s, Billy Joel and Whitney Houston in the 1980s, Celine Dion and Hootie & the Blowfish in the 1990s. For those rooting for change, the format was a waste—too little current music mixed in with oldies. But from 1960s AM stations whose "full service" MOR resisted Top 40 approaches, to 1970s FM AC perfecting the power ballad as reconciliation with rock, to 1980s AC and Hot AC emphasizing office listening or aerobics, MOR/AC filtered the new.

For women in particular, MOR/AC and Top 40 were the closest music got to a targeted format. Longtime radio analyst Sean Ross told me, "Just as she graduates up from *Seventeen* to *Glamour* to *More*, a female is expected to squeal for Top 40, recuperate from her first job listening to Hot AC, and then turn AC when kids and mortgage have left her only open to musical comfort food." That sounds demeaning, but theorist Tia DeNora provides more active language. Music, she writes, is "a device or resource to which people turn in order to regulate themselves as aesthetic agents, as feeling, thinking and acting beings in their day-to-day lives."[7] To listen commercially with Ertegun's second ear, to listen as a working woman to music whose mood gets your head right: these strategic acts of empathy and self-regulation made pop's impact nearly universal.

In studying how the music industry grew from a fringe business into a wing of multinational capitalism with billions at stake, one perennially sees record men trying to reconcile corporate logic and art: tensions between a need for coherent business practices, an instinct to flout boundaries of taste, and a bias toward appearing forward thinking and modern. To produce mass music by the 1980s and 1990s was to think like a record man. And increasingly, to consume culture—aware of, but not fully invested in, a range of genres and formats—was to think like a record man as well.

Whipped Cream and Lonely Bulls: The Easy Listening 1960s

"The Lonely Bull," which in 1962 became Herb Alpert's first hit, began as "Twinkle Star," written by his friend Sol Lake. Alpert, trying, he later said, to make instrumental music "palatable to radio," created an exotic setting: a bullfight in Tijuana. Nascent technology let him incorporate audio of a bullfight audience and achieve a signature trumpet sound by doubly recording his playing at slightly different pitches. It was inconsequential how well he knew Mexican mariachi. Session musicians worked the recording, but Moss merchandised a band: "The Tijuana Brass Featuring Herb Alpert." A number 6 single, "The Lonely Bull" inspired an album of the same name. "This is Tijuana music," proclaimed the liner notes. "The noisy Mexican-American voices in the narrow streets. . . . Tijuana is a spectacle, a garish border town."[8] Alpert's masquerade—there were no Mexicans in the Tijuana Brass—was unremarkable in 1962. The entertainment that Alpert was schooled in valued "spectacle" and "garish border" crossings. Within such eclecticism resided, among other things, the machinations of the record man. Alpert's 1960s success shows how, far into the decade, a stylish and profoundly unreflective staging could still reconcile youth and adult culture.

"The Lonely Bull" had many forebears. The record industry emerged as the aural imprint of the minstrel show, vaudeville, and variety approach to entertainment—global and heterogeneous from the start. What William Kenney calls "circles of resonance" ranged from the "Coney Island crowd" of urbane ethnic performers such as Irving Berlin to thirty thousand foreign recordings released domestically between 1900 and 1950. The pivotal American blues label, Okeh, home to Mamie and Bessie Smith, was founded in 1918 by a German Jew, Otto Heinemann, who reported to a European company, Lindstrom AG, with studios and pressing plants in Germany, Switzerland, England, France, Poland, Austria, Spain, and Brazil. Record sales surged before radio networks and the Depression arrived, dropped radically during the 1930s, then rebounded after World War II when the LP and single vinyl configurations again made records a consumer staple. Rock and roll was only part of postwar music, which ranged from 6 million "kiddie players" sold in 1952 to adult show soundtrack LPs.[9]

Record men prided themselves on fluency in a Babel of taste. George Martin, an artists and repertoire (A&R) manager for EMI before he produced the Beatles, wrote, "Where else would you be working with Albert Finney and Shirley Anne Field one day, Jimmy Shand the next, auditioning a 'rock' group between dubbing on sound effects for a 'Toytown' children's record, or perhaps supervising the editing of a new revue?" Mitch Miller, who ran Columbia Records A&R in the 1950s, was an oboist who played with Stokowski. But he convinced pop's Tony Bennett to cover country's Hank Williams, paired vocalist Dinah Shore with bagpipes, telling an interviewer, "It's a hook." Miller conceived the "Greatest Hits" LP with Johnny Mathis and sold 22 million albums of his *Sing Along with Mitch* series. "I think that's the success of the record business," he said. "The variety that you can choose from." As Capitol's Dave Dexter put it, "A well-rounded stable of artists is the goal of every discery."[10]

For Jews in particular, commercial music's irreverence toward identity offered a chance to entertain their way into the heart of American life: to don blackface, as Michael Rogin argued, and become white. Josh Kun places Alpert in a long lineage:

> Berlin and Gershwin dreaming up plantation fantasies of a mythical south or black romance on Catfish Row, Eli Basse and the Barry Sisters dreaming up fantasy versions of Cuba and Puerto Rico, the Urick Brothers becoming the Ames Brothers and swirling up some of the best '50s audio vanilla, Leiber & Stoller writing songs as if they were black men and black women, Herb Alpert putting on a sombrero and inventing what Tijuana sounds like, Phil Spector speaking through black girl groups and releasing Christmas albums, Peretz Bernstein (son of a Queens diamond dealer) inventing LA narco-decadence as Perry Farrell, and David Lee Roth (grandson of Ukrainian immigrants in Indiana) keeping his name and his nose, while using Borsht Belt tummeling to re-invent rock and roll theatrics.

Jewish entertainment gave priority to creative misappropriation. The year "The Lonely Bull" hit the charts, folk-music parodies by comedian Allen Sherman became the first number 1 album for the California company that within a decade would steer the industry: Warner Bros. Records, founded by the parent film studio in 1958.[11]

There could be a political streak to variety performers. Alpert, like another top-selling ethnic impersonator, calypso act Harry Belafonte, came into popularity at the tail end of what Michael Denning has called "the cultural front," a Depression-era left movement extending into mass culture that celebrated urban working-class unity across race and ethnicity. The melting-pot Americanism of the cultural front was at heart internationalist. It ranged from commercialized folk music to the swing bands, with their collective ensembles and global dance rhythms. The Tijuana Brass was a throwback.[12]

Yet by the 1950s and early 1960s, the cultural front and swing's rhetoric of solidarity had become adult entertainment and the masculine

swinger. Frank Sinatra, Keir Keightley suggests, was pivotal as he transformed from 1940s bobby-soxer idol to the male-admired "Chairman of
the Board" who made standards albums, started the Reprise label, and
associated with gangsters and presidents alike. Equally masculinized was
the home hi-fi system, marketed, Keightley demonstrates, "as a virtual
escape from domestic space." Exotica LPs fantasized global locales—for
example, Martin Denny's evocations of Hawaii. The swinger's hi-fi played
what Barbara Ehrenreich calls a "male revolt" against the nuclear family.
Playboy proclaimed, "We enjoy mixing up cocktails and an hors d'oeuvre
or two, putting a little mood music on the phonograph and inviting in
a female acquaintance for a quiet discussion on Picasso, Nietzsche, jazz,
sex."[13]

   Al Jolson had put on blackface. Hugh Hefner put on some mood music.
When Alpert, to use Kun's language, put on a sombrero, he mixed both
these strategies. The goal, remember, had been something "palatable
to radio." In 1962, that gave him a choice. After television, the medium
had shifted to "format radio," meaning a continual sound targeting some
listeners rather than varied programming targeting all. Top 40 aimed at
youths appealed to modern sensibilities and did well in the ratings that
Pulse and Hooper now offered. But there was a less-heralded genre, which
a new *Billboard* chart called Easy Listening in 1961, some stations called
Good Music or Beautiful Music, and disparagers termed MOR. This was
mood music broadcast for housewives rather than bachelors. If advertisers valued the demographic, the music industry was far less enchanted, assuming female listeners were undiscerning and unlikely to purchase discs.
Yet as Alpert admitted in 1966, "Good music stations played us right from
the beginning. That gave us our initial boost." "The Lonely Bull" crossed
into Top 40 from easy listening, not the opposite.[14]

   At a time of youthful brides and mothers, many in the MOR demographic were like Alpert and Moss: older than rock and roll fans but children of postwar affluence. Raised in Los Angeles by Eastern European
Jewish immigrants (his father manufactured women's apparel), Alpert
appeared on television first in 1950, at fifteen, when his Colonial Trio's
appearance on the local *High Talent Battle* earned regular ballroom
and hotel work. He formed a songwriting partnership in 1956 with kindred spirit Lou Adler. They demonstrated the fluidity of Top 40, land-
ing two hits with crossover rhythm and blues (R&B) performer Sam
Cooke ("Wonderful World" and "Only Sixteen") and then overseeing
surf duo Jan & Dean. Moss, the same age as Alpert and son of a men's

clothing salesman in the Bronx, worked behind the scenes: as a page for ABC-TV before becoming a "promotion man," responsible for badgering and sometimes bribing DJs. Moss sought entry into a life about "having fun" at "the entertainers' table," not "family and work hard and go home and complain." He loved the hurly-burly of promotions. "This was a burgeoning industry, and it was amateur sport all the way, but money was being made. . . . I just wished I liked the music better."[15]

When Alpert and Moss chanced forming a label in 1962, there were three thousand operating in the United States. It cost less than $1,000 to produce and press a single, *Fortune* noted, and indie-label songs made up over half the singles chart. Estimating his costs even lower, Alpert later told colleague Joe Smith,

> In those days, for a couple of hundred bucks, you could make a record, have it pressed, put a label on it, and put it out. If somebody bites, you either turn it over for distribution, or you try to hold it for yourself and get paid by the distributors, which was pretty impossible. . . . "The Lonely Bull" was one of those rarities. It took off. . . . Basically, we were just trying to hang on. . . . Distributors were crying out for us to put out *The Lonely Bull* album. . . . However, before a distributor received one album, Jerry made sure they were all paid up on the single. That gave us operating cash, and essentially that was the beginning of A&M Records.

Smith, who arrived from Boston in 1961 to run Warner Bros. Records, recalled that Los Angeles was "just a sleepy little village as far as the record people were concerned."[16]

But California was also, as of 1962, the largest state in the nation, with a tenth of the nation's children but 40 percent of its pools. The state represented "the quintessence of life in a capitalistic society" to *Esquire* in 1963 and "the holy temple of the American cult of youth" to *Time* in 1966. Southern California, from Dodger Stadium replacing Brooklyn's Ebbets Field to Disneyland replacing Coney Island, had become the white suburban revision of ethnic urbanism. Even Tijuana, just across the border, kept the foreign at a carnivalesque remove.[17]

The California culture Alpert perpetuated was sunny and bouncy—an easy sell. After "The Lonely Bull," he resurfaced when his "Mexican Shuffle" was licensed by a chewing gum for commercials that showed stiffs—a bank teller, a Buckingham Palace guard, a housewife carrying groceries— becoming as animated as the dancing graphics. "Have a little fun. Try

Clark's Teaberry Gum," was the simple tag. *South of the Border,* featuring "Mexican Shuffle," became Alpert's first LP hit, followed by *Whipped
Cream & Other Delights,* which remained top 10 for over a year. With a
cover model gowned in shaving foam, *Whipped Cream* centered Alpert
in Ehrenreich's "male revolt." When *The Dating Game* debuted in 1965,
California bachelors and bachelorettes vying through sexual innuendo,
"Whipped Cream" became the theme. By April 1966, the Tijuana Brass
(or TJB), now a touring unit, had five albums in the *Billboard* top 20.[18]

Alpert's huge popularity fused show-business variety, Jewish parody
of identity, the internationalist cultural front, the swinger's male revolt,
California youthfulness, and the crossover needs of Top 40 and MOR.
With a jovial trumpet leading the melodies, prominent drums for an upbeat, comic flourishes, and allusions to international sounds, TJB easy
listening, without exclusivity, affected a hi-fi ideal of cosmopolitan fun.
Time called Alpert "the middle-aged man's answer to rock 'n' roll." A TJB
program elaborated, "Since the rise of Elvis in the mid-Fifties, the popular music scene had been divided in half. . . . Onto this scene the Tijuana
Brass came like a healing, swinging salve. The middle-roaders dug the
sound (and their stations played it) and the Top 40 fans dug it (and their
stations played it)." Singer Sewing Corporation, sponsors of an Alpert
TV special, called it "The swinging sound of our cool generation and its
foremost musical interpreter in a lively hour filled with rich, flamboyant
arrangements."[19]

Herb Alpert & the Tijuana Brass, aired in April 1967, drew 57 percent of viewers: hardly underground totals. Alpert was putting on cool
the way he once had a sombrero. Nor was he alone. *Time* named as its
"Man and Woman of the Year" for 1966 everybody under twenty-five.
Businessmen were infatuated with youth culture. An ad man said, "The
youth market has become the American market. It now includes not only
everyone under 35, but most people over 35." Beatles-style youth culture,
represented in collegiate *Big Ten* magazine, blurred with its jet-set older
counterpart. American Airlines, marketing youthful vigor, had an A&M
channel on its AstroStereo in-flight entertainment. *Parade,* with a color
ad for the A&M catalogue, highlighted new sitcom *The Monkees,* reporting, "The kid audience likes it but many of the adult TV viewers are resistant to mopheads, find difficulty in following a program which has little or
no story line, is based on wild camera work and a special hipster, juvenile
vocabulary." Alpert's TV specials pursued a parallel hip adult illogic, as
when on *The Brass Are Comin',* sponsored by BankAmericard, he and

THEY CAME THIS-A-WAY!

Over 125 million people watched the "Brass Are Comin'"
NBC-TV Special October 29!

Hundreds of thousands more will see Herb & The Brass in person
on their current 16-city U.S. tour!

"The Brass Are Comin'" is coming! Right Now! Run with it!

 SP 4228

P.S. A SMASH SINGLE, "YOU ARE MY LIFE" • "GOOD MORNING, MR. SUNSHINE" • #1143

FIGURE 3.2 November 15, 1969, *Cash Box* advertisement for Herb Alpert & the Tijuana Brass, *The Brass Are Comin'* (A&M, 1969). The group's massive late 1960s popularity briefly created a global pop culture phenomenon, presenting music as carnivalesque self-transformation. Countercultural radicalization brought the semi-hip party to a close. Author's collection.

singer Petula Clarke parodied a film scene as conceived by Federico Fellini and Andy Warhol.[20]

To skeptic Thomas Frank, the "sudden mass defection of Americans from square to hip that distinguished the culture of the 1960s" was "as much a product of lascivious television specials and *Life* magazine stories as it was an expression of youthful disaffection." Indeed, the *Life* advertising department wrote A&M as a kindred spirit, promoting the magazine as "your marketing medium for the coming holidays." Terry Murphy argued that his magazine's wide demographics matched A&M's, where "grandparents consider the 'We Five' for their grandchildren, the kids buy the 'Baja Marimba' for their elders, and the TJB are gift candidates for all those between the ages of 7 and 10." *Esquire*'s Burt Leach, however, also seeking ad placements, stressed his publication's sophisticated readership: "Among consumer magazines *Esquire* has one of the highest concentrations of ownership of record playing equipment and for many years we have run more record club advertising than any other consumer magazine." A&M split its media purchases between connoisseur publications (*Playboy, Esquire*) and mainstream ones (*TV Guide, Parade*), playing to swingers and squares alike.[21]

The label marketed Alpert across the rudimentary segmentation of the 1960s, pitching men and women, older and younger listeners, within a middle-class frame. Alpert the upscale male cosmopolitan was photographed with "his hi-fi complex" and shown at his Malibu beach house. Alpert the MOR star sang "This Guy's in Love with You" to his wife and high school sweetheart, which became his first number 1 single. Alpert the show-business loyalist appeared on variety TV programs like *The Andy Williams Show* and *The Hollywood Palace* and in gossip columns. Alpert the leader of a group whose average age in 1966 was twenty-five received mentions in "Teen Talk" newspaper columns, teen newspaper *The Beat*, and *Teen* magazine, which called the TJB "the only new sound that has made a dent since the Beatles conquered America." The fantasy Alpert created and Moss packaged had room for nearly everybody.[22]

Lawrence Welk for the Acid Set?: The Fall of Easy Listening

By 1969, the Tijuana Brass had become untenable; it can seem amazing that it took so long. In concerts, Alpert typically termed his group's ethnicities as "four lasagnes, two bagels, and one American cheese." Bantering with Alpert on television, Andy Williams joked, "Sounds like they should be called 'The Neapolitan Italian Brass.'" "We don't have that problem anymore," Alpert replied. "You see, we were made honorary citizens of Mexico by the Mayor of Tijuana." "What was his name?" "Giuseppe Ravolini." *Time* wrote, "Ameriachi was born not in Old Mexico but in the recording studios of Hollywood. Alpert is of Jewish descent, his sidemen of Italian and Russian," taking pains to note that *Whipped Cream* was a hit in Mexico City as well. The TJB became a parodic standby, from Al Tijuana and His Jewish Brass to *Tijuana Bach*, Kentucky Fried Chicken's *Tijuana Picnic* LP, and a *Get Smart* episode.[23]

Politicians endorsed Alpert's racial charade as benign inclusiveness. Actor Ricardo Montalban handed Alpert a citation from Los Angeles mayor Sam Yorty "for promoting Mexico and our Mexican folk music throughout the world." Senator Thomas Kuchel lauded the TJB in the *Congressional Record*: "This team has contributed immeasurably to international understanding." Lyndon Johnson's party planners had the group play for the Mexican president; the program notes read, "While they do not pretend to absolute authenticity, the distinctive two-trumpet sound of Mexican music has been so successfully blended with the most appealing elements of the popular music of our own country that the Tijuana Brass sound has become a staple of popular composers, arrangers, and conductors everywhere."[24]

"At that moment," Moss later recalled of A&M as a whole, "I think our image was of a sort of semi-hip, jazz, Latin-sounding label using MOR stations to sell albums." The compressed jargon speaks to the globalizing complexity of what passed as "easy listening." A&M hitmakers included TJB spin-off the Baja Marimba Band, another faux exotica troupe; Sergio Mendes and Brasil '66, led by an actual Brazilian achieving MOR hits with bossa novas; the French chanteuse Claudine Longet (married to easy-listening king Andy Williams); Chris Montez, a Mexican American LA rocker whom Alpert produced as a lounge performer; and the Sandpipers, a white California male vocal trio whose "Guantanamera" hit was learned from the cultural front's Pete Seeger. Alpert's success became as international as "The Lonely Bull" imagined, tapped into a unified global pop emerging with the Beatles. A fall 1966 European tour included France, Germany, and England. In 1967, the TJB took 1,290 pounds of musical equipment to the Far East. A 1969 A&M memo noted thirty-two foreign countries an Alpert TV special had aired in, tracking for many locales the effect on TJB album sales after ninety days. He judged a song

festival in Rio in 1967. At MIDEM, a newly formed convention dedicated to the international record market, he was honored for having sold
the most albums in the United States and Europe in the previous twelve
months.[25]

Yet sales and global reach aside, to be MOR belied grandiosity: Alpert and his label mates were only novel entertainment. A nursing-home
resident wrote Alpert, "It was wonderful to hear you say in your very
pleasing, soft-spoken voice, 'I hope I can make you happy tonight because it makes me happy if I can bring happiness to other people.'" A
Pennsylvania fan wished, "Merry Christmas to the man who has given
happy music back to the world." Alpert never pretended rebellion, preferring assimilation—one TV special set at Ellis Island began, "The
sound of America is a strange mixture of countries, religions, people
and pastimes—all mysteriously blended together." The trumpeter said,
"All music is getting together—symphony, folk, jazz, far eastern, country western, everything. . . . What we've got now is homogenized music
from all over the world." With, by 1969, a "$30 million empire," Alpert
and Moss were "non-establishment tycoon[s]." Mendes opened concerts
in Portuguese, then joked, "Translated, that was a commercial in Portuguese for a Brazilian coffee company."[26]

The self-effacing humor was meant to inoculate Alpert and his cohort from the taint of MOR popularity. Scoring the James Bond parody
Casino Royale or being the youngest named to the Playboy Jazz Hall of
Fame showed cool; being name checked by a Chicago station that billed
itself as "No Bach. No rock." aligned Alpert with the middlebrow. Least
acceptable were comparisons to Lawrence Welk, the TV bandleader of
polkas and "champagne music." *Whipped Cream*'s liner notes caught the
tension: "One admirer, who looked as though he stepped from a page in
Esquire said, 'You would think that a lot of these people would be home
watching the man who serves the bubbles.'" Welk jokes became regular
Alpert stage patter: "They finally found a way to clear up the congestion
in West Hollywood: Lawrence Welk." But analogies persisted: "By the
way, I read somewhere that you were considered the 'Lawrence Welk' of
the 'Acid Set' (smiles)," Gaynel Hodge, coauthor of the doo-wop classic
"Earth Angel," wrote Alpert. One reviewer called him "a kind of Mex-
Tex Lawrence Welk for swingers."[27]

The Lawrence Welk of the Acid Set or a Lawrence Welk for swingers?
Initially, hippies appeared to be another fad of affluence. Warren Hinckle
wrote, "If the people looking in from the suburbs want change, clothes,

fun, and some lightheadedness from the new gypsies, the hippies are delivering—and some of them are becoming rich hippies because of it." Alpert saw hippies as exotica to transform. He joked about Berkeley students "on a riot scholarship" and "a combination LSD and birth control pill—so people can go on a trip without the kids." He also said, earnestly, "The young people of today, the hippies in San Francisco who drop out of society . . . they may not be doing it right, that remains to be seen, but they're trying." Young people were invited to an Alpert TV taping, but warned, "No extreme clothing of today, i.e. mini skirts, Long Hair, etc."[28]

Yet by 1968, blithe balancings between jet sets and mopheads became harder to sustain. The Tet Offensive in January, the murder of Martin Luther King Jr. in April, and May's international protests all radicalized youth. Robert Kennedy, chased like a Beatle by those reporter David Halberstam called "the squealers," might have extended Camelot. He was murdered in June. Alpert's new concert script addressed the improbability of "Whipped Cream" in a time of bullets. "To tell the truth, our thoughts are on the needs of our country," he would say. "What can we do? . . . Andrew Jackson once said, 'One man with courage makes a majority.' There are ___ thousands of us here tonight plus seven. Thank you." Richard Nixon made use of such concerns. Alpert's untenable position resembled losing Democrat Hubert Humphrey's proclaiming "the politics of joy."[29]

In the battles between New Left and cultural-front variety, younger radicals branded the earlier style "easy listening." Van Gosse's Left history captures the hypocrisy. While the counterculture "embedded within a commercialized, intensely capitalist popular culture," movement figures pretended otherwise. "The word they used to describe their desire was 'authentic,' meaning a passion for the real and natural rather than the processed and synthetic." The irony, as shown by Harry Belafonte, who found himself culturally marginalized even as he bankrolled civil rights, was that many MOR artists were as politically active as their "underground" counterparts. Alpert publicly canceled a Brigham Young University appearance in 1968 after officials refused his interracial opening act, Checkmates Ltd. Ralph Abernathy of the Southern Christian Leadership Conference wrote thanking him for a fund-raiser with Belafonte and Barbra Streisand.[30]

Nonetheless, Alpert's reception changed dramatically. He was dismissed by rock-identified critics as an "uppity brand of Muzak" and "music that simulates excitement." Al Aronowitz found that "Herb's music comes out of the same culture as Mod Squad, where you don't get your images from the reality that surrounds you but from the film that it comes wrapped up in." Aronowitz revived Alpert's own insecurities: "Poor Herb Alpert, he's such a misfit, too corny for the kids, too acid-headed for the Lawrence Welk generation." Transcending the generation gap was no longer an option. Aronowitz declared, "If President Nixon ever wanted to erect a monument to America's great silent majority, it would have to be a statue of Herb and his trumpet."[31]

Cultural allegiances had polarized, but in a manner that can easily be misconstrued. Alpert's remaining support came from MOR, the "middle Americans" who *Time* in 1969 gave its Man and Woman of the Year Award, instead of the people under twenty-five who'd won three years earlier. Yet a carefully framed notion of youth and experimentation retained considerable appeal to this older cohort. ABC president Elton Rule told *Variety* that what mattered was to be "younger-thinking," which could include those thirty-five (as Alpert had become) to even forty-five. Richard Atcheson, a former Hefner employee Alpert's age, wrote that when he dressed as a hippie, businessmen would approach and "start almost at once to inquire into my sexual habits." As David Allyn's history notes, "swinging hit the suburbs," with John Updike writing a novel, *Couples,* on the phenomenon. Still, and this is critical, refusing to "think of sex in political terms" meant that "swingers were the laughing stock of the sexual revolution."[32]

A laughing dismissal equally characterized the response to Alpert's adventure-seeking audience. A reporter from Philadelphia mocked, "The 'straight' people had their night Friday and they showed the more flamboyant generation that anyone can groove if he sets his mind to it." These were "office girl types and their Beau Brummel escorts," the latter "middle-age men . . . wearing turtle-neck shirts (white) to show that they know where it's at." A security guard remarked, "I didn't think there was this many average people left in the world." The journalist contrasted fans of the Doors, Los Angeles's most popular rock group, whose leader, Jim Morrison, called himself an "erotic politician" and had been arrested for indecent exposure during a concert. Entertainment standards had changed. The swinger's carnival notion of escape lost out to fixed oppositional identity.[33]

There were still writers praising Alpert along earlier lines: "It is relaxing as one basks in the mental trip south of the border and forgets taxes, wars, bills, and the upcoming holiday shopping madness." But he was unwilling to embrace the role of easy listening musician. "Muzak picked up my sound. You heard it in every elevator in the world. Even I got tired of it." He had sold 45 million albums by the end of the 1960s, yet found himself battling a psychological difficulty lipping the trumpet. And the crowds for his final tour with the TJB were smaller. Disbanding the TJB, he told his harshest critic, Aronowitz, "I might get back to L.A. and watch my hair grow for a while."[34]

Contemporary Adults: From MOR to AC

Billboard marveled in 1971 at labels aligned with rock. Warner-Reprise, $3 million in debt a decade earlier, now stood second in sales only to venerable and also rock-savvy Columbia. And a "less noticed, but equally spectacular turnaround came at A&M." Like Warner, it had "pioneered in the hip, non-hype style of underground publicity," turning artist bios into "a nearly surrealistic prose poetry style." From staff to packaging, companies "put themselves through massive changes in order to compete." A&M had remade itself from "the least hip record label in LA," to quote one chronicler. A Christmas ad exulted, "This year, along with making a lot of records, we set a few."[35]

A&M's rock rebranding, however, still needed an MOR fast becoming AC. The Carpenters' 75 million album sales exceeded TJB totals, and Carole King's feminist *Tapestry* became the biggest seller ever, winning a *Billboard* award "for bringing personal statement songs into a pre-eminent position within the mainstream markets." "Peace Train," by British "soft rock" or "lite rock" singer Cat Stevens, topped Easy Listening charts. Labels like A&M knew each big genre had become a mainstream. While rock held sway ideologically, what triumphed commercially was a range of revamped pop centers. As A&M demonstrated, hip was a continuum, not an absolute.[36]

Moss had been aware of A&M's growing irrelevance since the 1967 Monterey International Pop Festival. "The so-called underground emerged," he said. "I went to Monterey and we didn't have anybody there, and it was a *drag*." Industry attitudes toward rock were effusive. *Billboard* editorialized after Monterey, "Pop music has taken on the aspects of a serious art form." The magazine's radio editor stressed freeform FM's classiness: "Its listeners, so far, are above the common breed—they're doctors, lawyers, college students, young adults who're bored with regular music, ex-classical music fans." Clive Davis, the trendsetting young head of Columbia Records, told distributors, "Pop music has achieved the most respectable state ever, in its lyrics, philosophy and musicality."[37]

Unsure of the new music, Moss took dramatic measures. He changed the label's look, recalling, "We got the guys that were Monterey's art department . . . hired them, took the whole package. Decided to get a hipper art department and start moving." He updated A&M's artist roster: "I started buying finished records from England, which helped, because you could buy a record and just put it out in America, so that got you immediately on the radio." He quietly had Island Records founder Chris Blackwell, later to launch reggae's Bob Marley, steer A&M England. ("We are not interested in publicizing the fact that we are being guided by the Island executives," said a memo to staffers.) And he picked a new signature artist for his label, replacing Alpert: "The company really turned in 1969 on Joe Cocker. . . . We threw everything behind him." By Woodstock, thanks to Cocker, A&M did have a festival performer.[38]

The bluesy British singer, who told *Rolling Stone*, "Colored people have given America the only culture it has, and probably ever will have," credentialed A&M's remodel. "All small companies need one winning act. Right now, Joe Cocker makes everybody else on the label just a bit more believable," Moss wrote.[39] He invested heavily to document a tour by Cocker and a forty-five-member troupe. The movie *Mad Dogs & Englishmen* began with a plane, emblazoned "Cocker Power/A&M Records," touching down in square America. Viewers met a groupie named the Butter Lady, grinned at a middle-aged DJ determined to prove "well, yeah, I'm hip," and saw a drugged-seeming Cocker channel sweaty authenticity. "If I hadn't been a singer I probably would have murdered somebody," he said in one scene. "So many people have no release."

Moss may have worried over rock's break with entertainment niceties—he wired Australia to ask about "Joe's general deportment while performing and doing any press or promotion." But record men mostly embraced anti-commercial affect as a new wrinkle. Columbia's Davis gleefully recounted Janis Joplin's wanting sex to consummate her contract. Warner Bros. suits enjoyed meeting the Grateful Dead in a Haight-Ashbury acid haze. Labels deflected issues of commerciality by emphasizing a populist bigness, as with the "Cocker Power" plane. "Blockbusters are built on Epic Records," trumpeted ads by the sister label of Columbia, whose own slogan read, "The Columbia Rock Machine Turns You On!" Atlantic spent $200,000 to sign Led Zeppelin; A&M $400,000 on

FIGURE 3.3 Advertisement, *National Lampoon*, October 1974, for Joe Cocker, *I Can Stand a Little Rain* LP. Cocker's connection to the rock "underground" was pivotal to A&M's post-Alpert rebranding. The photo and sales copy position Cocker as outside of traditional show-business convention, yet the album's hit single, the ballad "You Are So Beautiful," relied on its appeal to older listeners. Author's collection.

Humble Pie. Ads promoting arena rockers Grand Funk Railroad, Steve Waksman's hard-rock study finds, made the size of the group's audience a legitimizing device.[40]

Leaders who mastered the new context dominated record selling for decades. They were not particularly rock fans, though many on staff were; asked what he listened to at home, Warner's Mo Ostin replied, "Oh, Andy Williams maybe." Walter Yetnikoff, Davis's protégé at Columbia, suggests a second reason record men enjoyed their relationship to rock: "If we were square businessmen watching the sexual revolution play out in the music we sold, we sure as hell wanted free and easy sex for ourselves. Some execs were growing long hair, smoking pot and sporting beards, but most were just Old School horny." The crassness of music-industry figures has long provoked outrage: the difference between Cocker, who remembers not arguing his payday for *Mad Dogs & Englishmen*—"Back then, the feeling was, it was a crime to have money anyway"—and Moss, said to have told engineer Michael James Jackson, in an A&M job interview that included the offer of cocaine, "I have no social responsibility. I'm here to make money." To Denny Bruce, a longtime rock-scene fixture, "Before Monterey, the music business was still making it up as it went along. When Clive Davis took over, he—and the whole New York business mentality—really ruined it. . . . Suddenly there was a whole New York Jewish management factor that everybody wanted."[41]

Yet Monterey, too, was organized by a Jewish manager, Alpert's old partner Lou Adler, a master at popularizing subculture. In 1964, he marketed discotheque singer Johnny Rivers to "adults dancing to rock'n'roll." He promoted a folk-rock exploitation, Barry McGuire's number 1 single, "Eve of Destruction." His Mamas and the Papas glorified LA youth culture with "California Dreamin'," but were from the East and as old as Alpert and Moss. To tap the summer of love, Adler pushed Scott McKenzie's "San Francisco (Be Sure to Wear Some Flowers in Your Hair)." Where Bruce cites New York as enemy, Californians had a nearer target. Adler remembered, "The San Francisco groups had a very bad taste in their mouths about LA commercialism. And it's true we were a business-minded industry. It wasn't a hobby. They called it slick, and I'd have to agree with them." Sellers like Adler appropriated the underground. But their concert circuits, radio networks, and studio and tour support made rock an international force.[42]

Carole King's album *Tapestry*, produced by Adler and distributed by A&M, epitomized transmission through incorporation; Robert Christgau's review called it "a triumph of mass culture." *Tapestry* charted 302 weeks on the *Billboard* Top 200. King, formerly a Brill Building writer, now sang her own tunes, in a conversational cadence unheard of from women. She lived in Laurel Canyon, divorced, just shy of thirty, and a close associate of those remaking Hollywood. *Tapestry's* cover showed her barefoot and in jeans, adult and sexual. Her one 1972 concert appearance was a Warren Beatty fund-raiser for George McGovern, with Barbra Streisand, James Taylor, and Quincy Jones—renewed MOR liberalism. Singer-songwriters were attacked for abandoning the communalism that made rock bands like "the movement." Their music, in Taylor's words, was "very self-centered, very autobiographical, and you could call it narcissistic." But as he noted, "The upside of that was that it was very accessible."[43]

As singer-songwriters personalized counterculture, a different California cohort did something similar with black power. Quincy Jones, a peer of Moss and Alpert, was a jazz musician, arranger, and producer whose history included a teen friendship with Ray Charles, work with Count Basie and Sinatra in Las Vegas, and film soundtracks. He'd also been a record man at Mercury, where "making hits turned out to be harder than I thought" and his key act was Top 40 singer Lesley Gore. On A&M from 1969 to 1980, Jones moved from swinger cosmopolitanism to racially centered statements, including a *Roots* companion soundtrack. *Smackwater Jack* included soul covers ("What's Goin' On") and a lesson on rock's black origins ("Guitar Blues Odyssey: From Roots to Fruits"). By *Body Heat* and *Mellow Madness*, the material was an R&B-MOR synthesis— that is, urban contemporary. Jones produced 4 million–selling albums on A&M of California "progressive R&B" group the Brothers Johnson, telling *Downbeat*, "The idea of finding musicians with raw ability and helping to polish that rough talent into a fine gem really gets me off." Jones, with the Brothers Johnson as musicians, later produced the huge hits *Off the Wall* and *Thriller* for Michael Jackson. "How's that for jazz?" he marveled.[44]

In a time remembered for rock and identity movements, growth in record sales owed much to MOR/AC success. *Billboard* admitted, "Aggressive easy listening stations have taken the play away from Top 40 as [the] key exposure medium for new product." The feeling in the industry was that "a new wave of 'moderation' has been working itself into the general life style of the country." Tony Zoppi of Las Vegas's Riviera said, "The trend is more to middle-of-the-road lyric singers who are young or have adapted their arrangements to appeal to youth." Harold Childs, A&M's

head of promotions, believed "progressive MOR stations have joined FM progressive rock and soul stations as today's most open routes to break an eventual Top 40 hit." A few such progressives now called themselves "adult contemporary": the term appears in *Broadcasting* as early as 1970.[45]

Yet "aggressive easy listening" was an oxymoron, and Childs acknowledged the negative associations still attached to MOR: the rackjobbers stocking department stores and the distributors supplying record stores "will not order product if it has only MOR airplay." To break Carole King, the Carpenters, and Cat Stevens, Moss went to KHJ, Bill Drake's influential Los Angeles Top 40 station. R. Serge Denisoff's 1975 study of the record industry called MOR "primarily the taste preference of married women over the age of 24." In an industry of record *men,* attitudes were traditional enough to allow a 1970 memo from A&M's first employee and office manager, Jolene Burton: "We have only one rule that applies to office attire. All female employees are expected to wear dresses to work." Patriarchal assumptions fed stereotypes that housewives were not "serious" enough to buy albums.[46]

The Carpenters showed how MOR remained the least-vaunted pop category. The family of Richard Carpenter, born in 1946, and his sister Karen, born in 1950, went to Downey, California, from Connecticut in 1963, enchanted by sunny TV images of the Rose Bowl parade. The duo defined a suburban Southern California that Eric Avila has called "popular culture in the age of white flight." In hippie 1967, Richard and a friend performed on Coke Corner at Disneyland. Karen collected Mickey Mouse items. Before signing to A&M, Richard and Karen became musical spokespeople for the youth-oriented Ford Maverick on *Your All American College Show*. Their second hit single, "We've Only Just Begun," originated as a bank ad aimed at the quintessential MOR demo: young marrieds. "Sing" was taken from the children's TV program *Sesame Street*. Nixon, beset by Watergate, invited the politically Republican Carpenters to play a function, calling them "Young America at its very best."[47]

"I know we're not rock," Richard Carpenter said. "We're pop. But we're not that kind of bland, unimaginative pop music that is so often associated with the term easy listening." Critic Tom Smucker contrasts the "whiteness" of the Carpenters and earlier MOR-fixture Welk, a midwestern bandleader who moved to California. "Under Welk's accommodating baton the ethnicities, or maybe genres, were gathered in: there was the Irish Tenor, the accordion playing Polka guy, the tap dancing black guy, the Mexican singer, the Dixieland instrumentalist, the country singer. . . .

It was music about mainstream social cohesion." Welk famously made "champagne music," what Smucker calls "the idea of post-war fun." He was not expected to project an inner life. "With the Carpenters," Smucker concludes, "the issue of control went from the social to the personal, from maintaining the norms of the musical family to a lonely inner battle, retrospectively intensified by Karen's death from anorexia."[48]

As attitudes shifted, it became a liability for the Carpenters to be wholesome—still living at home at roughly twenty-eight and twenty-four in a 1974 *Rolling Stone* profile. Richard vented to a reporter, " 'The stickysweet Carpenters—*still smiling those Pepsodent smiles!*' This . . . *thing* they've built up, where it's implicitly understood the Carpenters don't smoke, the Carpenters don't drink. Never would swear. Never would listen to rock music. They can't figure out how the fast car could have gotten in there. It's like we're Pat Boone, only a little *cleaner.* As if all we do all day is drink milk, eat apple pie and take showers. I don't even *like* milk. Not that we're totally opposite from that; we're not. But there's an in-between, you know what I mean? I don't drink a whole hell of a lot. I do have wine with dinner. I voted to make marijuana legal. I believe in premarital sex." "We would get critics reviewing our concerts, they'd review the AUDIENCE," Karen complained. "They'd say how ridiculous that somebody came to see the Carpenters in a tie!" Sure enough, when Lester Bangs, the definition of rock critic, reviewed a Carpenters concert for *Rolling Stone*, he wrote, "Something about band and audience both at this one just gave me the creeps. Mom and Dad come and learn to Dig the Kids' Music."[49]

Like Alpert a few years earlier, the Carpenters prided themselves on cross-generational appeal. "Our type of people would like the Fifth Dimension, Elton John, David Gates, Carole King—right down the middle," said Karen. The hit that launched them, "(They Long to Be) Close to You," was recorded earlier by Alpert as a failed demo. The contrasting versions support Smucker's analysis: Alpert's version comes off as worldly, a seduction over a Brazilian samba, but not particularly personal. The Carpenters removed jet-set rhythm for the controlled emotion of an inexperienced woman confessing feeling. The AC being heralded was not for would-be swingers; it translated countercultural liberation. "Superstar," a Carpenters hit, was a groupie's lament written by Leon Russell and first heard in *Mad Dogs & Englishmen.* "Goodbye to Love" featured an electric guitar solo to help create a critical AC category: the power ballad. For rockers, none of this mattered. "People who liked us were cast as having no musical sophistication or any idea of what was hip," Richard recalled. "They could not appreciate Led Zeppelin *and* the Carpenters."[50]

FIGURE 3.4 A&M Records promotional photo for Carpenters, early 1970s. A&M's biggest 1970s act was a young suburban duo with a clean-cut image, flirting with the counterculture's songs, sounds, and social changes. "I voted to make marijuana legal," Richard Carpenter protested. "I believe in premarital sex." Author's collection.

Some of the duo's frustration aimed at A&M, where they were often disparaged. Derek Green, who ran the English branch, later said, "Record company staffs are young, and young people want to be hip. Those in the company who did like the music were very much in the closet." It was more than an issue of respect: being seen as pop affected A&M's willingness to invest in the Carpenters. "Management invariably took a

short term view," an industry veteran told a biographer, and Richard said
in 1976, "It seems that if you're in country and western and you make a
couple of hit singles, you're there for life. Not in pop. We can go down as
quickly as we came up if our records are not selling." Once the Carpenters' vogue passed, they like Alpert plummeted in popularity, with AC
stations declaring it would alienate listeners to play them.[51]

In many ways, A&M as a label shared the Carpenters' insecurities. It
was a "family company," known for long relationships with artists and
employees. But what made A&M, in Denisoff's study, "*the* hot company
of the 1970s" had less to do with rock authenticity than mainstreaming
unlikely music. Publicist Bob Garcia said, "There was no market for Herb
Alpert when he first broke; he created his own market and there's never
been a waiting market for any act that we've put out." Producer Bones
Howe explained, "There was a very, very specific philosophy at A&M.
It was that there should always be some place else that you can get your
record played. If you can't get it on Top 40 radio, you should be able to get
it on a late-night MOR station." Moss fondly recalled breaking a novelty,
"The Lord's Prayer," on MOR. "I came back with this record that was this
huge hit in Australia, by a nun, Sister Janet Mead, and the guy gave it to
me at this convention. It was a record by a nun, no one was excited, no
one wanted to even take it out. And I said well get it played, get one guy
to play the record, one guy to tell us he played the record. . . . Finally, they
played the record. KMPC, somebody played the record. Switchboard lit
up. Record sold a million four singles. I mean, the album did nothing."[52]

A&M's marketing turned on courting multiple categories. Music
promotion remained how Moss started, pushing stations in a region to
play singles, but now a team of forty hectored nationally across formats.
The weekly document sent to promotions people illustrates the range. A
Quincy Jones song got "heavy R&B play on the east coast stations and
in San Francisco"; a sales guide noted his top five urban regions, as well
as those for the rock band Spooky Tooth. "All MOR stations should be
playing the LP by the Carpenters," one memo insisted. Another stressed
the youth market: "It is most important for you as promotion men and
salesmen to contact and obtain a solid rapport with your college radio stations and college people. The majority of our sales for Free Form product
is sold to these people." Childs told *Billboard*, "Our promotion men cover
all stations in their area, Top 40, progressive, soul and country."[53]

Like the Carpenters as a group, and A&M as a label, MOR as a format had a weak identity. *Radio & Records* listed dozens of variants, ask-

ing "Where (What?) Is M.O.R.?" There were contemporary MOR formatting hits, stations driven by DJ personalities, broadcasters building R&B, country, and pre-rock pop middles. "Full service" stations resisted song formatting altogether—music a placeholder for traffic, news, and weather. A WNEW-AM New York City aircheck (taped broadcast) from 1975, hosted by comedic morning man Gene Klavan, there since 1952, reveals impressive range: the Elvis Presley "Help Me Make It through the Night," Shirley Bassey's "Capricorn," "Rhinestone Cowboy," the Supremes' "I Hear a Symphony," 10 CC's "I'm Not in Love" with its 256-voice "virtual choir," Vikki Carr's cabaret "One Hell of a Woman," Keith Carradine's "I'm Easy" from *Nashville*, the Esther Phillips version of Dr. John's "Such a Night," and Herbie Mann's disco hit "Hijack." Klavan teased listeners about the variety of sounds given—akin to Johnny Carson welcoming his next strange guest.[54]

The presence of open-collared grown-ups in an arena-rock decade, incipient if uncertain AC music, and formats in the golden age of adventurous genres, has bequeathed ambivalence to accounts of early seventies music. For some, it was the height of serious listening, as hip capitalists challenged large audiences. Moss recalls, "In 1972, the people I knew would go to the market, get a couple of steaks, broccoli, and at the same time stop in at Tower Records and get two or three records they had heard about. And people would listen. You could go through a couple of hours of listening to music without anybody uttering a word." When Steven Ross purchased Warner Bros. for Kinney, he was told, "It's not a movie company, it's a record company. Essentially, all the earnings come from the record business." Others bemoaned the end of innocence. Elektra president Jac Holzman wrote, "The *music* business—which was where I had started out and where I was happiest—was becoming the music *business*." These differing paradigms speak to arguments about seventies America generally. From a left perspective, "it seemed like nothing happened," a "Me Decade" of corporate rock and smiley-face shallowness. But from another vantage, the first half of the 1970s extended the last half of the 1960s: widening countercultural attitudes. Few could fully romanticize segmenting markets purveyed by consolidating conglomerates. "The same distrust of the powers that be that undermined traditional sources of authority and fractured public life also spurred creative, personal, highly charged art that addressed just that discontent," writes Bruce Schulman. "But this rebellious streak remained knowing, jaded, circumspect. It lacked the utopian naivete of the Sixties."[55]

Long after hip marketing campaigns faded into painful memory, it remained the achievement of labels such as A&M that music had diversified its portfolio. The record industry had transferred its "serious" designation, in part, from classical and jazz to rock. Arguably, it had done poorest not by rock purists so much as by the MOR fans who confirmed or, as with the Carpenters, created its greatest sales achievements. At a time when African Americans used music to explore black power, country fans to modernize the South, and counterculturalists to draw boundaries across age, MOR fans were quiescent by definition. Yet this older listenership had varied tastes, more open than rockers admitted. They too found in music an interior reflection on what it meant to live in an affluent society whose norms had shifted.

The Making of Superstars: Blockbuster Pop

By 1977, A&M could tout massive hits such as the Captain & Tennille's "Love Will Keep Us Together" and Peter Frampton's *Frampton Comes Alive!* As the *Los Angeles Times* reported, it had "a roster of artists that spans the entire spectrum of contemporary music, including Peter Frampton, Brothers Johnson, Cat Stevens, Chuck Mangione, Gato Barbieri, L.T.D., Quincy Jones, Styx, Captain & Tennille, and Carpenters." A&M enjoyed "a reputation of maintaining long term relationships with its artists" and latitude for "progressive acts," such as black female rocker Joan Armatrading. *Billboard* hailed A&M's stable executive team and one hundred people marketing product. The Recording Industry Association of America named Moss president. The following year, number three executive Gil Friesen said, "We are not only developing a 'multi-departmental' consciousness, we are developing a multi-national marketing consciousness."[56]

Come 1979, A&M nearly went bankrupt, as Alpert and Moss were forced to secure $10 million by mortgaging their homes and purged 14 percent of the label's employees. A&M surrendered its fabled independence, entering a distribution deal with RCA. Now the *Los Angeles Times* reported a different opinion of the company: "For years, A&M has been viewed—not altogether unfairly—as a bloodless, middle-of-the-road label. . . . The label's meal tickets—the Carpenters, Carole King, Cat Stevens and the Captain & Tennille—have rarely strayed from the safe confines of the pop mainstream." An unnamed "industry insider" said,

"A&M's biggest problem has been that its big stars from Carole King to Peter Frampton could never sustain their appeal over a long period of time." The success of the industry, too, turned precarious. *Solid Gold*, Denisoff's first account of the record business, became *Tarnished Gold* in the sequel.[57]

A common view, in need of deconstructing, is that popular music at the end of the seventies became too middle of the road: grouped in formats so defined, musically and demographically, and so expensive to penetrate, that newcomers had little success. Bruce Schulman's influential decade history offhandedly comments, "A&M Records discovered a mediocre, undistinguished British rocker named Peter Frampton and packaged him as something for everyone. . . . *Frampton Comes Alive*, like most other Seventies corporate rock, offered music with no soul, no message, no recognizable quality to distinguish it from what came before. Yet it became the biggest-selling album of all time—the first multiplatinum record." Difficult as a business model, the imperial record industry was culturally unpopular. Equally transgressive and banal, it had something to offend everyone. John Leland argues in his history of hip, "Youth culture turned not against the establishment but against itself. . . . The enemy was not your dad, but Peter Frampton and the corporation supporting him." The backlash against disco and Frampton fed off misgivings about indulgence creating economic stagnation, social unraveling, and cultural mediocrity.[58]

An early illustration of the fragile status of an omnivorous music industry had been Clive Davis's 1973 firing by CBS. In seven years, Davis had brought annual revenues to half a billion dollars, signing rockers while cultivating MOR, country, and R&B. He'd just staged a genre-spanning "Week to Remember" concert series in Los Angeles to show the label's progress from Broadway hits and classical. Still, he was dismissed amid whispers of police investigating payola to R&B DJs by Columbia's newly formed black-music department. (No criminal charges were brought, though Davis admitted to exaggerated business expenses.) "Goddard [Lieberson] was the gentleman executive, Clive the hungry go-getter," Walter Yetnikoff wrote about Davis and the man, famous for backing *My Fair Lady*, who CBS now hired back. Frith, ever sympathetic to those devalued by unexamined cultural hierarchies, argues, "Much of the creative energy that has shaped the history of mass mediated music has been generated at the margins of the legal music world by music makers and hustlers, whose only means of access to audiences and markets has been illicit." Lieberson quickly proved unfit for 1970s

industry economics and was replaced by Yetnikoff: tone-deaf and attracted to "street characters." "Corporate rock" was, the point is, for
many in a boardroom, *not corporate enough*, with suspect promotions and
a product hard to legitimize.[59]

A&M epitomized the challenges. The label accounted for 4 to 7 percent of hit records, making it the biggest of the independents—more varied than Motown and the model for Davis's new imprimatur, Arista. A
feature on Harold Childs, A&M's vice president for promotions, captured
him frenetically managing campaigns for artists as different as teen idol
Frampton, fusion jazz-pop trumpeter Chuck Mangione, arena rockers
Supertramp, standards singer Peggy Lee, arty college favorites the Tubes,
folksinger Joan Baez, and R&B singer Billy Preston, calling staff around
the United States and writing Japan. Childs was said to ask repeatedly,
"What's happening with sales on the streets?" Given A&M's fifty-one
charting albums in 1975, there was much to learn. The label created a
"management information services department" to be "involved in studies concerning demographics and audience penetration."[60]

Topping the US charts now had international consequences. When
"The Lonely Bull" came out, Moss fielded a call from Australia and licensed the song for $500. In the latter 1970s, letters from the RPM label
recounted selling A&M product in South Africa, where a Frampton promotional film—a marketing innovation for hard-to-reach areas—arrived
late and Quincy Jones's *Roots* soundtrack could not be cleared politically.
A memo proposing an A&M French subsidiary reviewed the national
rules to follow, yet stressed the "American attitude" of the lawyers involved. A&M's Japanese representative for the King label, Kuna Murai,
telegrammed Moss to come host a Tokyo party for country singer Rita
Coolidge, push a Supertramp promotion, and further the Brothers Johnson. A manager's panel at an A&M gathering itemized a 130-date Styx
world tour.[61]

The bigness of the industry became a matter of public fascination, centered around what one book called *The Making of Superstars*. The new
industry measure was platinum sales, 1 million shipped, twice gold-record
status. Touring acts might earn $150,000 for a single sports-arena date.
Leading radio consultant Lee Abrams pioneered a "Superstars" approach
that emphasized name artists over novelties by unknowns. Consolidating
to white male guitar acts, freeform stations renamed themselves album-
oriented rock (AOR). One manager hung a sign "The Age of Aquarius is
over—and now it's time to kick ass." A&M's album promotions director

Rich Totoian agreed, "The free ride is over. We must be more specialized and committed." His colleague Al Moinet declared, "It's the advertising agencies that are controlling Top 40 because the station must appeal to the right demographics or they won't buy time." Al Edmondson, A&M director of R&B special projects, said, "Black radio realizes it's a business now."[62]

A&M vice president Bob Fead reported in 1977 that it cost $300,000 to create a charting LP before the first copy sold, including production, marketing, and artist fees. (*Tapestry* cost about $10,000.) As early as 1973, UK managing director Derek Green warned, "We can't continue to hide behind the old A&M image that we are a small creative company surrounded by large companies forever." Yet this remained the habit. Friesen insisted, "The reason for our success is the company's ability to properly market product . . . quickly and efficiently." Moss, who purchased English acts in the late 1960s, claimed that A&M was "maintaining its philosophy of concentrating its efforts into developing and breaking new acts instead of the outright buying of labels and established acts." He praised his label's rockers for having "broken the strict confines of Top 40 radio"— though they fit the now equally strict confines of AOR. Clive Davis also used an MOR/AC success, Barry Manilow, to fund his new label's growth, while insisting that Arista, "Where Careers Are Launched," was an artist-oriented brand.[63]

A&M's biggest successes remained open to derision. In 1975, the label had the year's top-selling single for the first time, the Captain & Tennille's "Love Will Keep Us Together." Daryl Dragon, son of a conductor and perennially outfitted in a yachting cap, resembled Alpert in some ways: "I waited 12 years for the happy sound to come back," he told the recently launched *People*. "I couldn't relate to dope groups." Toni Tennille, daughter of a swing band musician and a TV talk show host, was looser than Karen Carpenter, noting she and Dragon had lived together before marriage and grew "organic crops" in their garden. The TV variety series that followed had no such currency: sitcom stars, disco numbers, pre-rock standards, and strained appearances by older showmen. *People* labeled them "TV's square Sonny & Cher," and the program ended after a season, with the duo leaving A&M by 1979.[64]

The rise and fall of Peter Frampton on A&M was even more dramatic. A guitarist in Humble Pie, the group Moss signed for $400,000 to take A&M rock, Frampton relocated to California and became a solo act who crossed down in age the way Alpert had, but for even younger fans, combining "at one end of the scale the pubescent teenybop faction and at the other end, college students who see him as the new British rock guitar supremo." At Moss's urging, Frampton released a double live LP that rewarded the label's patience and became a sales phenomenon on par with *Tapestry*. But as a *Rolling Stone* cover story noted, success made him the unhappy subject of a new celebrity journalism, fascinated with money more than music.

> Frampton's album has sold 7 million copies in America and another 3 million worldwide; in the same period, Frampton sold nearly 2 million concert tickets. At a royalty rate of "approximately" 67 cents per album (according to A&M Records), this makes for a prodigious one-year income. *People* magazine captioned a photo of Frampton with ". . . His GNP? 50 million." The figure upset Frampton: "I'd like the people to know that figure is nowhere near what was actually earned," he said. "A lot of people came up to me and said, 'Do you really have that much money?' And I have to say, 'No, not on me, no.' They don't realize that Gross National Product is income generated in the music business, in the photography business, with posters, the T-shirt business . . . for other people, including myself."

As with Alpert, gender prejudices shaped Frampton's fears of being a mass idol. He recalled, "My credibility as a musician got lost. I was overmarketed. . . . Suddenly, I was appealing just to teenage girls. Everyone forgot that I could play the guitar." Talking about the "MOR musical stamp" attached to Frampton, veteran manager Dee Anthony blamed "rock critics not knowing what the word *entertainment* means." Jerry Moss recalled in his UCLA oral history, "The thing about rock is it's sort of dark and mysterious; you don't have to see people that close up, just get their music and let your emotions and imagination carry you. And Peter's a charming guy, and what they were trying, he and his manager, were trying to do was, I think, make a short cut into movies or whatever it was, and trying to show the many dimensions of Peter, which I can understand. But I don't think it helped his rock fans; it looked like he might have sold out." Frampton was dropped by A&M in 1982 and floundered for decades.[65]

Glenn Frey of the Eagles told California rock's best chronicler, Barney Hoskyns, "There was a time during 1976–77 when the record business went crazy, with *Hotel California*, *Rumours*, *Frampton Comes Alive!*, and then *Saturday Night Fever*. That was the decadent zenith of the music business." The comment invokes record sales, drug use, and lavish spending, conflating a disco soundtrack with adult and youth rock. Many disco his-

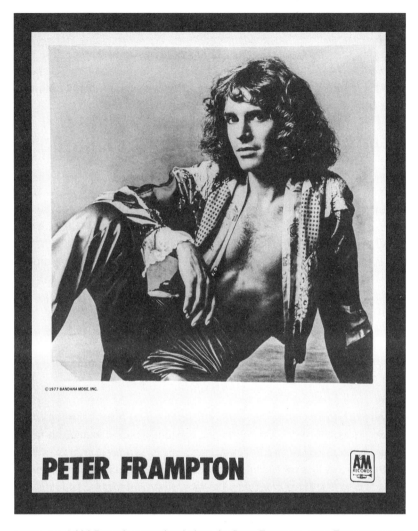

© 1977 BANDANA MDSE. INC.

PETER FRAMPTON

FIGURE 3.5 A&M Records promotional photo for Peter Frampton, 1977. Frampton was a rocker whose group Humble Pie was part of A&M's rebranding. *Frampton Comes Alive!* became one of the most successful, and scorned, albums of the 1970s. The singer-guitarist became ashamed of his sexual marketing. Author's collection.

tories see a black, Latin, gay, and female-oriented sound opposed by rock racism, sexism, and homophobia. But the dance music's appeal shared much with Fleetwood Mac and the Eagles' "life in the fast lane" narratives of Southern California recklessness, and Frampton's alteration from rocker to pin-up. The music industry emblemized unrestrained lifestyle. Bud Scoppa, an A&M employee, recalls constant cocaine use: "By the end of 1975, there'd be a weekly marketing meeting in a big conference room, and people would get up and leave the room all the way through the meeting. *Everybody* was doing it. I thought it was devastating."[66]

A&M's format-friendly acts personified dubious contemporaneity. "The vast chunk of audience in the middle has settled down to 'listen' with Supertramp," Canadian *MacLean's* reported. *Time* had proclaimed Alpert "the middle-aged man's answer to rock 'n' roll"; Supertramp was "for people who do not like their rock 'n' roll scary." The band's co-leader, Rick Davies, a British welder's son who wore designer jeans and was moving to Beverly Hills, said, "Don't forget we're a very manufactured group." Equally slick were A&M trumpeter Mangione, who turned *Tonight Show* appearances into hit albums of accessible jazz with rock guitar touches, or the Brothers Johnson and L.T.D., staples of New York's WBLS, billed as "geared more to contemporary black lifestyles."[67]

Across multiple formats, upwardly aspiring centrist acts created a musical variety responsive to social experimentation. But accompanying this was hostility to extremes of sound and ideology. The upheavals in MOR/AC taste reflected what Daniel Bell's landmark analysis called "the cultural contradictions of capitalism": an industrial ethos of hard work meeting a leisure economy's need for consumer release. "A corporation finds its people being straight by day and swingers by night," Bell wrote in the 1978 paperback edition. If the hostility directed in the late 1960s toward swingers and Alpert owed to radicalization, the late 1970s version aimed at disco and corporate rock reflected broader disquiet. In an era of rising prices and stagnant growth, the consumer sector seemed to fiddle while the nation burned. Jimmy Carter's speech about American "crisis of the spirit" asked for consumption limits; Christopher Lasch had an unexpected best seller, *The Culture of Narcissism: American Life in an Age of Diminishing Expectations.*[68]

The most controversial pop sound, disco, was much like the music of 1962: driven by MOR and Top 40 singles, a pleasure product open to international beats and created, primarily, by independent labels. Casablanca, home to disco queen Donna Summer and face-painted heavy metal act Kiss, now occupied A&M's former offices on Sunset Boulevard. *Saturday Night Fever,* the 1977 film that turned disco from pop music to pop culture, was the brainchild of Robert Stigwood, a contemporary of Alpert and Moss, and released on his independent RSO. Alpert enjoyed his first hit in a decade, "Rise," played in black discos and later sampled by Puff Daddy for Notorious B.I.G.'s "Hypnotize." The connection between Alpert and

MOR women revived: "Rise" soared when soap opera *General Hospital* featured it on a program.[69]

Key record sellers attacked disco. Some had prospered in the "serious" early 1970s, when rock's dominance masked the MOR nature of much of the industry. Stan Cornyn, long a hip executive at Warner, warned about "pure commercialism overwhelming and dictating our lives," saying of Stigwood's record label, "Just as man should not live by Big Macs alone, nor should he live only by RSO. . . . When popularity becomes the product itself, then popular art tends to feed on its own popularity, to idolize its own success, and eventually to parody its own standards." Consultant Lee Abrams advised clients to abandon the disco format, saying—in loaded language reflecting the sexism often behind attacks on MOR—that polling indicated that active fans found it "superficial, boring, repetitive, and short on balls." The assumption that MOR audiences were not reliable, buying only big hits, reemerged. One retailer said, "People came in for *Saturday Night Fever* who I've never seen and won't ever again."[70]

Will Straw, whose dissertation on this era is the most systematic study, makes a contrasting argument to period claims: record companies overvalued rock and "serious" music and failed to validate MOR and AC. Record companies, Straw argues, overinvested in rock career artists at a time when AOR was relatively closed to new performers. AOR acts formed a "canon," he notes, while MOR/AC acts were not given "contextualizing discourses wherein the coherence and continuity of particular performer careers were established."[71]

As part of a severe global recession, sales slumped 10 percent in 1979, 20 percent between 1979 and 1982, and would not hit 1978 levels until 1984—the first serious downturn to hit records since the Depression years. A&M, like many, found itself buried in returned product. "It's getting harder for an independent label to survive," Alpert told *Rolling Stone*. "Our mistakes are now a lot costlier than they used to be. . . . It used to be the two of us and then the three of us. Now it's the 350 of us." Moss explains A&M's difficulties as "basically the decline of the independent distributor." As record selling centralized, with national "super stores" and record chains, A&M decided it required major-label distribution and arranged an RCA deal. Former distributors held up payment. Though A&M would not be sold for a decade, the biggest indie needed corporate affiliation. "The record business is no longer an individual entrepreneur's heaven, it belongs to the really big guys, to the conglomerates," said a label executive.[72]

As recordings struggled, AC radio became as powerful as the chorus of Journey's "Don't Stop Believin'." *Billboard* noted "the shift of many MOR stations to adult contemporary formats, eschewing show tunes and soft pop for playlists that are often nearly indistinguishable from the Top 40 listings." Helping this, "rock music is edging toward a slice MOR approach, suggesting that both forms are borrowing from each other." Radio responded to a down economy and ad market by programming to the 25–34 demographic sponsors preferred over youth: a "move toward mass appeal formats." Bob Paiva, program director (PD) of WCMB and WSFM in Harrisburg, stressed class: "We are attempting to appeal to an upwardly mobile white collar adult who still wants to maintain a contemporary outlook and not be what we called an MOR listener." Rock-oriented label execs were said to "find themselves wistfully yearning for the days when AOR meant AOR, and not a combination of AOR, Top 40, and adult pop." But creative radio programmers at last targeted women deliberately, respectfully. Dwight Douglas, of the consultants Burkhart-Abrams-Michaels-Douglas, imagined a "Femme FM" aimed at the "hip young woman" and "more like a Perrier station rather than a beer station." After all, he said, "women are a different breed from several decades ago. They tend to control the radio a bit more. . . . The males are more passive than they used to be."[73]

The 1970s music industry proved unable to sustain mass appeal. Successful performers met backlashes. Companies were unable to legitimize the "eclectic, reminiscent, amused, fickle, perverse" qualities required of record men. Preferring to be seen as progressives, they overvalued "serious" rock and devalued female, older, and casual consumers. Even so, they could not escape public scorn. Punk took countercultural anti-commercialism to new levels. The Sex Pistols were signed to A&M, then dropped after only a few days. "The reason, if you want to call it that, we were given was that the Sex Pistols would tarnish the kind of quality MOR image A&M has," said band manager Malcolm McLaren. Once again, A&M would have to reinvent itself.[74]

"We Are the World": The Adult Contemporary 1980s

Herb Alpert and Jerry Moss struggled to raise funds in 1979. A decade later they sold their company for $500 million, with a subsequent $300 million for its publishing. Assumptions about pop weakness proved inaccurate in the 1980s, as centrist approaches dominated. Videos-oriented cable channel MTV launched in 1981, with an AC counterpart, VH-1, added in 1985; visuals revitalized the making of superstars. The more expensive compact disc replaced the LP, adding profit per sale and empowering reminiscence—audiences repurchased old favorites. The strategy of multiple formats and genres expanded: new age, college radio, and Christian music blossomed. "We Are the World," sang the USA for Africa stars, gathered at the A&M studios. The power ballads beloved by the dominant AC format, often attached to Hollywood soundtracks, made sure of that global reach.

A&M revived in part by again pursuing adventurous rock. Where Chris Blackwell and Lou Adler had steered A&M into the 1970s, "new wave" manager Ian Copeland revamped A&M by bringing the Police, Squeeze, and label IRS, whose acts included the Go-Gos and R.E.M. Moss heard Human League in England, secured US distribution on unfavorable terms ("We ain't got no leverage," a note attested), and broke synth-pop into the American Top 40. Distribution of Minneapolis's Twin/Tone, home to the Replacements, connected A&M to an emerging college radio network. The Police in particular became A&M's leading group. A commercial act with new wave trappings ("we're just carpet baggers," drummer Stewart Copeland said), its leader Sting was a jazz and world-music fan who preferred yoga to drugs and rejected punk's ideas of authenticity. But the band avoided late seventies excess. Sting recalled, "We never asked our record company, A&M, for an advance, so we never had that kind of feudal relationship with them. They never felt as if they owned us, and the partnership continues today." The globally popular Police played bullrings Alpert once had, and venues in India, Egypt, Greece, and Argentina. Sting avoided the downfall of earlier A&M acts, dissolving the Police in 1984 for a solo adult pop career that relied on the support of a steadily more consistent AC radio format.[75]

But much A&M prosperity came once more from niches outside rock. Windham Hill specialized in new age, updated mood-music LPs with a counterculture emphasis on spirituality and radio support on stations such as The Wave in Los Angeles. A&M began distributing it in 1983, responding to an article Childs passed on to Moss with the note, "Jerry, Windham Hill is the jazz label that I told you about. Geffen is after it." A&M dealt with Word Music in 1985 to secure Amy Grant. The twenty-four-year-old evangelical may have amused the Jewish-owned label execs, saying, "We all would choose to live in a world built on Christian principles"; she proclaimed herself "totally against" abortion and "sleeping around." Yet the leopard-skin jacket on her album cover showed AC

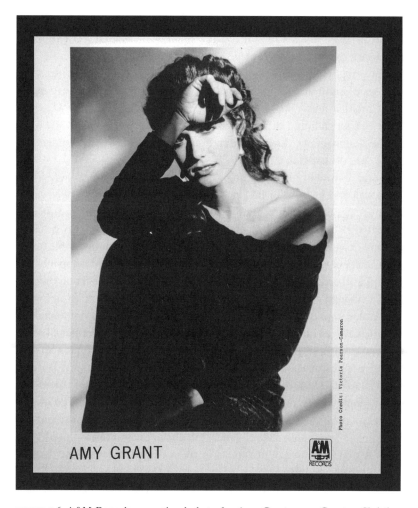

FIGURE 3.6 A&M Records promotional photo for Amy Grant, 1991. Grant, a Christian-music performer, fully accepted the importance of branding and marketing, making her a successful adult pop crossover figure for decades. Grant, Sting, and other 1980s figures helped AC finally solidify its concept. Author's collection.

instincts. Her husband stated, "I think she wants to say that it's okay to be a Christian and have fun," and she admitted, "I'm trying to look sexy to sell a record." A&M took an ad out in *Billboard* challenging a liberal industry: "You may not know this artist by name. But a million know her music by heart." Another A&M co-venture, children's music Shoreline, made Raffi the leading artist in that genre.[76]

Testing A&M more than these genre turns was its decision to invest heavily in R&B. A&M had insisted its promotions people work all fields—Childs, who oversaw the department, was African American but responsible for every music format. Now, John McClain created a separate black-music department. His coup was shepherding Janet Jackson into commercial success comparable to her brother Michael's. In a classic record man's move, McClain paired his Jackson with producers who had worked with Michael's rival Prince. The aggressive promotion McClain favored, a staple of black departments, created tensions within the laid-back A&M culture. Jeff Gold, a longtime employee, wrote a memo to the label heads after a physical altercation with McClain, complaining, "I understand the contribution he's made to the bottom line of this company, but he's also rewritten many a rule, and created a climate of fear and intimidation—not only with me."[77]

"Welcome to the boomtown," an A&M one-hit-wonder act named David & David sang in 1986. "All that money makes such a *succulent* sound." As with Michael Douglas's famous "greed is good" speech in *Wall Street*, Reagan-era pop culture contemplated changed standards. Michael Jackson, Prince, and Janet Jackson—like Madonna and Bruce Springsteen, both MTV and VH-1 favorites—redefined blockbuster success. "When we came out with *Rhythm Nation 1814*," Moss said in his oral history, "we spent about $700,000, which at the time was a ton of money, on essentially making like a 20-minute film, which encompassed three real videos of the three first singles that we were releasing from the album. And it turned out to be a brilliant way to go. . . . Janet could go on the road and not have to worry about getting back to do anything. . . . We'll do the videos and we'll tell you when they're coming. . . . Of course she approved who the film director was. . . . I mean, in a way, the record business grew up." Less glamorously, "independent promoters" were paid heavily to secure airplay for these enormous label investments, resurrecting controversies that had dogged Alan Freed and Clive Davis. When the industry debated an internal legal investigation, a crucial vote against taking such a step came from Jerry Moss. *Musician* asked if A&M's "just-folks image" was now a sham: the label's day-to-day head, Gil Friesen, had the nicknames "the Baron" and "Prince of Darkness." Friesen responded, "Personally, I don't like the word 'family.'"[78]

A&M could be as tough minded as anybody. The promotions summaries of 1970 are quaint next to a marketing plan preserved for R&B singer Jeffrey Osborne's 1983 track "Stay with Me Tonight," which aimed to move Osborne "from a major Black artist to a Pop album seller with the start of his own dual CHR/A-C hit base." This included "the 'personality' positioning of Jeffrey Osborne through cable/broadcast TV." The presence on the video of a rock guitarist, Queen's Brian May, was noted for its crossover implications, as were scheduled Osborne appearances on *The Tonight Show*, *David Letterman*, and *Friday Night Videos*. With equal candor, a 1984 memo assessed A&M's foreign distribution deal with CBS. For CBS, A&M was attractive because "A&M also has connotations of 'quality' and 'art' which help to soften CBS's 'hard-nosed' business image." For A&M, CBS could ensure maximum sales for established stars. The goal was to increase "the number of developing acts reaching the level at which the CBS machine is ready to take over."[79]

AC radio took a back seat to resurgent Top 40 (now contemporary hit radio, or CHR) in the early 1980s moment of MTV's emergence, but grew dominant again as the decade progressed, emphasizing current songs that fit its scope. "Programmers at old-line, full-service giants today feel like visitors to Mars when we look at the A/C charts," Carl Gardner of KEX Portland complained. Indianapolis PD Scott Wheeler had a ready answer: "We thought that artist identification would be a problem. But when you look closely at our listeners, they are familiar with most of these artists anyway. For example, if you walk into an aerobics class, you'll hear the Pointer Sisters, Madonna, Huey Lewis, and Prince all the time. It's not foreign to them." Ballads launched on (essentially black AC) Quiet Storm R&B led to AC playing more black music, some years, than CHR. *Billboard* warned in 1985 that AC's need to tap, yet not resemble, CHR left it vulnerable to fragmentation along age and style lines. A 1988 *Radio & Records* overview noted a "new variation" called "Hot AC"—positioned between CHR and AC. But there was room for both, because ACs now understood their key demo—working women. In Cleveland, WDOK—"Our in-office and workplace listening clearly put us over the top"—battled WLTF: "We're still number one 25–54 *women*, which is our target."[80]

Many artists heard on AC radio gathered in January 1985 at the A&M Studios, with longtime A&M artist Quincy Jones producing, to record "We Are the World." Activist and MOR entertainer Harry Belafonte suggested the project to Ken Kragen, who managed AC stalwarts Kenny Rogers and Lionel Richie; Richie and Michael Jackson wrote the song together. Soloists included Stevie Wonder, Paul Simon, Rogers, Tina Turner, Billy Joel, Willie Nelson, Bruce Springsteen, Bob Dylan, Ray Charles, Cyndi Lauper, Journey's Steve Perry, and Huey Lewis. Rock critic Greil Marcus blasted the recording as "desperately MOR music. . . .

The point is voracious aggrandizement in the face of starvation—a collective aggrandizement, what those in the industry are most proud of . . . projecting themselves on the world, the USA for Africa singers eat it." In response, Robert Christgau hailed the African American–led nature of the project, which connected black gentility to universal humanism. Calling the song, as he had *Tapestry*, "a triumph of mass culture," he found in the voices a string of qualities longer than the *New Yorker* description of Ertegun: "This isn't superstar arrogance at all—just superstar affluence. Its vocal bounty—sincere, childlike, foolish, pretentious, zany, overstated, gorgeous, sentimental, profound, vulgar, expert, soulful—incarnates the emotional and spiritual potential of America as material world."[81]

Regardless of how one judged it, "We Are the World" was a commercial triumph: flying out of stores "at a rate 20 times greater than the average popular single," *Billboard* reported, for multiplatinum certification. The same issue bannered that recording sales had finally surpassed the 1978 pre-crash high. One key was "a dramatic rise in shipments of Compact Discs." Moss remembered, "The CD just exploded the value of record companies, because we could charge three and four times more, wholesale, for the product, same information. The artists were excited about the new technology, therefore they were allowing us to take some packaging deductions. And so the result was that record companies became extremely profitable with hits. I mean, the hits became exponentially bigger, more rewarding."[82]

It can be as easy to mock the successes of 1980s mainstream pop as the failures of the 1970s. Joe Cocker, no longer the engaging sociopath of *Mad Dogs*, sang the AC love duet "Up Where We Belong" on the *Officer and a Gentleman* soundtrack. A&M's biggest AC rocker, Bryan Adams, hit with the nostalgic "Summer of '69" and power ballad "(Everything I Do) I Do It for You," featured in Kevin Costner's *Robin Hood*. Slotted and safe, adult pop fed on movie synergy and overpriced CD profits, not risk taking—hip-hop was marginalized. AC, aimed at women, was hardly programmed by them: a 1983 survey found only one of 136 station program directors was female. Nonetheless, the biggest songwriter of the era, Californian Diane Warren, specialized in therapeutic love songs popular across all major formats. Little known when her cowrite "Find a Way" became the breakout AC hit on Amy Grant's first A&M album, Warren's anthems included "How Do I Live," "Unbreak My Heart," "I Don't Want to Miss a Thing," and "If You Asked Me To." They were sung by rock's Aerosmith, Latin pop's Exposé, AC's Michael Bolton, R&B's Aaliyah, and country's Mark Chesnutt. They were lip-synched by the scandalous

Milli Vanilli. But mostly, they were performed by the women central to AC: Celine Dion, Whitney Houston, Mariah Carey, Gloria Estefan. AC had stabilized its place in the record industry.

A&M Becomes Universal

Toward the close of his oral history sessions with UCLA, Jerry Moss talked about staking horses on the urging of a friend, a record presser:

> Herbie and I could make a record at night and take the master over to Monarch, and they would press records, and the next night . . . go to a radio station and get somebody to play it maybe in the middle of the night so we could hear it in our cars to see if that sound was really the kind of sound we were looking for. . . . The spontaneity was so incredible. . . . [Wallach's] Music City used to be located on the corner of Sunset and Vine, and they'd catalogue the records, and on the back of the sheet where the 45s were you could . . . see how many records were sold at the end of a 24-hour period. . . . That kind of spontaneity and that kind of excitement over very little things, seemingly modest events, were very [much] part of that thing.

The anecdote seamlessly fed into Moss's much later horse adventures: "Got some young horses with a guy named Brian Mayberry and said, 'Boy, one day I want to win the [Kentucky] Derby.' Lo and behold, we happened to breed a horse that won it. . . . Only in America, huh?"[83]

For Moss the record man, the spontaneity of breaking new music resembled winning a big race. Had the music business, as it evolved, fulfilled his ambitions, betrayed them, or does that question even make sense? The king's ransom paid for A&M belonged to still bigger processes. Columbia sold to Japan's Sony; Arista and RCA went to Germany's BMG; A&M and Motown passed to Dutch PolyGram, a subsidiary of the electronics firm Phillips. A&M's purchase took place in 1989, as the shattered Berlin Wall marked Cold War dynamics replaced by amorphous globalization. Warner Bros. became the only US-owned major. Alpert and Moss were ousted from A&M's executive leadership in 1993, leaving behind acts like grunge's Soundgarden and incipient AC star Sheryl Crow. They created Almo Sounds, signing roots revivalist Gillian Welch, Mexican American alt-rockers Ozomatli, and powerpop Garbage, but found no joy competing with megacorporations to influence the radio chains of hundreds of stations formed after unlimited ownership was permitted by the 1996 Telecommunications Act. PolyGram merged with MCA to become Universal, the largest music conglomerate in the world, owned by a French water company. The Universal website delineates artist rosters for North America, Europe, Latin America, and Asia Pacific, noting that its publishing administers a million copyrights through forty-seven offices in forty-one countries. The A&M lots were sold off in 2000.[84]

Nonetheless, as corporate consolidation accelerated, the overall number of American radio formats kept increasing, fostering sonic diversity. Technological shifts—Internet downloading, iPods, satellite radio, *American Idol*, YouTube, social networks, and so forth—ensured that commercial pop remained far from static. From hip-hop to boy bands, the content continued to require a balancing act between margins and mainstreams. John McClain, for example, after controversially steering Janet Jackson at A&M, worked with Jimmy Iovine, a longtime A&M associate who'd modernized the company's studios in the 1980s, to create Interscope and push it into industry preeminence through Dr. Dre's *The Chronic*, the first blockbuster gangsta rap album. That Dre and his protégé Snoop Dogg were California rappers transforming a New York–centered field continued the story of rock and pop. Daniel Bell cited Interscope in a reissued *Cultural Contradictions of Capitalism*, to show that the contradictions persisted: "The buyers . . . are white, suburban, male youths, and the singers are black, inner-city thugs."[85]

Many A&M artists thought consigned to history enjoyed revivals that demonstrated the persistence of show-business values: novelty, eclecticism, and the oddities of mainstream appeal. Herb Alpert and the Tijuana Brass are now sampled and called "honorary Latinos" by postmodern Latin American artists who relish inauthenticity. (The animated sitcom *The Simpsons* also regularly uses TJB themes to parodic effect.) An early 1990s "lounge music" revival resurrected much of A&M's 1960s easy listening material, heard once again in films such as *Pulp Fiction* and *Swingers*. The Carpenters, too, enjoyed a revival, with the tribute album *If I Were a Carpenter* and an unreleased, yet widely circulated, film by director Todd Haynes. "White, suburban, drugged, anorexic [*sic*]: read cynically, as pop-cultural icons, Richard and Karen would seem to be the perfect patron saints for the mall-dwelling, vagued-out Generation X-ers of mid-Nineties America," one commentator wrote, while songwriter Linda Perry simply said, "I adore the cheesiness of them." Peter Frampton had his story retold more sympathetically on a popular cable series, *Behind the Music*, where every episode narrated the rise, downfall, and redemption of a different icon. Musicologists now study the category "music we love to hate."[86]

To look at the evolution of a single record label, A&M, between the 1960s and the 1980s, as it sought to reconcile "quality" and "machine," the off-beat record pitched to a local DJ and the world arena tour, is to feel the dubiousness of rigid distinctions between individually owned companies and megacorporations, between rock and MOR/AC, between youth music and adult taste. Too much else was caught up in these valuations for them to remain stable: gendered, generational, and class conceptions of taste perpetually challenged by the experimentation consumerism reinforced. The MOR, adult, suburban, record industry experience of these transformations was a particular one: uncommitted to any one musical approach, open to entertainment as artifice and formula, but romanced by "serious" art as well; avowedly upscale and contemporary. We'd be remiss to describe this stance as passive, like the housewives it deprecated, but equally wrong to accept swinging bachelors as rebels.

Rather, the cultural middle in music acted as a counterweight, defusing the ideological tendencies of rock, R&B, country music, and other coherent genres, translating subcultural products into suburban staples. It kept any one sound from drowning out all others, accruing an enormous catalogue along the way, for the economic benefit of a few but the aesthetic benefit of a great many. If the great achievement of the decentralized popular music industry was sustaining multiple and rival formats that nourished disparate publics and could stretch globally, much owed to the record man's eclecticism and perverse fascination with music selling as a process—and to the fickle audiences who provided landmark sales to such a broad range of pleasure.

CHAPTER FOUR

Madman across the Water

Elton John and Top 40

For thirty years, 1970 through 1999, Elton John placed at least one song in the Top 40 of the *Billboard* singles chart. That accomplishment, which John has called his proudest, meant American radio stations with a hits-oriented format played his offerings and the public bought them—US charts combined sales and airplay. But a true valuing is more complicated. Why was the most consistently successful hitmaker in American pop English? Why, in an era vaunting rock authenticity, were his lyrics from a cowriter, Bernie Taupin, and delivered live in absurd costumes? Does it refigure his seemingly innocuous catalogue that, since first calling himself "bisexual to a certain degree" in 1976, he has come to rank with the planet's most famous gay public figures, committing to David Furnish in a civil union greeted like an affair of state?[1]

My focus on John's career emphasizes the format he chose to prioritize. Adopted by American radio after television captured network programs, Top 40 played pop as a category unto itself, guaranteeing a familiar experience each time listeners tuned in. Formats sustained both defined genres, such as rhythm and blues (R&B) and country, and crossover channels like middle of the road/adult contemporary (MOR/AC). Top 40, renamed contemporary hits radio (CHR) in the 1980s, was another genre-mixing format. History credits Top 40 with popularizing rock and roll. But, such narratives continue, the approach's commercialism came to seem corny. "Freeform" (free of format) rock took the Woodstock Generation forward.

Yet Top 40 remained powerful long after portions of the baby boom deemed it déclassé. New York's WABC-AM stayed number 1 nationally

FIGURE 4.1 Poster from *Rock Superstars Poster Magazine No. 1*, Penthouse Poster Press, 1975, photograph by Barry Bregman. As one of the ultimate 1970s pop superstars, Elton John used Top 40 to transgress within capitalism, taking what had been a British Invasion into cultural globalization and what had been coded gay identity to the brink of queer celebration. Author's collection.

from 1962 to 1978. *American Top 40*, the widely syndicated radio countdown hosted by Casey Kasem, launched only in 1970. MTV, recast from
a rock focus to CHR after Michael Jackson's *Thriller* in the early 1980s,
dominated music promotion for two decades. Presently, Ryan Seacrest,
host of *American Idol*, also hosts *American Top 40* and a daily syndicated
CHR program.[2] Top 40 endured as a space for new cultural arrivals to
announce themselves, resisting countercultural disparagement of bla-
tant promotional processes. At a US, Anglo-American, and then global
level, it gave a backbeat to a consumerism of youthfulness and novelty.
For gay performers and listeners, its virtual arena unveiled controversial
identities. And as a pop contrast, it spoke to the women, people of color,
and others who rock left unaddressed. If MOR/AC represented a bourgeois center, Top 40 brandished aspirational modernity. Chart climbing
equated with social mobility.

Top 40–style "pop modernity," as I will call it, registered as Americanization to Europeans, came back to the United States as a British Invasion, and multiplied as globalization. Nik Cohn, a leading Beatles-era
critic, captured its allure with a largely nonmusical definition: "The way
I like it best, pop is teenage property and it mirrors everything that happens to teenagers in this time, in this American twentieth century. It is
about clothes and cars and dancing, it's about parents and highschool [*sic*]
and being rich and breaking loose, it is about getting sex and getting rich
and getting old, it's about America, it's about cities and noise. Get right
down to it, it's all about Coca Cola." Reinhold Wagnleitner, an Austrian
scholar of "Coca-Colonization," recalls, "The United States signified
an amalgam of freedom, fun, modernity, wealth, mobility, and youthful
rebellion."[3]

Within splashy exchanges of transatlantic style, gay performers and
managers affiliated from a knowing distance or deployed openness. Judith
Halberstam and Ira Livingston posit of a country singer turned publicly
lesbian, "Queering makes a postmodern politics out of the modernist
aesthetics of defamiliarization. 'What intrigues me,' k.d. lang asserts, 'is
being alternative and completely conformist at the same time.' " Queering
pop was especially a British tradition. Longtime manager Simon Napier-
Bell explains, "In the British music business gay culture seemed to have
played the same creative role as black culture had in the American music
business." Jon Savage observes an enduring UK "equation": "gay desire = teenage female desire." The staging of British pop relied on these
linkages.[4]

Savage's equation recasts sounds heard as feminine, sentimental, and mediated. Simon Frith argues that after the counterculture, youth pop and rock norms were at odds: "The ideology of rock was explicitly anti-commercial, even if commercialism meant pleasing an audience of youth."[5] If rock challenged the mainstream, pop still sought to enter it. In the United States, as album-oriented rock (AOR) wrestled Top 40 for primacy, this divide became crucial to radio demographics, overtly in gender, age, and racial differentiation, more quietly in terms of sexuality.

In sum, youth- and modernity-oriented Top 40 staged identity explorations across physical (transnational), socially imposed (queer-inflected), and mass media (crossover pop) boundaries. Savage stresses that "pop was about one thing: self-recreation." If so, new identifications produced complex effects. Wagnleitner notes that within "Americanization" European youth embraced US minority culture in service to a consumerism not particularly American at all. Pop modernity took multiple forms: by 1967, as US investments in the United Kingdom reached $6 billion, the Sexual Offences Act decriminalized homosexuality and the BBC created its first pop music channel.[6]

John's arc subsumed these transformations. "We've only got one station. Coming on a station like this is unbelievable," he said during one of his first US radio interviews. Consumerism was his denied birthright: "I didn't start enjoying life until I was twenty-one, so I'm living through my teenage period now." Sexually, *Gay Times* explained, "his life story has neatly mirrored that of all gay men: repressed in the Sixties, a model of Seventies hedonistic excess, a victim of the Right's homophobic backlash in the Eighties, then fighting his way forward to something approaching sainthood today."[7]

At first a rock figure, John prioritized pop success, paying tribute in his first American chart topper, "Crocodile Rock," to early Top 40. British music historian Dave Harker complains that for staunch rockers, "*his* 'rock' isn't *really* 'rock' at all! At this point, the size of the canonical 'rock' repertoire and audience seems to shrink almost to a minority taste." A biographer concedes, "To me he belonged to the light entertainment side of the music business; I did not see him as part of rock culture." To Frith, "Elton John is a pop not a rock star because his authenticity—the authenticity of his expressed emotions—is not an issue." Rock in this view is realism: connection to subcultures and unvarnished experience. Pop offers melodrama to crowds, realms of artifice and theater.[8]

But John pledged glittery allegiance to Top 40 because as a secretly gay

man his rock authenticity was very much in doubt. The format, despite
its crossover orientation and blurriness of demographic address, served
particular performers and listeners. John's redone "Candle in the Wind"
at the funeral of Princess Diana demonstrated the size of this category,
as intense collective mourning for "the people's princess" made the royal
family bend to an openly gay star's cosmology. With airplay on a now international array of CHR stations, it became the biggest-selling single of
all time. Top 40 as a "mass appeal" format periodically resurrected itself
to address divisions created by rock and roll, rock, disco, hip-hop, and
globalized sounds. Each time, the coalition of listeners supporting pop
modernity grew larger.

It has often been remarked that if American pop combined consumer
affluence and generative African American sounds, "what British musicians have added is style, image, self-consciousness." British artists created Pop Art in the 1950s; British society presented Swinging London
in the 1960s; British academics cemented cultural studies in the 1970s. A
nation of art school graduates translated "revolt into style," what by Tony
Blair became the economics of Cool Britannia and television's *Pop Idol*,
American Idol in its US sequel. But we are still, you might say, settling
accounts with subcultures. Reread cultural studies classics such as *Subculture: The Meaning of Style* or *Art into Pop* and imagine John in the godfather role occupied by David Bowie. To do so substitutes a mainstream
with secretly gay elements for performed gayness as a theatrics of disaffection; predominantly female listeners for predominantly male ones;
a working-class consumerism blurring the definition of middle class for
middle-class consumerism blurring the definition of working class. Recent
LGBT theorists dissect unexamined norms within gay identity; extending
the approach reveals Top 40 mediation circulating a version of queerness
often critically neglected.[9]

Elton John's apprenticeship came during the 1960s, when British "beat"
music and American Top 40 merged to obscure race, class, gender, sexuality, and nationhood. His US breakthrough in the early 1970s, as such
divisions reasserted themselves, balanced a rock persona with a Top 40
informed by coded gay statements. His run as a superstar and even teen
idol re-created the British Invasion around a singular icon. John spent the
1980s struggling, reflecting the waning of Anglo-American-style pop modernity. Since the 1990s, a sober, domesticated John has become a global
aristocrat. The *Gay Times* rundown of John concluded, "He's done it all
on pretty much his own terms. He's said 'fuck you' and 'love me' in equal

measure. But is Elton John an example of gay men's liberation or merely our assimilation? I guess the answer is 'a bit of both.' "[10] Within Top 40's pop modernity, liberation and assimilation remain closely linked affairs.

Made in England: Pop Art and Fashioning "Elton John"

In the story Elton John told from his earliest interviews, Reginald Dwight was born in 1947 in a suburb of London to a strict Royal Air Force father of working-class origins and a tender mother who brought home pop discs. A piano prodigy at the Royal Academy of Music, Dwight by 1961 sang American songs by vaudeville's Al Jolson and countrypolitan Jim Reeves at his local pub. Buying an electric piano with the earnings, he joined Bluesology, which backed touring African Americans Patti Labelle and Billy Stewart, then fellow roots revivalist Long John Baldry. As renown came to British pop, Dwight quit school, securing a songwriting post at Beatles publishers Dick James Music. Soon he found lyricist partner Bernie Taupin, three years younger and fascinated by Americana. Invited to record, Dwight remade himself into the star Elton John.[11]

One additional anecdote only gradually entered John's known history. His 1975 album *Captain Fantastic and the Brown Dirt Cowboy* featured "Someone Saved My Life Tonight," explained—including in a cartoon that was part of the vinyl package—as a reference to John's staging a suicide attempt in 1968 out of despair over his engagement to a woman who hated his music. When John became public about his sexuality, that tale expanded. John explained that Baldry, himself gay, had warned John to reverse course: "He knew I was gay and told me I had to get used to it or else it would destroy my life."[12] John's elongated coming-out narrative thus belatedly intertwines with the oedipal drama, cross-racial longings, and notions of self-liberation standard to rock and roll mythology.

John was hardly alone in his experiences, which suggest a way to recast British pop music's alliance with American Top 40. Subcultural London's Mod (short for modernist) scene heralded its affection for soul. It was less known for gay bars such as Le Duce, where Peter Burton remembered, " 'This old heart of mine's been broke a thousand times . . .' sing the Isley Brothers, and a hundred or so voices are raised to echo the sentiment. Eyes lock for a brief moment as all those on the dance floor sing the words and a feeling of togetherness, of belonging—though few would admit that's what it is—surges through the place." At such spaces, polari,

FIGURE 4.2 Cartoon from booklet included with Elton John's 1975 *Captain Fantastic and the Brown Dirt Cowboy* LP. "Someone Saved My Life Tonight," illustrated here, was explained at the time as a song about John's avoiding marriage to a woman who hated rock and roll—and only later as a narrative of Long John Baldry warning Reginald Dwight against a heterosexual partnership. Author's collection.

subcultural slang, deflected eavesdropping. Biographer Philip Norman
claims in the documentary *Elton John: Someone like Me* that Baldry tu-
tored John in these metropolitan folkways, linkages between urban life,
modernity, and gay experience.[13]

We can recognize a similar coding in original British uses of "pop," employed in the art world as an ambiguous celebration of Americanization.
In 1956, the Independent Group exhibition *This Is Tomorrow* featured
Richard Hamilton's collage, "Just what is it that makes today's homes so
different, so appealing?" Hamilton juxtaposed a marquee of Al Jolson in
blackface, modern appliances, and a bodybuilder holding a large lollipop
with the word *Pop* on it. Hamilton defined pop art as "Popular (designed
for a mass audience) / Transient (short-term solution) / Expendable (easily forgotten) / Low cost / Mass produced / Young (aimed at youth) / Witty /
Sexy / Gimmicky / Glamorous / Big Business." Recrossing the Atlantic to
influence Andy Warhol, pop art was the first British Invasion—American
culture returned reinterpreted. In the rock era, pop art's Peter Blake designed the cover of the Beatles' *Sgt. Pepper's Lonely Hearts Club Band*
LP and Warhol the cover of the Rolling Stones' *Sticky Fingers*. The Who's
Pete Townsend insisted, "We stand for pop art clothes, pop art music and
pop art behaviour. . . . We don't change offstage; we live pop art."[14]

Early British teen pop, by contrast, remained local and disrespected—
the seeming antithesis of rock and roll. Impresario Larry Parnes renamed
his protégés with camp mockery: Tommy Steele, Marty Wilde, Billy
Fury, Georgie Fame. "British pop in the fifties was pure farce," Nik Cohn
scoffed. "Rock brought in operators who were younger, faster, tougher,
cleverer. . . . Most of them were homosexual. They'd see some pretty
young boy singing in a pub and fancy him and sign him up. They'd bed
him and then they'd probably very quickly get bored with him." John
Lennon called Cliff Richard, the period's biggest star but a nonfactor in
America, "everything we hated in pop." Colin MacInnes found palpable
a reverse colonization: "We have the paradox that teenagers like, increasingly, songs sung *by Englishmen in American.*" However, he also recognized self-consciousness: "The kids have transformed this influence into
something of their own . . . in a way that suggests, subtly, that they're
almost *amused* by what has influenced them."[15]

After the Beatles, youth music replaced art theory as England's signal
pop contribution. Iain Chambers observes, "Pop stopped being a spectacular but peripheral event, largely understood to be associated with
teenage working-class taste, and became the central symbol of fashion-

able, metropolitan British culture." But arguably, metropolitan channels established the Fab Four to start with. Paul McCartney remembered of manager Brian Epstein, "We got down to London and Brian had his contacts on the gay scene. People would say, 'How are your boys, Brian?' 'Well, they're doing rather well, they just had a hit.' 'Oh, marvelous, do put them on my show!' So obviously that didn't hurt us." Joe Lockwood, who ran the Beatles' label EMI, was gay, as were the managers of the Who, Cream, and other bands. Napier-Bell argues, "It was gay managers, and their friends in fashion and media, who were chiefly responsible for creating the image of British youth culture that was being sold around the world." Early rock historian Charlie Gillett agrees: "A new breed . . . maintained and exaggerated the resulting distinctions between 'pop' and 'rock.'" Parnes's successors packaged rebellion. Napier-Bell says of Andrew Loog Oldham, "He taught the Rolling Stones the importance of hating the record company. In doing so, he invented rock music."[16]

American Top 40, with its commercial populism, and British pop, with its self-conscious metropolitanism, used Beatlemania to form an enduring partnership. Like country and R&B, Top 40 faced advertiser skepticism. "The sponsors were afraid of the new music," recalled Rick Sklar of his late 1950s and early 1960s days at WINS, the station that rock and roll DJ Alan Freed built into a powerhouse. MOR-oriented WNEW received more ad dollars than its audience numbers justified, while WINS sold "pimple cream." Sklar learned "to go after everyone. . . . Each record would have to do triple demographic duty, or I could not afford to play it." Total listenership was measured; demographics were not. Steve Labunski remembered, "You had to dominate the market for it to work. If you had 60 percent of listeners, you had a lot of adults in there. But if you had 15 percent of the audience, those were just kids and you were in trouble."[17]

Beatlemania charmed adults into supporting a youthful format. If much previous Top 40 involved black or working-class white artists, the image-polished British bands carried no clear connotations. As Jonathan Gould points out, Epstein booked the Beatles into Carnegie Hall early to put them on par with Mary Quant fashions and bespoke tailoring, satirists like Peter Sellers, and sophisticates like James Bond. Sklar's new station, WABC, became "WA Beatle C," with Beatles records "programmed as soon as they came out—before they started to sell." Where one British record had entered the American top 10 in 1963, thirty-two did in 1964, and an additional thirty-six in 1965. Through the mid-1980s, British groups averaged 20 percent of the US singles chart and a third of the albums chart. Top 40 America was intoxicating, Lennon recalled: "We were so overawed by American radio that Epstein our manager had to stop us, we phoned every radio in town, just saying would you play the Ronettes? We didn't ask for our own records. We asked for other people's."[18]

Britain turned into a nation of chart watchers. George Melly wrote, "States Worship has been largely replaced by a cool if deep chauvinism." Chambers claims, "The Hit Parade, not aesthetic canons, firmly dominated the common understanding of pop music." *Top of the Pops*, launched in 1964, was seen by 17 million weekly, almost a third of the country. With the BBC limiting hits radio to Saturday mornings, pirate stations were essentially Top 40: Radio London was initially named Radio KLIF London after broadcasting pioneer Gordon McLendon's most successful US station. Structurally, Britain was well designed for breeding hits: about a fourth of the US population in a space the size of Tennessee. There was one industry center, London, an avid weekly music press, and charts based entirely on sales estimates, susceptible to "hyping"—buying placement. From 1967, BBC Radio 1 supplied a national station unlike any in the United States. British music also lacked strong country or R&B equivalents to complicate popular music's identity.[19]

Notions of a boundary-spanning utopia were rife on both sides of the Atlantic. "The pop music scene has become an arena in which the old lodestar divisions of class, age, sex, status and geography have been challenged and uprooted," Richard Mabey claimed. He linked teen girl fans, the art school "tradition of bohemian classlessness," and pop art's "insistent and continuous need for change—what one writer has labeled 'the tradition of the new.'" Richard Hoggart declared in *Time*, "A new group of people is emerging into society, creating a kind of classlessness and a verve which has not been seen before." The biggest sixties innovation in Top 40, "Boss Radio," launched by Los Angeles station KHJ, took its name from British slang and tightened its playlist to thirty tracks, restricting DJ talk—hits provided sense of freedom enough.[20]

The soon-to-be Elton John was an acolyte of Mabey's "tradition of the new." He fondly recalled early UK pop: "When I was a kid and went to see those Larry Parnes–Billy Fury packages, I was on my feet having a good time." Piano pounder Little Richard, as close to an open drag queen as rock and roll had produced, and the elaborately garbed MOR pianist Liberace provided a genealogy. John said, "When I first saw Little Richard, standing on top of the piano, all lights, sequin, and energy, I decided there and then that I was going to be a Rock'n'roll piano player." As for Liberace, "He was what every straight person wants to think gay people are—so camp, not at all threatening." John's record collection, fastidiously indexed, meant enough that even after his career took off he clerked at Music Land Record Store for access to US imports. With Bluesology, he entered a scene small enough for a minor figure to experience it whole. The group opened for Little Richard before an audience that included Mick Jagger and Dave Clark; a Bluesology member dated Cindy Birdsong, of Patti Labelle's Blue Belles and the Supremes. John worked as a session pianist and studio vocalist imitating chart toppers for knockoffs. At one such session, he later recalled, "in wanders [Paul] McCartney—he was in Studio 2 and thought he'd pop in and see what the peasants were up to."[21]

It is often argued that British "beat" groups reminded Americans of the value of rock and roll, in particular black artists. "Britain served the useful function of re-establishing popular music as a medium for personal expression rather than as the raw material for mass-produced entertainment, which it once again had become," Gillett concludes. Yet the British Invasion equally rethought mass entertainment, conjoining American Top 40, which required crossover demographics to flourish, and a UK pop process built on transforming US consumer culture. The full story was not simply Beatles and Stones, but figures like the man John partly named himself for: Baldry, who moved between R&B and gay subcultures and a number 1 song on *Top of the Pops*.

Different national encounters had produced kindred results—for a time. Lawrence Alloway revisited pop art in 1969 and warned, "We looked at the United States as our expected future form. . . . This outlook had a mood of optimism that is not in accord with present feelings, but the point remains that Pop Art is the art of industrialism and not of America as such." Even as John and Taupin began writing together, the unity of Anglo-American pop modernity was starting to unravel.[22]

Burn Down the Mission: Elton John Conquers America

"Stardom is a word that has been associated with Elton John ever since he made his American debut shortly before 10 p.m. on Tuesday, August 25, 1970, at Doug Weston's Troubadour," began a 1976 MCA Records bio. John's performance was instant legend. "Rejoice. Rock music which has been going through a rather uneventful period recently, has a new star," the first notice shouted. As John told it, "Robert Hilburn from the *Los Angeles Times* gave me the rave review of all time, and it spread across America, and I became like an overnight sensation." John's performance at the 250-person West Hollywood club marked his and Taupin's first trip to the country their music fantasized about. At the Troubadour, John later recalled, "I had just released the album *Elton John*, which was quite dark, and very orchestral, and the album cover was also very dark, with just my face with a pair of glasses—and I came onstage with a three-piece band and I'm sitting there in hot pants, winged boots, and a Mr. Freedom T-shirt, and I'm leaping on the piano, standing on it, doing handstands on it, and people went, 'Fuck! What's that?' For the first time in my life I felt released."[23]

As with "Someone Saved My Life Tonight," parts of the story only emerged later. During his Troubadour run, John had sex with a man for the first time. John Reid, a UK branch manager for Motown, became his manager and live-in companion. John would tell Neil Tennant, "At school I used to have crushes on people, but not really any sex at all, male or female, until about twenty-three. And then it was like a volcano. Out it came; it was such a relief." In life terms, Elton John's musical and sexual liberation coincided. His public persona required a considerable temporal gap, as in the disparity between the *New Yorker*, in 1996, noting "John Reid, who lived with Elton John for five years, and was the first man Elton slept with" and even his 1976 *Rolling Stone* coming out, where John still claimed, "The press probably thought John Reid and I were an affair, but there's never been a serious person the whole time."[24] As an extension of this blocked self-presentation, John's musical impulses became divided as well. Counterculture rock competed for youth in 1970 with Top 40. Rock fans romanticize its rhetoric of anti-commercial revolt but ignore how the genre's style drew boundaries. American rock fans made John a star. But he ultimately found this "progressive" category too restrictive. He turned first to an English rock subgenre, glam, which rejected countercultural authenticity. Ultimately, even a cohort of androgynous rockers claiming pop as a theater of the absurd proved confining.

The rise of rock to prominence created what Michael Kramer categorizes as a bourgeois public sphere within commercial culture, in the sense that rock fans participated in the discourse of publications such as *Rolling Stone* and *Creem*; were steered by, and steered, FM underground radio; and regularly gathered at psychedelic ballrooms, indoor arenas, and outdoor festivals. Rock, however commercial, was civic, mediating politics and business. Helping constitute this new sphere was disdain for the Top 40 mass. In *Rolling Stone*, programmer Tom Donahue called Top 40 "A Rotten Corpse, Stinking Up the Airwaves." In the United Kingdom, resistant to commercial radio from the onset, Stephen Barnard finds that BBC programming "implicitly legitimized the notion that progressive rock was culturally *superior* to Top Forty pop." The BBC did not answer to sponsors. For American radio, a cleavage of mass and class was risky. Stations that courted elites, Pittsburgh program director (PD) Donald Shafer warned, "left the listeners." Still, Ken Barnes observes, early rock stations sounded "as countercultural, hip, mellow, and un–Top 40 as possible."[25]

The audience at John's first American concert expected a progressive. He could play up-tempo boogie-rock ("Take Me to the Pilot"), or draw on his R&B training ("Border Song," quickly covered by Aretha Franklin), but most early recordings were chamber pieces with high-flown lyrics by Taupin and symphonic orchestration. John even auditioned for lead singer of two British art rock groups: Gentle Giant and King Crimson. His first BBC TV special, "In Concert: The Songs of Elton John and Bernie Taupin," positioned the duo as writers in the George and Ira Gershwin mode. John presented himself as experimental on evening Radio 1 programs like *Sounds of the Seventies,* aimed at fans who deplored chart material. In contrast, he mocked the leading TV hits show: "*Top of the Pops* doesn't really give anybody an idea of what you can do—in fact it gives them a totally wrong impression."[26]

If the Beatles and American Top 40 had once legitimized each other, something similar now happened with British arena rockers such as Led Zeppelin and Pink Floyd and a burgeoning US rock radio format. As labels like A&M learned, methods existed by 1970 to convert underground appeal into album sales. John's "overnight" triumph was highly staged. Russ Regan, who headed Uni Records, John's American label, hired eight independent promotions people to court FM radio with advance album copies. "There seemed to be some snob appeal for radio people to have those pressings," his promotions head, David Rosner, attested, and Hilburn noted that "his new Uni album has been aired extensively on local FM radio." Uni also coaxed industry figures to the performance: John said, "About 60% of the people in Los Angeles were from the music business." Rock promoter Bill Graham bragged, "Some of his immediate booking success around the country can in part be attributed to some maniac in New York paying $5000 sight-unseen for an opening act." The album charted on underground clamor alone. A bootlegged, then officially released set by John on WABC-FM, sister channel of the powerful

AM Top 40, showed a new way to make listening feel exclusive. Where Top 40 played hits, AOR radio would delve repertoire. "That more or less started the concert scene on FM radio in America," John said.[27]

A sense of John's time in the "underground" can be derived from an interview he gave then freeform WNEW-FM. DJ Pete Fornatale came off as erudite where a Top 40 DJ would have been exuberant, while John was sarcastic about his success: "We came to New York for ex-po-sure," he said. "We're just starting on our massive campaign to capture the hearts of American youths." He called his early work with Taupin "rubbish, just bubblegum stuff"—meaning Top 40 teen material. "Groups in England have a really hard time getting played. It's all bubble gum, really there's only about three to four [radio] programs a week that cater for the minority, actually it's a great majority now, that buy albums instead of singles." Defining his wide taste, John declared, "The only thing I haven't got in my collection is middle of the road stuff: Engelbert Humperdinck, jazz."[28]

In a soundscape of multiple formats, affiliation could be critical. John's first hit had ample MOR support. "Your Song," a love-those-eyes confession made winning by John's blend of crooner and singer-songwriter, became a 45 single B side after DJ Tony Blackburn of BBC Radio 1 mornings—the most MOR-oriented section of the channel's dayparted broadcast—promised to make it his song of the week. In America, John sang it on Andy Williams's TV program, which led to its crossing over to number 8 Top 40. Yet John fought attempts to market him as MOR, complaining, "'Your Song' was such a fucking misrepresentation of me, although it's become almost a trademark. From the first time we went on the road, we were rockers at heart and on stage."[29]

He was equally pointed about his transnational identification. "I feel more American than British. Really," he told *Rolling Stone*. His rapid US success had inverted the pattern of the smaller British market as proving ground: headlines like *Melody Maker*'s "Elton Storms the States" increased his UK sales. With *Tumbleweed Connection* imagining an outlaw West, John and Taupin's identification with the United States seemed complete. British writer Penny Valentine noted, "Elton and Bernie come and pay their respects from afar; they are British and rock & roll straight from the American womb." John's spring 1971 tour took him to large venues in Columbus, Omaha, Oklahoma City, Houston, Jacksonville, and St. Louis, among others, proving the reach of the underground. When *Madman across the Water*, an American hit, topped out in the United Kingdom at 41, John concluded he had wounded British pride: "The press

was resentful that I spent more time in America than I did in England."
The progressive rock album featured singles over five minutes long, which
US FM stations played but Radio 1 ignored.[30]

Still, John's newfound American following, suspicious of pop inauthenticity, constrained the showmanship that had established him—and,
I'd argue, the private behavior that accompanied his Troubadour eruption. John protested, "The most unfortunate, narrow-minded thing was
that people said, 'He plays good music. Why does he have to do this?'
And they wanted me to stay as little Elton John and dress somberly like a
Randy Newman. I wasn't like that. I was out to have a good time, bay*bee*!"
He also said, "They won't share me with a mass public—the snobbery in
rock is amazing." "All the Nasties," Taupin noted, from *Madman across
the Water*, "was a song for Elton when the press was really crucifying us."
If this was one meaning of "the way they publicize" and "the image in
their eyes," Taupin acknowledged after John finally addressed his sexuality the subtext to "If it came to pass that they should ask / What could I tell
them?" By contrast, "Tiny Dancer," sung to a "blue jean baby, LA lady,
seamstress for the band," was instantly declared Taupin's love letter to his
US girlfriend—met the week that John met Reid.[31]

Back in London, John began aligning with glam rock, a British trend of
limited American popularity that rejected progressive organics for deviant artifice. He made appearances with Marc Bolan of T. Rex, including
a *Top of the Pops* performance—reservations about the program now set
aside. Then he recorded his own version of a glam album—*Honky Chateau*. "Honky Cat" and "Rocket Man" produced a breakthrough: John
and Taupin combined rock and roll exuberance, searching power ballads,
and a plasticity of subject matter and upper-register vocalizing that felt
modern, youthful, but never exclusive. John's rhetoric also flipped: "I've
never regarded pop music as an art form—I think it is just entertainment
and I think that is why pop groups are coming back, because people are
fed-up with moodies and they'd rather go out and have a good time."[32]

Philip Auslander argues that glam's "central social innovation was to
open safe space in which to experiment with versions of masculinity that
clearly flouted social norms." It was, he suggests, "the first fully developed
post-countercultural genre of rock music." This included a preoccupation
with hit singles, theatricality, and visuals—the constructed spectacle hippies distrusted. For Auslander, that "glam destabilized conventional oppositions between rock and pop, art and commerce" connects directly to
how it also "offered a new, implicitly queer, image of masculinity in rock"

by "positing gendered identities as constructed rather than actual." John is marginal to Auslander's narrative: "Even popular music artists not specifically identified as glam rockers, such as Rod Stewart and Elton John, took on some of the visual aspects of glam, whether in costume, makeup, hairstyle, or onstage flamboyance." Yet for Americans, Bolan was commercially insignificant, and David Bowie, the other major glam figure, had not yet systematically toured US markets. Bowie's "Starman," a major British hit, only reached number 65 on the American charts, while John and Taupin's imitation, "Rocket Man," rose to number 6 and *Honky Chateau* became John's first number 1 album.[33]

Where John's relationship with Reid remained secret, Bowie told *Melody Maker* in 1972, "I'm gay . . . and always have been." Yet the article's author spotted "a slight jollity about how he says it, a secret smile at the corners of his mouth. . . . The expression of sexual ambivalence establishes a fascinating game: is he, or isn't he?" Bowie was married at the time and would generally have heterosexual relationships. His positioning was recognized as a pose: what Andy Gill calls "the Queer David myth." Robert Duncan wrote, "Being homosexual, or at least seeming homosexual, was the new way to be black in rock 'n' roll. To seem homosexual was the new way to be different, cool, special, a romantic outlaw (and in this case, truly a *romantic* outlaw)." Duncan added, tellingly, "Not that it was all right actually to *be* homosexual." Thomas Geyrhalter has bemoaned the "constant disappointment to be experienced from a gay perspective as these so-called radicals 'come out' as normal heterosexuals, revealing that their act, that promised more, was just an act, therefore commodifying the flirt with the sexually diverse."[34]

Auslander opposes any argument that "recuperates glam rock for the very discourses of essentiality and authenticity it sought to resist." But glam hardly resisted essentializing the authentic rocker as a romantic outlaw. The switch from appropriating non-"normal" (to use Geyrhalter's language) blackness to gayness changed nothing about a process that only opened space for those pushing out. John used glam to develop a pop style that domesticated the transgressive more than flaunted it. Taupin marveled at the refusal of subversive self-presentation: "Nobody but Elton could have sung that line from 'Rocket Man' about being as high as a kite without getting banned from the radio. It was a drugs song." It was also a song of suppressed identity, with the chorus "I'm not the man they think I am" open to many readings.[35]

To parade Queer David over codedly Gay Elton ignored the question of what expressed rebelliousness in rock's underground. Gary Osborne, a friend and later writing partner of John's, has recalled, with humor and understatement, "I think Elton slightly resented the fact that Bowie, who is substantially straight, made it partially by pretending to be gay, by courting a gay following, by propagating a gay mystique, whereas Elton, who is substantially gay, had for so long to conceal his real orientation from the public. From Elton's point of view, here was this guy who had made it as a pretend poof, and here he was, a real poof, having to be a pretend straight." John's insecurities were well founded. The UK 1967 Sexual Offences Act decriminalized homosexuality but increased penalties for public displays. The 1969 Stonewall Inn uprising in New York, followed by gay liberation marches a year later, represented "Americanization" to English homosexuals like the rest of pop modernity. Only in 1976, the year John acknowledged having had sex with men, did the first gay nightclub advertised as such, Bang, open. The disco was modeled on Los Angeles's Studio One. John was among Bang's first patrons.[36]

Glam helped John, searching to unify progressive and pop tendencies, make singles like his flashiest concerts and reconnect with audiences at home. Still, it demonstrated the limits of even an ideologically gay-friendly rock subculture. To capture all of what John had suggested about liberation with his performance at the Troubadour, leaping like Little Richard, dressed in a pop art Mr. Freedom shirt that flashed the phrase "Rock & Roll," he would have to resurrect the inclusive public the Beatles and their favorite format had once conjured. He would have to become a Top 40 star.

Crocodile Rock: Elton John, Superstar

"*Superstar* was a word he had learned from Marie," we are told of a character in Stephen King's 1979 novel *The Dead Zone*. "She had used it in connection with a balding, bespectacled singer with the unlikely name of Elton John." Something of what John pulled off in his heyday lives in footage of the performer rocking "The Bitch Is Back" with tennis star, feminist, but not yet out lesbian Billie Jean King to a packed Dodger Stadium in October 1975. John's performance that evening redirected rock and roll's liberatory energy to align with gay, feminist, and black freedom movements rather than hippie or glam tropes. Another song performed, "Philadelphia Freedom," written by Taupin at John's suggestion, used the name of King's World Team Tennis club to combine America's bicentennial and gay liberation in the City of Brotherly Love. John's music made

Elton swings: superstar combines flash with artistry during his Dodger Stadium concert.

Billboard photo by Terry O'Neill

FIGURE 4.3 Photograph by Terry O'Neill of Elton John in concert at Dodger Stadium, 1975, from *Billboard*, November 8, 1975, with original caption. John, at the height of his 1970s popularity, "combines flash with artistry," the trade explains, reflecting questions in a rock era about the singer's use of a kind of glitziness soon to be associated with disco. Author's collection.

a different pun, emulating Philly Soul's translation of black power into aspirational Top 40 dance anthems. The mostly white counterculture audience, bearded men and lightly dressed women, twirled casually on the stadium grass. John, in sequin-encrusted Bob Mackie team uniform, seemed ready for a night disco clubbing.[37]

A second glimpse of John in this period, however, suggests why it remains problematic to view him as wholly subversive. Rick Sklar, who ran Top 40 behemoth WABC-AM, recalls that the star "always operated with a fanatic determination to wring the last possible dollar out of each album. Elton worked every angle. You could tell when sales began to slump on a new Elton John album, because king-sized ads began to appear on the sides and back of New York buses." By 1976, John's promotions team was debating two possible singles. As a test, some stations were fed "Grow Some Funk of Your Own," others "I Feel Like a Bullet (in the Gun of Robert Ford)." Sklar added neither to WABC's playlist and was soon sent a large carton with an expensive cake, lettered, "GIVE ELTON A SHOT! FEEL LIKE A BULLET IS A HIT!" He remained unmoved. When John's team settled on "Grow Some Funk," a larger package arrived. "DISREGARD PREVIOUS CAKE."[38]

John's Top 40 ambitions, unlike his sexuality, were public record: "Tuesday morning when the trades come out, first thing I do is look at the Radio Active list, then Kal Rudman in Record World and the Billboard album chart," he told an interviewer. His first US number 1, "Crocodile Rock," quoted myriad early pop hitmakers. John signed one such, Neil Sedaka, to his label Rocket, made promo calls on his behalf, and even invited the programming head of RKO Radio for Christmas dinner. "Elton is an artist/businessman much more than the Beatles were," Rocket's Tony King said. "It's a vast amount of information to assimilate, but he knows every facet of American radio." John in his late twenties became the most popular artist to readers of *16 Magazine*. His "Bennie and the Jets" used R&B support to cross into Top 40. And his record company, MCA, advertised re-signing him in the *Wall Street Journal, New York Times*, and *Los Angeles Times*. "We wanted to show in these ads how far the business has come," said label president Mike Maitland. A resurgent Top 40, with John central, transgressed *within* capitalism, creating a superstardom privileged to ignore conventions.[39]

"In 1970, Top 40 was dead. It was officially pronounced dead by the trade and the broadcasting industry," Tom Rounds remembered years later. Yet in the face of FM rock, Top 40 made a comeback in the early 1970s, maintaining female listeners while exchanging middle-class young men for older, working-class, and minority groups. The syndicated program that Rounds helped launch in 1970, *American Top 40*, with Lebanese American DJ Casey Kasem, syndicated to five hundred stations and the Armed Forces Network by decade's end, rendering the Top 40 a realm of long-distance dedications and musical trivia removed from rock and soul countercultures. Scott Shannon and WMAK beat out country in Nashville, while Rick Dees and WHBQ won when they "recognized the ethnic population" in Memphis; both DJ-programmers would leave the South, Shannon to anchor Z100 in New York, Dees for Los Angeles titan KIIS-FM. By 1973, Top 40 stations were number 1 in six of the top fifteen markets, and number 2 in seven others. *Broadcasting* maintained, "Any attrition in contemporary radio's 18-to-24 count has been more than overcome by the added numbers it has found in the demographics above 30 years old." Another study found an economic shift: "listeners of this format appear to be mainly working class young adults." Bill Tanner, a program director in Miami, put that more bluntly: "Top 40 has a substantial number of 18–24 males. I believe a whole lot of 'em work at McDonald's or they're under grease-racks in garages."[40]

For Elton John—who loved playing "EJ the DJ" on radio and had a dozen songs reach the top 5 between 1973 and 1976—format support from this revived Top 40 could be taken for granted. Greg Shaw marveled:

> His songs are on every radio station, every hour of every day; the old ones as well as the new. If the singles charts were based solely on airplay, the Beatles' long-standing record of eight songs in the Hot 100 during one week would be quickly forgotten; it's been over a year since Elton had less than that many on the air. I've been spinning my dial for the last six hours, and there hasn't been two minutes when EJ wasn't on some station, with everything from "Your Song" and "Daniel" to "Saturday Night" and his three current hits: "Philadelphia Freedom," "Pinball Wizard" and "Someone Saved My Life Tonight." These, plus three or four others, seem to be on constant rotation. A leading LA Top 40 now calls itself "Your Number One Elton John Station," while another "Plays More Elton John Than Anybody," and in New York a major station claims to be "Your Official Elton John Spot On the Dial." Not since Murray the K was the Fifth Beatle has there been anything like it.

To UK observers, the superstar's US reception defied belief. John told an English music paper, "In America I get sick and tired of hearing myself on AM radio. It's embarrassing." Dave Croker, general manager (GM) of Rocket, said, "To explain to anyone in England how big Elton is in America is absolutely impossible. My mother and father went across and it wasn't until that point that they realized the size of EJ over there." John had come close to re-creating the Beatles' Top 40 coalition. Claiming that mantle, he reached number 1 covering "Lucy in the Sky with Diamonds" with John Lennon on guitar, sang on Lennon's "Whatever Gets You thru the Night," and brought the ex-Beatle on stage at Madison Square Garden in what proved his final public performance. "He is the big one now," Lennon said of John on WNEW-FM, while spinning old Top 40 tunes he worried might irritate hard rock "glitter kids."[41]

As Lennon understood, what John faced and the Beatles had not was the antipathy FM rockers aimed at Top 40—the commerciality, however self-conscious and campy, of a "Crocodile Rock" was beneath them. "John Lennon was trying to elbow his way through the crowd to get to Elton John's table, and that did not accord with our idea of reality," the *New*

Yorker reported, calling his music "disposable." Shaw, endorsing John's "demonstration that rock can be serious and fun at the same time," still suggested that the singer "reflects today's mood of caution, wariness to become involved in issues that are too confusing to be attractive, and eagerness to embrace the right kind of frivolous gaiety." Jon Landau, whose advocacy launched Bruce Springsteen, wrote, "Is Elton John something more than a great entertainer? I'm not sure."[42]

The singer threatened because to appeal across demographic lines he resisted strong signifiers of genre and counterculture. Regardless of music and audience, most stations now employed Top 40 methods, as *Broadcasting* affirmed: "Top 40 is the matrix of contemporary radio. . . . Even progressive-rock radio has found it necessary to take several more steps toward top 40 rather than away from it in the past year." John's position, writing format-friendly pop with an adaptable lyricist, sought ample distance from genre categories. If "Crocodile Rock" mocked progressive rock seriousness, for "Daniel" he deleted the explanatory final verse from a Taupin lyric about a wounded Vietnam veteran, retaining only the feel of countercultural protest. "If you don't tell people what they [songs] are about, sometimes they're more mystical," he argued.[43]

John did not only subtract: with the bravado that elevated his chameleonic musical gifts, he reached outside rock and roll. *Don't Shoot Me I'm Only the Piano Player* referenced Hollywood in its marquee-sign cover. *Goodbye Yellow Brick Road*, the biggest album of John's career, nodded to *Wizard of Oz*'s gay "friends of Dorothy" and what Savage calls its consumerist "dream economy." "Candle in the Wind," sung with the cinematic sweep of a new song form John would deploy time and again, the rock- and gospel-informed power ballad, was a melancholy celebration of camp icon Marilyn Monroe. One biography at the time called John a "million-dollar mix of rock and vaudeville." The performer drew too on pop art. John owned a Bryan Organ portrait of himself wearing an Andy Warhol T-shirt, taking from the man who called his studios the Factory a determination to de-romanticize creativity. He made a show of how quickly he set Taupin lyrics to music: less than an hour or put aside forever. In a 1974 documentary he declared, "To me songs are like postage stamps. You lick them, put them on a letter, and never see them again." He sang "Pinball Wizard" in the Who's film version of *Tommy*, directed by Ken Russell, who earlier made *Pop Goes the Easel* about pop art.[44]

John's obsession with shopping was core to his Top 40 persona, the flaunted wealth a path between rock rebellion and MOR containment. The bravura glasses he purchased from Los Angeles's Optique Boutique

FIGURE 4.4 Magazine photo of Elton John as the Pinball Wizard in Ken Russell's film of the Who album *Tommy*, 1975. Pop Art, the 1950s British recasting of American modernity that returned to the United States through Andy Warhol and others, remained central to John's 1970s performances, helping him maintain dual Anglo-American allegiances, connect rock and Top 40, and take camp messaging to spectacular extremes. Author's collection.

became a trademark: one set included windshield wipers and a battery pack. Interviewed by *Playboy*, he joked about surgery few rockers would have owned to: "I might have a hair transplant. It's just a matter of going down there with the courage to say, *'I want some more hair, please.'*" A friend described him shopping at the diamond merchant Cartier "as if he was going around Safeway with a trolley." Before his Dodger Stadium appearance, John told a British interviewer, "When you grow up as a child over here, everybody has a car when they're 16. I never had a pair of roller skates until I was 23."[45]

This notion of Top 40 consumption as an entryway to freedom appealed to many Americans less assertive than those in the counterculture. Barbara Kingsolver's novel *Pigs in Heaven* captures the rebellion perceivable inside even "Crocodile Rock":

> This one Taylor remembers from dances on the bleached wood floor of the Pittman High gym, with some boy or other who never could live up to her sense of celebration on those occasions. They were always too busy trying to jam a hand between two of your buttons somewhere. The song is about that exact war, and it excited the girls as much as the boys to hear it because you knew how Suzy felt when she wore her dresses—as the song says—tight. Like something no boy could ever touch. Taylor liked Elton John, his oversized glasses and preposterous shoes, laughing at himself—such a far cry from other rock stars with long limp hair and closed eyes and heads rolled back to the sounds of their own acid chords, going for the crucifixion look.

If the barbed Elton featured on WNEW radio in 1970 fit a swelling underground, the performer displayed in *16 Magazine* in 1975 for female readers like Taylor was an indulged teenager. Guarding fans, the magazine titled one feature "Elton/The Girl He Chooses—She Could Be you!" and reported, "the only woman Elton has publicly professed love for is Billie Jean King, the tennis pro. That mini-romance is in the past, though." A glossy published by *16* had him declare, "My life is just an extension of all the things I wanted in my teenage years—bright clothes and shiny things!" Photos of his "Treasure House" showed a four-poster bed modeled on Empress Josephine's, a day-glo pink bathroom, and a rec room with pinball machines and gold records.[46]

John's insecurities about his crossover identity made him one of the few to refuse a *16* interview, though the editors report, "Elton became the #1 most requested star by our readers." To be a teen idol still carried

FIGURE 4.5 Elton John photographed at home, as shown in a 1970s Japanese fan magazine. In the increasingly global 1970s version of Top 40 pop modernity, John's excesses of consumerism went undisguised even as his sexuality remained coded. Author's collection.

overtones of predatory managers and naive prey. Tam Paton, manager of the Scottish teenyboppers Bay City Rollers, was convicted later of child molestation. Les McKeown, the lead singer, admitted, "Maybe what people said was 'easy meat.'" As with English glam, the US rock magazine *Creem* admired sexual border crossing from figures presumed straight: punk pioneer Lou Reed burnished his credentials dating a transsexual. John featured in a *Creem* satire of *16* calling him "a biz whiz who sets pubescent labia majoras fluttering" and attributing the offensive quote "They call me the nicest guy in the music business and hell, I don't even eat dick."[47]

Similarly, rockers such as Mick Jagger assumed a blackness that Reed lampooned in his "I Wanna Be Black": "I wanna be black, have natural rhythm, shoot twenty foot of jism too, have a stable of foxy whores; I don't wanna be a fucked up middle class college student anymore." John's Top 40 centrism treated African Americans as constituents. Producer Gus Dudgeon, who said, "English audiences always clap on the on beat, they're always on when they're supposed to be off, which drives me crazy," used such claps to tag "Bennie and the Jets." John, stuttering words and hitting boogie-woogie piano licks, made a lyrical wink at Bowie's Ziggy Stardust but created inverted exotica: ridiculously white funkiness. DJ

Donnie Simpson of WJLB in Detroit approached PD Jay Butler about airing it. Butler told *Record World*, "There are often repercussions from the black community about one less space for a black artist on the play-list." But "within three days, it was our No. 1 request item." John, delighted to have R&B success, deferred promoting "Candle in the Wind"—it's on his first UK greatest hits compilation but not the US version because in *Goodbye Yellow Brick Road*'s promo cycle "Bennie" replaced it. He became one of the first whites to appear on *Soul Train*, Don Cornelius hailing him as an MOR hippie: "a very, very gifted young man who has combined absolute genius as a musician with a sort of psychedelic outlook on life, which causes everybody that comes near him to be thoroughly entertained."[48]

The Elton persona inspired many such fumbling formulations. Stephen Holden astutely concluded, "Like every other 1970's pop star, Mr. John has had to contend with the post-countercultural notion that popular art could or should be thought of as more than a disposable commodity— that it requires an intellectual as well as a commercial *raison d'être*. Mr. John has reacted to that idea ambivalently. If the rock idols of the '60s allowed themselves to be deified, he helped to demystify rock by presenting himself as a fan whose campy stagecraft and Warholian de-tachment mocked its seriousness." John, Holden argued, "helped lay to rest the countercultural assumption that rock music, in order to be good, had to be free of the taint of urban bourgeois pop influence." Even this nuanced description says more about what John detached himself from than what he stood for. His own self-descriptions were contradictory. "It's glamour, but I refuse to say it's showbizzy." "I do it tongue in cheek with an 'up yours' attitude."[49]

A closeted gay man representing pop modernity proved hugely attrac-tive to format programmers seeking a demographic mix and to aspira-tional audiences living in the most egalitarian years of the century. To *People*, he was "Elton John, 28, multi-multi-millionaire and the rock world's most engaging *enfant gauche*." A children's book published at the height of his fame began with his show at the Hollywood Bowl, introduced by a "hostess" who said, "Here he is, the *biggest, largest*, most *gigantic* and *fantastic* man . . . Elton John!" That the hostess was Linda Lovelace, star of *Deep Throat*, was not mentioned, nor that John was carried around during encores by former Mr. America and gay Hollywood notable Jim Morris, dressed in a loincloth.[50] John had a song for such moments, "The Bitch Is Back": Top 40 flinched but played it anyway. "I can bitch 'cause I'm better than you," he sang. "It's the way that I move, the things that I do."

Still Standing: Coming Out and Staying Afloat

"Divine took me to Crisco Disco," John said in 1976 to a *Rolling Stone* reporter, who explained, "Divine is the name of a well-fed drag queen who acts in underground films and Crisco Disco is a Manhattan gay bar, so named for the frying oil, which is also a popular sexual lubricant." John's manner of coming out removed the ambiguity his crossover persona had rested upon and was received far differently than Bowie's self-outing. Phil Sutcliffe wrote in *Sounds*, "Bowie saying it is one thing. It appeared much less safe for the boy-next-door Elton." "The effect is shattering," Lisa Crane of Provo, Utah, told *Rolling Stone*. As the editors of *16* described, "There was an incredible amount of mail . . . which went something like this: 'My older brother says he read that Elton John is a bisexual. He is making fun of me for loving someone he says is a fag.'" Ultimately, "Elton's fickle teenage fans dropped him like the hot potato he had made of himself." FM rock also turned, anticipating the assault on disco three years later. "America's supposed to be the great liberated free-minded society," John complained.[51]

But time again revised the story. In a 1991 David Frost interview, the singer placed a new interpretation on the previous fifteen years. Drinking had turned into drug use and bulimia, John confessed. His beloved mother, accepting of male partners but not drug binges, moved to Spain, saying, "I don't have a son anymore." Substance abuse, he insisted, proved his demon: "I've never had any problems with my sexuality. That's been one of the few things I've been able to accept in my life." Yet the two were bound together, since during this period he married a woman, recording engineer Renate Blauel; they soon separated and divorced. Asked if he had gotten married "to prove that you were not gay," John answered heatedly, "No. I got married because I didn't confront the real problem in my life, that I was a drug addict." The stories were surprising from a performer "far removed from a rock type" vis-à-vis drugs in his heyday.[52]

In seeing his troubles as behavioral, essentially as overconsumption, John universalized them—befitting his crossover gifts. Just as gay subculture deserves a central place in accounts of transatlantic pop modernity, the backlash against homosexuals in the disco and AIDS era must be set against broader splinterings in Anglo-America's "tradition of the new," dwarfing earlier rock/Top 40 frictions. Both the United Kingdom and United States experienced a conservative insurgence that Stuart Hall called "The Great Moving Right Show": the inability of liberal social democracies to maintain public legitimacy, creating a crisis of representation.[53] American Top 40's rhetoric of classlessness and democratizing consumerism came under question, as the format twice, at the beginning of the 1980s and then 1990s, saw its commercial viability questioned.

As the 1970s ended, that challenge took two seemingly opposite paths, disco and punk. Punk, hyped most heavily in Britain, relied for all its radicalism on image-savvy managers: Malcolm McLaren changed Sex Pistols singer John Lydon's name, Larry Parnes style, to Johnny Rotten. And if rock managers encouraged charges to scorn the music industry, punk managers like McLaren and the Clash's Bernard Rhodes scorned America itself, urging songs like "I'm So Bored with the USA." Disco, with its prominent black and Latin rhythms and stress on DJs rather than bands, undercut not only rock but Top 40 norms existing since the British Invasion. An all-disco station, WKTU, dislodged WABC-AM from ratings primacy. Marc Fisher rhapsodizes, with baby boomer nostalgia, "It was time to say goodbye to everyone's song, to the idea that a vast nation could build its shared memory from one set of voices in the night." Where British punk rejected America, American disco largely rejected Britain. The results were disastrous for record and radio industries alike. Album sales plunged between 1979 and 1983. Falling ad revenues prompted a move within Top 40, defensively renamed CHR (contemporary hit radio), toward safer adult pop sounds by white performers, with resistance to black records declared at "an all-time high" in early 1982. Disco died, but rock suffered as well: Polydor executive Jerry Jaffe explained, "Most Top 40 stations started hammering crossover disco. When that died down as an audience grabber, they went for an older demographic that shunned high decibel rock music."[54]

As Top 40 and rock foundered, John's personal behavior problematized ideals of pop modernity as progressive. He initially viewed drugging as akin to discovering his sexual preferences late and acting the adult teen. Cocaine, he told Frost, made him feel "I'm finally accepted. I'm one of the in-crowd." A comrade in partying was Queen's Freddie Mercury, secretive about both his sexuality and his upbringing in India as Farrokh Bulsara. Mercury maintained a garden where men, at John's suggestion (channeling Baldry), used female pet names and drugs were spread in a buffet. If pop offered re-created identity, this elitist variant came when tens of thousands of Londoners lived in squats. John, as Edmund White portrayed him later, resembled predatory British music managers: "In his old cocaine-snorting days, he liked to pick up boys and 'Eltonize' them—that is, give them clothes, jewels, hopes and aspirations." John remembered, "When I saw the Sex Pistols slagging me off on television, I thought, Yes you *are* a lazy fat cunt."[55]

The superstar singer also confronted the decline of the liberal consensus that Top 40 Beatlemania had once represented. Summing up 1980, the CHR columnist for *Radio & Records* wrote it had been "the year America elected a new conservative President and Contemporary Hit Radio adopted a new conservative music policy." Visiting the United States in what, punning on the Beatles, he called his "Back in the U.S.S.A. Tour," John appeared for the first time on *The Tonight Show* a night after Reagan's election, and branded himself outside the program's MOR address. He made a fish face at his father's becoming "typical middle class English," explained UK pop by claiming that "the English have a sense of vaudeville. . . . English men can't wait to get into drag," joked that Russians invading Afghanistan hurt his pot supply, was bleeped for cursing, and called his life "like a fairy tale, pardon the expression." Earlier that fall, he'd donned a duck outfit at a massive Central Park concert and quacked "Your Song." He also dedicated "Imagine" to the park's famous neighbor, Lennon; formerly, he'd sent the icon a rewrite: "Imagine six apartments / It isn't hard to do / One is full of fur coats / The other's full of shoes." In December, Lennon was gunned down in front of his apartment.[56]

The backlash against pop modernity had considerable support in Britain as well, where a quarter of manufacturing jobs were lost and AIDS appeared in 1982, a year after the United States, prompting physical, tabloid, and governmental assaults on the gay community. Activist Michael James writes, "The hatred that was coming out was totally naked from the *Sun* and the *Daily Mail* and all those papers. The gloves were off." Thatcher instituted Section 28, forbidding the "promotion" of homosexuality by local government. In polling, disapproval of homosexuality increased from 62 percent in 1983 to 74 percent in 1987. John came under fire from Rupert Murdoch's *Sun* in 1988, accused of orgies with "rent boys" that eventually won him a legal settlement of a million pounds.[57]

If political culture had become more conservative, John could take comfort in the widening of his previously Anglo-American appeal into pop globalization. *Blue Moves*, the album following his *Rolling Stone* interview, spawned a European hit, "Song for Guy." In 1979, he made a far-reaching tour that recalled journeys into the American heartland, but now to Sweden, Denmark, Germany, the Netherlands, France, Spain, and Israel. On a Russian tour undertaken at John's own expense, his consumerist avocations were again relevant: "I didn't expect to have kids come up to me asking for chewing gum or offering $100 for my jeans," reflected accompanying writer Robert Hilburn. Though the *Los Angeles Times* critic noted John's apolitical lyrics made him a "safe choice," Nikki Finke called kids rushing past party dignitaries "almost historic here." In years following, John would appear solo in China in 1983; tour Yugoslavia, Hungary, Czechoslovakia, and Poland in 1984; and meet with Polish dissident leader Lech Walesa. "He said, it's the only way I can get any media coverage," John noted. Working again with pop art director Ken Russell, he satirized pop modernity as liberation in his video for "Nikita," a romance between John—shown driving a sports car and parading gaudy leisurewear—and a Berlin Wall border guard.[58]

The revival of Top 40, as a format and as a bulwark of progressive Anglo-American pop modernity, came down once again to sexually ambiguous British hitmakers with US crossover potential. "New Pop," led by drag singer Boy George, embraced the *Top of the Pops* ethos as an eccentric British creation: "Britain was going pop crazy. The charts were all anyone cared about," wrote chronicler Dave Rimmer. Much like the Beatles with Top 40, and arena bands with FM rock, this latest British Invasion relied on and elevated MTV, which permeated America by 1983. The new Elton was Wham! singer George Michael, who wouldn't acknowledge his sexuality for years. At Live Aid in 1985, Michael brought John out to duet on John's power ballad "Don't Let the Sun Go Down on Me." John, a poor fit in subcultural rock, became a recognized progenitor of British pop tradition. His up-tempo "I'm Still Standing," filmed in the manner of younger UK band Duran Duran, proved a significant MTV hit.[59]

The CHR format, now moved to FM, resurged alongside MTV, consultant Mike Joseph persuading station owners that a youth-oriented mix could attract older listeners. "People like to think young," one heard radio people say again, and programmer Kent Burkhart argued, "I think that CHR radio compared to ten years ago is about the same, but the industry got nervous over Madison Avenue's quest for 25+ demos. As a result, we moved away from CHR, but the listeners didn't." Joseph noted, "Most important, we refocused the format back to the active listeners who buy records." Scott Shannon's Z100 in New York led that city's ratings with a "suburban lifestyle with an urban influence" strategy. Rick Dees had a similar reach at KIIS-FM, a station "built on promotions." The new stars of CHR—Michael Jackson, Prince, and Madonna—duplicated John's reach across demos and outside rock, routinizing what his concerts had hinted at.[60]

Radio & Records editor Ken Barnes traced at the time a "new golden age of hit radio" that mixed black and Latino performers with British New Pop and some guitar rock. Yet he spotted a looming schism: stations torn between "emphasizing rock and cutting down on urban crossovers, or the reverse." There were some "CHR-AOR 'modern rock' hybrids," notably KROQ. "These West Coast stations focus primarily on British acts." But most Americans looking for Top 40 sounds were not looking to England; most Americans looking to England were not looking for Top 40. The majority of Top 40 hits derived from R&B and dance music with strong appeal to black and Latino listeners, or from AC ballads. Simon Frith argued that the "special relationship" musically between the United States and the United Kingdom was fading, finding from a British perspective, "Europe is not only nearer than the USA, these days it also generates more music income."[61]

By 1989, the rising popularity of hip-hop and hard rock, favored by young listeners but disparaged by the adults that sponsors craved, further pressured the original hits format, prompting *Radio & Records* to ask, was CHR "Losing Its Niche?" A station like Z100, which claimed that the 75 percent of its listeners over the age of eighteen accounted for 90 percent of ad revenue, faced questions of whether to play all hits or just a slanted fraction. Race factored heavily into the answer programmers came up with, as the new category of "rhythmic CHR"—aimed at both black and, increasingly, Latino urban listeners, on stations such as LA's Power 106, vied with newly dubbed "mainstream CHR" stations.[62] Often, no answer worked: as of 1996, only 318 commercial radio stations in the United States were CHR, down from 951 in 1989. Programmer Jeff Pollack wrote, "I've never heard more indecision and confusion from top programmers about the direction of a major format in all my years in radio." To Z100, a mainstream CHR that programmer Steven Kingston called "the music 2.4 million white suburban females are passionate about," John remained a "core artist." At rival "ethnic" Hot 97, where GM Judy Ellis said, "We play hit music that sells, and I'm proud of our Hispanic audience," he was invisible. "All-things-to-all-people CHR is over in major markets," *Radio & Records* concluded.[63]

John, who ranked number 1 for cumulative US Top 40 hits during the seventies (the Beatles topped the sixties), was still tenth in the more difficult eighties. He was helped by the format he'd always spurned, MOR, now recast as AC and aimed at aging members of the former rock underground. "Sorry Seems to Be the Hardest Word," his first single after discussing his sexuality, topped AC charts while only reaching number 6 pop, an imbalance repeated with "Little Jeannie" and "Blue Eyes." John also drew on Britain to establish his songs, on MTV's pop art sympathies in picking videos, and even on his liminal relationship to soul: Stevie Wonder played on John's "I Guess That's Why They Call It the Blues" and featured John in the AIDS empathy anthem "That's What Friends Are For," *Billboard*'s number 1 pop single of 1986. Finally, John's growth into a truly international pop star reflected the extent to which conservative privatization deposited Top 40 across the world, licensing commercial radio in countries previously reliant on government stations.[64]

Though John was determined to show that his confrontational side remained intact, songs like the lacerating "Ego" and "Sartorial Eloquence," with lyrics by gay songwriter Tom Robinson, only scraped the American Top 40. Looking for alternatives, he bemoaned what had become of the rock format. "When I first came here, FM was like a gift from heaven, but they're still playing 'Stairway to Heaven' and 'Your Song.' They need to play more of the new people and play more varied music." Top 40's place as an Ellis Island into pop modernity—associated with Americanization, consumerism, and youth experimentation—had made rebellion mainstream. Yet many in the 1980s lost confidence about such processes. Growing income disparities froze standards of living for industrial workers. On US radio, former DJs Rush Limbaugh, Howard Stern, and Don Imus were now "shock jocks" playing to audience alienation. Gil Troy describes a resultant "culture of confusion, a culture of moral crusading and vulgar displays."[65]

John had never forgotten the image of America he had perceived in his records, in that first copy of *Life* magazine with its pictures of Elvis. Inducting the Beach Boys into the Rock and Roll Hall of Fame in 1988, he said, "If you lived in England, all you ever wanted to do was go to America. Everything you ever dreamed of was American." Yet the limits of that particular dream were now acutely visible to him. UK and US pop music had followed different trajectories, leaving diminished space for an artist who sought to embody the new for transatlantic audiences. And for a performer past forty, the appeals of a deferred adolescent ideal of behavior and the rock star peer culture he had created around him had long since faded into patterns of bulimia and incoherence. Two years before entering rehab, as the marriage his uncertainties had led him toward dissolved, John made a different effort at personal recovery, confronting the dissipation he associated with consumption with an auction whose Sotheby's catalogue filled four volumes. In the past, his embrace of a pop rather than rock persona had been vital to his sexual identity. Now, it was unclear what he could carry over with him.[66]

Rock and Royalty: Sir Elton John

For scale, no performance by John rivals his singing "Candle in the Wind" in 1997 at the funeral of Princess Diana to an audience estimated to include 50 million Americans and 60 percent of Britain. The recording made afterward, engineered by Beatles producer George Martin, gave John—twenty-eight years into his run on the American Top 40—the highest-selling single of all time at 33 million copies, topping charts in twenty-two nations. Knighthood followed. A recent film, *The Queen,* looks at how pop impacted royal tradition: newly elected Labor prime minister Tony Blair persuades Queen Elizabeth that mass sentiment requires "the people's princess" be buried with spectacular pomp. That meant reworking a song written about Marilyn Monroe by Englishmen infatuated with America to produce a global anthem. "The core of the teenage group—the boys and girls who will be the real leaders and creators of society tomorrow—never go near a pop concert," future Thatcher adviser Paul Johnson had declared in 1964. In 1997, a photo of Blair with supporter Liam Gallagher of the Britpop band Oasis sym-bolized Cool Britannia. The new administration set up a Department of Culture, Media and Sport, and a Creative Industries Task Force, not-ing that the return on capital of recorded music exceeded any other UK industry.[67]

Earlier sections of this chapter have juxtaposed a public Elton moment and a private one, but in this case, crucially, the personal passage was cap-tured on camera and aired extensively: the funeral, six weeks before Di-ana's, of murdered gay fashion designer Gianni Versace. John mourned with Diana to one side and his life partner, David Furnish, on the other—princess and pop star. Following Diana's death, John invoked as their bond the celebrity culture and therapeutic consumerism of pop modernity, and shared connection to the crises that had undercut it. "We were both bu-limic for a start, and we both had marriages that failed, and we were both extremely interested in AIDS. You could talk about those and other issues with her in a way that you probably couldn't with any other member of the royal family. That's why she was such a special person."[68]

The Elton John who emerged from rehab in the 1990s embraced his position as rock royalty, publicly asserting sexuality and status in place of

FIGURE 4.6 Princess Diana, Elton John, and John's partner, David Furnish, at the funeral of fashion designer Gianni Versace, 1997. This widely circulated image of John and Furnish, grieving together alongside a British royal, ended the long schism between John's public persona and private life, and connected to a refashioning of pop modernity, in the era of leaders Bill Clinton and Tony Blair, as Anglo-American "soft power." © Luca Bruno/AP/Corbis Used by permission.

private explorations and coded pageantry. Aligned with an international fashion designer and media-savvy princess, his new role illustrated how culture, politics, and capitalism had converged to produce a celebrity immune to both counterculture and backlash. The difference with rock stars of old can be felt in Rolling Stone Keith Richards's dismissal of John's performance at Diana's funeral: "I'd find it difficult to ride on the back of something like that myself, but Reg [Reginald Dwight, John's birth name] is showbiz." Or in Barbara Walters's equally dismissive reference, from the opposite perspective, to a now hoary countercultural triangulation of rebellion while profiling John: "We talked about everything: sex, drugs, and rock 'n' roll, sure. But tonight he goes on record to reveal himself as he's rarely done before."[69]

This Elton John, making his personal life public record, was documented in *Tantrums and Tiaras*, filmed by Furnish. John was shown livid—disturbed at tennis in the south of France by an admirer—and tender, teasing his manager and ex-lover, Reid, "the fabulous Beryl." He wrote in a private journal the US and UK chart positions of his latest single. "I've always been fascinated with that," he said. He remained the opposite of a tortured artist: a sequence had singer Lulu bring him a lyric at 4 p.m. that he set to melody, rehearsed with her, and after proclaiming "tea break!" still had recorded by five. Yet he remained passionate about new music, plugging favorites Mary J. Blige and Massive Attack. Viewers met his therapist, saw him at an AIDS benefit with drag queen RuPaul, and contemplated the empire of clothes in his closet. Furnish asked, did he feel guilty about such excesses? "I have to be honest with you," said the man named British pop's top moneymaker. "No."[70]

Three subthemes have run throughout this chapter: pop modernity as it extended from Americanization to globalization; the evolving place of gay identity within that youth-identified realm; and the conflict between a rock notion of authenticity and its Top 40 inverse of theatricality and mediation. It is worth considering these once again, from John's most recent experiences.

As an international superstar, John exemplified the permeation of consumerism's "dream economy" across geography, age, and cultural lines. His first world tour after rehab, from 1992 to 1993, with sets and outfits designed by Versace, saw him play one hundred concerts to over 3 million people on five continents. His work with lyricist Tim Rice on *The Lion King* signified rock-era pop's primacy in the contemporary Broadway musical and resurrected his 1970s all-ages appeal—"it hit every market: the children, their parents, and also the existing Elton John fans," Rice said. John's AIDS foundation, to which he donated all income from his singles—the essence of Top 40 success—drew praise in philanthropic journals for its efficiency. A 1997 *Vanity Fair* issue featured John, and an ad for the Elton John AIDS Foundation Visa, alongside a "Portrait of World Power" gallery of politicians (including Clinton and Blair) and businessmen such as Bill Gates, shot by Annie Leibovitz and other long-time pop photographers.[71]

Culture was now understood, internationally, to represent what Joseph Nye, an assistant defense secretary under Clinton, called "soft power," the ability to prevail "through attraction rather than coercion." The results, most acknowledge, went beyond McDonaldization. Richard Pells sees "reinforcement of cultural diversity," Peter Taylor argues that "a hybrid culture is produced in which American influences are clear but where national cultures remain intact," and Andrew Blake suggests, "There was dialogue, differentiation and divergence, rather than the simple adoption of American models." Sociologist Jeremy Tunstall, who titled a 1977 analysis *The Media Are American: Anglo-American Media in the World*, named his follow-up study *The Media Were American: US Mass Media in Decline*. Tunstall found MTV channels globally began with a 70/30 mix of US versus native pop, but fully reversed that ratio over time.[72]

The pop modernity that John represented could provoke a resentment aimed at its power. British public intellectual Bryan Appleyard, who protested, "I defy anyone to study Elton John," worried that Cool Britannia "in terms of GNP, marketing, and electoral success" threatened "the idea of excellence and coherence in high culture." When Billy Joel performed "The Bitch Is Back" in front of George W. Bush as John received a Lifetime Achievement Award at the Kennedy Center, *Washington Times* columnist Diana West observed, "This was another transgressive moment of pomp and punkiness, a mix of cultivation and coarseness, but no one noticed the clash *because there wasn't any.*" If pop modernity and the Top 40 had signified an outsider cohort buying the center, John's luxury life as what Edmund White called "the ultimate shopper" typified a newly constituted elite. It was revealed, after he sued manager John Reid, that John had spent 40 million pounds between 1996 and 1997. A book on John's mansion, built for Henry VIII's physician, noted, "After coming out of rehabilitation he wanted to get rid of the rock-star image—he had been very unhappy in those days. So he shed all the rock-star glitter." John's former discotheque room was replaced by chintz sofas.[73]

Some of the same contradictions—liberation for whom, exactly, and to do what?—applied to John's position as what the *Advocate* called "arguably the world's most famous gay person and certainly one of its most vocal spokespeople and fund-raisers." Barry Walters conjectured, "His eventual coming-out in the early '90s as gay—not bi—was part of a larger effort to heal himself. The public sensed the difference and supported him." John's civil partnering with David Furnish was described in the *Advocate* as "the most media-saturated U.K. union since Charles and Diana's." *People* magazine, in 1978, had called John's announcement of his sexuality "pretty alarming" and later assured readers with the cover line, "The New Elton John: He's given up touring and those nutty glasses—but not lasses." Now, the tone was dramatically different. "Elton John and longtime partner David Furnish had long wanted to make honest men out of each other. Finally, the law cooperated." Yet a more skeptical *New York Times* article declared, "Celebrity Trumps Sexuality." One writer, discussing how "Liberation" evolved from black, women's, and gay freedom struggles, charged, "Today the gay man is Sir Elton John and the black woman is Condoleezza Rice. They rather need liberation from themselves." John said to David Frost, "I'm a celebrity, I've had no problems."[74]

Musicologist Judith Peraino has outlined three varieties of "queer icon." Judy Garland represented an ambivalent relationship to normalness: "Camp shares with melodrama excessiveness as a mode of imagination or a register of performance." Lesbian rocker Melissa Etheridge, by contrast, earned "a guest pass into the patriarchy" with her younger lover and mainstream sound enacting an "idealized entry into normalcy." Madonna, Peraino's third icon, gained a "guest pass into the queer community" by appropriating "their power to offend via sexuality" and displaying "an ideal of gender and sexual fluidity." A reviewer, commenting on Peraino's triad, places Elton John in the Etheridge category. John's ability to be mainstream icon and out gay man made him an arbiter of pop norms: both Axl Rose and Eminem, accused of homophobia, gave performances with John to defuse accusers. And an "idealized entry into normalcy" is at the heart of Top 40 assimilation. Yet, as with Auslander assigning "fluidity" to Bowie's experiments with homosexuality but disparaging John's importance, one needn't devalue the idea of diversifying the center.[75] "Don't Let the Sun Go Down on Me" became, in this period, the song that John poignantly sang in Laramie, Wyoming, in 1998 after two homophobes left Matthew Shepard tied up to die, while "The Last Song," a somber 1992 hit about a gay son dying of AIDS reconciling with his intolerant father, ran in the credits sequence of the epidemic's docudrama *And the Band Played On*.

Recent work in queer theory helps conceptualize John's Top 40 impact, how his blurred-identity pop and sentimental register could globalize LGBT experience. In *Another Country*, Scott Herring argues against urban subcultures as the inevitable location of queer identity, repositioning rural queer life as a mediated "social fantasy whose cartographies are as much psychic, emotive, stylistic, and relational as they are geographically or spatially realized." Karen Tongson then extends Herring in *Relocations* to suburban queers of color. For Tongson, the "amorphous urbanism" of queer children of immigrant workers made suburbs something other than white-flight sterility. The multiracial, queer-influenced gatherings Tongson unearths at amusement park Knott's Berry Farm's Studio K in the 1980s depended on "remote intimacies" like CHR listening. Tongson writes, "Playing on its Orange County setting, the nascent form of suburban expression practiced by queers and youth of color at Studio K transposed the very principles of security, spatial isolation, and a service-driven economy—as well as the weekly Top 40—into their repertories of rebellion." Assimilation balanced against delineated identity, rebellion located within the semiotic boundaries of an increasingly worldwide pop modernity: that has been the register of Elton John's Top 40 queering.[76]

A final consideration of the format and its relationship to clearer genres is useful in understanding this nebulous but important crossover sphere. CHR stations in the 1990s remained divided over playing rap tracks and aggressive guitar rock songs. While MTV enjoyed the functional monopoly that sustained an inclusive Top 40 approach, few CHR stations aired everything in the charts. The syndicated *American Top 40* found it difficult to secure sponsoring stations open to rap, rock, and sentimental ballads like "Candle in the Wind." ABC radio network executive Corinne Baldassano said, "They weren't ditching *AT40*—they were ditching the format." Yet CHR revived once more, as grunge, gangsta rap, and new country lost luster. "Pop Goes Back to the Center," *Radio & Records* declared at the end of 1996, and Mike Joseph was summoned again to repeat the verities: "I only fast-rotate mainstream music that is mass appeal to every demographic. I put a demographic, gender, and race on every tune, so I know who's buying that music. That's where dayparting comes in handy."[77]

The passage that same year of the Telecommunications Act, which in neoliberal fashion allowed giant chains of radio stations, proved a boon for CHR: the format that fantasized that mass-appeal broadcasting could be at once liberating and capitalistic. In 1997, as "Candle in the Wind" circulated, Randy Michaels, head of the dreaded behemoth Clear Channel, proclaimed Top 40 his special passion. It was easier to "live off cume," meaning large numbers of listeners rather than a qualitatively differentiated niche, when part of a chain whose sales managers could offer a balance of different demographics. And "CHR still has the most impact on retail cash registers," record labels agreed. It did not hurt that in the late 1990s, as the impact of Clinton's policies registered, income at the lower end finally rose for a time. "Advertisers Aren't Spending as Much in the 'Money Demo,'" *Radio & Records* reported. A new wave of boy bands (Backstreet Boys, 'N Sync), pop princesses (Britney Spears, Christina Aguilera), crossover R&B (Usher), and power balladeers (Celine Dion) pushed Top 40 into the next century. "Mainstream pop is here to stay," wrote a columnist in the journal. "Say what you will about consolidation," another story concluded, "but it has been great for CHRs by allowing them to finally focus on their specific audience, primarily the 18–34 demo, because chances are their sister station is covering 25–54."[78] Top 40 stations, despite subdivisions, remained the most likely to target racially mixed and working-class listeners and challenge niche capitalism with novel inclusiveness. John's final US Top 40 hit, "Written in the Stars," was a duet with teen country singer LeAnn Rimes, created for another Broadway musical.

Elton John was back circling the American Top 40 in 2008. The Kanye West track "Good Morning" was not released as a single, but many other hits by the rapper and producer appeared on *Billboard*'s multiple Top 40 variants, including Rhythmic Top 40, Top 40 Mainstream, European Hot 100 Singles, Latin Rhythm Airplay, and Hot Ringtones. Still, "Good Morning," with its video by Japanese pop art inheritor Takashi Murakami, commissioned for a museum retrospective that included a Louis Vuitton shop, stood as something of a commentary on Top 40 values gone global. Where rappers had once associated themselves with Malcolm X's credo "by any means necessary," West resisted hip-hop orthodoxy as John had the rock counterculture: "I'm like the fly Malcolm X, buy any jeans necessary," he joked in a lyric. The Chicago native stood apart in other ways. He told an MTV interviewer, "Everybody in hip-hop discriminates against gay people. Matter of fact, the exact opposite word of 'hip-hop,' I think, is 'gay.' . . . I wanna just come on TV and just tell my rappers, just tell my friends, 'Yo, stop it fam.'" For "Good Morning," he sampled a wordless vocal line from "Someone Saved My Life Tonight"; the sexual lineage, as so often with Top 40, was felt rather than stated.[79]

A crudely written marketing book that devoted a chapter to John's self-branding nonetheless summed up his unlikely achievement: "Fans have watched him transform from what might be described as the Liberace of rock and roll—clad in wild sunglasses, outrageously sequined outfits, and flamboyant hats—to respected artist, statesman, and AIDS activist." John kept his appeal with fans, the authors claimed, by being fully public and by ignoring rock aesthetics: "They've followed his personal life in the media, including his struggles with substance abuse, weight gain, sexual preference, and personal finances. They've also watched him push the envelope of artistry with his Disney movie soundtracks and his Broadway triumphs with *The Lion King* and *Aida*." John, from the "co-branding" of his duet with Rimes to the "enormous publicity value" of his defending Eminem and thus demonstrating cultural centrality, showed "how brand attributes work together to drive positioning and 'heart share.'"[80]

It may seem a backhanded compliment to celebrate Elton John for "positioning and 'heart share,'" the latter a marketing term for the psychographic intangibles that companies like Starbucks identify as crucial in creating the kind of customer identification that cements brand loyalty. But this is part of the interpretive challenge that the Top 40 format and Top 40 artists present. Top 40 preceded the rock and roll era, accompanied and then outlasted rock's dominance. It needs to be understood as an enduring, if less than clear, force for a different kind of popular music upheaval. Wed to the new, its Americanization became globalization, its coded messages and protest songs with the explanatory lyric cut out came to include queer royalty, and its pop tweaks to rock, hip-hop, and other genre verities became a reliable mass-appeal format. Rock and roll, the mythicized genre that John often saw himself embodying, may have splintered. But Top 40, and the pop modernity whose entry gates it maintained, seemed destined to endure forever.

CHAPTER FIVE

The Wrath of the Buzzard

WMMS and Rock

B etween 1975 and 1977, on the Cleveland FM album rock station WMMS, Murray Saul delivered "The Get Down" every Friday at 6 p.m., wrapping up another week on the punch clock.[1] "We're driving outta there, at full blast!" began one of his five- to ten-minute sermons, delivered in a vowel-extending, FCC-testing, half-retching moan of abject pomposity. "Ohh, the slavedriver brought out the meat grinder and the stomper. And after they pushed us through, grinding the *sheeeeeaaauught* outta us, they threw us on the grill, salt and peppered our wounds, and laughed as they squeezed the onion in our eyes. . . . They took the doors out of the stalls this week, just to speed things up a little bit! . . . That slave-driver just thinks of us as more machines, replaceable parts, and they built it so our tears keep the typewriters clean and our sweat oils the lathe."

The slave driver was a constant refrain in the Get Downs. And so was the arrival of the weekend, a time for the hallowed trio of sex, drugs, and rock 'n' roll—rarely clamored for in such an anti-work-discipline fashion. "It's Friday, Friday, Friday, Friday . . . now, we're ready to taste nothing but the best, because it's Friday, Friday, Friday, Friday! . . . Give me that weekend salute. We gotta gotta gotta get DOWN! . . . Turn on a friend! Get out the bong! . . . The beat of the street is in our feet. . . . Brothers and sisters, we've got our souls back. Our time is our own. The weekends must get longer than the weeks. And we gotta, gotta, gotta, gotta, gotta, gotta, gotta, gotta, gotta, gotta, gotta, gotta [speeding up], gottagottagottagottagotta-gottagottagottagotta get DOWN, damn it."

Heard today, Saul's ranting Get Downs evoke the edgy rock of period Cleveland bands such as Pere Ubu ("don't need a cure, I need a final

FIGURE 5.1 "The Wrath of the Buzzard" WMMS promotional picture, circa 1975. The Cleveland rock radio station became an industry trendsetter in the shift from an "underground" style to the blue-collar heartland rock represented by figures such as Bruce Springsteen. The aggressiveness of the buzzard as a logo represented the 18–34 male target audience, unabashed commercial ambitions, and the anger of a city succumbing to deindustrialization. Author's collection.

solution") and the Electric Eels ("I'm so agitated"). In 2005, New York–
area hipster station WFMU broadcast an hour of the thirty-year-old
broadcasts, marveling at their strangeness.[2] Yet, type Murray Saul into
YouTube and a far less fringe picture emerges. He is on stage at baseball's
Cleveland Stadium, delivering his broadside to some eighty thousand people, assembled for what WMMS called its World Series of Rock concerts,
with headliners such as the Rolling Stones, Pink Floyd, and Fleetwood
Mac. Saul, almost fifty at the time, is bald on top and bespectacled—
portly. But his blue Oxford shirt has been partially unbuttoned, his
scraggly beard makes him a longhair in spirit, and his arms are waving:
Uncle Stoner, leading ecstatic young adult rockers, WMMS's 18–34 demographic, through his fabled chant. This is not punk provocation: it's a TV
ad for 101 FM.

In the 1970s, as Cleveland and industrial centers like it festered, a
radio station renamed itself "The Buzzard" and made a commercial music
format out of the carnage. The station was remarkably popular into the
1980s, leading the effort to secure Cleveland the Rock and Roll Hall of
Fame, a designation that honored the city's listeners more than its artists. Other stations, such as WNEW/New York, WMMR/Philadelphia,
WBCN/Boston, KLOS/Los Angeles, and KSHE/St. Louis, took a similar path, creating what became known as album-oriented rock (AOR),
the most successful new radio format of the 1970s. In the process, rock,
a refashioning of 1950s rock and roll for the late 1960s counterculture,
took on a new identity: blue collar as much as collegiate. WMMS presents
this transformation, and its ambiguities, in a highly influential microcosm.
Late 1960s rock had refused Top 40 radio formats, with underground stations proclaiming themselves "freeform." The anti-commercial insistence
concealed far less progressive tendencies, including a severing of rock
from contemporary black-music making and female audiences. Still, the
most complicated dynamic involved the class position of the young white
men who anchored the format that did emerge. AOR's insistent populism
fantasized the music as both maverick and massive—amplified rebellion.
But with advertisers to please, and working-class income declining, a format built on the loyalty of fans in black T-shirts at arena shows struggled
with the implications of a new media fetish: the yuppie.

Rock occupies a humbler cultural position now than in its heyday. The
notion of "rockism," introduced by British subculturalists who listened to
Boy George in the 1980s, mocked a fixed language of guitars, bass, and
drums, nostalgia for the peak years of Dylan and the Stones, and ideals

of sweaty authenticity. Nineties alternative fans traced different lineages than the rock history reified in *Rolling Stone*. Scholarship and criticism have reflected these shifts. Keir Keightley argues that rock's contradictions were fundamental: millions buying a mass product, each feeling like a personal rebel. Alice Echols and Elijah Wald confront the whiteness in rock's conception of itself as art, while Carl Wilson and Kelefa Sanneh interrogate rockism in twenty-first-century guises. Labor historian Jefferson Cowie presents a counterculture severing itself from industrial workers. Steve Waksman and Ryan Moore show punk rebellion masking deeper connections to heavy metal and neoliberal niche culture. Most recently, Michael Kramer has demonstrated that "hip capitalism" was neither the antithesis nor guilty secret of sixties rock, but something more basic: the stage upon which a movement's spreading idealism had to be performed.[3]

Rock radio, the original example of hip capitalism, offers an important corollary to these efforts, since AOR, a format, extended countercultural rock's reach but unmade many of its ambitions. Studying rock as radio represented or misrepresented it demystifies the category—reinserting it back into the pop landscape. Rhythm and blues (R&B) as a commercial format absorbed soul, funk, and hip-hop to ensure black pop's "changing same." Country, an industry of southern modernization, took pride in its status as a consumer mainstream, keeping the format from subdividing. In rock, by contrast, structured formats were an insult to the countercultural music's founding principles. "Rockism is imperial," Sanneh could still write in 2004; "It claims the entire musical world as its own. Rock 'n' roll is the unmarked section in the record store, a vague pop-music category that swallows all the others." This book, in recasting the "rock era" as a time of flourishing pop categories, secured by the rival mainstreams of format radio, challenges such assumptions. But rock radio challenged them too, by delineating specific listeners and sounds as rock. The process created a cultural behemoth. Yet AOR the format stifled rock the genre, shunning vital newer artists out of anxiety over the taste and clout of its public.[4]

My look at WMMS relies on a remarkable set of primary documents, files kept between 1974 and 1986 by WMMS program director (PD) John Gorman. From this material, used alongside trade magazine reporting, additional interviews, and Gorman's own memoir, we can see the evolution over time of a particularly successful station's format: its methodology of structuring, daypart by daypart, an eclectic flow of songs, DJ banter, promotional material, and advertising to address and grow a particular audience. On a station like WMMS, the niche targeting involved in maintaining a viable format was not an abstraction: it was a praxis philosophized upon constantly by Gorman and his peers and then carefully enacted in everything from the categorizing of albums to DJ techniques and the style and placement of advertising. A station like WMMS lived "book to book," meaning the Arbitron listener diaries that were collated and summarized into ratings every three months. As competitors appeared, trying to carve off pieces of the Buzzard's large audience by deploying kindred formats, Gorman and his successors had to respond and recalibrate; "progressive rock" bred a range of "AOR," "Superstars," "classic rock," "modern rock," "alternative rock," and "active rock" approaches. To sell a set of sounds, formats constructed and revised group identity.

One other point should be made about Murray Saul's Get Downs. In the WMMS Friday-night countdown, they always followed DJ Kid Leo's playing of Bruce Springsteen's "Born to Run," a song not yet commercially available when the ceremony began. It has become customary to contemplate Springsteen's complex relationship, in the years between "Born to Run" and the megastardom inspired by his 1984 album *Born in the U.S.A.*, to a white working class suffering the displacement of factory closings. WMMS's experience contextualizes both the music and its listeners in a larger, contested debate over the meanings of heartland rock. To step into the AOR world was not always to be as working class in address as a Get Down or a Springsteen song, yet the notion of rock as a realm apart, the realm of the weekend, conveyed a fantasy that appealed across class lines in a way few other 1970s cultural forms attempted. WMMS fixes Springsteen next to Murray Saul and Kid Leo within a music format whose links to working people were contradictory, lucrative, but also intense.

Freeform Progressive: The Birth of WMMS

In 1968, WHK-FM, the perennially struggling counterpart to WHK-AM, was renamed WMMS by owners Metromedia and given a chance to prove itself as radio aimed at hippies. The stakes were low: the FCC now required that stations stop simulcasting AM and FM content, so something was needed, but only Beautiful Music, a Muzak-like stream of instrumentals for older listeners, had garnered ads on FM, which few received on transistors and virtually nobody could hear in cars. WMMS failed at underground rock the first time, tried big band jazz instead, then resumed the rock experiment under PD Billy Bass. As Martin Perlich, an early station DJ, recalled, the moment demanded a new ideal: "It was rock, it wasn't rock 'n' roll. People said rock, meant the new alive, living art form. Everything was carried in it. All the social messages, all the cues." Bass programmed with a sense of cultural politics: one DJ for his sound experiments, another for her feminism, a third for his mix of "gay liberation news" and unexpected pre-rock pop: "It was like a *Saturday Night Live* entourage," he now says. WMMS ads claimed the call letters stood for "Where the Music Means Something." Former Top 40 DJ Dick Kemp reported of his time at the station, "It was the hardest transition in my life. No more hollerin', no more bubblegum. No tight playlist."[5]

This was intentional: underground radio had been created as the antithesis of the Top 40 approach that popularized rock and roll and spread into R&B, country, and middle of the road (MOR) varieties. In 1967, San Francisco's Tom Donahue, the most visible programmer in the new radio category, wrote in the equally new *Rolling Stone* that Top 40 was a "rotting corpse . . . stinking up the airwaves." To Donahue, "The music has matured, the audience has matured, but radio has apparently proven to be a retarded child." Rock, in positioning itself as countercultural both topically and formally, created a space, as Keightley has shown, between earlier notions of youth and adult pop. "Freeform" did this for the binary split between Top 40 and MOR. It was FM rather than AM, played long songs from albums, and established a stoned vibe as laid back as hits DJs like Wolfman Jack were hyperbolic. Kramer describes a "Republic of Rock": a civic quest to create community within a mass media. By 1972, it was natural for Jack Nicholson and Warren Beatty to appear on WMMS to promote the liberal candidacy of George McGovern. And rock DJs had become icons. Richard Neer, then on Metromedia's flagship station in New York, writes, "The absolute coolest place to work in radio was WNEW-FM. The disc jockeys had total freedom to play whatever records they chose. They could say what they wanted, whenever they wanted."[6]

Celebrations of this first era of FM rock inevitably bemoan where it all ended: "FM became a great success by late in the 1970s," one history tells us, "but at the cost (to many of its adherents) of losing its programming soul to the bean counters." We should resist this romanticization. Rock radio was commercial from the beginning, only shifting in tone as the audience expanded from a version of class to a version of mass.

Underground stations were launched by the savvy owners of chains such as Metromedia, ABC, CBS, and Century because the vanguard they reached was tangible and growing. Bass told me, "We had a small, loyal audience. We knew them because we would go out and be among them. We would see them at concerts. If we played a song that reached our audience, it would sell at our record stores, the hippie record stores. We didn't want everybody—we were trying to serve the hippest, coolest people in town . . . that weren't just getting up and going to work." Elsewhere, he has connected the approach to a Cleveland classical station. "I wanted to build WMMS as a radio station similar to WCLV at the time. WCLV had all the great, classy Cadillac ads and made enough money to sustain themselves, but they didn't have the big numbers." In a 1970 *New York Times* report, station managers "requesting anonymity" held that "the advantage of FM 'underground radio' was that it could survive economically by pinpointing its efforts rather than catering to the mass following that television and large AM stations must woo." Top 40 remained for "less sophisticated youths." Boston rocker WBCN's college girl listeners protested ads for standard cosmetics, requesting "innovations in sandals or dress attire."[7]

Advertisers sought in underground radio, as Michael Keith's history captures, this boutique quality: rock musically connected components of the new buzzword "lifestyle" to epitomize a segmented consumerism beyond simple demographics. Radio analyst Mike Harrison has said, "Everything from head shops to alternative clothing stores, nightclubs, boutiques, newspapers and magazines, movies, concerts, and a lot more sprang up, and this industry needed a place to advertise." *Advertising Age* editorialized in 1970, "Marketing's traditional demographic measurement yardstick will now have to be supplemented with studies of the new attitudes that are developing in our society toward possessions, fashions, quality of life and advertising." DJ Larry Miller points out that "our listeners were also perceived as using the same products as everyone else. They wore Levis, drank Coke, and drove VWs. By 1970, many ad agencies were doing spots especially for the underground/progressive FM stations." A promotion piece by ABC-FM sales trumpeted, "It is difficult to define and completely understand the audience that is listening and responding to progressive and 'freeform' programming on stereo FM stations. Yet, the nature of our industry demands that we accept the challenge of audience definition—for this audience must be described in terms of LIFE-STYLE, as it parallels demographics. LIFESTYLE is an extra meaningful word to America's youth, for a new generation of young people demand that 'life' and 'style' be an inseparable quality."[8]

Freeform adherents mythicized Tom Donahue's first broadcast, his wife and partner Rachael recalling, "The first phone calls were rather unbelieving, half-whispered questions along the lines of 'Is this really happening or have I fallen down some rabbit hole or am I dreaming or . . . ?' Two people by the names of Swan and Juju came to the studio loaded down with bells, tapestries, pieces of lace and velvet, a Viet Cong banner, incense, candles, and a couple of joints." George Duncan, who oversaw Metromedia's new FM programming, told a different story, about the mainstream potential of stations that in 1969 were playing sixty-eight of the *Billboard* top 100 albums. Scott Muni, WNEW's most iconic DJ and program director, left better-paying work for $175 a week in the "grand experiment." Yet Muni knew "there had to be the tag of familiarity. . . . You also have to regulate yourself. . . . You have to experiment, but you also have to be careful not to say, 'okay, here I am, and I'm going to do all new things today because there are so many new things.' " In *Rolling Stone*, Ben Fong-Torres complained in 1970, "It appears 'underground radio,' under the repressive nursing of network and/or corporate owners, is becoming just another spinoff of commercial, format radio." But what intrigued Duncan and successful rock radio participants was the challenge of format work: the balancing act of programming to a listenership. Donahue, who ultimately ran Metromedia's KSAN, likely agreed.[9]

ABC-FM, having failed with utter freeform, called a meeting in Chicago in 1971 of programmers from stations there and in six other large cities. It was decided, division president Allen Shaw recalled later, they would have no "long raps on the music and not any political comments by the disc jockeys, but just a very friendly kind of delivery, playing the music for the people, playing the best cuts from the best albums . . . structuring it in such a way as to make it well-balanced." The ratings gains were instant, KLOS in Los Angeles rising from five thousand listeners a quarter hour to forty-eight thousand within a few ratings cycles. Elsewhere, Century Broadcasting, with its flagship KSHE, reported that in 1970 "we got into the Doors, Cream, and Deep Purple, a much heavier sound." A group at CBS FM, by sonic contrast, worked on "Mellow," with KNX FM launching in 1971 as a singer-songwriter-focused channel that anticipated adult contemporary (AC) and adult album alternative (triple A).[10]

In 1970, Duncan and David Moorhead, who programmed Metromedia's KMET, flew to Cleveland and listened to radio for a couple of days. "I said to him, 'Do you hear what I hear' meaning do you hear what I don't? He said, 'Yep, there is a hole so big you could drive a truck through it.' I said that cuts it, we are going to do it here. . . . It was late that year that we turned WMMS into an AOR Progressive Rock station and it was immediately successful." This diminishes Bass, who for all his adventurous choices wanted a dynamic radio station: "I was sick of dull, pretentious, hippie bullshit," he told a reporter in 1973. "I wanted to prove that an FM station could make money and be interesting." For a time, the countercultural nature of stations had replaced sonic formatics. Denny Sanders, a DJ who survived the transition to AOR, explained to me, "The counterculture was the string that all of these beads were strung on. Talking against war, gay rights, these people's language. Drug culture. So people sat through music they didn't care for because they felt a kinship." By the early 1970s this wasn't enough. "Once the counterculture unraveled, there was nothing to hold those beads together. So you had a heavy metal person calling to say what are you playing that James Taylor fag for? You had the acoustic person calling up, what are you playing this electric crap, etc. Nobody could pull it off anymore." Bass, Sanders recalls, "always used to say, 'Let's not get too hip for the room.'"[11]

The epitome of WMMS, as Bass and Sanders at that point idealized it, came in 1972, when the station broke David Bowie's *Hunky Dory* and Cleveland became the first place the androgynous post-hippie rock star played in his inaugural US tour. WMMS had its first of many core artists, a sonic anchor: Bowie facing the strange in "Changes" merged highbrow pop and vintage rock and roll. Bass had already firmly rejected another possible alternative. "We started to get all these requests for this Southern rock. It drove us crazy. I'm gonna play some songs that got some Confederate flags? We were looking for a way to separate ourselves from these people. I told Denny, we gotta move into a different direction. He came to me with the *Hunky Dory*, said this is a little weird—I fell in love with it. We figured, this southern rock crowd is not going to like this glitter stuff." WMMS had played John Lennon and Yoko Ono's "Woman Is the Nigger of the World," with the African American Bass (who would later manage Luther Vandross) telling the *Cleveland Plain Dealer*: "It's healthy for the business to make people wake up and think. Lennon . . . takes for granted that free-thinking, liberal blacks and liberal whites will understand the usage of the word." But as rock became a white male army of seemingly apolitical youth, Bass lost faith. "The revolution is over. And we lost. At the Stones' show there were 40,000 or so kids. All of them looked alike. . . . I want no part of it."[12]

The revolution was over, and rock radio had barely begun. The issue wasn't selling out but who was buying in. Greil Marcus wrote in a lengthy 1971 *Creem* article, "As a dissolving community, we no longer want to listen to each other's records." Top 40, he recalled, had "given us an idea of the choices that we made and that were being made for us." Now, "the fragmentation of the audience, and its institutionalization into groups of consumers with specialized tastes which an industry can exploit and on which it can depend, releases the artist from the pressure of appealing to a vast community." There was still an undercurrent that Marcus identified as "POP": meaning a "sense of being where the action is." Lyrically simplistic hard rock band Grand Funk Railroad had it, despite rock critic disdain, which meant that for those who recalled sixties aspirations, "Grand Funk is not merely fragmenting the audience, like most everyone else; they may be dividing it." The fear inculcated was that "a new pop audience . . . may make the old one irrelevant." Steve Waksman's study concludes, "The crowd was becoming a commodity in popular music to an unprecedented degree." Arena shows, with little hint of sixties progressive politics beyond the fervency of the audience, called countercultural unity into permanent question. Was it elitist to prefer the artier Bowie to routinized Stones tours? Those like Marcus, who recognized artistry in AM Top 40, but equally valued the audience generated by rock, found no easy answer to a widening split. AOR, often charged with destroying adventurous rock, began as a commercial attempt to resurrect its air of common culture.[13]

The Wrath of the Buzzard: Creating an AOR WMMS

After Malrite Communications bought WMMS in 1973, Bass resigned, and a new program director, John Gorman, placed an exaggerated blue-collar populism ahead of arty progressivism. Gorman, born in 1950, had grown up in a working-class Irish section of South Boston, idolizing Top 40 for its aggressive DJs and unruly mix of hits by black and white singers. To Gorman, rock and roll was born out of this energy—what Susan Douglas calls "the euphoria of commercialism." Gorman had no qualms about Grand Funk Railroad: "Progressive rock stations said Grand Funk wasn't real rock and roll," he said to me. "But the people wanted to hear it. And our feeling was we were going to leave it up to our audience." DJ Donna Halper showed the explosive potential of trying to cater to, rather than shun, listener tendencies, when she played the

Canadian band Rush, still unreleased in the United States: "I dropped the needle on 'Working Man,' and the moment I heard it I knew it was a Cleveland record." The rabid response quickly led to the band's signing by Mercury executive Cliff Burnstein, later to manage Metallica.[14]

From a skeptic's view far down the road, a vision that moved from Bowie to Grand Funk Railroad and Rush, on the path to a 1990s marriage to Metallica, doomed rock radio to only interpellate white male rage. Gorman's intentions were far more inclusive. He orchestrated his station much like a Top 40, with promotions and tight DJ sets intended to build a large audience on principles of shared loud fun. Gorman merged the Top 40 pop need to make music where the action was and rock's countercultural exclusivity. And he insisted that black music, always a thorny issue in rock radio, be included. He writes in his memoir, "We believed we could do a mass-appeal album-rock station, where we could play the best progressive and mainstream cuts and even some Top 40 hits and oldies. We'd play progressive rhythm and blues. We'd sound like we were having fun. We'd jump on every fad, regardless of how weird or off-the-wall it might be. Our goal was to be a pop culture station, and the best rock and roll station in America."[15] Still, his programming, like the expanding AOR of the mid-1970s as a whole, mainly had a different consequence: uniting a white male 18–34 demographic across education and economic class.

This was no small matter, as Jefferson Cowie's eulogy for labor, *Stayin' Alive: The 1970s and the Last Days of the Working Class*, puts in context. Worker income, Cowie notes, peaked historically in 1972, having risen 42 percent since 1960, exceeding the country's overall gains. Fully entering into a life of leisure time and consumer goods were figures like Cowie's key example, Dewey Burton, twenty-six in 1972, with "long sideburns, slicked back hair, and mod striped pants" plus a taste for customizing cars. Burton would become a Reagan Democrat, frustrated over busing and welfare freeloaders even as his union auto-plant job started to wither. For Cowie, the symbolism is clear: "One of the great constructs of the modern age, the unified notion of a 'working class,' crumbled, and the new world order was built on the rubble." Yet his book hints at an alternative possibility: the striking Chevy Vega builders of Youngstown, Ohio, about seventy-five miles southeast of Cleveland. *Fortune* reported, "Along the main production lines and in the subassembly areas there are beards, and shades, long hair here, a peace medallion there, occasionally some beads—above all, young faces, curious eyes." Could more of such workers, getting high together and bonding across race lines, have built a road to a better postindustrial order? In Cowie's accounting, the anthemic laments of Springsteen represent a highway not taken. When Ohio next appears in his book, it's in the form of the late 1970s postpunk group Devo, short for devolution, whose members were alienated from the counterculture by the Kent State shootings and from the union traditions of Akron, the Rubber City, by a consumerism that rendered workers "Spuds."[16]

I'd suggest a different Ohio symbol: the Buzzard, icon of WMMS's approach to rock radio in the John Gorman era. As station sales manager Walt Tiburski told the story, "Gorman and I happened to have the identical poster on our office walls. It was a popular hippie poster showing two scrawny buzzards sitting on a wire looking at each other and one saying to the other, 'Patience my ass, let's go kill something.'" Appropriately, as progressive gave way to the harder sell of AOR, the Buzzard replaced a lysergic mushroom as the new station icon. The first ads to run were emblazoned "The Wrath of the Buzzard" and showed the warty creature cackling amid tombstones that represented rival radio stations. Len "Boom Boom" Goldberg, a deep-voiced barker with a note of irony, voiced promos in the same register ("the THUNDERING Buzzard, WMMS, Cleveland") for decades. Far from any countercultural stress on peace and love, the Buzzard was in-your-face rock personified. Gorman recalls, "It was the foundation of our new take-no-prisoners on-air attitude at WMMS. We were no longer content to be that hippie FM underground station. Our goal from that day forward was to become Cleveland's #1 radio station—and one of the most influential FM stations in America." But of course the Buzzard also stood for Cleveland, "the mistake by the lake," butt of jokes the whole country over and emblematic of industrial decay. "The buzzard sort of depicts the working class of Cleveland, the people who get up and fight the weather and go to work in the steel mills," said illustrator David Helton. An underground publication remarked, "It's a perfect image for rock and roll suiciders pushing thirty and stuck in jobs that they hate in a city that Gorman seems to be symbolizing in a rotting cadaver."[17]

Another key act of class positioning came when Gorman installed Kid Leo as the new afternoon DJ. The former Lawrence Travagliante, a Cleveland native of similar background to Gorman, said that in high school "I was what we called a 'greaser.'" Much like Gorman, who complained in memos about the Coventry neighborhood bohemians in

Cleveland, Leo had never connected to the collegiate counterculture. His on-air delivery, his sound in presenting other sounds, resembled that of a cast member of the fifties-themed musical *Grease* (which he appeared in during a Cleveland production). Gorman said at the time, "There's no difference between Kid Leo doing what he does and some guy his age doing a plumbing job. They're both listening to music, and they both go to concerts." David Sowd, then a mail sorter, recalled, "We could relate, from the perspective of our blue-collar gig, to the clichéd way he left the air every day without fail: 'It's time to punch out, wash up, come back and wrap it up!'"[18]

By the mid-1970s, WMMS was a phenomenon, garnering a number 1 rating with its core demographic group, 18- to 34-year-old men. Arty but hard-edged bands such as Mott the Hoople, whose leader, Ian Hunter, would later write "Cleveland Rocks" in tribute, found themselves more popular in Cleveland than elsewhere in America. The radio industry now agreed upon a name for the format WMMS belonged to: AOR. But Buzzard staffers took pride in stretching the format. Sanders, still the evening DJ, recalls:

> We played a variety of different music, but kept it within a rock 'n' roll attitude. So we weren't like the old freeform days. But within the intensity required you could play reggae, peripheral styles, as long as they had force and impact. We played oldies, Motown or Wilson Pickett, Stax/Volt. Leo in the afternoon used to love "Dancing Queen." When new wave and punk came in, we were careful, but we dabbled. Talking Heads, Boomtown Rats, Blondie. And the other aspect was the fact that we did hot walkups—walked songs up to the post [talked until the first words came in]. We had production, explosive station IDs, quite early on. That kind of is what made us famous. We were a Trojan horse. A mainstream, hotly produced radio station which played Funkadelic, *Harder They Come*, local music. We were playing it to the Sunoco station in the suburbs. There were more radical stations than WMMS, stations with bigger playlists, more musically sophisticated. But only MMS pulled it off as a huge, mega-rated radio station.[19]

The aesthetic here is worth underlining: WMMS had to break new music outside the elites; it had to deploy Top 40 devices, from DJ banter to station IDs, but with a sardonic and knowing belligerence. There would be room for "peripheral styles," from reggae to Abba, so long as there was no question about the station's unifying commitment to a white, guitar-driven, rock attitude. The "hotly produced," hyperbolically maintained

FIGURE 5.2 WMMS staffers, circa 1976. DJ Kid Leo in *Rocky* T-shirt, program director John Gorman above him, DJ Denny Sanders second from right. In trying to stretch the boundaries of AOR, the station's staff took on an attitude that blended aggressive self-promotion and older ideals of rock as revolution. Still from *Radio Daze: Cleveland's FM Air Wars* (DVD, Harvard 131 Films, 2008).

sound was the thread now, where previously, as Sanders has said, counter-cultural allegiances connected much more varied programming.

The determination to forge a format through the perfect stream of songs is evident in Gorman's extant station files. "We are the tightest (by that I mean flow, not music) we've ever been," he told the DJs. "Just keep it in mind that the year is 1975, not 1968, and you'll be all set." There were constant reminders: "Keep programming up tempo and bright. . . . Keep the familiar tunes in the sets to welcome new listeners with." "The morning format must be tight, familiar and informative . . . not loose and radical." Sanders was cautioned, "I notice you playing music like you are a rock critic. You try too hard to make a point with your music and it goes over the heads of your listeners." Gorman had a *Radio & Records* article, about the need for AOR stations to offer a "total environment" where "attitude is the key," copied for staffers. Gorman was quoted there on the need for ad agencies to let stations edit commercials that diminished AOR credibility. This, the trade publication concluded, was "not anti-commercialism. No more than tight playlists are anti-music."[20]

A WMMS competitor emerged in 1975. WWWM, or M105, played from a constrained list of arena-rock anthems and fit a broader pattern: stations that had professionalized freeform now found themselves pushed by stations that went further, often advised by radio consultant Lee Abrams and his Superstars approach to stress canonical artists. At a meeting of DJs in June, Gorman noted, " 'Elitism' was discussed. . . . This [not being elitist] is M105's strength by default. We should never take for granted that the average WMMS listener is as 'hip' as the airstaff." Kid Leo was instructed to avoid indulging in too hard rock, since "we don't want to scare the women or 25+'s away from the station." Ultimately, both stations did well enough for *Radio & Records* to conclude, "In Cleveland, AOR Radio, in the form of the legendary WMMS and newcomer M105, is not only 'coming on,' but is already dominant." But Gorman's memoir makes clear the stakes. "Incumbent album-rock stations were falling as new, tight-listed stations entered their market. . . . Wanting to avoid that, we had to take fewer liberties than we once could, while still breaking new music and taking a chance on a Labelle or Isley Brothers, moves that other album-rock stations wouldn't make." Tellingly, he cites two black groups as worth fighting to include.[21]

By 1977, Gorman's rhetoric had hardened: his air staff and listeners formed the "Buzzard Nuclear Army," his opposing program director at M105 was "the Chimp," and it was common humor for memos to staff to end "Die, Chimp, Die! Kill! Kill! Kill!" When a new DJ began at WMMS, Gorman wrote him,

> Al: Let it be known. You have joined The Buzzard Nuclear Army, otherwise known as WMMS. WMMS is the top AOR station, not only in Cleveland, but in the entire country. WMMS is a very unique radio station. We strive for creativity and we live to win. The many individuals making radio station WMMS are allowed and encouraged to be creative, but must also recognize commercial limitations in which we must live. We do not program for ourselves—we cater 101% to our audience. They will make or break you. Have fun. Remember our raps. Stay familiar. Get to know the audience as they get to know you. When in doubt—don't say it, don't play it! You're in The Buzzard Nuclear Army now. Good luck![22]

Gorman competed with the tightened playlists of Superstars rock by making the fabled station itself, and its nuclear fan base, the superstar to identify with—the by now ubiquitous Buzzard, visible on T-shirts, in ads, and on hundreds of thousands of printed bumper stickers. "To call WMMS/Cleveland a 'success' would be an understatement," *Radio & Records* gushed. "'A way of life' for the station's staff and listeners is a more fitting description." The trade magazine ran features on sales manager Walt Tiburski and promotions director Dan Garfinkel, eager to understand the station's balance of unhinged attitude and business acumen. AOR sales people, Tiburski explained, "must relate the most *important* factor of the AOR listener—the lifestyle (otherwise known to research fanatics as psychographics)." Psychographics served AOR well, suggesting that a hot musical format reflected broader commitments that went beyond demographics and could connect the right products and the right population.[23]

In 1978, *Radio & Records* published a stand-alone book: *The AOR Story*. The cover relayed a decade of rock in a nutshell: cartoon images of hippies pictured with references to Haight-Ashbury, *Hair*, and Vietnam giving way to the same people ten years later: playing tennis for exercise, watching *Star Wars*, reading the slicker New York version of *Rolling Stone*. AOR had been the portion of radio most attuned to these changes. And the rewards had been great. Scott Muni of WNEW boasted, "We are THE largest money-maker, from a standpoint of income and revenue. . . . A person who is involved in concerts doesn't look at Arbitron. . . . He buys his time on the station because he knows if he's got a shot at selling tickets to the concert, he better be here. This holds true for certain albums, and then because of our great young adult male audience, every automobile, every beer, all the national accounts are here." A rundown of some fifty radio stations, from Albany and Albuquerque to Toledo and Worcester, from a largely automated station in Birmingham to dueling outlets in Dallas, made clear AOR's national success. Bob Garrett, general manager (GM) of KYYS/Kansas City attested, "There's no other radio format that allows you this very clearcut audience lifestyle to appeal to." Rick Lee, GM of KMEL/San Francisco, agreed: "What is different about AOR is the tremendous response factor you get from the audience. They are particularly responsive to new ideas and products, which makes the station ideal for certain promotional or commercial tie-ins."[24]

If rock radio had originated by blurring the line between Top 40 and MOR, AOR blurred the line between class and mass. Yet this, as at least a few recognized in the midst of AOR's triumph, might be an unstable proposition. Dex Allen, who led KPRI/San Diego, was cautious: "In a market with no competition, an AOR station can afford to be progressive. In a competitive market you have to be more familiar, or you lose your entire upper demographic. I can't run a station that just sells to

18–24-year-old males. I'm not surprised to see AOR tightening up as more stations realize this." And Billy Bass, the original WMMS program director, now handling album promotion for arty acts like Blondie on Chrysalis Records, was still more sober about a transition he'd been leery of from the start. "AOR radio has become mass appeal radio. With its mass appeal has come tighter playlists. AOR is getting tighter and tighter and pretty soon its spring will snap and a new development will be born. AOR radio seems to be cyclical so it may become loose again; it may become New Wave, or whatever."[25]

As for WMMS, its own tenth-anniversary celebration led Cleveland's alternative newspaper *Scene* to proclaim "radio station becomes institution" and a longtime advertiser to exult "The Cult of 1968 Becomes the Masses of 1978." "We have a philosophy around here that in the morning we don't get dressed to go to work," declared station manager Carl Hirsch. "We get dressed to go to war. We are at war." Sanders admitted to the daily paper, "We're commercial as hell. . . . But we're commercial art, and we attempt to put some flair into what we do." WMMS was rare in AOR for stressing working-class affiliations. Told, "I've heard it said that WMMS captures the pulse of the 'blue collar' workers in Cleveland," Gorman replied, "Yes, we have. We all sort of come from that background. Before taking this job I was driving that station wagon around Boston. Kid Leo was a carnival barker. . . . We all seem to have come from blue collar backgrounds or neighborhoods." Typically, radio people asserted the rock versus pop divide as a gendered one, as when Abrams's partner Kent Burkhart discussed his "high school boyfriend theory. When the high school guy breaks at 15, when he gets out of the bubblegum at 15 and he moves into progressive, he is going with the same girl . . . and he more or less forces his girl to listen to progressive." A third way to frame things was as a balance of vanguard and mainstream: rock columnist Mike Harrison said that at AOR, "the sophisticated and hip must be blended with the commercial and mundane in a manner that lures the susceptible of each without tipping them off that the other exists premeditatedly within the context of their radio station."[26]

Back in 1968, *Billboard* radio columnist Claude Hall had assured his readers that "Progressive Rock Listeners Do Wash." In fact, they were classy: "above the common breed." Murray Saul, twenty-two years older than Gorman when he wandered into WMMS in 1973 looking for an ad sales job, took the opposite view. "The passport was the fact that I smoked dope," he said when I spoke with him. Cleveland was anything but classy:

"a blue collar town. I enjoyed calling Cleveland the Slush Capital of the World." But that in no way disconnected the city from a rock culture where "you had a T-shirt with the latest thing happening in the world instead of a *New York Times* front page." Gorman mostly wrote the Get Down scripts that Saul would read, and the salesman preaching dissolution became a Buzzard icon. The gig was short-lived: a couple of years. But this most sardonic of human beings remembered the station and the scene as an enormous family: "When I would go to the World Series of Rock, I was seeing my friends, that's how I saw them. . . . It was a big umbrella."[27]

Sales manager Tiburski, a less bohemian figure, took a different tone. Station rates, he noted, had recently gone as high as $101 for a sixty-second spot. Kid Leo could be hired to voice ads "for an extra $100, lending you his persona and credibility. We find customers quite responsive to that sort of packaging." He remembered, "I suffered through the biases of AM radio salespeople telling clients that dope-shooting hippies were coming in to see you next, telling them that all their stations appealed to were kids who didn't have any money. . . . The fact is that the 18–34 market right now is the most affluent and largest group numerically today. They are the biggest spenders." Tiburski concluded, "We can sell anything to our audience."[28]

"Born to Run": The AOR Soundtrack

Song 1: Biting electric guitar establishes a blues lick, drums arrive with a double blast and then a rhythm expertly miked to sit apart in the mix. More guitar and bass flow in, and a male singer strains his upper register to assert unhinged power and anticipate the shrieking solo to follow. Song 2: Glistening guitar and keyboard fade up to a mid-tempo beat and impassively vocalized lyric about getting lost inside music; crunching chords herald a multitrack chorus, then turbulence returns to reverie. Soft and loud, back and forth; pop harmonics and rock solipsism. Song 3: An even softer beginning, solo piano this time, then a full band working a mellow pattern; the first verse, sung with mannered dandyism, asserting the realm of the singer-songwriter. "On a morning from a Bogart movie . . ."

I am listening to an MP3 folder I have assembled of the forty-three rock radio cuts most played between 1968 and 1978, as determined by *Radio & Records* with input from reporting stations for *The AOR Story*.

Ted Nugent's "Stranglehold," Boston's "More Than a Feeling," and Al Stewart's "Year of the Cat" kick off the kind of countdown a station might have run on a Memorial Day broadcast. This was the soundtrack to AOR long after the counterculture emerged, warhorses played with a constancy that secured eternal album sales—Pink Floyd's *Dark Side of the Moon*, released in 1973, remained in *Billboard*'s charts for 741 weeks. Along with a fabled live Bruce Springsteen recording, performed in Cleveland for broadcast on WMMS in 1978, the set manifests the ways in which seventies AOR could strike listeners as both progressive and populist—a realm of cross-class freedom rooted in temporal abundance and a sonic multiplicity always harkening back to the dominant texture of full-on rock. Springsteen gave lyrical expression to what AOR-ready songs, in what might be called their musical formatics, accomplished structurally.

The three earliest songs included in the *Radio & Records* list, from 1965, established the rock template. The Beatles' "Yesterday" showed that Top 40 youth could make adult music, with strings, though it took the subsequent "A Day in the Life," also listed, to position experimentalism at the core of the new form's vision of maturity. The Rolling Stones' "(I Can't Get No) Satisfaction" was pure rock and roll, save for a self-conscious lyric and performance that pushed against mass-media conventions. Above all, Bob Dylan's "Like a Rolling Stone" merged electric blues and folk bohemianism, shattering rules of song length and lyrical clarity to pile on a Whitmanesque cascade of pop art delinquency. Rock, as created in 1965, was British—63 percent of the list—and it claimed a lot of time: 72 percent of the forty-three songs exceed four minutes. *Radio & Records* gave these stats, yet ignored that only one woman sang lead—Stevie Nicks in Fleetwood Mac's "Rihannon"—and one black man: Jimi Hendrix, covering Dylan's "All Along the Watchtower."

Yet the magazine was not wrong to twice mention the "diversity" of this playlist in its introduction; rather, we need to recuperate how range and adventurousness generated in such a white male temple. Part is the balance between the split that Sanders identified as a challenge for rock radio to encompass: singer-songwriter folksiness and heavy metal thunder. These songs fed both impulses, often in the same number, like the three biggest AOR hits. Eric Clapton's band Derek and the Dominoes' "Layla" moved from frantic guitar to a serenely contemplative conclusion. Lynyrd Skynyrd's "Free Bird" worked opposite, the confessional minstrel sent flying by a multi-guitar southern rock opera. Most iconic, Led Zeppelin's "Stairway to Heaven" matched the industrial and folk images on the gatefold sleeve of the unnamed album it derived from, ascending from acoustic to electric to seal arena rock's fantastic self-conception.

The meeting of two guitar sounds, of mellow and heavy, was only part of the aesthetic range. Many songs, like Traffic's "Low Sparks of High Heeled Boys" and Van Morrison's scatted "Moondance," featured jazz. The Doobie Brothers ("Let the Music Play"), Jefferson Starship ("Miracles"), and especially Hall & Oates ("She's Gone") evoked soul sounds that AOR largely refused from black performers. Reggae syncopated Pink Floyd's "Money," while Led Zeppelin's "Kashmir" offered notes of the Orient. Aerosmith's cover of "Train Kept a Rollin'" looked back to rockabilly, while the Mississippi blues song "Loan Me a Dime" was covered by Boz Scaggs with slide guitar from Duane Allman, and Yes's prog-rock "Roundabout" layered in Baroque-era classical references. Pop artifice also had its day: Peter Frampton's "talk box" in "Do You Feel Like We Do," the early synthesizer used in the Who's "Won't Get Fooled Again." Virtually every AOR behemoth concealed a sleek Top 40 song within. As *Radio & Records* pointed out, 70 percent were ultimately singles, edited down after the longer version proved itself on rock radio.

Because AOR recurrents were long, combined into song suites ("Suite: Judy Blue Eyes"), offered in pairs (the opening tracks of *Sgt. Pepper's* and *Goodbye Yellow Brick Road*), or on their own approaching and exceeding ten minutes, they had time to veer stylistically and still arrive at a rock outcome, not unlike jazz solos returning to the head arrangement. In AOR, the genre experiments and pop components were a foil. Rock always won out—that was the dominant allegory in these anthems: triumph over the rest of music, past and present, over internal divides between subcategories of heavy metal, prog-rock, and singer-songwriter. In the same inclusive manner, where underground versus mainstream dichotomies haunted 1990s alternative rock, deviant AOR parables such as Jethro Tull's "Aqualung" or Supertramp's "School" didn't trouble who bankrolled or represented rebellion. Rock's impact on the uptight could be assumed.

It's easier, after spending almost five hours in the company of these forty-three classic rock recordings that Gorman would have called "power hitters," to understand why the class breakdown of AOR audiences was mostly an afterthought in 1978. The format led radio talk of psychographics by finding songs that formally positioned rock as a life path. Rock as formatted by FM radio invited listeners to remove constrictive reality and step into something larger. Radio stations mostly choose between programming that builds cume, the overall size of the audience, and programming that builds TSL, time spent listening. Rarely can a format audience swell to win a cume battle without diluting the passion that creates lengthy close listening. AOR, compressing commercials into three clusters an hour to permit long sets, upped TSL structurally—and built sizable cumes in the process—by offering what felt like the gift of extended time. Tracks had a catchy portion that could be extracted if Top 40 called, but that joined on AOR with an extended guitar or keyboard passage, or the repeated chorus that took the Beatles' "Hey Jude" from three and a half to a full seven minutes, or even, in the case of the Moody Blues' "Nights in White Satin," a poem. To listen in full, regularly, meant returning to a space of expansive leisure—cross-class psychographic affluence.

The artist who cemented the ritual, and WMMS and AOR's lifestyle claims, was Bruce Springsteen. "We couldn't have created a better artist to represent what WMMS stood for," Gorman writes. A superstar in the Lee Abrams sense, Springsteen also personified credibility as an innovator with strong ties to the rock and roll past. On the *Radio & Records* list, where he was called "a special cause for AOR since his debut," his earliest song was "Rosalita," an anthem of a working-class rocker winning his girl by getting a record-company contract, with notes of fifties doo-wop in the banter with his E Street bandmates. For Kid Leo, the protagonists in Springsteen songs resembled his own punch-clock persona: "You have given the greaser back his respect, and I thank you for it," he told Springsteen over the airwaves. Springsteen aligned rock allegiances for working- and middle-class listeners—"new," but not so much as punk; reverent of soul music, but framed as white; sparking a popular chord, but somehow, to use a word Gorman and Leo were fond of, "street." The DJ said, "'Born to Run' was the essence of everything I loved about rock 'n' roll. Bruce held on to the innocence and the romance. At the same time, the music communicates frustration and a constant longing to escape."[29]

Springsteen's concert at the thousand-seat Agora Theater in 1978, a celebration of WMMS's tenth anniversary, came to stand in as the classic WMMS moment. Denny Sanders began the radio broadcast by hailing other, all-midwestern stations carrying the show: WABX/Detroit; WDVE/Pittsburgh; WEBN/Cincinnati; WLVQ/Columbus; WXRT/Chicago; KSHE/St. Louis; KQRS/Minneapolis. Springsteen launched with the rockabilly employment anthem "Summertime Blues," then tore into originals largely from *Born to Run* and the new *Darkness on the Edge of Town*. "Badlands," about working guys off-clock looking to "spit in the face" of their daily fate, might have been a Murray Saul Get Down.

FIGURE 5.3 Bruce Springsteen in performance, 1978. Springsteen came to embody everything that AOR in the 1970s thought was best about itself: the ability to be populist and progressive, to be commercially successful across class lines, to make rock seem both work and play. © Lynn Goldsmith/Corbis. Used by permission.

Introducing "Factory," Springsteen recalled seeing his dad at night, sitting in the kitchen in the dark, smoking and drinking, then leaving at 6 a.m.: "He worked in a factory and his father did, I wrote this song for him." "Promised Land" used the still-germinating arena-rock power ballad—swelling keyboards, sax solo, midtempo pace, longing vocals—to yearn beyond "Working all day in my daddy's garage / Driving all night, chasing some mirage." "You want an autograph?" Springsteen said to a fan at one point. "I'm working here!"

For all the laboring grace notes, this was still at core a celebration of rock in the shape that AOR and Springsteen had defined. The music ranged aggressively across genres: harmonica and wordy verses nodding to folk and its singer-songwriter sequels, thick Clarence Clemons saxophone fills as partying R&B, Roy Bittan's keyboards gesturing toward art rock. But nearly every song started at, or built to, pounding full-band rock—"Racing in the Streets," the dispirited sequel to "Born to Run," was notable for withholding that release. Pre-counterculture rock and roll was celebrated: Springsteen explained "fraternity rock" as the joy of songs that were more about vomiting in your girlfriend's purse than anything terribly serious, then reworked Buddy Holly's "Not Fade Away" for Max Weinberg to thump its Bo Diddley beat and lead into Van Morrison's garage-rock perennial "Gloria." That nod to the past positioned Springsteen with punk, whose most shamanistic new artist, Patti Smith, also remade "Gloria." Springsteen and Smith had collaborated on another song he did at the Agora—"Because the Night." It could work on Top 40 but expand live to 7:30, epic like most of the Springsteen (and Smith) songbook—even the frat throwaways were patched into AOR-worthy suites. Springsteen's live banter was as mannered and showy as Kid Leo's, flirty masculine bravado relating the shaggy dog story of his "Growing Up" that ended with God telling the Boss "three words: let it rock!" Eddie Floyd's soul hit for Stax, "Raise Your Hand"—a part of rock too for Springsteen, though a minority presence, like his beloved Big Man on sax—ended the festivities, and Leo signed off the multi-station transmission: "Mid-America, good night."

Bruce Springsteen at the Agora in 1978 can certainly be heard on its own terms, and many like Cowie view him as a singular artist standing outside the contradictions of a splintering counterculture and worsening postindustrial economy. Yet for rock radio Springsteen was exactly the opposite: the distillation of a collective sensibility. Both WMMS and the Boss would have a larger audience in the 1980s. But these were recalled as the golden days: *Born to Run* and *Darkness on the Edge of Town* have regularly been voted by Springsteen fans their two favorite albums. In losing a "New Dylan" designation and recasting himself as a rocker with working affiliations and a strong sense of place, Springsteen subsumed divisions of class and education to concretize the AOR story.[30]

Most of his peers were not so explicit, and the reasonable charge is often made that AOR drained politics from rock just as the United States as a whole moved rightward. Can we hear in the soundtrack of the format a politics nonetheless, rooted in elongated time and collective catharsis? George Lipsitz, thinking about why R&B, honky-tonk country, and fifties rock and roll—all loud, masculine, apolitical working-class forms— emerged in a time of political retrenchment, suggests we learn to hear "blasted hopes and utopian aspirations" in "nonsense syllables and scat singing," because "if one defines politics as the social struggle for a good life, then these songs represent politics of the highest order." Lawrence Grossberg adds another key idea: rock, he argues, supplied "affective alliances": a means to create "resistance for generations with no faith in revolution," rooted in fun, distinctiveness in relationship to pop, and a generational politics of distended youth. Even as rock fragmented, artists

like Springsteen, in Grossberg's opinion, "make the two registers of rock
and roll's diversity [a singer-songwriter consciousness and a hard rock
reinvestment in the body] . . . parallel." AOR as a whole, and the music it
favored, often crafted explicitly for such airplay, achieved the same sym-
metry. The politics were in the formatics.[31]

From Mass Back to Class: AOR Meets the Yuppie

In 1983, ten years into his run as WMMS program director, John Gorman
made a big decision, announced in a memo to Kid Leo, still afternoon
DJ and now also music director. "We are playing black music," Gorman
wrote.[32] By 1985, WMMS was officially not an AOR station. It reported
to *Radio & Records* as a contemporary hit radio (CHR), the name for
Top 40 channels on FM. But where did that leave those who identified
with the wrathful Buzzard? The sound of WMMS in 1972 was David
Bowie, and in 1978 Bruce Springsteen. Could the sound of WMMS by
1984 be Michael Jackson? The story of WMMS and AOR in the decade
following its triumphant first ten years reflected many such unlikely
choices, as the unities sustaining AOR broke down. Some in rock radio
experimented with new wave and Top 40, others classic rock; all felt pressure to reach older and more affluent listeners.

The collective value of particular format demos was always murky in
radio, exacerbated by differences between that industry and the record
business. Arbitron ratings gave explicit numeration only to age (12+,
18+, 12–24, 18–24, 18–34, 25–34, 25–54, etc.) and gender, not income.
"Qualitative" data from Simmons, Scarborough, and Arbitron's own
Qualidata were available, but as competing ratings company Birch's CEO,
Tom Birch, complained, "After all these years, most agency buyers are still
buying on the basis of age and sex!"[33] Those buyers, all agreed, preferred
well-to-do 25- to 54-year-old listeners, making older listeners to AC a cash
cow for station owners but of less use to labels. Record companies recognized younger, not particularly affluent fans as a core market, so CHR
was the gold standard for record selling, receiving the most promotional
label support and mass-appeal ads for its cross-generational listenership.
Early AOR created an alternate new-music route, and garnered significant record ads and promo spending, but as boomers aged and lucrative
AC-type ads became winnable, there was pressure to be "classic rock":
AOR for older men. Blue-collar rock populism faced potent competing

format/audience paradigms in the 1980s, as its original audience aged, replaced by a shrinking post-boomer demographic.

WMMS and AOR's high-water moment had come at a low point for working-class politics and cultural status. Cowie sees 1978 as "Waterloo for unions, regulators, Keynesian tax reformers." Efforts like the Humphrey-Hawkins full employment bill failed amidst a politics of resentment, a resurgent business lobby, the anti-tax Proposition 13 in California, a new Moral Majority, and outflows of jobs and people from industrial cities like Cleveland. In this climate, the AOR audience, Gorman's Buzzard Nuclear Army, now came off like losers; the World Series of Rock audience remade as Kiss fans, at the invocation of Chicago AOR announcer Steve Dahl, blowing up disco records at a 1979 White Sox game. Lee Abrams, the most influential programmer in AOR, instilled a "modal" rock radio with no room for acoustic types or other non-rock genre luxuries, writing later, "Never again was Carly Simon, James Taylor, or Carol King heard on AOR. It was now Heart, Journey, Foreigner, and Ted Nugent. Stations burned disco records on the air and adapted 'street' logos and attitudes." After not only disco but punk and new wave, one-time progressive rock sounds now seemed reactionary. *Creem*, Cowie remarks, made the class disparagement explicit, setting the blazingly ironic Ramones against "ponderous middle-aged labor unions like Zep, Bad Co. and Foghat." Springsteen's class protagonists, by the halting 1982 album *Nebraska,* seemed less psychographic than psychopathic.[34]

Gorman encouraged the air staff to retain an everyman address. "The other day I heard the unemployed referred to as 'bums' on our air. Wanna lose your audience? That's the way to do it. Right now, everyone feels (and rightly so) they're getting ripped-off-blind by big oil and big business. Talk up that point. Talk up how expensive everything has become. Take the side of the vast majority getting screwed over. It costs a small fortune just to gas up a car for an afternoon of cruisin'. Our prime demo is smack-dab in the middle of getting screwed-over by big biz." He wrote on another occasion, "With the collapse of the American Automobile Industry, which directly affects other industries such as steel, glass, auto parts, etc. combined with runaway inflation, high interest rates, and the return of The Cold War . . . the so-called post-war American dream is dead. The people most affected by these changes are our audience. . . . Read the papers, read Time and Newsweek. Relate to the current mood of the country. Don't editorialize, but don't hesitate to make mention in the on-air raps about current events." Ronald Reagan won forty-four states in

1980, including Ohio. Gorman editorialized, "Expect 'witch hunts' along the lines of Senator Joe McCarthy's in the early '50s. Welcome to 1953! Strom Thurmond? Alexander Haig? The Moral Majority? Shit . . . it's gonna be a rough four years!"[35]

Yet the program director was far less sure how to respond to new radio realities. Instead of a tightly formatted AOR station like M105, the main competitor was now WGCL, a CHR, which meant repositioning WMMS as less traditionally AOR, not more so. BLF Bash, an overnight DJ, was cautioned not to play Rush's "Working Man," the song that helped center the station's sound years previously: "too long drum solo," Gorman wrote. The sales crew remained far less populist than the air staff, using a new slogan, "WMMS Means Business." Tiburski said, "Our audience means a lot of disposable income. These are the people who are setting up bank accounts, and buying big-ticket items like cars and furniture. Today, banks and supermarkets share a big piece of commercial time with record stores and jean shops."[36]

For Gorman, playing black music meant WMMS could compete with hits on WGCL. He continued in his memo to Leo, "We are being attacked from the left. We, therefore, build-up our left. . . . We're getting a little risky, but not enough to alienate the mainstream." If earlier Gorman tightened playlists in response to "the right," superstars AOR, he would now loosen format restrictions. He also engaged artier, less guitar-driven rock, telling staff, "The New Wave influence is starting to make inroads to the mainstream." Tiburski was informed, "The 'heavy metal' fringe is actively writing letters, accusing WMMS of 'selling out' to Blacks and 'New Wavers.' We expected this response." By summer 1983, Gorman claimed, "We are successfully defusing WMMS' image as a 'hard rock' and/or 'A.O.R.'"[37]

Gorman's memoir defends this substantial redefinition in terms of WMMS's tradition of breaking new music and openness to at least some black artists. Rock definitionally excluded the black performers central to an earlier era's rock and roll. Elijah Wald tracks a separation that caused original rock critic Paul Williams to declare, even as James Brown revolutionized funk, "One of the curious things about the year 1966 is that for the first time in the history of America, the best contemporary music is not being made by the American Negro," and Michael Lydon to argue with Smokey Robinson in a 1968 *Rolling Stone* about the artistic legitimacy of editing down a classic Motown groove for Top 40 needs. A decade later, Alice Echols writes, "the color line in popular music had reemerged and felt nearly as solid as the days before Chuck Berry and Little Richard broke through it." Artistry was irrelevant: "AOR listeners," Echols bemoans, "would never know that black rock was not an oxymoron, that Nona Hendryx and Parliament-Funkadelic rocked with the best of them." Yet core WMMS listeners certainly knew P-Funk: if Springsteen at 6 p.m. Fridays was one ritual, another was BLF Bash's weekly airing of "Maggot Brain" at 1 a.m. on Saturday night. The Isley Brothers, long victims of AOR, were photographed at a 1975 Buzzard visit: Gorman reflects, "Few rock stations played their music, but at WMMS their songs were among the most requested. This was the first time the Isleys visited a rock format station." Gorman and Leo wrote *Radio & Records* congratulating a label executive who had protested stations that made excuses for not playing black music and asked, "Don't you want black listeners?"[38]

Nonetheless, Gorman was equally dismissive of black listeners in a memo speculating on the success of his CHR competitor: "We don't have demo breakouts. WGCL could very well be all teens and blacks." Gaye Ramstrom, sales manager for the station at the time, agrees that women and older listeners, not African Americans, were the key targets of the new format modifications: "With Top 40 you were assuming that the moms and dads were listening along with the kids. . . . We were trying to go for the earlier baby boomers, to boost up our 25–49 numbers of the 25 to 54. We could own that demo which at the time had the most avails, the most ups for advertisers. They wanted people with money in their pockets who had jobs. Eighteen to 24 was kind of suspect, dirtbags, blue collar image, even though it may not have been true." Going after more women meant "getting on some female buys, the adults. Fashion Bug, the Casual Corner, more department stores like the May Company, Higbee's, Hallee's."[39]

Working-class male listeners were less valuable. Gorman reported to management, "Negative reaction toward our airplay of black and CHR product has been very small, coming from the 'earthdog'-types only. We are noticing an increase in female calls." *Earthdog* as a term referred to guys who might have proudly carried a Wrath of the Buzzard emblem on their chests or car. Morning host Jeff Kinzbach was advised, "We are working at building our 25+ audience. They are turned off by juvenile, dumb, or stoned-out callers. Get a higher class of listener on-the-air." To *Radio & Records*, Gorman complained, "AOR is no longer a salable format. The big-buck ad agencies are going to A/C and CHR." He explained in 1985 to an industry tip sheet, "Let's face it, some agencies immediately close the door when they hear you're AOR. That wasn't true 7 or 8 years ago when AOR was coming into its own. Unfortunately we have to look at the direction that some of the consultants took us in the mid 70s. The change to a much more hard rock/modal approach did provide short term gains in terms of 12+ numbers, but in the long run, it appears to have done major damage to our overall regard on a business level. . . . Banging away with nothing but Led Zep, Foreigner, and any band that sounded like them, did indeed pull teens and 18–24 males and jack the 12+ numbers through the roof. But what do you do for an encore?" Asked whether the switch in sound would secure "more national ad bucks," Gorman responded, "I'm certain it will."[40]

In 1984, WMMS spent some $250,000 and all of its promotional energy to guarantee that, with the Buzzard sponsoring, Cleveland would host a night of the Jacksons Victory Tour. The goal was not to target the city's 40 percent African American urban population; Cleveland councilman Jeffrey Johnson complained publicly about black-oriented radio's exclusion. Rather, WMMS hoped to put to rest its confrontational "Wrath of the Buzzard" image once and for all. Gorman contemplated pulling the Buzzard logo altogether. "Instead," a local business publication explained, "the Buzzard was given a makeover to match the new look of the station. The ominous-looking bird that was anti-everything in 1974 now sports a new haircut, better clothes, a nice car and other expensive accessories." The station now truly was a hybrid. A *Radio & Records* columnist, studying the new format variant, concluded, "Its jocks, while lively and energetic, aren't as frenetic as many CHRs'. They show a musical knowledge and project a street-smart attitude more commonly found at AOR. While 'MMS uses a touch of reverb and fabulously produced IDs, it doesn't employ a jingle package, as most CHRs do." Playing 80 percent current music, station revenues in 1985 soared to $6 million, atop the market, though only somewhat more than lower-rated AC stations WLTF ($5.4 million) and WMJI ($5 million).[41]

WMMS was hardly the only AOR station in the early 1980s questioning its identity. *Radio & Records* asked in 1983, "Modern Rock and AOR, Will They Mix?" The Los Angeles channel KROQ, which played new wave with Top 40 repetitiveness, and the now-powerful national channel MTV, making CHR hits for new wave like Duran Duran (and then learning to play black hits as well), showed it could work. Abrams himself called music from 1969 "dinosaur rock . . . the music has changed, and so must we," ordering most of the AOR stations his firm consulted to play 70–80 percent current music. John Sebastian, another consultant, cautioned against provoking another disco-style backlash, however: "My company's existing clients are slaughtering the competition where those stations have taken this kneejerk reaction to modern music." PD Oedipus of Boston's WBCN was on Gorman's side, vowing "If AOR wants to expand on its 18–24 male base, it's got to take chances and play songs that don't have guitar breaks in the middle." Charlie Kendall, PD of WMMR / Philadelphia, declared, "I think AOR radio has ignored black music long enough. . . . Some hip black artists are now making songs that are not just targeted to black audiences—they're just good songs." Even Greg Solk of WLUP/Chicago, the original disco demolisher, had second thoughts: "We have an anti-dance music image, thanks to Steve Dahl's stay here, and we're trying to turn that image around. But it's a slow process." On the opposite side, WNEW's Scott Muni believed that "each day that passes, our consistency earns us more respect from the audience." Beau Phillips in Seattle worried, "The worst thing you can do is water down your station's image, and risk blowing your station's core." And Chuck DuCoty in Baltimore was sure that "part of the magic of an AOR station is what you *don't* hear. An exclusive cume listener to our station isn't looking to hear Ray Parker Jr., the Jacksons, or Prince."[42]

As Gorman summed up the moment, "Once upon a time, about a decade and a half ago, AOR radio served as the 'fresh air' format to a rock 'n' roll audience tired of Top 40's same rotated 30–40 currents and 200–300 oldies. Today, CHR serves as the 'fresh air' to listeners tired of AOR's same rotated 30–40 currents and 200–300 oldies." Once again, rock fans didn't like each other's record collections. More specifically, and as King Biscuit Flower Hour broadcasters Robert Meyrowitz and Peter Kauff wrote, the issue "wasn't conservative playlists. It was fragmenting audiences." The true culprit was "white males mostly, under 25, who don't want a broad spectrum of music, who still want a radio format that plays Quiet Riot and Black Sabbath." Rock radio, regardless of how programmers came down in the playlist debates, fought what Gorman called "the notion that the AOR listener is a long-haired kid wearing a torn Def Leppard shirt—the kind of person you wouldn't want in your store." In Chicago, which had three rock radio stations, two based on 12–24 appeal, all chased the 25+ market by mid-1985.[43]

If change was requisite, a new rock radio was problematic to define in the marketplace. Gorman sent Sales his complicated formula: "Definition of WMMS: WMMS is a hit-oriented rock station playing contemporary hits, mass-appeal album tracks and highly selected 'oldies.' Target: 18–34 adults. Originally an AOR station, WMMS is now considered a 'hybrid' of CHR, AOR, and A/C." But strong concerns clearly persisted: a later memo protested, "Why can't WMMS be sold on its excellence, its reputation, its 31 straight #1 Arbitrons in 18–34 Adults or the 4 straight (one year's worth) double digit #1 12+ domination in the Cleveland Metro? How about selling WMMS as Cleveland's radio station? Gaye, you've been given dream numbers to sell—continuously—book after book after book. I cannot even begin to comprehend the 'panic' running rampant at your end of the hill."[44]

WMMS had risked its rock identity—but without fully embracing a Top 40 identity. New York's Z100, a hugely successful CHR station owned in common with WMMS by the still Cleveland-based Malrite Communications, used the sales slogan "Z-100 Is Mass Appeal Radio!" and offered advertisers an "ethnic audience composition" of 63 percent white, 20 percent black, and 17 percent Hispanic, closely mirroring the citywide population. (New York's leading rock station, WNEW-FM, by contrast, was 91 percent white, 9 percent black, with no claimed Hispanic listeners, while urban contemporary leader WBLS reported a 16 percent white, 71 percent black, 13 percent Hispanic audience.) WMMS was marketed as "reaching more well educated, affluent, upscale adults than any other radio station in the market," with Red Carpet Airport Car Care claiming those who could afford the service preferred WMMS to its AC rivals. Tiburski said the station relied on "careful dayparting" and "John Gorman's intuitive ability to be able to play to both ends of the AOR audience spectrum."[45]

The shift from AOR to CHR was an undeniable ratings success, WMMS winning a 14.5 share by 1986, but many in Cleveland felt betrayed. Morning DJ Kinzbach, reliant on listener calls, remembered broadcasting "Billie Jean" the first time. "You should've seen the phones light up after that song played. After all, that was *their* radio station, *their* music. And suddenly it wasn't just theirs anymore. What it did was bring in a whole new group of listeners." Dan Garfinkel, whose promotions made the Buzzard ubiquitous, said, "A lot of people felt, well, how could they add Michael Jackson? That wasn't rock and roll." A letter writer to *Scene* complained later, "WMMS ceased being a 'Rock Station' five years ago, yet has continued to pass itself off as an innovative, trend-setting radio programmer." Another echoed in revealingly stereotypical language: "One has to feel kind of sorry for Jeff, . . . Flash, Kid Leo, et al., aging has-beens reduced to playing Michael Jackson and Whitney Houston for housewives and teenyboppers, trying desperately to buy back their once glorious past." The new WMMS confused listeners, advertisers, and even some on staff.[46]

Was it politically progressive, given rock's legacy of racism and sexism, or regressive, given the anti-working-class sales goals, for WMMS to play Michael Jackson? The results could not be untangled. Gorman told staffers in 1985, "The WMMS of today is different than the WMMS of '82, '83 or, for that matter, 12 months ago. Our audience today is more balanced by sex, age, income, and region than in the past." Gorman went on, "In specific, we are no longer male dominant." The Buzzard would have to rethink its address, the programmer elaborated: "You're talking to, and play music for, both sexes and a wider demo of both sexes. Besides getting your message across in the fewest amount of words, you must make every attempt to avoid sexist remarks." Yet Gorman also had a much less inclusive rationale: "Another way to put it: upscale and Yuppie." Chasing the "elite" listeners he once mocked, Gorman and WMMS had come full circle: when new promotions head Jim Marchyshyn requested a Mercedes giveaway, specifying, "We are aiming to have 'Yuppy' [sic] prizes and this is the key," he echoed Bass's fantasy of progressive radio earning Cadillac-type sponsors. Rock radio had become yuppie obsessed. GM Tom Connolly of WKLS/Atlanta said, "With the format's metamorphosis, a lot of upscale advertisers are realizing that we now appeal to 'yuppies'—the guys that are 25–35 years old with nice cars, good jobs, and some income to spend." WMMR GM Michael Craven bragged, "We've gotten stock brokerage firms, exotic car companies, most of the major airlines, and two major real estate companies."[47]

In truth, as Gerry Boehme, vice president of radio research for Katz, finally pointed out in 1987, "If you look at the figures on how many yuppies there actually are, compared to the amount of attention everybody spends trying to get them, it seems like a case of overkill." At WMMS, the "Morning Zoo," which had the station's largest listenership (typical for radio but newer in the 1980s for the first late-night, then afternoon-oriented FM rock format), was anything but managerial. Kinzbach, the host since 1978 alongside sarcastic news reporter Ed "Flash" Ferenc, oversaw a cast that included Kenny Clean, the station janitor before he was put on the airwaves, whose signature phrase "sho' yo' rite" evoked minstrel dialect comedy, and a woman named Ruby Cheeks who supplied feminist banter. There were Token Jokes, initially a play on pot tokin' but now focused on a "certain ethnic group" (Cleveland lingo for Polish). Other bits targeted punch-clock listeners: in Go Back to Bed, a boss was asked if the winner might just stay home. For many averse to Top 40, Kinzbach and crew's modulated rudeness now defined WMMS.[48]

Had the morning team picked music themselves, it likely would have resembled the trend that succeeded on rock radio where new wave and CHR encroachment failed: classic rock. Consultant Fred Jacobs's innovation, overtly aimed at an older demographic now viable as some boomers approached forty, took hold by 1986 and proved enduring: nearly five hundred such stations broadcast today. The synchronicity with reissues of older material on compact disc lent currency to the approach, but it was also consistent with new wave– and CHR-leaning predecessors: radio, said St. Louis programmer Bob Hattrick, was "no longer attempting to address that mythical AOR core audience of rock dogs." Heavy metal was not the only contemporary rock shut down. Kevin Sutter, Chrysalis national director of album promotion, complained, "The funnel for new music is being squeezed tighter and tighter every day." New York's classic rock WXRK battled venerable WNEW, helped by one element of the new: shock DJ Howard Stern, who ruled mornings. In Cleveland, the emergent classic rock station, WNCX, put local heartland rocker Michael Stanley on afternoons in 1990; he has remained ever since.

WMMS fell apart under the strain of its identity conflicts by the late 1980s. Gorman and Sanders departed in 1986, resenting Malrite meddling in programming and seeking greater financial rewards, though they never created their desired rock-hybrid station and wound up primarily employed at AC channel WMJI. Stanley's classic-rock installment placed him in the afternoon slot abdicated by Kid Leo in 1988 when he left WMMS for Columbia Records. The revelation in 1987, after WMMS was voted Best Radio Station for the ninth year running in a *Rolling Stone* poll, that the Buzzard had stuffed the ballot box, also affected Cleveland's pride. Tiburski, now working for a competitor, said listeners no longer saw the station as "anti-establishment underdogs." WMMS's final gift to Cleveland might have been the Rock and Roll Hall of Fame and Museum, as Gorman, Leo, and Sanders organized the Buzzard Army in a 1986 campaign that outshouted all other locales. Was rock in Cleveland now essentially a shrine? As the 1980s ended, WMMS again reported as an AOR targeting 18 to 34. *Friday Morning Quarterback Album Report*'s Paul Heine argued, "Stations are focusing on smaller audience segments and finding success through that, and WMMS really needed to pick a niche and serve it." With ratings down in the summer book, operations manager Rich Piombino knew "I have something to prove here." PD Chuck Bortnick said they wouldn't play "Madonna and artists of her genre any more."[49]

WMMS's retrenchment was duplicated throughout AOR. Lee Abrams had given up consulting the format, telling *Radio & Records*, "I've been bored with the existing state of AOR," but his late 1970s conservative approach prevailed: "'Modal' radio is back with a vengeance," the trade's rock radio columnist declared. Pierre Bouvard, from research firm Coleman, explained, "Every PD has a 'sound' that defines his/her station. That sound is comprised of a group of songs that represent the 'narrowest' definition of the station." Increasingly, that core sound was vintage: the average AOR in 1990 played 26 percent currents and 7 percent recent material, the rest drawn from the past. If, in the seventies, AOR offered a "diversity" of sound that allegorically affirmed rock's conquest, eighties AOR built what scope it still possessed on filtering the present to attest the primacy of rock's golden age. The category's leading acts for the decade according to *Radio & Records*, figures such as U2 and John Mellencamp, joined by one woman (Pat Benatar) and veterans Springsteen, the Rolling Stones, Eric Clapton, Tom Petty, and Rush, evoked heartland seventies rock more than punk or new wave. Only one, Van Halen, was heavy metal, the decade's most popular rock genre but too "earthdog" for AOR.[50]

Even Bruce Springsteen reflected the category confusion. The single "Dancing in the Dark," with accompanying video of a buffed Boss dancing with a young Courtney Cox, launched *Born in the U.S.A.* in 1984 and let him rival Jackson, Prince, and Madonna within pop's new blockbuster economy. *USA Today* quoted Gorman approving "the most commercial sounding" song Springsteen had done: "it sounds like he's looking for a hit record." But by the end of the 1980s, Springsteen, alienated by his pop omnipresence, dissolved the E Street Band. Rock seemingly did not know how to win. Larry Bruce, PD of a station in South Dakota, japed, "We spend so much time mentally masturbating over the music mix—should we play Madonna, modern, or metal." The format that led 1970s radio limped, however profitably, through the 1980s, unsure which sound should govern the others.[51]

The Next Generation: WMMS and Alternative Rock

Nirvana, grunge, and alternative rock broke in the 1990s on my watch: at the *Village Voice* and *Spin* the children of college radio rather than AOR radio focused on artists and scenes, wondering as indie rock became mainstream whether to celebrate or worry. As Pearl Jam was replaced by Korn, most leaned toward answer two. The anthemic Radiohead of *OK Computer* became the enigmatic Radiohead of *Kid A*. *Spin*, an alternative *Rolling Stone*, became *Pitchfork*, unworried about its indie niche. Later scholarship challenges alternative-era assumptions: problematizing rock's oppositionality helps explain why punk shrine CBGB merited replacement by a John Varvatos boutique in neobohemian New York.[52] Back issues of *Radio & Records* offer an equally revisionist perspective. In these pages, alternative is not about mainstreams and undergrounds so much as how different commercial categories bullied each other. Was alternative the natural province of a small but growing number of stations that played it exclusively? Of longtime rock stations ready to play new bands again? What did it mean if the Gin Blossoms were hot AC? Rock radio satisfied niches—but failed to craft an umbrella format that could sustain the genre.

When Nirvana's *Nevermind* became a surprise number 1 album at the beginning of 1992, longtime AOR stations were still suffering an identity crisis. Howard Stern was now syndicated in half the ten biggest morning markets, usually on classic rock stations that challenged "heritage" broadcasters. Stern could pitch himself at earthdog listeners due to what he called "an active and aggressive audience": his TSL was high, and his endorsement of products such as Snapple had instant results. As album rock toned down for 25–44 appeal, Stern wired himself up. The traditional Top 40/CHR answer to having a less than desirable demo for advertisers was to build cume: generate a big audience of multiple categories. But this no longer tempted many AORs, as Top 40 appeared in desperate straits: the number of CHR stations plunged from 951 in 1989 to just 318 in 1996 as programmers lost faith in their ability to mix hard rock, hip-hop, and power ballads. Finally, "new rock" or "modern rock" stations stressed their upscale base, just as progressive stations once had. Minneapolis PD Tony Powers claimed his listeners "have money and are, in general, more educated than the average radio listener." Larry Nielson, PD of KDGE (The Edge) in Dallas, called his listeners as being "into high-tech stereos, cars, computers, and the cutting edge of 1991." Still, this was a cume sliver. Programmer Max Tolkoff admitted, "There are basically a handful of commercial New Rock stations around the country. It's unfortunate, but most of the music that's happening today appears only on those stations."[53]

Grunge, as it broke big, became hugely attractive to AOR: culturally important and distinct from classic rock, Top 40, or synth-driven new rock. Brew Michaels, a Seattle PD, reported, "We don't really view 'Smells Like

Teen Spirit' or 'Alive' as alternative songs." Ted Utz, a consultant, said, "For the first time in over two decades, there's new music that has really captured the imagination of a generation." WMMS PD Chuck Bortnick talked about "all of the heritage stations" that had had "a real morale problem" but now could again declare, "We're a rock station—let's just be that." By the end of 1992, *Radio & Records* called Nirvana and Pearl Jam AOR "stalwarts," and the format was playing more new music than it had in years.[54]

The first onset of corporate consolidation also helped embolden rock radio. Local marketing agreements (LMAs) allowed two stations, a "duopoly," to market together to advertisers, offering combined demographic coverage. New Orleans operations manager Brian Thomas said, "This LMA allows CHR to be more of what it's designed to be—a 12–34 female format—while the AC or duopoly sister takes care of the upper-end demos." Thomas noted that such deals "will actually help foster and develop some specialized formats, like New Rock . . . which couldn't survive as stand-alones." Flipping to alternative was now compelling. KROQ in Los Angeles was format leader, with PD Kevin Weatherly applying Top 40 rotations to Beck and his peers. The station reached top 5 overall cume and number 1 English for 18–34. By the end of 1993, national listenership to alternative rock overall was up 59 percent for the year, 120 percent from the summer of 1991, and 176 percent from the summer of 1990. *Radio & Records* declared, "The format has arrived." Jeff Pollack stated consensus wisdom by the mid-1990s: "You'll find strategic duopolies . . . allowing Alternative programmers to remain pure to their core's interests. . . . Gone is the obsession with trying to be all things to all people."[55]

With Gorman returning as program director, WMMS flipped to alternative in 1994, using the *Star Trek* slogan "WMMS: The Next Generation" and switching from 20 percent current music to 70 percent. Being in a duopoly helped, Gorman said: "WMJI has been dominant 25–54 since 1991 and we didn't want to cannibalize our sister station. We wanted to build a strong 18–34 station." If alternative wasn't *that* alternative, as many charged, what was being resurrected was not only vintage rock sounds but progressive and early AOR rock radio ideals. The new WMMS was overtly modeled on KROQ, offering a Buzzardpalooza promotion and a Green Day show for eighteen thousand; but then KROQ was in the path of the 1970s WMMS, which featured mostly new music, big concerts, and an amped, close to Top 40 DJ style, too. Old dilemmas of blue collar and collegiate, hard rock and too hard rock did assert themselves.

To avoid one pitfall, Gorman says, he never used the word *alternative* on the air in branding the station. Still, that was his impulse, as he told the staff: "The majority of our audience is new, younger, and better educated than the (many) formats the previous owners of this station had." The "Next Generation" Buzzard published *Buzzard Bone*, an alternative magazine that gave short shrift to 1960s to 1970s "dinosaur rock," but also to hard rock groups such as Metallica. While many cheered, Dave Lombardi, Warner Bros. national promotions director, complained about WMMS going alternative: "They think that name makes them more competitive—especially for concert 'presents'—and gives them more record company attention. I don't agree. . . . We need stations like that in Rock. . . . It's disappointing because most of the music is mainstream rock. Candlebox used to be alternative, but Alternative didn't want to play them until they got too big to ignore." Lombardi thought rock needed to grow, not subdivide.[56]

Class bias permeated the shift to alternative. Frank Copsidas, a PD in Augusta, Georgia, said, "This format attracts real hip, cutting edge high school kids, college students, and people in their 20s, 30s, and 40s. . . . If you've been in college within the last 15 years, you're familiar with some of this music." Even in a period of niche formats, could elites from the less attractive and demographically smaller 18–34 set be enough? New York programmer Tom Calderone wasn't convinced: "A cumer would feel uncomfortable listening to the 'Alternative' station. . . . Rock is a universal term that feels comfortable." Success brought its own dilemmas. Boston PD Kurt St. Thomas reflected, "There's almost something really wrong with Green Day selling as many records as they are. Punk bands aren't supposed to be big. Anytime something gets too big, it's very vulnerable to being torn down." Media buyer Harvey Rabinowitz noted, "Its ironic conflict is that it wasn't designed for, nor should it try to sell itself to, the masses. That defeats its 'hip' cachet, its cutting edge position."[57]

Notably, nothing about grunge and alternative radio stopped the ongoing rise of Howard Stern, whose syndicated morning show appealed to exactly the white male demographic, blurred between working-class and collegiate, that AOR had pioneered. Stern, with his Gay Dial-a-Date and Butt Bongo provocations, his stripper obsession, his persona Fartman, exhumed all that AOR's emphasis away from earthdog listeners and heavy metal had purged. Where Jeff Kinzbach had "Spousal Arousal," Stern turned sexuality into a wrestling match of the male id. After Stern triumphed in a new market, he'd appear to publicly stage a "funeral" for

FIGURE 5.4 Morning-radio host Howard Stern beheads the WMMS mascot, the Buzzard, during a "funeral" for his Cleveland competition, 1994. Stern's shock-jock provocations appealed
to the same cross-class male listenership that in an earlier era had supported rock that presented itself as blue-collar. Still from *Radio Daze: Cleveland's FM Air Wars* (DVD, Harvard
131 Films, 2008).

his competition. Stern began syndication in Cleveland in 1992. Kinzbach
was forbidden to respond to Stern's jabs and provocations. "By the time
Howard Stern arrived we had already been hogtied and horsewhipped
by our own people," he has said. Kinzbach's show was pulled in 1994, the
final piece of WMMS's longtime daily lineup. Stern shortly after became
number 1 in the Cleveland marketplace and readied his funeral ceremony,
complete with topless women, appearances by tabloid celebrity Joey
Buttafuoco and former Van Halen singer David Lee Roth, and an estimated crowd of ten to twenty thousand. Nodding to earlier radio wars,
the Buzzard struck back. A WMMS engineer cut the cable during the
funeral broadcast. But the incident only redounded onto Stern, who said,
"As you notice, I am dressed as a general. And that is because it is D-Day
here. It is war. I am in the middle of war. I am in my bunker right now."
It was another echo of WMMS, where the internal slogan had long been
"We don't go to work, we go to war."[58]

Consultant Tom Barnes astutely predicted, in the early 1990s, "Hard Rock and Alternative will become—for all intents and purposes—the same successful format for the male demo." By the latter 1990s this new reality had asserted itself. The "active rock" subformat played new bands without pretending cultural forwardness. Stations that couldn't get Stern got Mancow Muller, who said, "It's a show that talks to the regular guy who's not being served by other radio shows. . . . There's a lower class that's getting lower, and a middle class that's disappeared, and nobody's speaking to them." Yet it proved as difficult to extricate class sympathy from gender and race belligerence as earlier to separate an allergy to earthdogs from anti-sexism. Greaseman, who had 2.5 million listeners daily via Infinity Broadcasting Syndication, fouled the planet and ended his career when, in the wake of James Byrd's murder in 1998, and after playing rapper-singer Lauryn Hill, he actually said, "No wonder people drag them behind trucks." Once again, said saleswoman Lisa Amador, the "image of the Rock listener is of someone who drives a truck, is either a grungy contractor or unemployed with no money to spend."[59]

Women still heard rock, but in non-rock crossover formats. Back in 1993, Lauren MacLeash, a PD in Norfolk, had hoped, "Alternative is becoming more mainstream. You can hear Soul Asylum on just about every format." Her wishes came true if you sub Gin Blossoms for Soul Asylum. With Top 40 struggling, music by Alanis Morissette and Green Day replaced hip-hop and R&B, prompting talk at *Radio & Records* of a new category: pop/alternative. Most Top 40 by the late 1990s returned to beats: Tom Poleman, the new PD of Z100, said, "Alternative wasn't as hot as we thought it was." But alternative remained a strand, part of what Poleman called "balance. . . . We don't want to overdose on one particular style." And hot AC, aimed at women just older than CHR, kept fervency: *Radio & Records* noted how "artists such as Melissa Etheridge, Natalie Merchant, and the Gin Blossoms supplant '80s artists such as Phil Collins and Elton John at the top of their music tests."[60]

Hot AC flourished, active ate up new rock, and radio lost faith in alternative. New Orleans PD Vince Richards reflected, "The early '90s was a result of a generation having its needs overlooked by Classic Rock–based radio. Everyone signed everything in sight, expecting it to gain acceptance under the Alternative banner. . . . It's evident we don't know how to pace ourselves, so forced corrections are taking place." WMMS fired Gorman and ended three years of alternative, with new PD Bob Neumann saying, "I'm glad to be out of the self-indulgent, whiny Alternative world." The new WMMS "positioning liner," "The Real Buzzard is Back," was meant to "highlight the return of such Rock staples as Ozzy Osbourne, AC/DC and Aerosmith." Chicago programmer Dave Richards argued that rock was core based. "Not to pick on one artist, but some people loved Hootie & The Blowfish a few years ago; these people don't necessarily love Hootie & The Blowfish anymore. At the same time, there were a lot of people who loved Led Zeppelin and Metallica years ago; they still love Led Zeppelin and Metallica."[61]

Against the rest, KROQ continued to win—Kevin Weatherly said he resisted "the elitism that can exist in this format," kept the high rotations on his biggest songs, and made key delineations: "Nine Inch Nails is vital to KROQ's core and Prodigy has the potential to do so. An act like Jewel gives the station greater cume potential. The core audience may not have the same passion for acts like her, but these artists have broader appeal. You have to find the balance, a representative center." Outside Los Angeles, that balance seemed hard to strike. WPLY/Philadelphia PD Jim McGuinn said, "Alternative stations used to have so much more space that had more room for error and experimentation. You could think more long term when it came to the music. Now, there's so much more taking place: the consolidation at radio, Pop/Alternative and Active Rock playing alternative music, and Alternative stations becoming addicted to ratings."[62]

By the end of the 1990s, alternative-oriented music had two widely divergent options. Groups like the Goo Goo Dolls or Maroon 5 pursued hot AC success and stopped worrying about credibility. Angela Perelli of KYSR, whose young DJ Ryan Seacrest was soon to host *American Idol*, said, "This station works for 30-year-old women because it makes them feel hip. But cutting-edge stations are hip; we're pseudo-hip. . . . We don't have a bunch of people calling and questioning why we're playing these artists." The other choice was what *Radio & Records* called "conservative hard-rock stations," playing oldies mixed with new bands in the vein of Metallica. A study of rock radio found alternative stations imposing a "virtual embargo of female pop/alternative artists." A subdivided rock had no chance of producing a new Nirvana: earthdog rapper Eminem broke on MTV, not radio. The biggest sellers, like Creed or Nickelback, hit both active and hot AC rock categories, but minus any aura of what AOR had offered: progressive music. John Wozniak of Marcy Playground said of alternative radio, "It's a dying format. I'm sorry to say that, because I love it, but it's definitely on the way out." Some pushed to steer alternative toward adults, with triple A as male-driven but affluent and older. Here, purchasing data that aligned formats to consumers, where 100 was average and 200 a clear preference, found microbrews getting a score of 282.[63]

Looking at the grunge and alternative era from radio's perspective, a story about indie versus major labels, creativity versus commerce, becomes something else: a case study in the construction not of art but of audiences for that art. Radio could drive a song or sound into the permanent memory bank of listeners. It could turn new rock into the long-awaited continuation of old rock, or make alternative into a form of Top 40, or offer a female audience a place to rock out, or accentuate the precarity of postindustrial masculinity. Radio did all these things, often very well, in the 1990s, helped by forces we instinctively demonize, like consolidation of ownership. To understand, for example, why bands such as Green Day, the Offspring, and No Doubt not only achieved popular success but built the expectation of success into their presentation, their arena-ready performativity, requires honoring the world that KROQ made. Yet, despite considerable radio-industry efforts to achieve something larger, alternative ultimately returned to what it had been before Nirvana: a minor format. It persists alongside active rock, mainstream rock, triple A, and hot AC as a feeder channel of certain kinds of sounds and attitudes, though arguably exceeded by noncommercial music radio channels; synchs in the soundtracks for television, movies, and ads; or editorial coverage on NPR. Howard Stern is on SiriusXM, with many other shock jocks, and most of the biggest remaining rock stations are classic rock stations—now they often include a chunk of 1990s memories.

If one can take any comfort in the failure of rock radio to seize the grunge moment in a way that paved a path into the future, it's in thinking about what did succeed. Niche programming allowed for dominance in Cleveland to be shared more broadly than when WMMS ruled. As hip-hop challenged the musical primacy of rock in the late 1980s, urban contemporary WZAK became powerful on Cleveland radio. Sales vice president Mike Hilber discussed his strategies for getting ad buys: "In many of the demographic sales, WZAK covers 80% of the total black population in a given week." WGAR-FM offered "new country," hitting number 1 in 1992. Relaxed WDOK, programmed by women, stayed top 4 in ad billings by reaching 35+ females, more often white-collar workers than housewives: "It is the station whose music is most often found playing in offices throughout the Northeast Ohio area, whether you notice it or not."[64] In addition, some radio formats defied fragmentation. Country, which resisted subdivision, survived as a format that could introduce and culturally frame new music. And Top 40, written off in the early 1990s, grew in listenership and station count afterward. Rock failed not because Kurt Cobain was on a major label but because programmers resisted a vision like KROQ's in the 1990s and the first decade of the 2000s or WMMS's in the 1970s and 1980s, fusing not only rock and Top 40 sensibilities but a young demographic across class lines. That's what, ultimately, was needed to sell like 18–34 spirit.

WMMS–Clear Channel: Rock Radio and Consolidation

The Buzzard had cackled over expired competitors; Stern staged pompous funerals. Another death loomed, this time for radio as it had been. The 1996 Telecommunications Act, which allowed virtually unlimited ownership of radio stations, transformed an industry whose biggest players had only a dozen or so properties collectively into behemoths of a thousand stations. WMMS went to Nationwide, which sent a national programmer to Cleveland. Gorman recalls, "They hired a guy named Bob Bellin, he came in and said this is the most unlistenable station I ever heard in my life. There was no way I could work with this guy. He turned it into Active Rock, the numbers took a dive and the numbers never recovered. It had gone backwards." In other words, Bellin steered the station back in the direction of aggressive rock bands aimed at a blue-collar as much as a college male audience. Nationwide then sold its properties to Jacor, which subsequently merged with Clear Channel, the scourge of many a radio history, which quickly staged its own stunt: pretending to kill off the Buzzard to raise ratings. An NPR story on WMMS, aired as Gorman's memoir was published, concluded, "Today, WMMS is owned by Clear Channel and The Buzzard has been grounded."[65]

But are there more nuanced ways that we might see the trajectory of WMMS, AOR radio, and the kind of borderline-anarchic young male energy summoned variously by Murray Saul, Bruce Springsteen, and Howard Stern? What makes radio *work*? What is the sound that forges the other sounds? One hint is provided by Clear Channel president Randall Mays, who says in an authorized book about the company, "Everybody who has taken an economics class knows that if you owned every station in the market, none of them would play the same format. There's absolutely no need to." Gaye Ramstrom, who remained with WMMS from

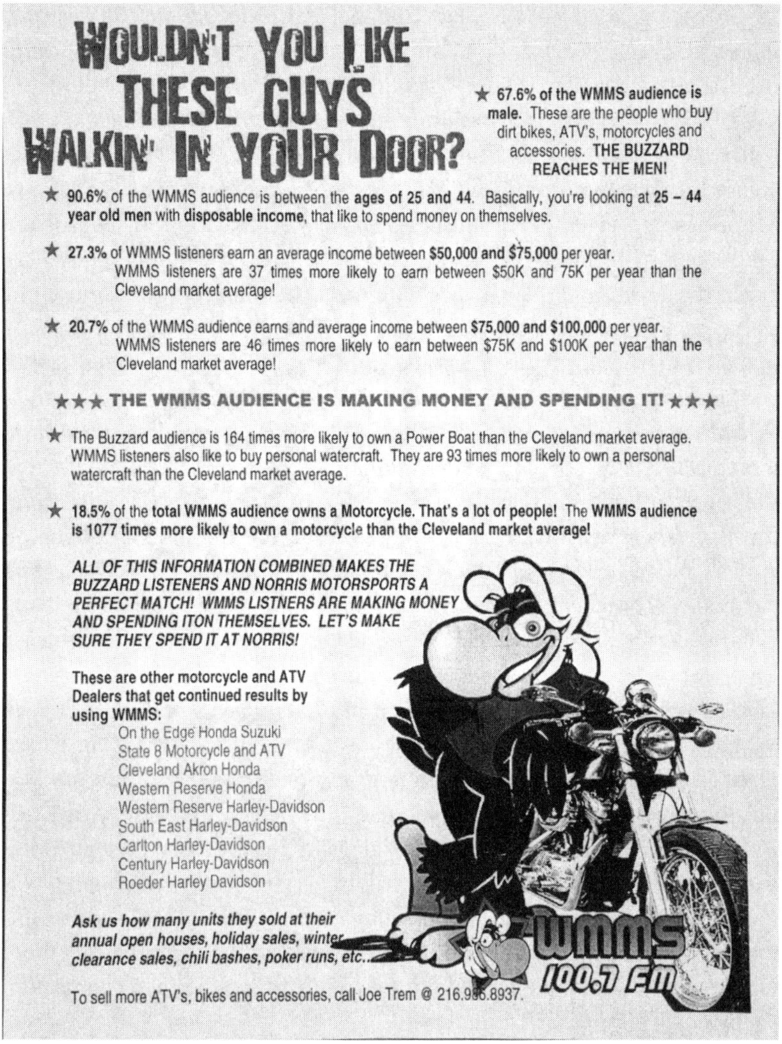

FIGURE 5.5 WMMS sales flyer, circa 2000. Radio stations by the era of corporate consolidation emphasized not only particular demographics but particular products that such listeners were disproportionately likely to buy. Yet the bias of advertisers toward the 25–44 age set, and affluent listeners, hurt stations with a younger, more working-class appeal and altered how WMMS presented itself. Author's collection.

1978 to 2004, is no fan of Clear Channel but concedes that it was only under their corporate consolidation that a secure answer was found to the "AOR, blue collar, dirtbag" stereotype that had for so long hampered sales. Today, WMMS is a station of music inspired by Metallica, a later-generation version of the Grand Funk Railroad and Rush arena rock that John Gorman once embraced over the cooler preferences of Billy Bass. Mornings and afternoons, music gives way to talk inspired by Howard Stern: guys being guys. It is not programming to inspire books and DVDs. But it does continue the career of the original, non-preppy Buzzard, just as the decline of Cleveland continues—declared the most miserable city in the United States in 2010, even before losing LeBron James to Miami.[66]

For more than forty years, through shrewd programmers and bad ones, WMMS and the 18–34 male demographic it has principally served have illustrated the frustrating intersectionalities of the cultural world that radio formatting left us with. Was the best version of WMMS the free-form station that Billy Bass created, with its room for female, African American, and gay DJs and near-complete programming freedom? You can believe so, but then you are endorsing self-conscious hipster elitism. What about the WMMS of "Born to Run" and Murray Saul's Get Downs? That station reconciled collegiate rockers and blue-collar ones within a kick-ass mix. Yet it also marginalized music by blacks and women. The WMMS of Michael Jackson and new wave alongside "Dancing in the Dark" was the highest-rated Buzzard ever. So why, as the station reached out to women, did so many people feel betrayed? Were they sexist, racist, and rockist? Or were these "earthdogs" right to notice that WMMS's fortunes no longer hinged upon a rallying cry of *sheeeeeaaauught*? Was Howard Stern, in this context, a plague or a deliverance? Did reconstituting radio into a small number of mega-chains end the format altogether? Or did it mark the moment, finally, when advertisers learned to make an "active rock" approach profitable?

There will be no absolute answers to these questions, in part because there was never absolute information for programmers and sales managers to steer by. Radio charts monitored the age and gender of listeners, but not their income or race. In every period, confusion reigned as to the rules of the road, as FM made its way into cars, as the baby boom aged into the 25–54 power demographic, as a format system built upon the entry of workers, blacks, southerners, and women into a poorly delineated middle-class continuum contemplated the yuppie: that token of trends shifting new wealth toward elites. Despite this, formats, for all their

shifts and subdivisions, have proven enduring institutions: the plate tec-
tonics of sonic capitalism. What makes radio work is that a sound locks in,
a sound that can take the form of a record or a station promo, a singer or
a DJ or a talking personality cut from the same cloth who plays no music
whatsoever.

John Gorman knew this as well as anybody. "Music is the initial draw,"
he wrote in a 1978 memo to his Buzzard Nuclear Army. "But what makes
'em stay is warmth. Personality. Humor. We're a three dimensional station. Everyone's playin' good music . . . but only WMMS transmits a
vibe." What also makes radio work is that the sound, the format, speaks
to its time, sings out against history—in the case of the Buzzard taking
Cleveland beyond the ruins: The memo continued, "This city is crumbling.
The whole fucking city is in a down mood about [then-mayor Dennis]
Kucinich, the schools, busing, pot holes, the air . . . and everyone's dusting
themselves off after a shitty winter & a chilly spring. But the weather is
breaking! People are gonna charge into the streets like wild bulls! Give
'em the best fucking weekend they've ever heard!"[67]

CHAPTER SIX

This Generation's Radio

Music Formats in the Early 2000s

At the beginning of 2001, *Billboard* announced, "Album Sales In-crease by Only 4% in 2000." The *only* was proper for a record in-dustry that, a 1979–82 downturn aside, had expanded for a half century, establishing rival mainstreams. In the same issue country's Garth Brooks was certified the first solo act in any category with 100 million albums sold domestically, while Brad Paisley joined the Grand Ole Opry, having volunteered to play thirty-six times since May 1999. "That recharges me," he said, but he identified with country as an industry, too—"making a dif-ference in a positive way toward this format of ours." Among labels, the A&M equivalent now, that is, an indie rivaling a major, was Jive, selling 40 million albums with the millennial pop of 'N Sync, Britney Spears, and the Backstreet Boys. But rock remained gold: the Beatles catalogue scanned 18 million albums in 2000 ("almost 40 years later, and the Beatles are still saving the industry's ass," said the president of HMV America), an Eagles hits album pushed past *Thriller* at 27 million US copies, Car-los Santana moved 8 million *Supernatural* discs working with industry titan Clive Davis, and alternative rock collectively registered 131 mil-lion albums. The top Top 40 song, for the ninth week, was "Independent Women" by Destiny's Child, a Houston rhythm and blues (R&B) group introducing Beyoncé Knowles. R&B was also the best-selling format, its 197 million albums (105 million hip-hop derived) a quarter of the overall 785 million sold in the United States.[1]

If that was the picture then, nobody selling recordings has felt so con-fident since. Album sales dropped 2.8 percent in 2001, the top sellers es-pecially, with CD burning and MP3 downloads bringing the top 10 acts down from 60 to 40 million units, no release over 5 million. The summary twelve months later, to start 2003, was stark: "If the U.S. music industry hit a wall in 2001, when album sales declined for the first time in the SoundScan era [since 1991], last year the floor collapsed." This time the falloff was 10.7 percent, with five hundred record stores expected to close. The next year's report wondered, "Have Sales Finally Hit Bottom?"—the decline now "just" 3.6 percent. The 2004 results were promising, sales ascending a bit over 1 percent. Then another plunge: 7 percent in 2005, to the lowest album totals since 1994, only forty-eight titles selling a million against one hundred in 2000 and just thirteen multiplatinum. Sales were down another 5 percent in 2006, dipping to 1993 levels; 15 percent fewer still in 2007, another large whack in 2008. After the 2009 drop, the record industry left the decade almost chopped in half: 490 million "track equivalent albums" (counting downloads of a certain number as albums), including 374 million albums proper.[2]

The totals are not in question. What we should make of them remains less clear, so I want to use this book's conclusion to make a final quick study of music formats in the first decade of the 2000s, just far removed enough to allow for some historical conclusions. Doug Morris, a veteran record man who ran Universal, the biggest label of the decade, said, "It comes down to hits and developing artists. And it's still the same. Nothing has changed." Steve Knopper, longtime music journalist, responded, "He's wrong. Everything has changed. *Thriller* won't save the record business this time. Thinking differently will." Knopper got the last word, since it was his book, titled, typically for the mood of the era, *Appetite for Self-Destruction: The Spectacular Crash of the Record Industry in the Digital Age*. Still, this was not necessarily the biggest crash for recordings, given radio and the Depression hitting in the 1920s. And predictions can be humbled by subsequent events. In 2007, *Billboard* writers complained that it had been almost fifteen years since a story like Sheryl Crow, the A&M artist who took over a year to reach the album charts' top 10. "Record companies no longer have the time, the money, and the staffing to provide that infrastructure for an artist early on," said former A&M head Al Cafaro. In the same issue, Taylor Swift was number 17 in the album charts, forty-three weeks after the release of her debut, nurtured by the independent Big Machine Records and climbing inexorably toward the top. A similar contrast can be found in the best-selling coverage when Chris Anderson, editor of the technology magazine *Wired*, claimed in *The Long Tail* that Web economics favored niche markets. Checking the numbers, Harvard Business School's Anita Elberse demonstrated persuasively that blockbuster products remained dominant—if anything, cherished more by consumers than obscurities relinquishing the thrill of the consumer hunt with downloading.[3]

The transformative effects of the Internet in the first decade of the 2000s were mesmerizing—too much so. Writing in the indie website *Pitchfork*, Eric Harvey concluded, "The past 10 years could become the first decade of pop music to be remembered by history for its musical *technology* rather than the actual music itself." Jerry Del Colliano, publisher of *Inside Radio*, warned, "The next generation is not interested at all in radio. They don't need radio to find out about music anymore. The Internet is here. That's this generation's radio." Steven Levy exemplified the triumphal rhetoric: "Digital technology gathers, shreds, and empowers, all at once. Mix, mash, rip, burn, plunder, and discover: these are the things that the digital world can do much more easily than before—or for the first time. The iPod and the download dollar-store that accompanies it, makes sense of these things without making our brains hurt." Fred Turner, whose *From Counterculture to Cyberculture* is the most historically grounded writing of this period, calls the hype "digital utopianism." Rhetoric of "disintermediation" and "disaggregration" promised freedom from traditional media structures and major labels. In *The Future of Music*, David Kusek and Gerd Leonhard insisted, "The days of mass-marketing records via playlist-homogenized broadcast radio stations are thankfully coming to a close."[4]

Yet more skeptical critics of the "digital music wars" warned against the notion that a "celestial jukebox" would transform commercial culture; if anything, Patrick Burkart and Tom McCourt cautioned, "Industries have transformed the Internet from a public space into a private distribution platform for media conglomerates." This was, after all, the decade that saw *American Idol*, a musical talent competition, generate record profits in TV advertising and multiple other cultural categories (touring, iTunes downloads, celebrity branding). *Idol* defined what Henry Jenkins's influential formulation called a "convergence culture" that recast audiences as interactive and mixed old media with new rather than casting it out. Similarly, Apple, as Levy noted, transformed in the four years after the 2001 launch of the iPod "from a computer company to a consumer electronics giant deriving almost 60 percent of its income from music-related business," driving the company's stock price up 700 percent on its way to topping Microsoft. If record stores, record labels, radio, and MTV had weakened, now the "digital music commodity" was a battleground for Internet providers, social networks, gamers, and YouTube. Their content options were greater, but it was more restrictive to switch between streaming from Spotify or Rhapsody, which required personal user data to access a cloud-based jukebox, than in the older model—changing radio stations.[5]

Radio formats deployed rudimentary notions of "psychographics," the idea that taste shaped identity as much as demographics. As the value of music became indeterminate, such arguments proliferated into business models. An anonymous music-industry executive told one researcher, "All of our evidence points to the issue that people like music more than ever. Nothing can replace it in terms of the emotional connection it makes." Hence the heightened use of music in marketing strategies, a way for brands to "amplify" their message and a further blurring of music and capitalism, as Timothy Taylor's history bemoans. But to focus on com-modification alone ignores an issue this book has turned on—the rockist rejection of established format categories accrued resale value because its putative anti-materialism asserted privilege. Musicians who lacked hit records and blamed tight radio playlists earned substantial licensing revenues when advertisers paid for their aura of exclusivity: "We had this very simple idea," said Eric Hirshberg, executive creative director of Deutsch LA in 2001. "Let's make the Mitsubishi owners into a cool club. If they were all singing a Britney Spears song, the specialness of driving a Mitsubishi would have gone away." That dynamic, manna for the edgy electronic band Dirty Vegas, differed significantly from Wrigley's putting seed money into a single by Top 40 star Chris Brown for future use in a gum ad.[6]

So, to bring to a close this study of the multiple formats that shaped American pop music in the final decades of the twentieth century, I'll sur-vey how those formats—plus one new one, the increasingly important category of Latino-oriented radio—persisted into the twenty-first. If the new buzzwords were "convergence culture" or Aram Sinreich's similar concept of "configurable culture," the nexus of radio and records, after all, had been the original laboratory for capitalizing on musical multiplic-ity.[7] Many asked whether radio could survive a brave new world that had removed receivers from the home and might soon take them from cars as well. But more critical was the question of how the collective categories that formatting supported—absorbing unresolved issues of race, region, age, class, gender, and consumerism itself—would newly assert themselves. The talk of the time was the clustering of social networks. The musical result, surprisingly, was a resurgence of Top 40 crossover pop. Radio was archaic; even radio companies no longer called themselves that. But formatting lived on.

Rhythm and Bullshit?: Urban Contemporary Unsung

The legendary first black-oriented radio station, dating to 1948, Memphis's WDIA had by the 2000s become just another entry in the Clear Channel ledger of broadcasters. Told this way, the endpoint of R&B might truly be what leading soul scholar Mark Anthony Neal calls it, "Rhythm and Bullshit." Urban stations, he charged in 2005, "all sound the same," a homogenized palette of mega-acts like Usher recording for multinational corporations, played by syndicated air personalities who felt no local or community responsibility. He concluded, "The current radio and label consolidation, along with the emergence of hip-hop as the dominant cross-over genre and the perceived aging of traditional R&B audiences, has created the situation where the best R&B being recorded is simply not heard by the audience that would be attracted to it."[8]

Yet Neal also qualified his argument in revealing ways, noting that the syndicated *Tom Joyner Morning Show*, if a "digitized version of the chitlin' circuit," was also "potentially a formidable political force" and that radio consolidation prompted by the 1996 Telecommunications Act had likely helped southern crunk hip-hop break nationally. Radio homogenization, whatever else its effects, was not eradicating black-produced and black-oriented sounds. The R&B format, in the first decade of the 2000s, remained what it had been: a division of the cultural industries that made more room for African American voices than any other, creating enduring success at rising levels of wealth and power for some artists and executives, allowing for both crossover and targeted communal niches, *but* structurally precarious and inequitable compared to other formats.

Back in Memphis, for example, Clear Channel regional vice president Bruce Demps, an African American, oversaw four top-rated stations: two hip-hop and R&B focused, one adult R&B, and one classic rock, with a new gospel station launching as well and two news/talk stations. Demps told the trades, "At the end of the day, if you think of hip-hop, we want you to think of WHRK first. When you think of legendary call letters, it's WDIA first and foremost. Contemporary adult R&B? KJMS. And when you think of gospel, we want you to think of WHAL first." What had been a single R&B format, aimed at many kinds of black listeners, now broke into youth and adult subcategories, anchored by hip-hop and R&B sounds and prominent morning hosts.[9]

Black pop proved vital to Top 40 in the early 2000s, helped by a *Billboard* reformulation that tallied singles airplay across all broadcast formats, not just Top 40; R&B radio now launched over a quarter of the top hits. "We've obliterated the color line," said A&M president Ron Fair. "An awful lot of people of all colors worked on these Hot 100 records, black and white artists, producers, label execs. Call it 'hip-hop' or 'R&B,' but it's the universal language of today's music and it's pop." One programmer worried, "My R&B colleagues have had to deal with hearing their top 40 competition play the music they thought they owned." His advice? "Remember who you are," and then the pragmatic minutiae radio turns on: "R&B lean brings in enough adults to offset the teens that punch back and forth to any station that is pleasing them at the moment. Protecting TSL means that I can't match CKEY by playing [Missy Elliott's] 'Work It' 95 times this week, but I can still jump on a strong Musiq or Jill Scott record." It was threatening to urban stations to see rapper 50 Cent release an "In da Club" remix that hailed Clear Channel's Top 40 "Kiss" stations ("Go Kiss! It's your birthday"). But earlier, Clear Channel had sold R&B holdings to the black-owned Radio One chain. Now it competed, speaking to the format's strength, as in Philadelphia, where the Clear Channel–owned heritage station WDAS battled Radio One's WRNB for adult R&B, with powerful syndicated morning host Tom Joyner moving to WRNB.[10]

Nor did it appear that black-oriented radio had abandoned community involvement; a stress upon such connections was part of how urban stations distinguished themselves from Top 40 competitors. In Cincinnati, the home town of the Isley Brothers, for example, Radio One's WIZF PD, Terri Thomas, spoke about responding to race rioting with a variety of youth initiatives to accompany music by T.I. and Lil Jon, and said of her pop radio competitor, "Catering to the lifestyle is the subtle difference. They may get the music, but we get the lifestyle." Black radio, most observers agreed, influenced elections, with the millions of listeners reached by Joyner and NPR's Tavis Smiley affecting specific senate and congressional races. "If you're in politics, there's no greater power than black radio," said Jesse Jackson. "Only black radio has the capacity and the will to change our communities."[11]

However, while individuals such as billionaire power couple Jay-Z and Beyoncé Knowles achieved unprecedented influence, mingling in the Obama White House, the early 2000s boom in hip-hop and R&B music and urban radio was only short-lived. *Billboard* reported in 2005 that 7 percent of stations had left the format the previous year, as once again advertiser resistance to targeting black consumers proved unyielding. "Urban music is a ratings getter. But high ratings do not mean revenue will follow," said Mychal Maguire, former program director (PD) of a station that had flipped to talk in South Carolina. The sale of BET to Viacom in 2005 symbolized the failure of African Americans to retain cultural ownership. As record sales plummeted, a *Billboard* cover story claimed—in an echo of sentiments that Keith Negus had found prevalent in black corporate sectors in the 1990s—that despite producing 25 percent of album purchases, "black execs are first to be 'downsized' because most of the financial decision-makers are white." As one industry figure, speaking anonymously, put it, "You're not going to cut one of your own if you can cut a black person." Top 40 programmers, fearful of how hip-hop and R&B the sound had become, lobbied for more "pure pop." Guy Zapoleon, an influential format figure, said, "Thank God for Kelly Clarkson and 'American Idol' for keeping pop front and center." Increasingly, from Usher and the Black Eyed Peas to Clarkson and Katy Perry, the rhythmic underpinning of Top 40 shifted to a global dance beat reminiscent of disco, leaving R&B less able to launch crossover hits. "More than three years after Top 40 radio took a hard right toward dance-pop, urban music has been left to founder," charts analyst Chris Molanphy concluded. Urban radio also faced ratings challenges, as the new Portable People Meters (PPM) devices used by Arbitron to replace listener diaries led to reduced ratings for black-oriented stations, perhaps because of sampling imbalances, perhaps because the diary system had overstated listening times.[12]

Once again, R&B success had proven fickle even while R&B itself remained eternal, a paradigm dominating the narratives in the series *Unsung*, airing on the TV One channel—a cable version of the Radio One chain, still owned by Quiet Storm pioneer Cathy Hughes. Each episode hinged on cheating contracts, a biased music industry, and ruined lives, yet magnificent and still treasured music—the hour on David Ruffin, the immortal voice of Motown's Temptations, who died after an evening in a crack house, might have been the most gut wrenching. The duality was striking: for all its failures, the R&B format remained a crucial pathway, the product of decades of black aspiration. If corporate skepticism about African American wealth weakened the "power ratio" (listeners to revenues) of urban radio, a Nielsen study found that advertisers spent $805 million on black-oriented radio in twelve months from 2006 to 2007,

35 percent of their total spending in black-oriented advertising, a far higher percentage than radio's usual portion of ad revenues and a figure exceeding that for magazine, network, or cable television. The biggest syndicated morning hosts—including Joyner, Steve Harvey, and Michael Baisden—were heard by millions each morning. Joyner argued, "My show is not really that regionalized or age-specific because, honestly, the needs of black people are the same everywhere." And if hip-hop, always a problematic sound for adult-oriented R&B, faced challenges, other black performers such as Ne-Yo and *American Idol* winner Fantasia gained from the rise of an urban AC blend—the balancing act of musical emphasis that formatting encouraged. Critic Kelefa Sanneh said, parodying a longtime hip-hop station's positioning slogan, "These days, Hot 97 is where R&B lives."[13]

"Admit It. You Love It": Country on the Fence

Early in the 2000s, the Country Music Association (CMA), Nashville's venerable trade organization, suggested a new slogan for the music— "Admit it. You love it." The defensiveness inherent in the much disliked, quickly withdrawn branding effort suggested that, Garth Brooks and 1990s "new country" or no, perceptions remained that listeners were trashy, hopelessly uncool rubes. Ratings for country radio peaked in 1993. New York City lost its country station, WYNY, in 2002, and was without one for the next ten years, with San Francisco and Los Angeles following by 2006, three of the top five media markets. In an increasingly multiracial America, country was a holdout: "we can't even do bilingual IDs without significant listener backlash," said the program director of a Miami station. *Radio & Records* country columnist Wade Jessen wrote angrily that the CMA-led claim "we're sorry you had that silly old stereotype that our audience is mostly working-class white folks. We're the new American pop music" was the problem. "That was essentially the marketing message from 1989 until the bottom fell out five years later, and the town was left dazed by how quickly its newfound audience had left the building." Jessen thought country had to face facts: "working-class whites— country's largest constituency—is an ethnic group unto itself."[14]

As country questioned its image once more, women continued to personify the temptation to cross into middle-class pop, particularly adult contemporary (AC) pop. The Dixie Chicks were a throwback to "real country" after the pin-up Shania Twain, and even bashed country radio on "Long Time Gone" for not supporting artists like Merle Haggard. Yet they too were expelled from country, after criticizing George W. Bush in the run-up to the second US war in Iraq. This came amid a twenty-two-month stretch in which no solo female performer had a number 1 country hit. Only four of the thirty-four top 10 country hits in the first half of 2003 featured women, compared to fourteen in 1998. Mike Dungan, CEO of Capitol Nashville, said, "Women, for the most part, were making very, very pop records. We finally pushed the format too far in that direction." The woman who broke the drought, Gretchen Wilson, constructed herself as a virile "Redneck Woman," avowedly working class, a Walmart shopper, and identified with a communal chant of "hell yeah." Faith Hill, a new country figure accused of becoming too AC, released "Mississippi Girl" to court country radio. Carrie Underwood's "Jesus Take the Wheel" and "Before He Cheats" were country-credential assertions by a polished *American Idol* winner releasing different songs to AC. Her label head, Joe Galante, said, "My experience is that country gets upset when you take a record to top 40 or AC before you take it to them or if you're working on a record simultaneously, but we're not. We're working two separate records."[15]

The tensions existing within the Nashville "community"—always (as Negus pointed out in his 1990s study) a complicated construction given the need to balance local and multinational business concerns that intersected creativity—were not limited to gendered categories of "hardcore" (traditionalist) and "soft shell" (pop leaning). After all, Toby Keith, the most belligerent traditionalist, and Taylor Swift, the most pop-leaning figure, both recorded for indie labels, a rising presence in a longtime major-label company town, and experimented with new business models. Keith left Universal division DreamWorks for his own Show Dog, rising to the number 3 highest-paid music star in all pop from mid-2007 to 2008 for a mix of record sales, concerts, merchandise, and Ford endorsements. If Keith presented himself as a soldier-loving iconoclast, feuding with the crossover-crazed CMA, he still courted country radio, at one point flying one hundred programmers to his home in Oklahoma for a golf tournament. Swift, a far from working-class or southern figure, brought teen romantic sensibilities to her songwriting and rapped Eminem lyrics in concert. Label head Scott Borchetta said, "We wanted her to be viral, and she was—particularly with the younger, internet-savvy crowd," while Seattle programmer Becky Brenner noted, "Her popularity on MySpace was a big deal for us." But Swift too knew where country was defined: "So many people tell me that radio won't play me because I'm too young. Because of that, radio is the biggest priority for me and building those relationships." As it had once with Dolly Parton, Nashville accepted success: Swift won Entertainer of the Year at the CMA Awards in 2010, alongside MTV video awards, and moved crossover country from AC to Top 40.[16]

The paradox of country music in the early 2000s was that its anchorage to a radio format devoted to breaking new material gave it a coherence no other style of music could match, but did nothing for the genre's anti-contemporary image and issues with class, race, and gender. The touring organization Live Nation's country music president, Brian O'Connell, expressed the music's strengths perfectly: "In rock you have seven or eight different sub-categories, in country you have country, period. People keep trying to divide it up into classic country, traditional country, pop country, but it still boils down to country." Meanwhile, country power couple Faith Hill and Tim McGraw, political liberals whose messages of racial inclusion ("Southern Voices") and unapologetic sexuality ("Breathe") tested radio regularly, opened shows on a joint tour with a cover by the rock band favored by hot AC and the TV show *Grey's Anatomy*: Snow Patrol. Was that country? The format system, in its multiplicity, ultimately supported *both* entrenchment and crossover explorations, which resonated with twenty-first-century technological shifts. Jennifer Nettles, the woman who led the duo Sugarland when not duetting with Jon Bon Jovi, said, "I call it the 'iPod nation.' You look on somebody's iPod and they've got Johnny Cash, Missy Elliott, Emmylou Harris, whomever. It's an exciting time to be in music because boundaries are being crossed and stretched right and left. Consequently, if we want to cross over or those doors were opened, the sky's the limit."[17]

Country music began the 2000s with "Murder on Music Row": two of its most established stars, George Strait and Alan Jackson, accusing Nashville of betraying the style's legacy. The multiplatinum album success of the *O Brother, Where Art Thou?* soundtrack, with the traditional "I Am a Man of Constant Sorrow" performed comically and "O Death" utterly seriously, eclipsed almost every mainstream country release. One exception, the Dixie Chicks, were kicked out of the category altogether—less, it appears in scholarly retrospect, because of the conservative politics of the consolidated radio chains that now ruled country radio and more because "true" country fans demanded it. Because those fans were slower to download MP3s or shift from radio to the Internet, something like the traditional industry of radio and records persisted longer in country than

other categories, though this too prompted anxiety, as country-single marketing costs became the costly equal of pop singles and Epic/Monument
Records senior vice president of promotion Larry Pareigis bemoaned the
"million-dollar cost to make someone a country star," meaning only a first
hit single.[18]

Yet it was still possible to have a more-than-solid career following
the country format rulebook. Thirty years after CMA Female Vocalist of the Year Olivia Newton-John had embarrassed herself by asking
to meet the deceased Hank Williams and vowing to someday set foot in
Nashville, fellow Australian Keith Urban was far more respectful. The
operating manager of the Emmis chain's Los Angeles station, KZLA,
R. J. Curtis, saluted his recent visit of more than an hour. "Keith and two
other people came walking up the street and into the station," Curtis says.
"No entourage, no limo with dark-tinted windows, no guys in suits with
radios. . . . It was real, and so is he." For this courtesy and others, Urban
enjoyed two songs atop the 2005 country charts, more than 6 million in
album sales as of 2006, 2005 tour revenues of about $11 million, and an
award as CMA Entertainer of the Year. His sound, a mixture of country
and rock, with room for AC hits and an eventual role judging *American
Idol*, prompted no complaints from the industry or fans whatsoever. Men
flirting with rock were making acceptable genre moves; women flirting
with pop continued to make the country format nervous.[19]

Staind: Rock Music in a Post-Rock Era

It is not precisely equivalent to the AOR all-time playlist that *Radio &
Records* constructed in 1978, but a sample Friday afternoon hour of programming on WMMS in 2003—the DJ Kid Leo's old slot—shows how
rock radio had changed a quarter century later. Uniformly white and
male, the acts on this playlist responded to a more extreme version of
the old challenge to at least create sonic diversity nonetheless. A Led
Zeppelin obscurity ("Hey Hey What Can I Do") represented acoustic
music; Beck's "Loser" stood in for hip-hop and blues; Green Day's "When
I Come Around" enacted something like Beatlesque pop; Pearl Jam's
"Daughter" might have been singer-songwriter rock; Metallica's Queen
cover "Stone Cold Crazy" revisited the freedoms of vintage rock and roll.
The rest—Taproot, Staind, Puddle of Mudd, Trapt, Stone Temple Pi-
lots, Godsmack—anchored on the crunch of guitar chords originating in

hardcore punk and thrash metal, slowed down by 1990s grunge, and now
heavily processed into an active and/or alternative rock radio staple—
apocalyptic impulses rendered quotidian moodiness music. Joshua Clover
has written of grunge's "inward turn," flipping the target of rock rebellion
to the shattered self. These anthems to disintegration—typically by bands
from flyover America, a white working class on the wrong side of shifts to
a multiracial, creative class urbanity—were a far cry from album-oriented
rock's (AOR's) earlier allegories of emboldened everyman affluence, still
heard on hundreds of temporally fixed classic rock stations.[20]

Rock radio had narrowcast itself into a frustrated howl. Steve Dahl, the
demolisher of disco records, could only chuckle, "When I started doing
this back in the mid-'70s, I was in my mid-20s, and nobody in that demographic was really doing anything except playing records and backselling
them. Anybody that got on and did anything else was considered outrageous and shocking. And it's kind of funny to see that as time goes on,
guys like Opie & Anthony make me look like a choirboy." The precarity
of rock as a format, especially stations that played new releases, could be
illustrated with one nipple. Janet Jackson's exposed breast during a Super
Bowl halftime show broadcast in 2004 led to heightened FCC scrutiny
of TV and radio broadcasts. Howard Stern, the most famous envelope-
pusher, drew repeated citations. So Stern and other shock jocks skipped
category, for the unregulated satellite radio of SiriusXM, leaving behind
no-longer-viable "terrestrial" stations. New York City, for one, lacked a
radio station playing new mainstream rock as the decade ended.[21]

As had long been the case, much perfectly commercial music eluded
the format, due to the reluctance of musicians and listeners to accept rock
as a diverse pop category. Bruce Springsteen's *Rising*, an emotional response to the September 11 attacks, sold more than a half million copies
its first week in 2002, but outside of the smaller adult album alternative
(triple A) format, rock radio had abandoned singer-songwriters. The
Strokes and others like them received disproportionate record-industry
support in hope that hipster rock might replace the aggressive sexism of
bands like Limp Bizkit. "What makes these bands special helps to make
the format special," said WBCN's Oedipus, a longtime proponent of progressive radio. But such efforts were equally biased, against the bulk of
rock radio listeners. By contrast, Keith Hastings, PD of WAAF, WBCN's
more successful rival, would not even play the more populist, but female-
fronted, Evanescence. "I saw no sense in playing Evanescence's 'Bring
Me to Life,' even though I fully agreed it was a hit record," he said. "It

didn't make sense for me to try to own that with so many other stations playing it. Part of our focus is to differentiate ourselves where it makes sense. There's a new Type O Negative record that's flying out of the stores here, and that's enough to tell me that it's a record that I can differentiate my radio station with. . . . I'm fighting for a smaller piece of pie in a bigger market." In 2004, Oedipus was fired as program director, and in 2009, WBCN signed off after forty-one years; WAAF became Boston's most long-standing rock radio station.[22]

Fighting for a smaller piece of pie, instead of competing in the pop universe, diminished rock. It was forbidding to make pop-friendly music with rock-friendly attitude. Linkin Park, equally popular on Top 40 and hot AC, refused to do events at such stations, leaving them, in *Airplay Monitor*'s words, "able to maintain their rock radio credibility." The issues, to a hugely male listenership, were transparent: pop was girly and corrupt. To quote three rock program directors with varying opinions but the same basic worldview: "Linkin Park is one of those bands that's too mainstream for the hardcore listeners, but as one of them put it, 'Hey, if cool chicks dig it, I'm not gonna turn off the station!' "; "Their credibility as a rock band comes into question as soon as the top 40 station plays the record. Rock fans don't want their favorite band played on the 'uncool station.' That's the station that plays Madonna, not Linkin Park"; 'I think it's pure pop crap. . . . They're not really a rock band. A frequent comment from listeners is that they're just a boy band with tattoos." Ever a student of format positioning, Clive Davis wrote appreciatively but measuredly of the band best at navigating the subcategorizing of rock—the Foo Fighters, led by former Nirvana drummer Dave Grohl: "Their albums consistently go double platinum, and the band thrives in the rock world and dominates rock radio from the moment its albums are released. . . . Dave, of course, has grown into a charismatic, outspoken front man and personality himself—a musician who deeply believes in and understands rock 'n' roll, but doesn't take himself too seriously . . . so the media loves him. Within and beyond the music industry, the Foo Fighters have come to be seen as rock 'n' roll standard-bearers, as evidenced by the band's twenty-five Grammy nominations and eleven Grammy awards. I realize that in some critical quarters, the Foo Fighters may not be granted as high a place in the pantheon of rock bands as I would accord them." Female rockers like Avril Lavigne and Pink were left to court hot AC.[23]

Restrictive sonically, rock radio could encompass a range of political valences. The Democrat-driven Rock for Change tour in 2004, featuring

Pearl Jam, divided programmers, who loved the bill but saw their audience as "split down the middle." Post-grunge Mississippi band 3 Doors Down made their video for "Citizen/Soldier" ("I stepped forward when the towers fell") to support a US Army National Guard recruitment campaign. Underoath, a Christian rock band, reached number 2 on the *Billboard* album chart with the 2006 album *Define the Great Line*, critiquing the idolization of pop stars in "Regards to Myself" and feuding with the band NOFX on the annual punk tour Warped. On the other hand, Trent Reznor devoted a Nine Inch Nails album, *Year Zero*, to what one academic calls "an intersection of the politics of media convergence with the biopolitics of control"—grunge's inward gaze recast as the product of surveillance and the War on Terror. And Green Day's *American Idiot* made "Sing along to the age of paranoia / Information age of hysteria" the stuff of a multi-hit triumph and eventual Broadway musical.[24]

If rock anger found multiple avenues, other bands and listeners pursued a different politics—removal from major record labels and distaste for radio hits of any kind. This rock adhered to the growing category of the indie hipster, as elites returned to colonize urban spaces in Williamsburg, Brooklyn; Wicker Park, Chicago; and the portion of Oregon that a TV show on the apropos Independent Film Channel satirized as *Portlandia*. The Montreal band Arcade Fire, recording for the long-standing North Carolina indie Merge, could sell out Madison Square Garden, come one spot from the top of the *Billboard* albums chart, and headline the hipster-oriented Coachella festival in Southern California without courting rock radio. Radiohead challenged the record-selling system altogether, having fans pay a sum of their choosing to download an album. Yet when Wilco, having made an experimental album (*Yankee Hotel Foxtrot*) that its major label Reprise rejected, wound up switching to a different Warner Music Group division, Nonesuch, designed for hipsters, the spectacle said less about artistic resistance than about the removal of elites from the rock mainstream. When Joe Pernice of the Pernice Brothers argued, as many did, "It's almost like commercial and television placement are the new radio," the reason this made sense was that indie acts exiled from mainstream rock radio were now preferred by ad buyers proud of their edgy taste. The dream of a new "middle of the rock" radio went largely unfulfilled, even as the one enduring counterexample, Los Angeles's KROQ, became radio's highest biller of any station in 2006, and the *Guitar Hero* and *Rock Band* video games proved the continuing appeal of spectacles of cross-class rock unity.[25]

Hurban Blues: The Dilemmas of Latin Radio

No category of music on US radio grew as quickly in the early 2000s as Spanish language—up to 685 stations by 2005, a rise of 230 (or 50 percent) since 1996, and that from 376 in 1990 and just 67 in 1980. (The 2012 figure was 825.) Similarly, the percentage of total listenership such broadcasters claimed rose from 6.7 percent in 1998 to 10.1 in the summer of 2005. But what was this format or formats? One subcategory, regional Mexican, dominated the overall numbers but produced almost no crossover figures. Crossover itself was a complicated question in this globalized mainstream: crossover into a pan-Latin world market or into English-language pop? Many listeners were also US born and bilingual, as likely to listen to Top 40 channels, prompting efforts to create "Hurban" (Hispanic urban) approaches. Latin music intersected hip-hop with the explosive rise of reggaeton. It intersected technology as CD pirating crippled the recordings market before many fans entered the digital age. And the Latin format proved the political power of radio when DJs helped lead immigration marches in 2006.[26]

For record sellers, Ricky Martin's 1999 Grammy performance ushered in a new pop category. Tommy Mottola, chairman of Sony Music Entertainment, "had it in his mind that he was going to create this Latin revolution," said awards producer Ken Ehrlich. Martin, a Puerto Rican–born former Menudo singer, Mexican and American soap opera star, and Broadway actor, was a creature of media and mediation. He'd later, like Elton John, acknowledge his homosexuality, in his case with a memoir that noted his first serious male lover had been a radio DJ: "He would play certain songs and say certain things that only I could understand. He would scream his love out to me over the airwaves, but the really incredible, powerful, magnificent, and devastating thing about it was that only I knew it." Martin sold 7 million copies domestically and almost seventeen worldwide of his English-language debut album, through the hit "Livin' la Vida Loca," but only after a decade-long process of breaking him across Latin America and globally, including singing the 1998 World Cup theme in several languages. As manager Angelo Medina put it, "I always say Ricky's crossover wasn't in English." Artists such as Marc Anthony, Jennifer Lopez, Shakira, and Enrique Iglesias followed Martin's global path. What was their ethnicity? Martin found it odd that "I was known as 'the international artist.' But when I arrived in the United States, I was 'the Latino phenomenon.'" From his vantage, "I am a mestizo."[27]

By contrast, the Mexican-derived sounds of groups like California-born Los Tigres del Norte remained avowedly regional. "We are the hicks, the rednecks of Latin music," said one vendor. And yet, with Mexican Americans two-thirds of the swelling Latino population in the 2000 census, rootsy albums made for under $50,000, certified gold at just 100,000 copies, and performed by self-contained bands that could be found on the road virtually every weekend collectively dominated US Latin sales. Much as had happened with country music, regional Mexican was viewed as the antithesis of bigger but ephemeral sounds. Leila Cobo, the leading reporter, wrote in *Billboard*, "Unlike fickle pop customers, regional Mexican buyers are considered loyal fans who stick with such acts as [Joan] Sebastian, Vicente Fernandez, Banda el Recodo, and Los Tigres for 10, 20, or 30 years." In 1992, Los Angeles station KLAX shockingly topped the market playing the regional sounds of polka-inflected banda. Regional Mexican featured few women in its accenting of tradition, but it was avowedly working class in address, like the Michoacán-born morning-drive hosts Juan Carlos Hidalgo and Jesus Garcia. Hidalgo said, pointedly, "When there are problems in the community, like in the case of Governor Wilson attacking immigrants, we don't have, as we say, hair on our tongues keeping us from telling the truth." Dolores Inés Casillas argues that listening to regional Mexican stations was more "communal and classed" than the privatized "white collar mode" in cars and earbuds, with programmers emphasizing "discursive gestures of belonging."[28]

From a US record-selling vantage, Spanish-language music occupied three categories: tropical (salsa and related beats), regional Mexican, and global pop-rock, each with further subcategories. As the leading share of record sales passed from Fonovisa to Mexican TV company Univision in 2002 and then Universal in 2008, album sellers struggled to apply their balanced-portfolio format strategies to domestic, international, and transnational paradigms. Carlos Sanchez, president of Universal Music Latino, said, "Within Universal, we're not a label; we're a division," hoping the synergies would help artists cross category. But the chains that dominated this radio format, Hispanic Broadcasting Corporation, Spanish Broadcasting System, and Mega Communications, responded to prosperity in the reverse direction, creating tight playlists and showing resistance to new artists. Arnulfo Ramirez, operations manager for two Houston stations—a Spanish contemporary and regional Mexican—told *Billboard*, "Five years ago, Spanish stations played a little bit of everything. You'd hear a ballad, then a banda song. Now, Spanish radio is very defined."[29]

If musical hybridity threatened the defined formats of Spanish-language stations, English-speaking Latinos were demographically desta-bilizing. As far back as the 1980s, their presence had reconstituted Top 40 and urban R&B as Madonna-friendly "rhythmic CHR" (contemporary hit radio) or "Churban." Then, there were "Latin freestyle" acts and sta-tions like New York's WKTU, whose PD Carlos DeJesus said, "Our audi-ence breakdown has been 1/3 Latino, 1/3 black, and 1/3 white. Latinos are our base." By 2004, as Los Angeles Top 40 channel KIIS passed Spanish stations for top cume, Latinos comprised KIIS's largest listening group, rising from 40 to 60 percent in three years. Clear Channel announced in 2005 that it would flip twenty-five stations to Latin, emphasizing a Hur-ban approach, with playlists half in English, half in Spanish. "The audi-ence we're going after is a bilingual audience," senior vice president of Hispanic radio Alfredo Alonso said, "that young Latino whose needs, for years, weren't served. They do become acculturated, but they still are Latinos, and they still have interests that are very different from the gen-eral market." Univision's La Kalle franchise made similar moves. Hurban formats failed, however. By 2007, Alonso concluded, "It's very difficult to sell a radio station where the age that sells the largest portion of the audience are teens. A lot of the advertisers are not interested." As for English-speaking Latinos preferring a Spanglish mix, "The reality was, that never materialized."[30]

A similar fate befell reggaeton, the hip-hop and dancehall reggae-inflected beat of Puerto Rican artists such as Pitbull and Daddy Yankee, called "real street music" in its first *Billboard* mention. The explosive popularity of this transnational Spanish sound, which as Wayne Marshall notes worked to address a pan-Latin audience while refusing "tropical" signifiers, broke open Latin radio playlists. "It crosses into all the listening groups of the station," said one programmer of the first hit, "Gasolína," and *Billboard* concluded, "The Spanish-language radio we hear today is not the radio we heard even three months ago." Top 40 also took notice: at the revived rhythmic WKTU, programmer Jeff Z said, "Daddy Yankee was a star in the Latin market long before WKTU started playing 'Gaso-lina.' We kept hearing this extremely infectious hook at every club we were attending." The mainstream Top 40 Z100 followed. "We've found that the appeal of reggaeton is universal," said PD Tom Poleman. "It's not just about Latin listeners. White suburban kids have a lot of passion for it." The boom proved somewhat ephemeral—anchored only in the weak Hurban format. But reggaeton's legacy was critical: carnal sex music, viewed (in the words of Frances Negrón-Muntaner) as "cultural trash" from the Puerto Rican lower classes, became what reggaeton performer Tego Calderón called "a movement were we get respect, where we can celebrate our blackness without shame."[31]

Latino alternative rockers, in keeping with rock tradition, chafed at formats and crossover strategies. Only three stations in Mexico were said to play such bands, and the situation was no better in the United States. Josh Kun, an advocate, said, "Latin radio does not support Latin alternative music. Period." The comments of Sergio Arau, leader of Botellita de Jerez, made his attitudes clear. "I would never listen to any of those horrible stations, knowing that at any time they can play some romantic garbage in between some badly chosen rock songs." Alex Gonzalez, the drummer for Mexico's Maná, sometimes called the U2 of Latin pop, disliked groups who "stop looking Latin because they're so Americanized, because they're into making things sellable." As in English-language rock, however, "alternative" Latino groups could benefit from exclusivity. Mexican rockers Kinky, only selling twenty-four thousand albums in the United States, earned a good living through synch deals with *Felicity*, *Six Feet Under*, and *Alias*, plus ads for Honda, Motorola, and Smirnoff.[32]

Had the Latin-music boom heralded, quixotically, by the internationalist Martin in 1999 proven to be a hype? Mottola himself told *Billboard* in 2004, "There never really was a Latin explosion. It was a mirage. And two of the biggest stars [Jennifer Lopez and Marc Anthony] were from the Bronx." CD burning crippled sales eventually, as SoundScan figures, rising against prevailing trends early in the dismal decade (perhaps mom and pop stores were being supplanted by bar code–tracked chains), crashed 15 percent in 2006, then 21 percent in 2007. Digital sales were hugely lower than in other categories: more than five times less as late as 2009. The US Latino youth demographic, 25 million under age thirty, its buying power said to grow twice as fast as consumers as a whole since 1990, remained fragmented: 42 percent under eighteen preferred English, 28 percent were bilingual, and 30 percent spoke Spanish. "It's an elusive experience, people living simultaneously in two cultures," said music manager Jorge Hernandez. And yet, as Enrique Iglesias, releasing his first all-Spanish hits album in 2008, knew full well, "radio is the best instrument you have to sell records." The overall boom in Spanish broadcasting only continued, a new idiom of Top 40 democracy's interweaving of genre, format, and group identity.[33]

An example of radio's power came on May 1, 2006, as marchers gathered in about seventy cities across the United States for a national "Day without an Immigrant," including over half a million in Los Angeles and four hundred thousand in Chicago. Popular DJs such as Renán Almendárez Coello (El Cucuy), Eduardo "Piolín" Sotelo, and Rafael Pulido proposed that all would wear white and carry the US flag: "even in the age of iPods and blogs, radio is as effective as ever," a *New York Times* reporter concluded. It helped nationalize the protests, first staged only in Los Angeles on March 25, that a DJ like Almendárez, heard by 3 million weekly in that city, was syndicated by Spanish Broadcasting System to such locales as Denver, Seattle, Tulsa, San Francisco, Atlanta, Salt Lake City, Minneapolis, Jackson (Mississippi), and Greenville (South Carolina). Regional Mexican music had long served migrants as what Sony Music's Miguel Trujillo called "the only way to link to those places they left behind." But radio sealed the bond: "we identify the relationship between Spanish-language radio DJs and their publics as one of mutual trust, reciprocity, and solidarity," an academic study concluded. Now Los Tigres del Norte walked down Wilshire Boulevard, singing, a cappella, "El Mojado Acaudalado" (The wealthy wetback), "De Paisano a Paisano" (From brother to brother), and "Tres Veces Mojado" (Three times a wetback). Rival morning DJs from KXOL, KLAX, and KBUE marched side by side.[34]

20 on 20: Top 40 Forever?

As the first decade of the 2000s came to a close, those who followed radio from paradigm shift to paradigm shift savored an outcome that few would have predicted generations earlier, when original rock programmer Tom Donahue declared Top 40 a "rotting corpse." The original, most basic approach to music on radio was bidding to become the last format standing. Without citing the twist or disco, though she might have, Julie Pilat, music director for powerhouse KIIS, noted that "the format has swung back to more of a dance sound." Explaining in contemporary terms a musical multiplicity that dated at least to 1960s "Boss" Top 40 in her city, the mix of rock and soul displayed in the *T.A.M.I. Show* concert that featured James Brown and the Rolling Stones, Pilat claimed, "More and more I'm seeing the iPod generation cross format lines and fuse things together." Sean Ross, commercial radio's most astute analyst, concluded, "The surprise is that the music also works fine for today's 16-year-olds and their very mainstream taste. If there's music they consider hipper, it's not what's on hip-hop or alternative radio; it's the indie rock that isn't on the radio in most places." Top 40, said Ross, "is all alone in the end zone."[35]

For many advocates of diversified airwaves, groups such as the Future of Music Coalition, the tight playlists of Top 40 had long represented a betrayal of a public sphere. Yet when satellite radio, offering dozens of different streams of sound, became viable in the 2000s, with the combined SiriusXM reaching a subscriber base of 24 million by 2013, the most popular music offerings remained the likes of "Top 20 on 20" and "Hits 1." Dave Reynolds, Virgin vice president of promotions, said with satisfaction, "It's very rare to find a station like Sirius Hits 1 or XM 20 on 20 that will put in a new song and play it 21, 28, 35 times a week right off the bat. That's really exposing a new record." The PPM devices gradually introduced in different cities by Arbitron to measure ratings automatically also helped Top 40 and its adult-skewing crossover kin, demonstrating that radio listening tended to involve shorter bursts of attention from listeners seeking a range of sound, rather than the genre and station loyalty of longer TSL reflected in diary estimates. The twenty-first century had not really left behind the mythical progenitor of Top 40: the waitress at the jukebox, feeding quarters to again hear songs that had been playing all day.[36]

If crossover pop on radio was outpacing targeted approaches such as country, R&B, and rock, record executives excited by multiple mainstreams continued to define what remained of the post-Napster industry. Jerry Moss and Herb Alpert no longer ran A&M Records, but Ron Fair, who oversaw the label from 2001 to 2006, seemed cut from the same cloth, promoting the new tween pop category dominated by Radio Disney with S Club 7, repositioning the hip-hop-identified Black Eyed Peas as a pop act through an opening slot on a Justin Timberlake and Christina Aguilera tour, and celebrating the range of commercial sound, "whether it goes to the standards thing, like what we've got going with Queen Latifah, or the breakthrough of Hoobastank or Maroon 5 at Top 40, or what we're achieving with Snow Patrol and Keane, or Kanye West's incredible rise." What fascinated Fair, like many record men before him, centered on format and the channels that connected artists to publics, not genre and authenticity: "It's all going to come down to 'What are the songs? What are they saying?' If somebody has a great viewpoint or something to say or an incredible hook, even if it's a simple and mundanc hook, if it has something to say, it *is* valid."[37]

The longtime behemoth stations of Top 40 flourished late in the decade, as the format moved from a hip-hop emphasis to again embrace
what *Radio & Records* hailed as "all the different factions of pop music,
including female pop/rock artists like [*American Idol* winner Kelly]
Clarkson, pop/rock like Nickelback, pop/hip-hop like Chamillionaire,
pop/alternative like Panic! at the Disco and pop/reggae like Sean Paul."
Z100 in New York, which had helped define CHR on FM in the early
1980s, again topped all others in total listenership—heard by 2.7 million
in an average week. Ryan Seacrest, "America's Host," commanded attention on *American Idol*, replaced Casey Kasem on an *AT40* (American
Top 40) broadcast heard on five hundred affiliates worldwide, and helmed
mornings on KIIS, with segments like "The Sleaze" delivering what station PD John Ivey called "on-air and online content aimed squarely at a
YouTube- and TMZ-savvy audience that deeply desires its daily fix of pop
culture and celebrity dirt, backed by the musical soundtrack KIIS provides." Seacrest said, "I still get excited about which jingle to pick after a
talk set or going into a song. I still love when I nail the right tempo jingle
into the right song, at just the right beat." Clear Channel syndicated "On
Air with Ryan Seacrest" nationally as well.[38]

American music fans seemed intrigued by crossover pop of all kinds
in the early 2000s. The most popular new musical concept, the mash-up,
took tracks from different genres or different levels of artistic credibility
and combined them. An early example blended pop princess Christina
Aguilera's vocal for "Genie in a Bottle" with hip alternative rock from
the Strokes. The mash-up concept could be almost infinitely extended, if
copyrights were set aside: Girl Talk, the name used by Pittsburgh DJ Greg
Gillis, mixed layers of rock, hip-hop, and pop into a stuttering symphony
of beats and braggadocio for works that were distributed free, performed
live, and deconstructed on fan sites. But mash-ups worked symbolically
too: as critic Sasha Frere-Jones noted, the effect of "A Stroke of Genius"
was more than musical, because "each song targets a demographic that
wants nothing to do with the other." On the TV show *Glee*, mash-ups
like the combination of Katrina and the Waves' 1980s hit "Walking on
Sunshine" and Beyoncé's current "Halo" served the show's desire to mix
new and vintage hits, the theme of geeky glee club outsiders achieving a
reconciliation with the world, and an ecumenicalism about pop authenticity that Karen Tongson noticed: "*Glee* plays upon our nostalgia for the so-
called 'naked voice,' even as the show itself employs post-digital modes of
mixing, distribution and dissemination." On radio, the mash-up was represented by the Jack format, which transformed oldies and AC radio by

mixing hits from multiple decades of the past, from pop, R&B, and rock, with the slogan "playing what we want." "This whole format is about programming a potential train wreck," said one programmer. "You'll have 'Wild Thing' by Tone-Loc, 'Hotel California' by the Eagles, 'Soak Up the Sun' by Sheryl Crow, and Supertramp in a music sweep. But the format works because it addresses the variety issue. Listeners get music from so many places these days that their palates have become broader."[39]

Had palates become broader, or was Top 40 simply as much of a force as ever in keeping them that way? Format consultant Guy Zapoleon's theory of the ten-year cycle of Top 40—extremes of concentration around one sound hurt the format, but it inevitably rebounded—was now taken as gospel. "Unlike 10 years ago, where a full 500 stations left the format, you have companies like Clear Channel that are believers in the format," said Zapoleon. The key was to keep the proper focus, "on 16–24, because that's who is the most passionate about the format." Looking ahead, years before the Korean pop star Psy generated a number 1 hit via social networks recommending his viral YouTube video "Gangnam Style," Zapoleon predicted a global Top 40: "I think you will continue to hear sounds from Asia, Africa and the Middle East, mixed in with more traditional music types, which will ultimately breed entirely new styles of music."[40]

In a Top 40 tradition, a payola scandal broke mid-decade in the 2000s, as then New York attorney general Eliot Spitzer's investigation of independent promoters led to penalties for record labels and radio chains. Yet analysis by both industry observers and outside scholars challenges assumptions that deregulated chains shut out worthier material. Sean Ross of *Airplay Monitor* and *Billboard*, looking closely at the many Clear Channel Top 40 stations, found only a 65 percent overlap in their top songs in 2003, "considerably less than what was perceived by format observers" and similar to non-chain outlets. Gabriel Rossman, a sociologist examining the diffusion patterns of hits reaching radio, found for both a particular song (Rihanna's "Umbrella") and a sample of one hundred songs per year from 2002 to 2007 that chains were not being programmed in lockstep. Rossman called payola "a permanent feature of the music industry," cyclically rising because too effective to resist but offering "little or no aggregate gain in promotional exposure" when everybody did it and particularly valued by independent labels as a tool. Ross took issue with the idea that restraining payola led to unleashed creativity: "Viewed over several decades' perspective, radio does seem to become more aggressive musically when the labels are throwing money around to work their product, by whatever means, than when they're not." Richard Peterson's

notion of a tension between entrepreneurial business styles and bureau-
cratic ones applied here—apparently, a more payola-driven Top 40 was
also more hip-hop friendly.[41]

What exactly was Top 40 supposed to ideally deliver? Strikingly, Rossman, building on criticism by Hua Hsu in *Slate*, found that one of the most
critically scorned songs of all time ("interminable," "cringe-inducing,"
"embarrassing," "laughably bad"), the Black Eyed Peas' "My Humps,"
an ode to singer Fergie's "lovely lady lumps," was a rare example of a hit
with a fully endogenous curve—proof of slow-building, unmanufactured
support, or as Hsu put it, "the most successful unsolicited single in history." Here was the paradox of Top 40 democracy in a nutshell: a song
that confirmed the worst fears of elite tastemakers, including some at the
record label, proved dramatically successful with actual listeners.[42]

After all, the commodified sexual crassness of Fergie was far from singular. "Wake up in the morning feeling like P. Diddy," began the breakout
hit by a white female rapper of sorts, with a dollar sign in her name. "Tik
Tok" was made for a Top 40 radio clock: catchy, novel, a blur of category,
edgy via consumerism and leisure—and by women for women. "Before
I leave, brush my teeth with a bottle of Jack. 'Cause when I leave for the
night, I ain't coming back." Ke$ha, born Kesha Rose Sebert, was second-
generation format pop: her mother Patricia Sebert had a cowrite of Dolly
Parton's country chart topper "Old Flames Can't Hold a Candle to You."
Now, Ke$ha worked for Dr. Luke, whose pop pedigree traced to creating,
alongside Swedish guru Max Martin, *American Idol* winner Kelly Clarkson's pop-rock breakout "Since U Been Gone." The women Luke produced formed a category—Ke$ha, Clarkson, Pink, Avril Lavigne, Katy
Perry, Miley Cyrus, and the godmother of them all, Britney Spears. These
women *had* to be controversial and never put on airs. It was their brand,
but also their social role—the "democratization through exploitation"
that sociologist Joshua Gamson found in Jerry Springer's TV talk-show
guests.[43]

Fergie's group, the Black Eyed Peas, embodied another consequential Top 40 trend: multiracial collectivities and/or multiracial performers.
Ethnically blended pop was not new to Top 40's inherent multiplicity—
similar forces produced Richard Berry's "Louie Louie" in 1950s Los Angeles, "Twist and Shout" for the Isley Brothers in Brill Building–era New
York City. But the process took on new relevance, given rising Latino
and Asian populations in the United States. The supposedly "contentless" Black Eyed Peas, Rachel Devitt noticed, put songs in Tagalog, the

FIGURE 6.1 Bruno Mars performing at radio chain Clear Channel's iHeartRadio music festival in Las Vegas. Mars, with his complicated ethnicity, avowed commerciality, and musical blend of genres, represents the continued centrality of Top 40 pop in the twenty-first century. © Steve Marcus/Reuters/Corbis. Used by permission.

language of the Philippines, on their album: member apl.de.ap, or Allan Pineda, had been born there, to a Filipina mother and departed black American soldier. Filipino Americans' roles in pop, as Devitt points out, have been all too often "glossed over," yet gloss is itself an important story. The multiculturalism that she calls "a kind of pliable, 'something for everyone' chicness"—very much the tone of a Black Eyed Peas hit— pushes against the more righteous but also essentializing "resistance vernaculars" of hip-hop, like rock before it. Similarly, Bruno Mars, raised imitating Elvis Presley in Hawaii by a Puerto Rican father and Filipina mother ("an offspring of the 1898 axis of two former US imperial possessions," quips one scholar), has his music singled out for "placelessness" by *New York Times* critic Jon Caramanica, one of many avowedly pop critics replacing earlier generations of rock and rap critics. I'd argue that Mars's concerts reveal that he does have clear roots—in Top 40. "Billionaire," the single by Gym Class Heroes that he wrote and performed on, starts with the Berry Gordy Motown number it takes melody and chord structure from: "Money (That's What I Want)."[44]

Radio On: *Is* Top 40 Democracy?

One might conclude an overview of recent Top 40 with any of a few examples, each delivering a different moral. The abrupt shuttering of the trade publication *Radio & Records* in 2009 reflected the weakness of radio after a decade in which new ad dollars had gone to Internet companies, TSL overall had steadily declined, and supposed behemoth Clear Channel sold hundreds of channels. A second viewpoint might look at Pandora, Last. FM, Rdio, Spotify, iHeartRadio, Beats Music, and other streaming services that make the radio experience more interactive and personal but struggle to replace the collective impact of formats, their links to social needs beyond particular songs. A third glimpse might utilize Clive Davis's recent memoir. There was an edge to the 1975 book where Davis, fired by Columbia Records, justified his ecumenical, some might say crass, approach to a recognition that record cultures in an era of identity needed diverse handling. By 2013, Davis was the man who built Arista, was forced to retire, then built J Records to boot. He bookended his life story around examples of inclusiveness: his yearly Grammy party, which featured a range of different performers to showcase pop multiplicity, and his sexual identity: bisexuality. For Davis, pop was still a match game, artists and repertoire, sounds and formats, Alicia Keyes sold through Oprah Winfrey, Rod Stewart revived with standards. Nothing had changed.[45]

But since Top 40 democracy rests on unanswerable questions—whether one identity is worth furthering over another, especially where money is involved—I will end with a recent values tester. A *Billboard* article recently asked, "Why Isn't R&B Radio Shopping at the 'Thrift Shop'?" The white Seattle team of rapper Macklemore and producer Ryan Lewis, joined by hired black R&B singer Wanz, had an enormous hit, number 1 for digital downloads and number 2 on the Hot 100, which it would shortly top. It was also considered the number 1 R&B/hip-hop song in the country. Yet it could not be found, at all, in the fifty-position R&B/Hip-Hop Airplay chart. Indeed, two program directors of R&B stations said, "I have never heard of the song," which had never been serviced to them. The song's promoters, Alternative Distribution Alliance (ADA), had first targeted alternative rock, then rhythmic Top 40, and then mainstream Top 40. So while "Thrift Shop" fully fit the sonic genre definition of hip-hop and R&B, it in no way sought to belong to R&B as a format—and by extension to the R&B format's privileging of black listeners. *Billboard*, in shifting its rules for charts like R&B/Hip-Hop Songs to include tracks that sonically belonged and were played elsewhere on radio ("Gangnam Style" was another example), favored musical genre over demographic format, collective sales over the traditional way that charts like R&B allowed a minority population a category to dominate numerically.[46]

Was *Billboard*'s decision correct? Is the core issue the deplorable existence of racially separate music categories, such as R&B, country, and rock (Karl Hagstrom Miller called his study of the subject *Segregating Sound*[47]) or the laudable success of popular music in creating enduring spaces for different populations to express themselves with the confidence of insiders? Should we valorize music that crosses between categories, like "Thrift Shop," or worry about white men usurping black forms and about how easily creative capitalism transforms underground and communal styles? Capitalism, after all, has been at this game for a while. The linkages back can be seen in the vaudeville troupe the Brown Skin Models that the father of the Isley Brothers toured with; in the Chattanooga Medicine Company, who sponsored *The Porter Wagoner Show* that launched Dolly Parton; in the decision of Herb Alpert to dress himself and his band up as Mexicans and create an imaginary Tijuana that made A&M Records viable; in Al Jolson, the vaudeville star who blacked up in the film

The Jazz Singer, who Elton John sang in pubs growing up and who British pop art cited as a touchstone.

But the deeper connection, the connecting thread, is in the continuum of Top 40 formats. Radio apportioned brief songs, briefer DJ commentary, station promotions, and targeted ads, in a virtual embodiment of the oldest linkage of capitalism and culture: the theater alongside the marketplace. Radio was a "social lubricant" and "human surrogate," a 1962 study commissioned by Top 40 station WMCA concluded. Marshall McLuhan wrote of radio's power to "retribalize mankind, its almost instant reversal of individualism into collectivism." The collective audiences conjured by Top 40 music formats in the rock era would have suffered if efforts to separate rock from pop, or true country from a feminized, AC-leaning country, or soul and hip-hop from a corporate urban contemporary, had ever fully succeeded. In the "placelessness" of Top 40, to use Jon Caramanica's word, its endless retweaking of identity categories that some preferred to see remain stable, music did not just sell out communal impulses; it subsidized new publics, or at least glimpses of social relationships still being cemented.[48]

This is not to argue that Top 40, AC, R&B, and country listeners represented a coherent challenge to policies of neoliberalism and widening wealth inequality. If anything, the crossover and assimilationist tendencies of pop formats favored the blurring of social, cultural, and political differences. Yet Top 40 and its offshoots have made their biggest impact when place was in question: for the diaspora of white and African American southerners nationally and into cities that James Gregory has observed, for suburbanites testing social "containment" (to use Elaine Tyler May's phrase), and for youths, gays and lesbians, blended ethnicities, and other "new" cohorts moving into the spotlight of pop modernity. Against such shifts, the placeless markets of the Top 40 formats and their intimate publics offered a vital, diverse center, a feeling of home. They did their most democratic work simply by prioritizing, or making space for within an eclectic mix, the cultural needs of particular audiences and artists. It is remarkable how much value resided in the creation and ongoing existence of rival musical mainstreams. Rock may, at times, have been what critic Robert Christgau calls a "monoculture"; pop, the more encompassing category, never was, once five (going on six) formats of radio music established themselves.[49]

Many people hate what's on the radio, especially "these days," and they have been expressing such sentiments for generations. "You had better do what you are told, you better listen to the radio," Elvis Costello famously sang in his punk rock period, and recently the jazz pianist Robert Glasper won the R&B Grammy for an album pointedly titled *Black Radio*—Glasper knew he would never fit that box and showcased a range of sounds that he thought jazz as a genre and urban as a format should be open to, including a cover of Nirvana's grunge anthem "Smells like Teen Spirit." The stylistic diversity of commercial radio often is viewed as a sham, the equivalent of different fast-food chains and no more nourishing. There was a time when grabbing a burger and driving a freeway to have fun, radio blasting, felt like what Bruce Schulman calls "the great American ride"—democratized leisure for a population enjoying a rising, shared prosperity that opened up consumer culture. Few would now celebrate a "Fast Food Nation."[50]

But hit songs are not Quarter Pounders; each one contains a story that involves people trying to get their music heard at a particular instant, even as the rules of the game are changed by technology, social shifts, and the music of others. When a bunch of songs sound alike, for a time, that is not a problem—it's a history lesson. When a format cycles back and forth over an unresolved issue that returns again and again, that is proof that history isn't as quick as a pop tune. We can, of course, bemoan aspects of what makes it onto the charts; that's a national and now global pastime. Yet we should be glad that music created so many paths for the sounds of different cities, different parts of the same city (and suburb), to rise to the top. And we should never lose sight of the trap that a manufactured Top 40 democracy sets for all critics: our antipathy to packaged sound, to format callousness, always seems to spring from self-congratulatory entitlement. If we get frustrated with radio, is the issue that it's corrupt or that its buckshot form of address unsettles us? And when we confess to guilty pleasures, or sing karaoke, isn't that about the recognition that a commercialized packaging of identity turned out to capture something interstitial about who we were, and are?

As I noted at the start of this book, my first involvement with radio was college radio, where DJs could play whatever we liked, though we nonetheless created a fairly tight playlist of indie rock bands and their progenitors—an attempt to tell a story other than the hippie-dominated, *Rolling Stone*, Rolling Stones, "Like a Rolling Stone" classic rock version. It would take decades for most of us to see that the way around uncritical rockism led back to pop. But one of our legends, Jonathan Richman, had never been confused. In the early 1970s, he steered his band, the Modern

Lovers, to critique the counterculture just as it started to dominate. There was "I'm Straight," where he told us he wasn't stoned "like hippie Johnny." There was "Modern World," a place "not so bad / Not like the students say." But most of all there was "Roadrunner," a song about the great American ride. FM underground stations were broadcasting, but Richman was having none of it as he went fast on Route 128, late at night, revved up on the AM "rockin' modern neon sound," open to all that was out there. Listening to Top 40 democracy, despite what his hero Lou Reed called, in his Velvet Underground tribute song to the same thing, all the computations and all the amputations. Radio on.

Acknowledgments

I began this book project convinced that rockism and poptimism needed to be understood as part of a larger history and that, more than ever, scholarship on popular music was now in a position to provide it. I owe thanks to the *New York Times*, who commissioned an early essay on the "Ancestors of Pop" that got me going. But my biggest intellectual inspiration has been the Pop Conference, which I cofounded for the Seattle museum EMP (then Experience Music Project) in 2002 and have been overseeing ever since. Watching a diverse community of academics and critics form through these gatherings has been one of the great satisfactions of my life. I thank all those who have presented—many will see their work mentioned in my endnotes, framing how I conceptualize this large subject—but the collective effect has been even more important: making pop, that shiny beast, a subject of study to rival rock, hip-hop, and jazz.

When I began this book, I was a former alt-press critic and editor who worked at a music museum; now I teach American studies. My thanks to the *Village Voice* and *Spin* gang for getting me started: Robert Christgau, Craig Marks, Joe Levy, Doug Simmons, Rob Sheffield, and of course Ann Powers (who will come up again). Thanks to Bob Santelli and Jim Fricke for bringing Ann and me to EMP, to Dan Cavicchi for sharing that first Pop Conference year, and to Jasen Emmons for keeping the connection vital. At UC Berkeley, where I belatedly dissertated, Paula Fass continued as longtime mentor, Waldo Martin saved the day when things foundered, and Scott Saul was both a needed peer and vibrant friend. Lynne Adrian and the American studies gang at the University of Alabama have been incredibly nurturing as I began to teach, with Stacy Morgan, Rich Megraw, and Edward Tang always available across the hallway and the school's research grant committee making summer writing far easier. It was a delight to serve as an officer of the International Association for the Study of Popular Music's American branch (IASPM-US) with Barry Shank, Beverly Keel, Karl Hagstrom Miller, and Caroline O'Meara, and as a *Journal of Popular Music Studies* associate editor with Karen Tongson and Gus Stadler.

Many other peers and inspirations have kept me going in writing this book, presenting on panels, and conference organizing. Forgive me if your name was inadvertently omitted, but beyond those already mentioned here are at least a few: Daphne Brooks, Joshua Clover, Drew Daniel, Joel Dinerstein, Alice Echols, Robert Fink, Holly George-Warren, Michelle Habell-Pallan, David Hesmondhalgh, Hua Hsu, Keir Keightley, Jason King, Josh Kun, Eric Lott, Greil Marcus, Michaelangelo Matos, Charles McGovern, Katherine Meizel, Mark Anthony Neal, Ali Neff, Keith Negus, Sean Nelson, Tavia Nyong'o, Lauren Onkey, Diane Pecknold, Tim Quirk, Guthrie Ramsey, Sonnet Retman, Jody Rosen, Carlo Rotella, the greatly missed David Sanjek, Kelefa Sanneh, RJ Smith, Ned Sublette, David Suisman, Greg Tate, Alexandra Vazquez, Steve Waksman, Elijah Wald, Gayle Wald, Oliver Wang, Carl Wilson, and Ken Wissoker.

John Gorman opened his files, Rolodex, and home to me in Cleveland; thanks as well there for WMMS interviews with Billy Bass, Jeff Kinzbach, Gaye Ramstrom, Denny Sanders, and the late Murray Saul. Herb Alpert and Jerry Moss gave me a helpful interview about A&M Records. John Rumble was a gracious host at the Country Music Hall of Fame, and I was also aided by staffers at the New York Public Library for the Performing Arts and Schomburg Center for Research in Black Culture, UCLA's A&M Records and film and TV archives, Bowling Green's recorded sound archives, the Paley Center for Media in Los Angeles, and the University of Maryland Library of American Broadcasting. *Radio & Records* was not an archive, but the besieged staff gave me leather-bound volumes of a scarce resource; thanks to Cyndee Maxwell and Darnella Dunham. Robert Devens was kind enough to bring me to the University of Chicago Press, then skipped town; Tim Mennell has been his enthusiastic and rock-solid replacement. David Barker let me write a weird little book about Guns N' Roses for Continuum when I was tired of scholarly immersion.

Oh, who am I kidding, it really all comes back to Ann Powers. It isn't every day that one's husband says there is this book he wants to write, and maybe it could double as a diss, and there could be a teaching gig someplace. I said that and Ann, amazingly, at no small cost, said *sure*—that makes total sense. Our daughter has hit double-digits along the way, old enough to make Top 40 democracy the subject of every car drive—thanks for keeping me current, Rebecca! And my parents have been generous and steadfast. WPRB friends, I love you and owe you. But really, Ann, this one is all about a quarter century of arguing music and music writing together, watching empires of records rise and fall (and *Empire Records* fall and rise). I'll never see the light on Nick Drake, but your love of music and me has shaped every sentence here.

Notes

Introduction

1. Ben Fong-Torres, *The Hits Just Keep On Coming: The History of Top 40 Radio* (Miller Freeman Books, 1998), 37–39; Eric Rothenbuhler and Tom McCourt, "Radio Redefines Itself, 1947–1962," in *Radio Reader: Essays in the Cultural History of Radio*, ed. Michele Hilmes and Jason Loviglio (Routledge, 2001), 367–87; Marc Fisher, *Something in the Air: Radio, Rock, and the Revolution That Shaped a Generation* (Random House, 2007), 3–28.

2. Richard Peterson, *Creating Country Music: Fabricating Authenticity* (University of Chicago Press, 1997), 17–32; Tim Lawrence, *Love Saves the Day: A History of American Dance Music Culture, 1970–1979* (Duke University Press, 2003), 70–72; Andreas Huyssen, "Mass Culture as Woman: Modernism's Other," in *After the Great Divide: Modernism, Mass Culture, Postmodernism* (Indiana University Press, 1986), 44–64; Jennifer Scanlon, ed., *The Gender and Consumer Culture Reader* (New York University Press, 2000); David MacFarland, *The Development of the Top 40 Radio Format* (1973; reprint, Arno Press, 1979), 298, 536; *Time*, June 4, 1956, cited on 187.

3. MacFarland, *Top 40 Radio Format*, 267; Fong-Torres, *Hits Just Keep On Coming*, 49, 56–57.

4. Karl Hagstrom Miller, *Segregating Sound: Inventing Folk and Pop Music in the Age of Jim Crow* (Duke University Press, 2010), 6.

5. William Howland Kenney, *Recorded Music in American Life: The Phonograph and Popular Memory, 1890–1945* (Oxford University Press, 1999), 158–81; Mark Katz, *Capturing Sound: How Technology Has Changed Music* (University of California Press, 2004), 8–47; Lewis Erenberg, *Swingin' the Dream: Big Band Jazz and the Rebirth of American Culture* (University of Chicago Press, 1998), 35–64; Elijah Wald, *How the Beatles Destroyed Rock 'n' Roll: An Alternative History of American Popular Music* (Oxford University Press, 2009), 138–49.

6. Andre Millard, *America on Record: A History of Recorded Sound*, second

edition (Cambridge University Press, 2005), 172; Richard Peterson, "Why 1955? Explaining the Advent of Rock Music," *Popular Music* 9, no. 1 (1990): 97–116; John Broven, *Record Makers and Breakers: Voices of the Independent Rock 'n' Roll Pioneers* (University of Illinois Press, 2009).

7. Susan Douglas, *Where the Girls Are: Growing Up Female with the Mass Media* (Times Books, 1994), 83–98.

8. Jean-Christophe Agnew, *Worlds Apart: The Market and the Theater in Anglo-American Thought, 1550–1750* (Cambridge University Press, 1986), 202; Eric Lott, *Love and Theft: Blackface Minstrelsy and the American Working Class* (Oxford University Press, 1993), *Tribune* quote on 49; W. C. Handy, *Father of the Blues: An Autobiography* (1941; reprint, Da Capo Press, 1991), 33.

9. David Suisman, *Selling Sounds: The Commercial Revolution in American Music* (Harvard University Press, 2009); Keir Keightley, "Tin Pan Allegory," *Modernism/Modernity* 19, no. 2 (2013): 717–36; Jody Rosen, *White Christmas: The Story of an American Song* (Scribner, 2002); Timothy Taylor, *The Sounds of Capitalism: Advertising, Music, and the Conquest of Culture* (University of Chicago Press, 2012), 11–100.

10. Thomas Streeter, *Selling the Air: A Critique of the Policy of Commercial Broadcasting in the United States* (University of Chicago Press, 1996); Michele Hilmes, *Radio Voices: American Broadcasting, 1922–1952* (University of Minnesota Press, 1997); Susan Douglas, *Listening In: Radio and the American Imagination, from Amos 'n' Andy and Edward R. Murrow to Wolfman Jack and Howard Stern* (Times Books, 1999); Jason Loviglio, *Radio's Intimate Public: Network Broadcasting and Mass-Mediated Democracy* (University of Minnesota Press, 2005); Elena Razlogova, *The Listener's Voice: Early Radio and the American Public* (University of Pennsylvania Press, 2011), 108.

11. *Billboard*, September 26, 1942; *The Billboard 1944 Music Year Book* (Billboard, 1944), 57–58.

12. Edd Routt, James McGrath, and Fredric Weiss, *The Radio Format Conundrum* (Hastings House, 1978), 11.

13. David Riesman, "Listening to Popular Music" (1950), reprinted in *On Record: Rock, Pop, and the Written Word*, ed. Simon Frith and Andrew Goodwin (Taylor & Francis, 1990), 4–10.

14. Grace Hale, *A Nation of Outsiders: How the White Middle Class Fell in Love with Rebellion in Postwar America* (Oxford University Press, 2011); Gerald Early, "Pulp and Circumstance: The Story of Jazz in High Places," in *The Jazz Cadence of American Culture*, ed. Robert O'Meally (Columbia University Press, 1998), 393–430; Michael Denning, *The Cultural Front: The Laboring of American Culture in the Twentieth Century* (Verso, 1997), 323–61; Andrew Ross, *No Respect: Intellectuals & Popular Culture* (Routledge, 1989), 65–101; John Leland, *Hip: The History* (Harper Perennial, 2005).

15. Bill Malone and Jocelyn Neal, *Country Music, U.S.A.*, third revised edition (University of Texas Press, 2010), 242; Miller, *Segregating Sound*, 6.

16. Franco Fabbri, "A Theory of Musical Genres: Two Applications," in *Popular Music Perspectives*, ed. David Horn and Phillip Tagg (International Association for the Study of Popular Music, 1981), 52–81; Simon Frith, *Performing Rites: On the Value of Popular Music* (Harvard University Press, 1996), 75–98; Jennifer Lena, *Banding Together: How Communities Create Genres in Popular Music* (Princeton University Press, 2012); Fabian Holt, *Genre in Popular Music* (University of Chicago Press, 2007); Eric Weisbard, "Beyond Category? Never! The Game of Genres in Popular Music," *Journal of Popular Music Studies* 25, no. 3 (2013): 401–5.

17. Eric Porter, *What Is This Thing Called Jazz? African American Musicians as Artists, Critics, and Activists* (University of California Press, 2002), 51; Elijah Wald, *Escaping the Delta: Robert Johnson and the Invention of the Blues* (Amistad, 2004). For an outraged response to Wald, see Greil Marcus, *Mystery Train: Images of America in Rock 'n' Roll Music*, fifth revised edition (Plume, 2008), 208–10.

18. Robert Christgau, *Any Old Way You Choose It: Rock and Other Pop Music, 1967–1973* (Penguin, 1973), 1; Ellen Willis, "Records: Rock, etc.— the Big Ones," *New Yorker*, February 1, 1969, reprinted in *The Pop, Rock, and Soul Reader: Histories and Debates*, ed. David Brackett (Oxford University Press, 2009), 234.

19. Alice Echols, *Shaky Ground: The Sixties and Its Aftershocks* (Columbia University Press, 2002), 159–92; Bernard Gendron, *Between Montmartre and the Mudd Club: Popular Music and the Avant-Garde* (University of Chicago Press, 2002), 161–247; Wald, *How the Beatles Destroyed Rock 'n' Roll*, 230–47; Devon Powers, *Writing the Record: The Village Voice and the Birth of Rock Criticism* (University of Massachusetts Press, 2013); Simon Frith, *Sound Effects: Youth, Leisure, and the Politics of Rock 'n' Roll* (Pantheon, 1983), 11; Steve Chapple and Reebee Garofalo, *Rock 'n' Roll Is Here to Pay: The History and Politics of the Music Industry* (Nelson-Hall, 1977); Keir Keightley, "Reconsidering Rock," in *The Cambridge Companion to Pop and Rock*, ed. Simon Frith, Will Straw, and John Street (Cambridge University Press, 2001), 109; Kelefa Sanneh, "The Rap against Rockism," *New York Times*, October 31, 2004.

20. Michael Kramer, *The Republic of Rock: Music and Citizenship in the Sixties Counterculture* (Oxford University Press, 2013).

21. Jim Ladd, *Radio Waves: Life and Revolution on the FM Dial* (St. Martin's, 1992).

22. Kim Simpson, *Early '70s Radio: The American Format Revolution* (Continuum, 2011); Simon Frith, "Pop Music," in Frith, Straw, and Street, *The Cambridge Companion to Pop and Rock*, 100–101.

23. Keir Keightley, "You Keep Coming Back like a Song: Adult Audiences, Taste Panics, and the Idea of the Standard," *Journal of Popular Music Studies* 13 (2001): 7–40; Keightley, "Long Play: Adult-Oriented Popular Music and the Temporal Logics of the Post-war Sound Recording Industry in the US," *Media Culture Society* 26, no. 3 (2004): 375–91.

24. Clive Davis with James Willwerth, *Clive: Inside the Record Business* (William Morrow, 1975), esp. 53, 94–95, 140, and 143–48.

25. Timothy Dowd, "Concentration and Diversity Revisited: Production Logics and the U.S. Mainstream Recording Market, 1940–1990," *Social Forces* 82, no. 4 (2004): 1411–55; Motti Regev, *Pop-Rock Music: Aesthetic Cosmopolitanism in Late Modernity* (Polity, 2013); Eric Weisbard, "Pop in the 90's: Everything for Everyone," *New York Times*, April 30, 2000.

26. Keith Negus, *Music Genres and Corporate Cultures* (Routledge, 1999); Negus, *Producing Pop: Culture and Conflict in the Popular Music Industry* (Edward Arnold, 1992), 49.

27. Adam Green, *Selling the Race: Culture, Community, and Black Chicago, 1940–1955* (University of Chicago Press, 2007); Kathy Newman, "The Forgotten Fifteen Million: Black Radio, Radicalism, and the Construction of the 'Negro Market,'" in *Communities of the Air: Radio Century, Radio Culture*, ed. Susan Merrill Squier (Duke University Press, 2003), 127; Robert Weems, *Desegregating the Dollar: African American Consumerism in the Twentieth Century* (New York University Press, 1998), 71–79.

28. NAACP Report, "The Discordant Sound of Music" (1987), reprinted in *R&B Rhythm and Business: The Political Economy of Black Music*, ed. Norman Kelley (Akashic, 2005), 44–58.

29. Jefferson Cowie, *Stayin' Alive: The 1970s and the Last Days of the Working Class* (New Press, 2010); David Harvey, *A Brief History of Neoliberalism* (Oxford University Press, 2005).

30. Stuart Ewen, *Captains of Consciousness: Advertising and the Social Roots of the Consumer Culture* (McGraw-Hill, 1976); Roland Marchand, *Advertising the American Dream: Making Way for Modernity, 1920–1940* (University of California Press, 1985); Jennifer Scanlon, *Inarticulate Longings: The Ladies' Home Journal, Gender, and the Promises of Consumer Culture* (Routledge, 1995); Lawrence Glickman, *A Living Wage: American Workers and the Making of Consumer Society* (Cornell University Press, 1997); Thomas Frank, *The Conquest of Cool: Business Culture, Counterculture, and the Rise of Hip Consumerism* (University of Chicago Press, 1997); Taylor, *Sounds of Capitalism*; Charles McGovern, *Sold American: Consumption and Citizenship, 1890–1945* (University of North Carolina Press, 2006), 18; Lizabeth Cohen, *A Consumers' Republic: The Politics of Mass Consumption in Postwar America* (Knopf, 2003), 292–344.

31. Michele Hilmes, "Rethinking Radio," in Hilmes and Loviglio, *Radio Reader*, 4.

32. Diane Pecknold, *The Selling Sound: Commercialism and Country Music* (Duke University Press, 2007).

33. George Lipsitz, *Footsteps in the Dark: The Hidden Histories of Popular Music* (University of Minnesota Press, 2007), viii; Lauren Berlant, *The Female Complaint: The Unfinished Business of Sentimentality in American Culture* (Duke University Press, 2008), 10; Loviglio, *Radio's Intimate Public*.

34. Jason King, "The Sound of Velvet Melting: The Power of 'Vibe' in the Music of Roberta Flack," in *Listen Again: A Momentary History of Pop Music*,

ed. Eric Weisbard (Duke University Press, 2007), 172–99; Alice Echols, *Hot Stuff: Disco and the Remaking of American Culture* (Norton, 2010); Aretha Franklin with David Ritz, *From These Roots* (Villard, 1999).

35. Jacqueline Dowd Hall, "The Long Civil Rights Movement and the Political Uses of the Past," *Journal of American History* 91, no. 4 (2005): 1233–63.

36. Guthrie Ramsey Jr., *Race Music: Black Cultures from Bebop to Hip-Hop* (University of California Press, 2004).

37. Gary Burns, "A Typology of 'Hooks' in Popular Music," *Popular Music* 6, no. 1 (1987): 1–20; Antoine Hennion, "The Production of Success: An Antimusicology of the Pop Song" (1983), reprinted in Frith and Goodwin, *On Record*, 185–206; Charles Kronengold, "Accidents, Hooks, and Theory," *Popular Music* 24, no. 3 (2005): 381–97.

38. Magazines in James Baughman, *The Republic of Mass Culture: Journalism, Filmmaking, and Broadcasting in America since 1941*, third edition (Johns Hopkins University Press, 2006), 190; Letterman in Gil Troy, *Morning in America: How Ronald Reagan Invented the 1980s* (Princeton University Press, 2005), 128; Jeremy Tunstall, *The Media Were American: U.S. Mass Media in Decline* (Oxford University Press, 2007), 253; David Hesmondhalgh, *The Cultural Industries*, third edition (Sage, 2013).

39. Joshua Gamson, *Claims to Fame: Celebrity in Contemporary America* (University of California Press, 1994), 149; Rob Drew, *Karaoke Nights: An Ethnographic Rhapsody* (AltaMira, 2001); Katherine Meizel, *Idolized: Music, Media, and Identity in American Idol* (Indiana University Press, 2011); Henry Jenkins, *Convergence Culture: Where Old and New Media Collide*, revised edition (New York University Press, 2008).

40. Rick Perlstein, *Nixonland: The Rise of a President and the Fracturing of America* (Scribner, 2008), 178; Christopher Waterman, "Race Music: Bo Chatmon, 'Corrine Corrina,' and the Excluded Middle," in *Music and the Racial Imagination*, ed. Ronald Radano and Philip Bohlman (University of Chicago Press, 2000), 167–205; Regev, *Pop-Rock*, 58; Mitchell Morris, *The Persistence of Sentiment: Display and Feeling in Popular Music of the 1970s* (University of California Press, 2013); Simpson, *Early '70s Radio*; Gabriel Rossman, *Climbing the Charts: What Radio Airplay Tells Us about the Diffusion of Innovation* (Princeton University Press, 2012); David Hesmondhalgh, *Why Music Matters* (Wiley Blackwell, 2013).

41. Richard A. Peterson, "The Dialectic of Hard-Core and Soft-Shell," *South Atlantic Quarterly* 94, no. 1 (1995): 273–300.

42. Lani Guinier, *The Tyranny of the Majority: Fundamental Fairness in Representative Democracy* (Free Press, 1994), 1–20.

Chapter One

1. Isabel Wilkerson, "Separate Senior Proms Reveal an Unspanned Racial Divide," *New York Times*, May 25, 1991.

2. There has never been a book about the Isley Brothers. The single best source for information is the booklet accompanying the boxed set *It's Your Thing: The Story of the Isley Brothers* (Legacy, 1999). For other good overviews, see their entry in the All Music Guide (www.allmusic.com); *Goldmine*, November 29, 1991; and the Vocal Group Hall of Fame website, http://www.vocalgroup.org/inductees /the_isley_brothers.html.

3. The strongest revisionist arguments are Alice Echols, "Shaky Ground: Popular Music in the Disco Years," in *Shaky Ground: The Sixties and Its Aftershocks* (Columbia University Press, 2002), 159–92; and Elijah Wald, *How the Beatles Destroyed Rock 'n' Roll: An Alternative History of American Popular Music* (Oxford University Press, 2009), 230–47.

4. Howard Brick, *Age of Contradiction: American Thought & Culture in the 1960s* (Cornell University Press, 1998), 13; Donald Katz, *Home Fires: An Intimate Portrait of One Middle-Class Family in Postwar America* (HarperCollins, 1992), 94; Maureen Mahon, *Right to Rock: The Black Rock Coalition and the Cultural Politics of Race* (Duke University Press, 2004), 9–10; Peter Guralnick, *Sweet Soul Music: Rhythm and Blues and the Southern Dream of Freedom* (HarperCollins, 1986); Richard Green and Monique Guillory, "Question of a 'Soulful Style': Interview with Paul Gilroy," in *Soul: Black Power, Politics, and Pleasure*, ed. Richard Green and Monique Guillory (New York University Press, 1998), 251; Nelson George, *The Death of Rhythm and Blues* (Pantheon, 1988); Mark Anthony Neal, "Rhythm & Bullshit," PopMatters.com, June 3, 2005, http://www.popmatters.com /pm/feature/050603-randb. For a more sophisticated treatment of rock's role in southern integration, see Michael Bertrand, *Race, Rock, and Elvis* (University of Illinois Press, 2000).

5. Robert Self and Thomas Sugrue, "The Power of Place: Race, Political Economy, and Identity in the Postwar Metropolis," in *A Companion to Post-1945 America*, ed. Jean-Christophe Agnew and Roy Rosenzweig (Blackwell, 2002), 20–43; Jacqueline Dowd Hall, "The Long Civil Rights Movement and the Political Uses of the Past," *Journal of American History* 91, no. 4 (2005): 1233–63; Nikhil Pal Singh, *Black Is a Country: Race and the Unfinished Struggle for Democracy* (Harvard University Press, 2004); Eric Avila, *Popular Culture in the Age of White Flight: Fear and Fantasy in Suburban Los Angeles* (University of California Press, 2004).

6. Tera Hunter, "'Sexual Pantomimes,' the Blues Aesthetic, and Black Women in the New South," in *Music and the Racial Imagination*, ed. Ronald Radano and Philip Bohlman (University of Chicago Press, 2000), 145–64; Preston Lauterbach, *The Chitlin' Circuit and the Road to Rock 'n' Roll* (Norton, 2011).

7. *Radio & Records*, May 25, 1979; May 24, 1985.

8. James Snead, "Repetition as a Figure of Black Culture," in *Black Literature and Literary Theory*, ed. Henry Louis Gates (Methuen, 1984), 59–79; Amiri Baraka (then Leroi Jones), "The Changing Same: R&B and New Black Music" (1966), reprinted in *The Leroi Jones/Amiri Baraka Reader*, ed. William Harris

(Thunder's Mouth, 1991), 186–209; Guthrie Ramsey Jr., *Race Music: Black Cultures from Bebop to Hip-Hop* (University of California Press, 2004); Adam Green, *Selling the Race: Culture, Community, and Black Chicago, 1940–1955* (University of Chicago Press, 2007).

9. George Lipsitz, *Footsteps in the Dark: The Hidden Histories of Popular Music* (University of Minnesota Press, 2007), x–xi.

10. Ramsey, *Race Music*, 51; for *Ebony*, Green, *Selling the Race*.

11. Jeff Greenfield, *No Peace, No Place: Excavations along the Generational Fault* (Doubleday, 1973), 29.

12. Liner notes, *It's Your Thing*.

13. Like the Isley Brothers, the Mills Brothers have not received their historical due, but for an overview see Will Friedwald, *A Biographical Guide to the Great Jazz and Pop Singers* (Random House, 2010), 336–40.

14. Anthony Heilbut, *The Gospel Sound: Good News and Bad Times*, 25th anniversary edition (Limelight, 1997), comment about promoters on 257; Robert Darden, *People Get Ready! A New History of Gospel Music* (Continuum, 2005); Jerma Jackson, *Singing in My Soul: Black Gospel Music in a Secular Age* (University of North Carolina Press, 2003); Ramsey, *Race Music*, 48–75.

15. Samuel Floyd Jr., *The Power of Black Music: Interpreting Its History from Africa to the United States* (Oxford University Press, 1995), 38. The anthropologist Melville Herskovits argued most forcefully for notions of retention, beginning with *The Myth of the Negro Past* (1941; reprint, Beacon, 1990); the case was far from resolved in 1959, a year that saw the publication of Herskovits and William Bascom, eds., *Continuity and Change in African Cultures* (University of Chicago Press, 1959); Lawrence Levine traces the debate in *Black Culture and Black Consciousness* (Oxford University Press, 1977), uncovering an 1862 white ancestor of Jeff Greenfield: "To-night I have been to a 'shout,' which seems to me certainly the remains of some old idol worship. . . . I never saw anything so savage. They call it a religious ceremony, but it seems more like a regular frolic to me."

16. *Ebony*, March 1964; Green, *Selling the Race*; Ramsey, *Race Music*.

17. Charlie Gillett, *The Sound of the City: The Rise of Rock and Roll*, second edition (1983; reprint, Da Capo, 1996), 153–59; Philip Ennis, *The Seventh Stream: The Emergence of Rocknroll in American Popular Music* (Wesleyan University Press, 1992), 211–12; Jay Warner, *American Singing Groups: A History from 1940 to Today* (1992; reprint, Hal Leonard, 2006), 312–14; Henry Sampson, *Swingin' Ether Waves: A Chronological History of African Americans in Radio and Television Broadcasting, 1925–1955* (Scarecrow, 2005), vol. 2, 1016, 1175.

18. Sampson, *Swingin' Ether Waves*, vol. 2, 942, 1033, 812.

19. Nikki Giovanni, *The Prosaic Soul of Nikki Giovanni* (Harper Perennial, 2003), 405–6, 491–92; Henry Louis Taylor Jr., ed., *Race and the City: Work, Community, and Protest in Cincinnati, 1820–1970* (University of Illinois Press, 1993), esp. 14–15 and 175.

20. Kathy Newman, "The Forgotten Fifteen Million: Black Radio, Radicalism, and the Construction of the 'Negro Market,'" in *Communities of the Air: Radio Century, Radio Culture*, ed. Susan Merrill Squier (Duke University Press, 2003), 122; William Barlow, *Voice Over: The Making of Black Radio* (Temple University Press, 1999), 98–103; George, *Death of Rhythm and Blues*, 41.

21. *Jet*, July 14, 2003; liner notes, *It's Your Thing*.

22. Brian Ward, *Just My Soul Responding: Rhythm and Blues, Black Consciousness, and Race Relations* (University of California Press, 1998), 20; Keir Keightley, "You Keep Coming Back like a Song: Adult Audiences, Taste Panics, and the Idea of the Standard," *Journal of Popular Music Studies* 13 (2001): 7–40; *Ebony*, November 1957; Rob Bowman, *Soulsville, USA: The Story of Stax Records* (Schirmer, 2000), 105–6; *Soul*, June 10, 1974.

23. Gavin Petrie, *Black Music* (Hamlyn, 1974), 77–78; Katz, *Home Fires*, 93; *Goldmine*, July 23, 2004.

24. John Broven, *Record Makers and Breakers: Voices of the Independent Rock 'n' Roll Pioneers* (University of Illinois Press, 2009), 234–38, 248–53.

25. Thomas Sugrue, *Sweet Land of Liberty: The Forgotten Struggle for Civil Rights in the North* (Random House, 2008), 159.

26. *New York Times*, November 20, 2003.

27. Louis Masur, *Runaway Dream: Born to Run and Bruce Springsteen's American Vision* (Bloomsbury, 2009), 85.

28. Petrie, *Black Music*, 78; *Billboard*, February 3, 1990; liner notes, *It's Your Thing*.

29. Wald, *How the Beatles Destroyed Rock 'n' Roll*, 221. All Music Guide, www .allmusic.com, is the most useful discographical source.

30. Ward, *Just My Soul Responding*, 124; Cleaver cited on 166–67. See also George Lipsitz, "Land of a Thousand Dances: Youth, Minorities, and the Rise of Rock 'n' Roll," in *Recasting America: Culture and Politics in the Age of Cold War*, ed. Lary May (University of Chicago Press, 1989), 267–84.

31. Brian Ward, *Radio and the Struggle for Civil Rights in the South* (University of Florida Press, 2004), 7, 116, 190–204.

32. Ken Emerson, *Always Magic in the Air: The Bomp and Brilliance of the Brill Building Era* (Viking, 2005); George Lipsitz, *Dangerous Crossroads: Popular Music, Postmodernism, and the Poetics of Place* (Verso, 1994), 162, for Berns, *Mojo*, March 1998.

33. *New York Times*, June 25, 2000; Stanley Dance, *The World of Swing* (Da Capo, 1979), 202; *New York Times*, May 2, 1993.

34. Sugrue, *Sweet Land of Liberty*, 455; Reginald Damerell, *Triumph in a White Suburb* (William Morrow, 1968).

35. Suzanne Smith, *Dancing in the Streets: Motown and the Cultural Politics of Detroit* (Harvard University Press, 2001).

36. Steven Stark, *Meet the Beatles: A Cultural History of the Band That Shook Youth, Gender, and the World* (HarperCollins, 2005), 28–29.

37. *Newsweek*, September 10, 2001.

38. Berry Gordy, *To Be Loved: The Music, the Magic, the Memories of Motown* (Warner Books, 1995), 204–5, 245–46.

39. King speech cited in Ward, *Just My Soul Responding*, 232; liner notes, *It's Your Thing*.

40. Advertisement, *New York Times*, March 13, 1961; James Brown with Bruce Tucker, *James Brown: The Godfather of Soul* (Macmillan, 1986), 104.

41. Kevin Phinney, *Souled American: How Black Music Transformed White Culture* (Billboard, 2005), 265; John Edgar Wideman, "Michael Jordan Leaps the Great Divide," in *Signifyin(G), Sanctifyin', & Slam Dunking: A Reader in African American Expressive Culture*, ed. Gena Dagel Caponi (University of Massachusetts Press, 1999), 399.

42. David Roediger, *Colored White: Transcending the Racial Past* (University of California Press, 2002), 217.

43. Larry Neal, "Black Art and Black Liberation," *Ebony*, August 1969.

44. Amy Ongiri, *Spectacular Blackness: The Cultural Politics of the Black Power Movement and the Search for a Black Aesthetic* (University of Virginia Press, 2010), 16.

45. Robert Weems, *Desegregating the Dollar: African American Consumerism in the Twentieth Century* (New York University Press, 1998), 70–79; Lizabeth Cohen, *A Consumers' Republic: The Politics of Mass Consumption in Postwar America* (Knopf, 2003), 309.

46. David Greenberg, *Nixon's Shadow: The History of an Image* (Norton, 2003), 136; Paul Gilroy, "Wearing Your Art on Your Sleeve: Notes toward a Diaspora History of Black Ephemera," in *Small Acts: Thoughts on the Politics of Black Cultures* (Serpent's Tail, 1994), 237–57; Kim Simpson, *Early '70s Radio: The American Format Revolution* (Continuum, 2011).

47. "It Really *Is* Their Thing," *Soul*, June 16, 1969.

48. Ibid.; *Sepia*, December 1969.

49. *It's Your Thing* (Medford Films, 1970), viewed at the UCLA Film and Television Archive. Poster reprinted in *It's Your Thing* box set.

50. *Billboard*, September 13, 1969.

51. "A Study of the Soul Music Environment Prepared for Columbia Records Group" (1972; not published; copy in author's possession); David Morse, *Motown and the Arrival of Black Music* (Macmillan, 1971), 136–37; Clive Davis with James Willwerth, *Clive: Inside the Record Business* (William Morrow, 1975), 148.

52. *Mix*, November 1, 2003; *New York Times*, October 7, 1973.

53. Barlow, *Voice Over*, 234–35; Harry Allen, "Frankie Crocker," *Vibe*, January 2001; February 2001.

54. Barlow, *Voice Over*, 226–41.

55. See, for example, Robert Palmer, "Black, Proud, Not Ashamed to Be Loud: The Isleys Keep On Fighting the Power," *Rolling Stone*, August 28, 1975; *Sun Reporter*, March 22, 1979.

56. Weems, *Desegregating the Dollar*, 80–90; Russell Sanjek, *American Popular Music and Its Business* (Oxford University Press, 1988), vol. 3, 640.

57. Rickey Vincent, *Funk: The Music, the People, and the Rhythm of the One* (St. Martin's Press, 1996), 193; Scott Poulson-Bryant and Smokey Fontaine, *What's Your Hi-Fi Q? From Prince to Puff Daddy, 30 Years of Black Music Trivia* (Fireside, 2002), 49; Carol Cooper, liner notes, Isley Brothers, *Funky Family* (Legacy, 1995); Dinah Shore performance and her response heard on *Live It Up* reissue (Legacy, 2004); *Billboard*, November 2, 1974; David Toop, *Rap Attack 3: African Rap to Global Hip Hop* (Serpent's Tail, 1999).

58. *Billboard*, November 8, 1975; Robin D. G. Kelley, *Race Rebels: Culture, Politics, and the Black Working Class* (Free Press, 1994), 71; Cedric the Entertainer, *Grown-A$$ Man* (Ballantine, 2002), 28.

59. *Black Enterprise*, December 1979; *Goldmine*, November 29, 1991.

60. Petrie, *Black Music*, 78; *Phonograph Record*, June 1976, archived at www.rocksbackpages.com; Chris Jasper in liner notes for *Live It Up* reissue.

61. *Blues & Soul*, November 19–December 2, 1974; Petrie, *Black Music*, 78.

62. *Blues & Soul*, October 1967; *Black Stars*, November 1975; June 1974.

63. Figures from Robin D. G. Kelley and Earl Lewis, *To Make Our World Anew: A History of African Americans* (Oxford University Press, 2000), 562–70; and William Chafe, *The Unfinished Journey: America since World War II*, fifth edition (Oxford University Press, 2003), 430–42; William Julius Wilson, *The Declining Significance of Race: Blacks and Changing American Institutions* (University of Chicago Press, 1978).

64. Kimberly W. Bentson, "Amiri Baraka: An Interview," in *Boundary 2*, vol. 6, no. 2 (1978): 312.

65. Carla Roney, *The Knot Guide to Wedding Vows and Traditions: Readings, Rituals, Music, Dances, and Toasts* (Crown, 2004), 3; Harriette Cole, *Jumping the Broom: The African-American Wedding Planner* (Owl, 2004), 172; Kalyn Johnson, *BAP Handbook: The Official Guide to the Black American Princess* (Broadway, 2001); Susan Newman, *Oh God! A Black Woman's Guide to Sex and Spirituality* (One World/Ballantine, 2002), 17; E. Lynn Harris, *A Love of My Own* (Doubleday, 2002), 118; Harris, *If This World Were Mine* (Doubleday, 1997), 12; Harris, *What Becomes of the Brokenhearted: A Memoir* (Doubleday, 2003), 101; Benilde Little, *Who Does She Think She Is? A Novel* (Free Press, 2005), 193; April Sinclair, *Ain't Gonna Be the Same Fool Twice* (Hyperion, 1994), 174; Trisha R. Thomas, *Would I Lie to You?* (Crown, 2004), 64; Ntozake Shange, *Liliane: A Novel* (Picador, 1994), 215. Stressed by work, human resources professional Robyn Sharpe puts on a mix CD with the Isleys in Joni Cole, Rebecca Joffrey, and B. K. Rakhra, eds., *This Day: Diaries from American Women* (Beyond Words, 2003), 198–99.

66. John Edgar Wideman, *Brothers and Keepers: A Memoir* (Holt, Rinehart & Winston, 1984), 126; John W. Fountain, *True Vine: A Young Black Man's Journey of Faith, Hope and Clarity* (Public Affairs, 2003), 11.

67. Gerald Early, *One Nation under a Groove: Motown and American Culture* (Ecco, 1995), 4; S. Smith, *Dancing in the Streets.*

68. Michael Patrick MacDonald, *All Souls: A Family Story from Southie* (Ballantine, 2000), 88.

69. Ralph Ellison, "Little Man at Chehaw Station" (1977), reprinted in *The Collected Essays of Ralph Ellison*, ed. John Callahan (Modern Library, 1995), 489–519, cited in Roediger, *Colored White*, 223.

70. Richard Corliss, "The Stones: Heady Promises," *New York Times*, April 28, 1968; *Sounds* cited in Iain Chambers, *Urban Rhythms: Pop Music and Popular Culture* (Macmillan, 1985), 118; Keir Keightley, "Reconsidering Rock," in *The Cambridge Companion to Pop and Rock*, ed. Simon Frith, Will Straw, and John Street (Cambridge University Press, 2001), 122.

71. Gene Sculatti, "Gator in the Candy Lab: A Brief History of Buddah Records," in *Bubblegum Music Is the Naked Truth: The Dark History of Prepubescent Pop, from the Banana Splits to Britney Spears*, ed. Kim Cooper and David Smay (Feral House, 2001), 232–35.

72. Howard Wuelfing, *3+3* review, *Rutgers Daily Targum*, April 2, 1973, available in the Isley Brothers clippings file, New York Library for the Performing Arts; *New York Times*, February 25, 1968; Charles Cross, *Room Full of Mirrors: A Biography of Jimi Hendrix* (Hyperion, 2005), 112.

73. *Billboard*, December 6, 1969; Palmer, "Black, Proud, Not Ashamed to Be Loud"; Abe Peck, "The Isley Brothers Are Ready for the Next Phase," *Rolling Stone*, August 10, 1978.

74. *Radio & Records*, April 1, 1977; August 19, 1977.

75. Frank Robertson, "Disco Tech: An All-American DJ Fights the Power," from *Dancing Madness*, ed. Abe Peck (Rolling Stone, 1976), cited in Peter Shapiro, *Turn the Beat Around: The Secret History of Disco* (Faber & Faber, 2005), 134; *Radio & Records*, December 8, 1978.

76. *Radio & Records*, December 8, 1978; Tricia Rose, *Black Noise: Rap Music and Black Culture in Contemporary America* (Wesleyan University Press, 1994); see also Ronald Radano, *Lying Up a Nation: Race and Black Music* (University of Chicago Press, 2003). For a defense of the Isleys' repetitiveness to a rock readership, Cliff White, *Go for Your Guns* review in *New Musical Express*, July 9, 1977, archived at www.rocksbackpages.com.

77. Richard Merelman, *Representing Black Culture: Racial Conflict and Cultural Politics in the United States* (Routledge, 1995), 16–18; Robert Hilburn cited in Reebee Garofalo, "Crossing Over, 1939–1989," in *Split Image: African-Americans in the Mass Media*, ed. Jannette Dates and William Barlow (Howard University Press, 1990), 106–7; Tim Lawrence, *Love Saves the Day: A History of American Dance Music Culture, 1970–1979* (Duke University Press, 2003), 376; *Radio & Records*, December 4, 1981; January 29, 1982.

78. Bruce Schulman, *The Seventies: The Great Shift in American Culture, Society,*

and Politics (Da Capo, 2002), 58; Lester Bangs, "The White Noise Supremacists" (1979), in *Psychotic Reactions and Carburetor Dung* (Knopf, 1987), 272–82.

79. Marc Weingarden, *Station to Station: The History of Rock 'n' Roll on Television* (Pocket, 2000).

80. *Rolling Stone*, August 10, 1978; Douglas O'Connor and Gayla Cook, "Black Radio: The 'Soul' Sellout," cited in Ward, *Radio and the Struggle for Civil Rights*, 344; NAACP Report, "The Discordant Sound of Music"; Pitts in Kelley, *R&B Rhythm and Business*, 56.

81. Nelson George quoted in Eithne Quinn, *Nuthin' but a "G" Thang: The Culture and Commerce of Gangsta Rap* (Columbia University Press, 2005), 143.

82. Jason King, "The Sound of Velvet Melting: The Power of 'Vibe' in the Music of Roberta Flack," in *Listen Again: A Momentary History of Pop Music*, ed. Eric Weisbard (Duke University Press, 2007), 172–99. For accounts of the Quiet Storm subformat, see *New York Times*, February 19, 1987; and *Billboard*, June 27, 1992.

83. Dan Charnas, *The Big Payback: The History of the Business of Hip-Hop* (New American Library, 2010); Charles Aaron, "What the White Boy Means When He Says Yo" (1998), reprinted in *And It Don't Stop? The Best American Hip-Hop Journalism of the Last 25 Years*, ed. Raquel Cepeda (Faber & Faber, 2004), 232.

84. Charnas, *Big Payback*, 460; Keith Negus, *Music Genres and Corporate Cultures* (Routledge, 1999), 83–102; Quinn, *Nuthin' but a "G" Thang*.

85. Weems, *Desegregating the Dollar*, 6; *Billboard*, August 7, 1999; *Black Enterprise*, December 2002; *Jet*, September 3, 2001.

86. Elizabeth Isley Barkley, *One Isley Brother's Daughter* (Xlibris, 2011), 32.

87. Kelley, *R&B Rhythm and Business*, 6–23; *Mix*, November 1, 2003; *Jet*, September 13, 1979; *New York Times*, May 13, 1990; decision in case of *Christopher H. Jasper, Marvin Isley v. Bovina Music, Inc., T-Neck Records, Inc.*, December 20, 2002, at http://laws.findlaw.com/circs/2nd/017628.html; Barkley, *One Isley Brother's Daughter*, 54.

88. Paul Gilroy, *Against Race: Imagining Political Culture beyond the Color Line* (Harvard University Press, 2000), 184, 272.

Chapter Two

1. Videos of Dolly Parton's *Tonight Show* appearances (the second was February 17, 1977) are available at the Paley Center for Media in Los Angeles and New York; her December 16, 1977, interview with Walters can be viewed at the Country Music Foundation Library and Media Center at the Country Music Hall of Fame and Museum in Nashville (hereafter CMHOF).

2. Aaron Fox, *Real Country: Music and Language in Working-Class Culture* (Duke University Press, 2004); Kristine McCusker and Diane Pecknold, eds.,

A Boy Named Sue: Gender and Country Music (University Press of Mississippi, 2004); Pamela Fox, *Natural Acts: Gender, Race, and Rusticity in Country Music* (Michigan University Press, 2009).

3. Mary Bufwack and Robert Oermann, *Finding Her Voice: Women in Country Music, 1800–2000* (Country Music Foundation and Vanderbilt University Press, 2003), 311.

4. Paul DiMaggio, Richard Peterson, and Jack Esco Jr., "Country Music: Ballad of the Silent Majority," and Jens Lund, "Fundamentalism, Racism, and Political Reaction in Country Music," in *The Sounds of Social Change*, ed. R. Serge Denisoff and Richard Peterson (Rand McNally, 1972), 38–56, 79–91; James Gregory, *The Southern Diaspora: How the Great Migrations of Black and White Southerners Transformed America* (University of North Carolina Press, 2005), 315; Richard Goldstein, "My Country Music Problem—and Yours," *Mademoiselle*, June 1973.

5. James Cobb, "From Muskogee to Luckenbach: Country Music and the 'Southernization' of America," in *Redefining Southern Culture: Mind & Identity in the Modern South* (University of Georgia Press, 1999); Robert Cantwell, *Bluegrass Breakdown: The Making of the Old Southern Sound* (University of Illinois, 1984); Richard Peterson, *Creating Country Music: Fabricating Authenticity* (University of Chicago Press, 1997); Joli Jensen, *The Nashville Sound: Authenticity, Commercialization, and Country Music* (Vanderbilt University Press, 1998); Diane Pecknold, *The Selling Sound: Commercialism and Country Music* (Duke University Press, 2007); Bill Ivey, "The Bottom Line: Business Practices That Shaped Country Music," in *Country: The Music and the Musicians*, ed. Paul Kingsbury and Alan Axelrod (Abbeville, 1988), 411–51.

6. Gregory, *Southern Diaspora*.

7. Dolly Parton, *Dolly: My Life and Other Unfinished Business* (HarperCollins, 1994); Alanna Nash, *Dolly: The Biography* (1978; reprint, Cooper Square Press, 2002); Willadeene [Parton], *In the Shadow of a Song: The Story of the Parton Family* (Bantam, 1985), 107. For television and plumbing, see Numan Bartley, *The New South, 1945–1980* (Louisiana State University Press, 1995), 269.

8. Stephen Whitfield, "Is It True What They Sing about Dixie?," *Southern Cultures* 8, no. 2 (2002): 9–37; Jack Temple Kirby, *Media-Made Dixie: The South in the American Imagination* (University of Georgia Press, 1986); J. W. Williamson, *Hillbillyland: What the Movies Did to the Mountains and the Mountains Did to the Movies* (University of North Carolina Press, 1995); C. Brendan Martin, "To Keep the Spirit of Mountain Culture Alive," in *Where These Memories Grow: History, Memory, and Southern Identity*, ed. W. Fitzhugh Brundage (University of North Carolina Press, 2000), 249–70; Nash, *Dolly*, 8.

9. David Whisnant, *All That Is Native and Fine: The Politics of Culture in an American Region* (University of North Carolina Press, 1983); Benjamin Filene, *Romancing the Folk: Public Memory & American Roots Music* (University of North Carolina Press, 2000).

10. Jeffrey Lange, *Smile When You Call Me a Hillbilly: Country Music's Struggle for Respectability, 1939–1954* (University of Georgia Press, 2004), 61.

11. *Newsweek*, August 11, 1952, collected in Linnell Gentry, *A History and Encyclopedia of Country, Western, and Gospel Music* (Scholarly Press, 1972), 108; Edward Morris, "New, Improved, Homogenized: Country Radio since 1950," in Kingsbury and Axelrod, *Country*, 89–107; Lola Scobey, *Dolly Parton: Daughter of the South* (Zebra, 1977).

12. Pecknold, *Selling Sound*; *Broadcast*, October 18, 1965; CMA news release cited in Jensen, *Nashville Sound*, 67. The walkway existed prior to the museum's opening.

13. William Nicholls quoted in Bartley, *New South*, 263; Jensen, *Nashville Sound*, 126.

14. Nash, *Dolly*. For sentimental songwriting, see Charles Hamm, *Yesterdays: Popular Song in America* (Norton, 1979), 284–325.

15. Parton, *Dolly*; *Vanity Fair*, June 1991.

16. *The Wilburn Brothers Show*, May 16, 1967, Connie Brick Collection, CMHOF.

17. "Country Music Television Programming, 1948–1987: A Preliminary Survey," prepared by the Country Music Foundation, March 1987, available at CMHOF. See also John Scott Colley, "The Sound Seen: Country Music on Television," *Journal of Country Music*, Fall and Winter (1973): 107–13. Parton quotes from Bufwack and Oermann, *Finding Her Voice*, 321, which has figures for Opry membership and recordings.

18. Steve Eng, *A Satisfied Mind: The Country Music Life of Porter Wagoner* (Rutledge Hill, 1992); *Country Song Roundup*, February 1972; March 1972.

19. Eng, *Satisfied Mind*; Colley, "Sound Seen."

20. Jane Becker, *Selling Tradition: Appalachia and the Construction of an American Folk* (University of North Carolina Press, 1998), 7.

21. Pecknold, *Selling Sound*; Bartley, *New South*, 145–46; David Carlton, "Smoke-Stack Chasing and Its Discontents," in *The American South in the 20th Century*, edited by Craig Pascoe, Karen Trahan Leathem, and Andy Ambrose (University of Georgia Press, 2005), 106; Douglas Hurt, ed., *The Rural South since World War II* (Louisiana State University Press, 1998), 2.

22. Video of historic CMA Awards can be viewed at the CMHOF.

23. Dan Carter, *From George Wallace to Newt Gingrich: Race in the Conservative Counterrevolution, 1963–1994* (Louisiana State University Press, 1996); *The News & Observer*, Raleigh, North Carolina, March 19, 1975—this and other subsequent regional newspaper coverage can be found in the CMHOF Dolly Parton clippings microfiche.

24. Everett Corbin, "Dolly Parton No 'Dumb Blonde,'" *Music City News*, September 1967; *Country Song Roundup*, May 1968.

25. "Moeller Talent Presents: Dolly Parton" (1968), Dolly Parton circular

folder, CMHOF; *Nashville Tennessean*, September 27–October 3, 1970; RCA bio in Dolly Parton folder.

26. Paul Hemphill, *The Nashville Sound: Bright Lights and Country Music* (Simon & Schuster, 1970), Singleton quote on 45. *Billboard*, April 25, 1970, stressed "Nashville has taken on a new pop image," noting the format now included 600 full-time and 1,400 part-time stations.

27. Malone and Neal, *Country Music, U.S.A.*, 271; Hemphill, *Nashville Sound*, 89.

28. Barbara Ching, *Wrong's What I Do Best: Hard Country Music and Contemporary Culture* (Oxford University Press, 2003), 4; Jesse Burt and Bob Ferguson, *So You Want to Be in Music!* (Abingdon, 1970), 127–28.

29. Edward Ayers, *What Caused the Civil War? Reflections on the South and Southern History* (Norton, 2005), 20; Corbin, "Dolly Parton No 'Dumb Blonde'"; Teresa Goddu, "Bloody Daggers and Lonesome Graveyards: The Gothic and Country Music," in *Reading Country Music: Steel Guitars, Opry Stars, and Honky-Tonk Bars*, ed. Cecilia Tichi (Duke University Press, 1998), 45–64.

30. *Music City News*, March 1970; Jocelyn Neal, *The Songs of Jimmie Rodgers: A Legacy in Country Music* (Indiana University Press, 2009).

31. Dan Carter, *The Politics of Rage: George Wallace, the Origins of the New Conservatism, and the Transformation of American Politics* (Simon & Schuster, 1995), 315–16; *Look*, July 13, 1971.

32. *Look*, July 13, 1971; *Radio & Records*, April 16, 1976.

33. Bill Malone, *Don't Get above Your Raisin': Country Music and the Southern Working Class* (University of Illinois Press, 2002), 211; Joan Dew, *Singers & Sweethearts: The Women of Country Music* (Doubleday, 1977), 38, 56; Bufwack and Oermann, *Finding Her Voice*, 281–309.

34. Patrick Carr, ed., *The Illustrated History of Country Music* (Random House, 1995), 312; for "vertical formats" see *Billboard*, December 11, 1971.

35. *Country Song Roundup*, November 1969. An early live version can be heard on the reissued *Just Because I'm a Woman* (RCA, 2003).

36. Eng, *Satisfied Mind*, 300; *Billboard*, February 2, 1974.

37. Burt and Ferguson, *So You Want to Be in Music!*, 83; Gregory, *Southern Diaspora*; *Billboard*, September 30, 1978.

38. Paul Hemphill in Goldstein, "My Country Music Problem"; Pecknold, *Selling Sound*; *Country Song Roundup*, May 1975.

39. *Radio & Records*, October 1, 1976; November 19, 1976.

40. *Radio & Records*, October 1, 1976.

41. *Country Music*, April 1973; Pecknold, *Selling Sound*.

42. Carole-Anne Tyler, *Female Impersonation* (Routledge, 2003), 105; *Tennessee Magazine*, October 20, 1974; Eng, *Satisfied Mind*, 287.

43. Parton, *Dolly*, 148–49; Eva Illouz, *Consuming the Romantic Utopia: Love and the Cultural Contradictions of Capitalism* (University of California Press, 1997); David Metzer, "The Power Ballad," *Popular Music* 31, no. 3 (2012): 437–59.

44. *Country Song Roundup*, April 1974; September 1974.

45. *Dolly* episodes in Connie Brick Collection, CMHOF.

46. Carr, *Illustrated History of Country Music*, 398; Bufwack and Oermann, *Finding Her Voice*.

47. Eng, *Satisfied Mind*, 333–34.

48. *Billboard*, May 20, 1978; *Radio & Records*, October 1, 1976.

49. *Country Music*, inaugural issue, Summer 1972; Dave Hickey, "In Defense of the Telecaster Cowboy Outlaws," *Country Music*, January 1974.

50. Cobb, "From Muskogee to Luckenbach"; *Country Music*, July 1976; April 1977; *Country Rambler*, October 21, 1976.

51. Marc Landy, "Country Music: The Melody of Dislocation," *New South*, Winter 1971; *Music City News*, October 1972.

52. Ed McLanahan, *My Vita, if You Will: The Uncollected Ed McLanahan* (Counterpoint, 1998), 159; *Country Style*, November 1976; *Tennessee Magazine*, October 20, 1974.

53. *Country Music*, May 1977; Scobey, *Dolly Parton*, 259; Eng, *Satisfied Mind*, 336.

54. Nash, *Dolly*; Philip Jenkins, *Decade of Nightmares: The End of the Sixties and the Making of Eighties America* (Oxford University Press, 2006); *The Today Show*, August 22, 1978, Connie Brick Collection, CMHOF; *Playboy*, October 1978; *Rolling Stone*, August 25, 1977.

55. *Pittsburgh Post-Gazette*, November 22, 1977; *Newsday*, date obscured, 1978 Dolly Parton clippings microfiche, p. 1, CMHOF.

56. *Esquire*, March 1977; Nash, *Dolly*, 259.

57. *Trenton Sunday Times Advertiser*, October 19, 1975; *News American of Baltimore*, November 30, 1975; *Music City News*, May 1972; *Rolling Stone*, August 25, 1977; *Pasadena Star News*, September 24, 1979; *Roanoke Times & World*, August 22, 1979; *Radio & Records*, December 8, 1979.

58. *Coronet*, July 1977; *Cosmopolitan*, January 1979; *Philadelphia Inquirer*, July 15, 1977; *Norfolk Ledger-Star*, May 9, 1978; *Rolling Stone*, October 19, 1978; December 11, 1980.

59. *Parade*, November 2, 1980; *Photoplay*, January 1979; *Enquirer*, July 31, 1979; *Us Weekly*, July 24, 1979; *Cosmopolitan*, January 1979; *Vanity Fair*, June 1991.

60. *Charleston Daily Mail*, May 6, 1978; *Tennessean*, October 12, 1978; Everett Corbin, *Storm over Nashville: A Case against "Modern" Country Music* (Ashlar, 1980).

61. Carr, *Illustrated History of Country Music*, 356; *Country Music*, April 1977; February 1978; April 1978.

62. *Atlanta Journal-Constitution*, May 20, 1978; *Hits*, September 16, 1979; *Knoxville News Sentinel*, May 7, 1978; *Philadelphia Inquirer*, October 21, 1979.

63. *E! True Hollywood Story: Dolly Parton*, March 7, 2005.

64. *Billboard*, March 17, 1979; *Radio & Records*, January 18, 1980; September 26, 1980; February 6, 1980.

65. *Radio & Records*, May 22, 1981.

66. Pete Axthelm, "Hello Dolly," *Newsweek*, June 13, 1977; Nash, *Dolly*, 228; Mitchell Morris, *The Persistence of Sentiment: Display and Feeling in Popular Music of the 1970s* (University of California Press, 2013), 198–208. Parton said the song arose "when child molesting and child abuse was in the news." To her, it was both traditional *and* contemporary. *Rolling Stone*, August 25, 1977.

67. Jack Hurst, "Dolly Parton," *Chicago Tribune*, February 18, 1979; Cantwell, *Bluegrass Breakdown*; *Tennessean*, September 5, 1979.

68. Barbara Walters interview with Dolly Parton, 1982, Connie Brick Collection, CMHOF; *Billboard*, July 7, 1984. Episodes of *Dolly* and *A Smoky Mountain Christmas* can be viewed at the Paley Center for Media.

69. *Radio & Records*, March 8, 1985; July 26, 1985; March 7, 1986; Malone and Neal, *Country Music, U.S.A.*, 369–415; Robert Palmer, "Nashville Sound: Country Music in Decline," *New York Times*, September 17, 1985.

70. Stephen Holden, "For Country Music, a New Sound Ends 5 Years' Stagnation," *New York Times*, April 21, 1987; *Radio & Records*, February 20, 1987.

71. *Chicago Tribune*, April 16, 1987; "The Relationship between Radio Audience Share and Revenue Shares," survey reported in *Radio & Records*, January 15, 1988; Craig Havighurst, *Air Castle of the South: WSM and the Making of Music City* (University of Illinois Press, 2007), 224–43.

72. Melissa Jane Hardie, "Torque: Dollywood, Pigeon Forge, and Authentic Feeling in the Smoky Mountains," in *The Themed Space: Locating Culture, Nation, and Self*, ed. Scott Lucas (Lexington Books, 2007), 23–38; Martin, "Spirit of Mountain Culture."

73. *Country Sounds*, May 1987.

74. *Dolly Parton: Country Music Honors* broadcast, February 6, 1993, available at CMHOF.

75. *Radio & Records*, April 28, 1989; Bruce Feiler, *Dreaming Out Loud: Garth Brooks, Wynonna Judd, Wade Hayes, and the Changing Face of Nashville* (Avon, 1998); Nicholas Davidoff, *In the Country of Country: People and Places in American Music* (Pantheon, 1997).

76. Peter Applebome, *Dixie Rising: How the South Is Shaping American Values, Politics, and Culture* (Crown, 1996).

77. *Vogue*, January 1994.

78. Pamela Wilson, "Mountains of Contradictions: Gender, Class and Region in the Star Image of Dolly Parton," in Ticchi, *Reading Country Music*, 107; Curtis Ellison, *Country Music Culture: From Hard Times to Heaven* (University Press of Mississippi, 1995), 188–97.

79. *People* figure cited in Ellison, *Country Music Culture*, 189; *Rolling Stone*, October 30, 2003.

80. *Ladies' Home Journal*, July 1995; Parton, *Dolly*, 189.

81. Keith Negus, *Music Genres and Corporate Cultures* (Routledge, 1999), 114, 121.

82. *Chicago Sun-Sentinel*, July 31, 1998; *Music Row*, March 5, 2009. Chris Willman, *Rednecks & Bluenecks: The Politics of Country Music* (New Press, 2005), offers the best contemporary overview. Charles Hughes finds interracial musicianship at the level of session players, producers, and repertoire in Nashville recording studios. But this rarely meant black or Latino lead performers. "The Country-Soul Triangle: How Southern Soul Changed Country Music," Experience Music Project Pop Conference presentation, April 21, 2007.

83. Peterson, *Creating Country Music*; Fox, *Natural Acts*, 5.

Chapter Three

1. Jerry Moss, "A&M: Everything from A to Z," *Record World*, May 2, 1970, part of A&M Records Collection, University of California, Los Angeles, press clippings box.

2. Steve Chapple and Reebee Garofalo, *Rock 'n' Roll Is Here to Pay: The History and Politics of the Music Industry* (Nelson-Hall, 1977); Marc Eliot, *Rockonomics: The Money behind the Music* (Franklin Watts, 1989); Fred Goodman, *The Mansion on the Hill: Dylan, Young, Geffen, Springsteen, and the Head-on Collision of Rock and Commerce* (Times Books, 1997); Andre Millard, *America on Record: A History of Recorded Sound*, second edition (Cambridge University Press, 2005), 224; Keith Negus, *Producing Pop: Culture and Conflict in the Popular Music Industry* (Edward Arnold, 1992); Simon Frith, *Performing Rites: On the Value of Popular Music* (Harvard University Press, 1996), 42. Charlie Gillett, *The Sound of the City: The Rise of Rock and Roll* (E. P. Dutton, 1970), the first authoritative history, presented rock and roll's emergence as the triumph of independent record labels. William Straw argues that overvaluing "artist development" limited novelty and non-rock approaches. "Popular Music as Cultural Commodity: The American Recorded Music Industries, 1976–1985" (PhD dissertation, McGill University, 1990).

3. Jerry Moss, keynote to National Association of Record Merchandisers, March 16, 1972, transcript in A&M Records Collection, box 182.

4. William Howland Kenney, *Recorded Music in American Life: The Phonograph and Popular Memory, 1890–1945* (Oxford University Press, 1999); *Los Angeles Times*, March 23, 1980; George W. S. Trow Jr., "Eclectic, Reminiscent, Amused, Fickle, Perverse," *New Yorker*, May 29, 1978.

5. Motti Regev, "The 'Pop-Rockization' of Popular Music," in *Popular Music Studies*, ed. David Hesmondhalgh and Keith Negus (Oxford University Press, 2002), 261; Richard Peterson and Roger Kern, "Changing Highbrow Taste: From Snob to Omnivore," *American Sociological Review* 61, no. 5 (1996): 900–907;

Joshua Gamson, *Claims to Fame: Celebrity in Contemporary America* (University of California Press, 1994); David Hollinger, *Postethnic America: Beyond Multiculturalism* (Basic Books, 1995); Chris Anderson, *The Long Tail: Why the Future of Business Is Selling Less of More* (Hyperion, 2006).

6. *Radio & Records*, October 7, 1983.

7. Sean Ross, author interview, April 2, 2009; Tia DeNora, *Music in Everyday Life* (Cambridge University Press, 2000), 62.

8. Josh Kun, reissue notes to Herb Alpert & the Tijuana Brass, *The Lonely Bull* (Shout! Factory, 2005); Joe Smith, *Off the Record: An Oral History of Popular Music* (Warner Books, 1988), 183–85.

9. Kenney, *Recorded Music in American Life*; Russell Sanjek, *American Popular Music and Its Business*, vol. 3 (Oxford University Press, 1988); Geoffrey Hull, *The Recording Industry*, second edition (Routledge, 2004).

10. Peter Martland, *Since Records Began: EMI, the First 100 Years* (B. T. Batsford, 1997), 225; Ted Fox, *In the Groove: The People behind the Music* (St. Martin's, 1986), 26–67; Dave Dexter, *Playback: A Newsman/Record Producer's Hits and Misses from the Thirties to the Seventies* (Billboard Books, 1976), 215.

11. Michael Rogin, *Blackface, White Noise: Jewish Immigrants in the Melting Pot* (University of California Press, 1996); Jeffrey Melnick, *A Right to Sing the Blues: African Americans, Jews, and American Popular Song* (Harvard University Press, 1999); Jody Rosen, *White Christmas: The Story of an American Song* (Scribner, 2002); Josh Kun, "Abie the Fishman: On Masks, Birthmarks, and Hunchbacks," in *Listen Again: A Momentary History of Pop Music*, ed. Eric Weisbard (Duke University Press, 2007), 63; Stan Cornyn with Paul Scanlon, *Exploding: The Highs, Hits, Hype, Heroes, and Hustlers of the Warner Music Group* (Harper-Entertainment, 2002).

12. Michael Denning, *The Cultural Front: The Laboring of American Culture in the Twentieth Century* (Verso, 1997), 47.

13. Keir Keightley, "Frank Sinatra, Hi-Fi, and Formations of Adult Culture: Gender, Technology, and Celebrity, 1948–1962" (PhD dissertation, Concordia University, 1996); Keightley, "'Turn It Down' She Shrieked: Gender, Domestic Space, and High Fidelity, 1948–1959," *Popular Music* 16, no. 2 (1997): 150–78; *Playboy*, undated first issue, 1953, cited in Barbara Ehrenreich, *The Hearts of Men: American Dreams and the Flight from Commitment* (Anchor Press, 1983). See also Timothy Taylor, *Strange Sounds: Music, Technology & Culture* (Routledge, 2001); Bill Ogersby, *Playboys in Paradise: Masculinity, Youth, and Leisure-Style in Modern America* (New York University Press, 2001).

14. R. Serge Denisoff, *Solid Gold: The Popular Record Industry* (Transaction, 1975); Joseph Lanza, *Elevator Music: A Surreal History of Muzak, Easy Listening, and Other Moodsong*, second edition (University of Michigan Press, 2004), 124; Tim Anderson, *Making Easy Listening: Material Culture and Postwar American Recording* (University of Minnesota Press, 2006). For stereotypes of women as

passive consumers, Janice Radway, *Reading the Romance: Women, Patriarchy and Popular Literature* (University of North Carolina, 1984); Andreas Huyssen, *After the Great Divide: Modernism, Mass Culture, Postmodernism* (Indiana University Press, 1986); and Jennifer Scanlon, ed., *The Gender and Consumer Culture Reader* (New York University Press, 2000). Herb Alpert quoted in *Los Angeles Times*, May 2, 1966.

15. Timothy White, "The Adroit Muse, the Artful Merchant, and the Appetite for Music," in *A&M Records: The First 25 Years*, ed. Jeffrey Gold and David Leaf (A&M, 1987); UCLA oral history with Jerry Moss, session 1, available at http://oralhistory.library.ucla.edu.

16. *Fortune*, May 1961, cited in Millard, *America on Record*, 229–30; J. Smith, *Off the Record*, 183–85; *Los Angeles Times*, August 23, 1981.

17. Kirse Granat May, *Golden State, Golden Youth: The California Image in Popular Culture, 1955–1966* (University of North Carolina Press, 2002); J. Hoberman, *The Dream Life: Movies, Media, and the Mythology of the Sixties* (Norton, 2003), 156; Eric Avila, *Popular Culture in the Age of White Flight: Fear and Fantasy in Suburban Los Angeles* (University of California Press, 2004); Rebecca Leydon, "Utopias of the Tropics: The Exotic Music of Les Baxter and Yma Sumac," in *Widening the Horizon: Exoticism in Post-war Popular Music*, ed. Philip Hayward (Indiana University Press, 1999), 30.

18. White, "Adroit Muse."

19. *Time*, November 21, 1965; Royal Albert Hall program booklet, October 7, 1966, A&M Records Collection, press clippings box; Singer promotional kit, 1967, A&M Records Collection, box 180.

20. Ratings in memo by Paul Cooper, May 20, 1968, A&M Records Collection, box 189; *Parade*, December 11, 1966, box 77. *The Brass Are Coming*, including original commercials, can be viewed at the Paley Center for Media, Los Angeles.

21. Frank, *Conquest of Cool*, 7; Terry Murphy to Gil Friesen, July 12, 1966; Burt Leach letter, circa 1966; "Media Analysis of Circulation," circa 1966; all in A&M Records Collection, box 77.

22. *Los Angeles Herald-Examiner*, October 29, 1967; cartoon about Alpert's stereo in *Stereo Review*, undated; syndicated columns by Joyce Haber, Florabel Muir, David McIntyre, and others; *Coronet*, June 1966; *Teen*, April 1966; Teen Talk column, *Van Nuys News*, January 21, 1966; *The Beat*, March 19, 1966; all in A&M Records Collection, press clippings box.

23. Concert script, circa 1968, A&M Records Collection, box 175; *Top 40 Reviewer* 1, no. 12, October 23, 1965, A&M Records Collection, press clippings box; *Time*, November 21, 1965; Josh Kun, notes to *South of the Border* reissue (Shout! Factory, 2005).

24. *Record World* and *Cashbox*, February 26, 1966; program, Herb Alpert & the Tijuana Brass at the White House, October 26, 1967; both in A&M Records Collection, press clippings box; *Congressional Record*, August 25, 1966, box 77.

25. White, "Adroit Muse"; "Europe Trip" memo, Gil Friesen to Herb Alpert, September 9, 1966; Harry McCune Jr., HM Sound Service, to Sal Monte, December 27, 1966; all in A&M Records Collection, box 77; memo, no author and undated (1969), box 83.

26. Bess Ann Jubert to Herb Alpert, October 16, 1967; Pat Horton to Herb Alpert, December 15, 1967; both in A&M Records Collection, box 188; *Des Moines Sunday Register*, March 9, 1969; *Austin American-Statesman*, September 28, 1969; *Schenectady Gazette*, n.d. [1969], press clippings box; *Beat of the Brass* script and Mendes script, box 175.

27. WFMF ad, *Chicago Tribune*, May 11, 1969, A&M Records Collection, press clippings box; concert scripts with jokes about Welk, box 175; Gaynel Hodge to Herb Alpert, September 15, 1967, box 185; *Philadelphia Inquirer*, October 25, 1969, press clippings box.

28. *Ramparts*, March, 1967, cited in Frank, *Conquest of Cool*; concert scripts, 1967–69, A&M Records Collection, box 175; invitation, February 13, 1967, box 189.

29. Terry Anderson, *The Movement and the Sixties* (Oxford University Press, 1995); script, June 1968, A&M Records Collection, box 197.

30. Denning, *Cultural Front*, 116; Van Gosse, *Rethinking the New Left: An Interpretative History* (Palgrave Macmillan, 2005), 207, 203; Brian Ward, *Just My Soul Responding: Rhythm and Blues, Black Consciousness, and Race Relations* (University of California Press, 1998), 303; Ralph Abernathy to Herb Alpert, August 2, 1967, A&M Records Collection, press clippings box.

31. *Boston Herald-Traveler*, November 19, 1969; *Toronto Star*, October 31, 1969; Alfred Aronowitz, "Pop Scene" column, *New York Post*, November 19, 1969; all in A&M Records Collection, press clippings box.

32. *Time*, January 5, 1970; Aniko Bodroghkozy, *Groove Tube: Sixties Television and the Youth Rebellion* (Duke University Press, 2001), 149, 202; Anderson, *Movement and the Sixties*, 280; David Allyn, *Make Love, Not War: The Sexual Revolution, an Unfettered History* (Little, Brown, 2000), 206–27.

33. *Philadelphia Inquirer*, October 25, 1969, A&M Records Collection, press clippings box.

34. *Pittsburgh Press*, November 18, 1969; *Los Angeles Times*, June 8, 1975; *New York Post*, November 19, 1969; all in A&M Records Collection, press clippings box. Trumpet problems in *Los Angeles*, May 1, 2011.

35. "Top Quality Rock Helps Labels Turnaround Their Profit Picture," *Billboard*, November 6, 1971; December 25, 1971; Barney Hoskyns, *Waiting for the Sun: Strange Days, Weird Scenes, and the Sound of Los Angeles* (St. Martin's, 1996), 165.

36. *Billboard*, December 25, 1971; December 11, 1971; for a full account, see Kim Simpson, *Early '70s Radio: The American Format Revolution* (Continuum, 2011).

37. White, "Adroit Muse"; *Billboard*, July 29, 1967; Claude Hall, "Progressive Rock Listeners Do Wash," *Billboard*, July 27, 1968; *Billboard*, March 15, 1969.

38. UCLA oral history with Jerry Moss, session 4; memo, Jerry Moss to A&M staff, March 4, 1969, A&M Records Collection, box 189.

39. *Rolling Stone*, March 1, 1969; Moss, "A&M."

40. Telegram, Jerry Moss to Alan Heley, August 3, 1970, A&M Records Collection, box 186; Clive Davis with James Willwerth, *Clive: Inside the Record Business* (William Morrow, 1975); Cornyn, *Exploding*; *Billboard*, November 16, 1968; Steve Waksman, *This Ain't the Summer of Love: Conflict and Crossover in Heavy Metal and Punk* (University of California Press, 2009), 19–21.

41. Cornyn, *Exploding*, 163; Walter Yetnikoff and David Ritz, *Howling at the Moon: The Odyssey of a Monstrous Music Mogul in an Age of Excess* (Broadway, 2004), 68; Fredric Dannen, *Hit Men: Power Brokers and Fast Money inside the Music Business* (Crown, 1990); Goodman, *Mansion on the Hill*; William Knoedelseder, *Stiffed: A True Story of MCA, the Music Business, and the Mafia* (HarperCollins, 1993). For Cocker, see J. Smith, *Off the Record*, 300. Michael James Jackson account in Michael Walker, *Laurel Canyon: The Inside Story of Rock and Roll's Legendary Neighborhood* (Faber & Faber, 2006), 171, 207. Denny Bruce in Hoskyns, *Waiting for the Sun*, 149, 223.

42. Hoskyns, *Waiting for the Sun*, 71, 84, 143.

43. Robert Christgau, *Any Old Way You Choose It: Rock and Other Pop Music, 1967–1973* (Penguin, 1973); Walker, *Laurel Canyon*; Hoskyns, *Waiting for the Sun*, 206, Taylor quotation on 108.

44. Quincy Jones, *Q: The Autobiography of Quincy Jones* (Doubleday, 2001), 173, 233.

45. *Billboard*, January 2, 1971; January 30, 1971; November 4, 1972; March 24, 1973; *Broadcasting*, August 24, 1970.

46. *Billboard*, March 24, 1973; Denisoff, *Solid Gold*, 32; Jolene Burton memo, April 17, 1970, A&M Records Collection, box 192.

47. Avila, *Popular Culture in the Age of White Flight*; Ray Coleman, *The Carpenters: The Untold Story: An Authorized Biography* (HarperCollins, 1994); *Close to You: Remembering the Carpenters* (1997; DVD, MPI, 2001).

48. *Billboard*, November 17, 1973; Tom Smucker, "Boring and Horrifying Whiteness: The Rise and Fall of Reaganism as Prefigured by the Career Arcs of Carpenters, Lawrence Welk and the Beach Boys in 1973–74," in *Pop When the World Falls Apart: Music in the Shadow of Doubt*, ed. Eric Weisbard (Duke University Press, 2012), 47–61.

49. Coleman, *Carpenters*, 108–9; Lester Bangs, "The Carpenters and the Creeps," *Rolling Stone*, March 4, 1971.

50. Coleman, *Carpenters*, 142.

51. Ibid., 96.

52. Denisoff, *Solid Gold*, 100, 264, 132; Jerry Moss, author interview, February 2, 2007.

53. "The A&M Sales & Promotion Rap-Up," April 13, 1970; April 20, 1970; May 4, 1970; May 18, 1970; "The A&M Hype & Hyperbole Mummy Wraps," April 1970; all in A&M Records Collection, box 194; *Billboard*, March 24, 1973.

54. *Radio & Records*, May 30, 1975; "Gene Klavan on WNEW 1130 New York, August, 1975," Airchexx, http://airchexx.com/2012/07/23/gene-klavan-on-wnew -1130-new-york-august-1975-10002/.

55. Moss, interview; Cornyn, *Exploding*, 132; Jac Holzman with Gavan Daws, *Follow the Music: The Life and High Times of Elektra Records in the Great Years of American Pop Culture* (FirstMedia, 1998), 308–9; Peter Carroll, *It Seemed Like Nothing Happened: The Tragedy and Promise of American Life in the 1970s* (Holt, Rinehart & Winston, 1982); Philip Jenkins, *Decade of Nightmares: The End of the Sixties and the Making of Eighties America* (Oxford University Press, 2006); Bruce Schulman, *The Seventies: The Great Shift in American Culture, Society, and Politics* (Da Capo, 2002), 146. See LeRoy Ashby, *With Amusement for All: A History of American Popular Culture since 1830* (University Press of Kentucky, 2006), 410– 13, for a typical treatment of "corporate rock."

56. "A&M Boasts Top Contemporary Artists," *Los Angeles Times*, November 16, 1977; *Billboard*, March 19, 1977; July 22, 1978.

57. Patrick Goldstein, "A&M Records: It's Off and Running," *Los Angeles Times*, March 23, 1980; R. Serge Denisoff, *Tarnished Gold: The Record Industry Revisited* (Transaction Publishers, 1986).

58. Schulman, *The Seventies*, 151; John Leland, *Hip: The History* (Ecco, 2004), 297. Dannen, *Hit Men*; Eliot, *Rockonomics*; Knoedelseder, *Stiffed*; and Goodman, *Mansion on the Hill*, all caricature a corrupt record industry.

59. Davis, *Clive*; *Billboard* coverage of A Week to Remember, May 19, 1973; and of Davis's firing, June 9, 1973; June 16, 1973; Yetnikoff, *Howling at the Moon*, 67, 111–12; Simon Frith, "Illegality and the Music Industry," in *The Business of Music*, ed. Michael Talbot (Liverpool, 2002), 197–212. For more critical appraisal of Davis's work at CBS, see Dannen, *Hit Men*.

60. "A Day in the Life . . . Harold Childs," *Billboard*, December 20, 1975.

61. Moss, interview; Matt Mann of RPM to Dave Hubert of A&M, March 15, 1977; memo, Festival Records to A&M, May 22, 1977; memo, Werner Wolfen to Jerry Moss, April 18, 1977; all in A&M Records Collection, box 85; telegram, Kuni Murai to Jerry Moss, May 18, 1979, box 186; Styx panel in *Billboard*, July 22, 1978.

62. Robert Spitz, *The Making of Superstars: The Artists and Executives of the Rock Music World* (Anchor, 1978); for Abrams and AOR, see Pete Fornatale and Joshua Mills, *Radio in the Television Age* (Overlook, 1980), 139–42; *Billboard*, July 22, 1978.

63. *Billboard*, May 7, 1977; December 20, 1975; September 3, 1977; March 10, 1973; September 10, 1977.

64. *People*, October 18, 1976; *The Captain & Tennille—Ultimate Collection* (Listen 2, 2005).

65. *Rolling Stone*, April 22, 1976; February 10, 1977; *ZigZag*, April 1976; *Creem*, October 1977; *Kerrang!* 1998, at www.rocksbackpages.com; UCLA oral history with Jerry Moss, session 5.

66. Hoskyns, *Waiting for the Sun*, 272; Barney Hoskyns, *Hotel California* (Wiley, 2006), 238.

67. *MacLean's*, August 6, 1979. *Rolling Stone* titled a feature on Supertramp "The Taking of America by Strategy" (June 30, 1977) and wrote of their "not-quite-progressive, not-quite-pop music." For a defensive Mangione in a jazz publication, see *Downbeat*, March 23, 1978. For WBLS and black radio's evolution, see the "Radio Today" supplement in *Advertising Age*, May 29, 1978.

68. Daniel Bell, *The Cultural Contradictions of Capitalism* (1976; reprint, Basic, 1996), xxv; Baughman, *Republic of Mass Culture*; Christopher Lasch, *The Culture of Narcissism: American Life in an Age of Diminishing Expectations* (Norton, 1979). See also historian Rick Perlstein's interpretation of Bell in *Slate*, November 20, 1996. P. Jenkins, *Decade of Nightmares*, argues that both Carter and Ronald Reagan shared a sense of American decline.

69. Peter Shapiro, *Turn the Beat Around: The Secret History of Disco* (Faber & Faber, 2005); Eric Weisbard, liner notes to *Rise* reissue (Shout! Factory, 2007).

70. *Billboard*, August 19, August 26, 1978; *Advertising Age*, May 29, 1978; *Village Voice*, February 12, 1979, and November 12, 1979, cited in Shapiro, *Turn the Beat Around*; Denisoff, *Tarnished Gold*, 124–25.

71. Straw, "Popular Music as Cultural Commodity," 229.

72. *Rolling Stone*, December 13, 1979; Moss, interview; Denisoff, *Tarnished Gold*, 124–28.

73. *Billboard*, May 5, 1979; December 27, 1980; *Radio & Records*, March 13, 1981; June 13, 1980.

74. McLaren in *Billboard*, August 20, 1977. Moss and Alpert, author interview, January 30, 2007, recall happily playing for each other the controversial "God Save the Queen," a song banned by the BBC, but claim the band's conduct, including physically attacking people in the A&M UK offices, was offensive to a "family" label.

75. Note attached to Human League draft contract, A&M Records Collection, 1981 folder, box 85; White, "Adroit Muse"; *Everyone Stares: The Police Inside Out* (DVD, VistaVega, 2006); J. Smith, *Off the Record*, 419; *Rolling Stone*, September 1,1983.

76. White, "Adroit Muse," summarizes A&M's early 1980s revitalization; Childs note, A&M Records Collection, box 86; Grant in *Rolling Stone*, June 6, 1985.

77. Memo, Jeff Gold to Herb Alpert, Jerry Moss, and Gil Friesen, August 20, 1987, A&M Records Collection, box 183. McClain apologized and left the company in June 1989, followed by Janet Jackson, returning later after Alpert and Moss sold A&M. For a different view of McClain, as a successful African American executive, see *Black Enterprise*, November 1987.

78. UCLA oral history with Jerry Moss, session 7; Dannen, *Hit Men*, 264–71; *Musician*, June 1988.

79. Marketing Plan, June 29, 1983, A&M Records Collection, box 86. In the end, "Stay with Me Tonight" remained an R&B hit, but Osborne gradually became an adult contemporary hitmaker; memo, Ross Curry to Gil Friesen and Jerry Moss, 1984, box 86.

80. *Radio & Records*, December 21, 1984; January 10, 1986; *Billboard*, August 31, 1985; *Radio & Records*, December 23, 1988; January 26, 1990.

81. Greil Marcus, "Number One with a Bullet," in *In the Fascist Bathroom: Punk in Pop Music, 1977–1992* (Harvard University Press, 1999), 280–84; Robert Christgau, "A Song for You," *Village Voice*, May 7, 1985.

82. *Billboard*, March 23, 1985; UCLA oral history with Jerry Moss, session 7.

83. UCLA oral history with Jerry Moss, session 7.

84. Hull, *Recording Industry*, 125–26; "Overview" at www.Umusic.com.

85. Bell, *Cultural Contradictions of Capitalism*, 323.

86. Rafael Perez-Torres, "Mestizaje in the Mix: Chicano Identity, Cultura Politics and Postmodern Music," in *Music and the Racial Imagination*, ed. Ronald Radano and Philip Bohlman (University of Chicago Press, 2000), 206–30; Josh Kun, *Audiotopia: Music, Race, and America* (University of California Press, 2005), 223; Guillermo Gomez-Pena, *Ethno-Techno: Writings on Performance, Activism, and Pedagogy* (Routledge, 2005), 151; script to *Superstar: The Karen Carpenter Story* in Todd Haynes, *Far from Heaven, Safe, and Superstar: Three Screenplays* (Grove, 2003); Michael Bracewell, *When Surface Was Depth: Death by Cappuccino and Other Reflections on Music and Culture in the 1990's* (Da Capo, 2001), 173–77; Christopher Washburne and Maiken Derko, eds., *Bad Music: The Music We Love to Hate* (Routledge, 2004).

Chapter Four

1. The best overviews are David Buckley, *Elton: The Biography* (Chicago Review Press, 2007); Elisabeth Rosenthal, *His Song: The Musical Journey of Elton John* (Billboard Books, 2001); and Philip Norman, *Sir Elton: The Definitive Biography* (Carroll & Graf, 2001). John's initial discussion of his sexuality came in Cliff Jahr, "Elton John: It's Lonely at the Top," *Rolling Stone*, October 7, 1976. For his wedding to Furnish, with congratulations from Tony Blair and Bill Clinton, see *People*, January 9, 2006; *Advocate*, January 31, 2006.

2. Susan Douglas, *Listening In: Radio and the American Imagination, from Amos 'n' Andy and Edward R. Murrow to Wolfman Jack and Howard Stern* (Times Books, 1999); Ben Fong-Torres, *The Hits Just Keep On Coming: The History of Top 40 Radio* (Backbeat Books, 2001); Marc Fisher, *Something in the Air: Radio, Rock, and the Revolution That Shaped a Generation* (Random House, 2007); Kim Simpson, *Early '70s Radio: The American Format Revolution* (Continuum, 2011);

Ken Barnes, "Top 40 Radio: A Fragment of the Imagination," in *Facing the Music*, ed. Simon Frith (Pantheon, 1988), 8–50; Rick Sklar, *Rocking America: An Insider's Story: How the All-Hit Radio Stations Took Over* (St. Martin's, 1984); Rob Durkee, *American Top 40: The Countdown of the Century* (Schirmer, 1999).

3. Nik Cohn, *Awopbopaloobop Alopbamboom: The Golden Age of Rock* (1970; reprint, Da Capo, 1996), 145; Reinhold Wagnleitner, *Coca-Colonization and the Cold War: The Cultural Mission of the United States in Austria after the Second World War* (University of North Carolina Press, 1994), xiii.

4. Judith Halberstam and Ira Livingston, "Introduction: Posthuman Bodies," in *Posthuman Bodies* (Indiana University Press, 1995), 14; Simon Napier-Bell, *Black Vinyl, White Powder* (Ebury, 2001), viii; Jon Savage, "The Simple Things You See Are All Complicated," in *The Faber Book of Pop*, ed. Hanif Kureishi and Jon Savage (Faber & Faber, 1995), xxiii.

5. Simon Frith, *Sound Effects: Youth, Leisure, and the Politics of Rock 'n' Roll* (Pantheon, 1981), 73.

6. Wagnleitner, *Coca-Colonization*, 4; Savage, "Simple Things," xxii–xxiii; Richard Pells, *Not Like Us: How Europeans Have Loved, Hated, and Transformed American Culture since World War II* (Basic, 1997), 189–90.

7. Elton John, interview with Pete Fornatale, WNEW-FM, November 1970, available at Paley Center for Media; *Time*, July 7, 1975; Richard Smith, "Elton John: Man of the Year," *Gay Times*, December 1997, cited in Rosenthal, *His Song*, 470.

8. Dave Harker, "Blood on the Tracks: Popular Music in the 1970s," in *The Arts in the 1970s: Cultural Closure?*, ed. B. J. Moore-Gilbert (Routledge, 1994), 240–58; Buckley, *Elton*, 9; Simon Frith, "Pop Music," in *The Cambridge Companion to Pop and Rock*, ed. Simon Frith, Will Straw, and John Street (Cambridge University Press, 2001), 94.

9. Simon Frith and Howard Horne, *Art into Pop* (Methuen, 1987), 1; George Melly, *Revolt into Style: The Pop Arts in Britain* (Penguin, 1970); Paul McDonald, "The Music Industry," in *The Media in Britain: Current Debates and Developments*, ed. Jane Stokes and Anna Reading (St. Martin's, 1999); Dick Hebdige, *Subculture: The Meaning of Style* (Methuen, 1979); Scott Herring, *Another Country: Queer Anti-urbanism* (New York University Press, 2010); Karen Tongson, *Relocations: Queer Suburban Imaginaries* (New York University Press, 2011).

10. R. Smith, "Elton John: Man of the Year."

11. Robert Hilburn, " *Elton John: A Super Rock Star Arrives on Scene,*" *Los Angeles Times*, September 13, 1970; Roy Carr and Charles Shaar Murray, "The Life and Times of Elton John," *New Musical Express*, February 22, 1975: Paul Gambaccini, *A Conversation with Elton John and Bernie Taupin* (Flash, 1975); Dick Tatham and Tony Jasper, *Elton John* (Octopus, 1976); Andy Peebles, *The Elton John Tapes: Elton John in Conversation* (St. Martin's, 1981); Dave Laing, "Nine Lives in the Music Business: Reg Dwight and Elton John in the 1960s," *Popular Music History* 2, no. 3 (2007): 237–61.

12. *Mojo*, October 1997.

13. Peter Burton, *Parallel Lives* (GMP, 1985), 30–41; *Elton John: Someone like Me* (DVD, Eagle Vision, 2007); John D'Emilio, "*Capitalism and Gay Identity*," in *Powers of Desire: The Politics of Sexuality*, ed. Ann Snitow, Christine Stansell, and Sharon Thompson (Monthly Review Press, 1983), 100–113; George Chauncey, *Gay New York: Gender, Urban Culture, and the Making of the Gay Male World, 1890–1940* (Basic Books, 1994).

14. Brian Wallis, Tom Finkelpearl, Patricia Phillips, Glenn Weiss, and Thomas Lawson, eds., *Modern Dreams: The Rise and Fall and Rise of Pop* (MIT Press, 1988); Marco Livingstone, ed., *Pop Art: An International Perspective* (Rizzoli, 1991), 154–55; Frith and Horne, *Art into Pop*, 101.

15. Cohn, *Awopbopaloobop*, 61–62; Michael Braun, "York," and Colin Mac-Innes, "Pop Songs and Teenagers," both in Kureishi and Savage, *Faber Book of Pop*, 191, 81–90.

16. Chambers, *Urban Rhythms*, 57; Napier-Bell, *Black Vinyl, White Powder*, 45, 61, 76–77; Gillett, *Sound of the City*, 257, 375.

17. Sklar, *Rocking America*, 91–93; Fisher, *Something in the Air*, 27.

18. Jonathan Gould, *Can't Buy Me Love: The Beatles, Britain, and America* (Three Rivers Press, 2008), 200–203; Sklar, *Rocking America*, 112–13; Gillett, *Sound of the City*, 283; Alan Wells, "The British Invasion of American Popular Music: What Is It and Who Pays?," *Popular Music and Society* 11, no. 2 (1987): 65–78; John Lennon, interview with Dennis Elsas, WNEW, September 28, 1974, available at Paley Center for Media; Stephen Barnard, *On the Radio: Music Radio in Britain* (Open University Press, 1989).

19. Melly, *Revolt into Style*, 8; Chambers, *Urban Rhythms*, 52; Paul Fryer, " 'Everybody's on Top of the Pops': Popular Music on British Television, 1960–1985," *Popular Music and Society* 21, no. 2 (1997): 71–90; Robert Chapman, *Selling the Sixties: The Pirates and Pop Music Radio* (Routledge, 1992); Don Cusic, "Basic Differences: The British and American Music Industries," *Popular Music and Society* 15, no. 4 (1991): 47–55.

20. Richard Mabey, *The Pop Process* (Hutchinson Educational, 1969); Piri Halasz, "London: The Swinging City; You Can Walk across It on the Grass," *Time*, April 15, 1966; Fisher, *Something in the Air*, 64–75.

21. Carr and Murray, "Life and Times of Elton John"; Charles White, *The Life and Times of Little Richard: The Authorised Biography*, third revised edition (Omnibus Press, 2003), 132; Darden Asbury Pyron, *Liberace: An American Boy* (University of Chicago Press, 2000), 175; Peebles, *Elton John Tapes*, 13; Ian Wallis, *American Rock 'n' Roll: The UK Tours, 1956–1972* (Music Mentor Books, 2003), 227; Gambaccini, *Elton John and Bernie Taupin*, 61; Buckley, *Elton*, 72–76.

22. Gillett, *Sound of the City*, 250; Andy Gill, *Queer Noises: Male and Female Homosexuality in Twentieth-Century Music* (University of Minnesota Press, 1995), 101–3; Paul Myers, *It Ain't Easy: Long John Baldry and the Birth of the British Blues* (Greystone Books, 2007); Lawrence Alloway, "Popular Culture and Pop

Art," in *Pop Art: A Critical History*, ed. Steven Madoff (second edition, University of California Press, 1997), 171.

23. Bio in New York Public Library for the Performing Arts, Elton John clippings file; Robert Hilburn, "Elton John New Rock Talent," *Los Angeles Times*, August 27, 1970; Peebles, *Elton John Tapes*, 16–17; Gambaccini, *Elton John and Bernie Taupin*, 25; *Interview*, April 1995. Mr. Freedom was a London boutique. The bright red shirt was lettered "Rock & Roll."

24. Buckley, *Elton*, 25–26; *New Yorker*, August 26, 1996; Jahr, "Lonely at the Top."

25. Michael Kramer, *The Republic of Rock: Music and Citizenship in the Sixties Counterculture* (Oxford University Press, 2013); *Rolling Stone*, November 23, 1967, cited in Fisher, *Something in the Air*, 158; Barnard, *On the Radio*, 55; *Billboard*, July 12, 1969; Barnes, "Top 40 Radio."

26. Rosenthal, *His Song*, 12–23; Buckley, *Elton*, 68–92; Susan Black, *Elton John in His Own Words* (Omnibus Press, 1993), 41.

27. Hilburn, "Elton John New Rock Talent"; Hilburn, "Super Rock Star Arrives"; Graham Q&A in "Elton John Spectacular" issue of *Record World*, January 31, 1976; Peebles, *Elton John Tapes*, 21.

28. Elton John, interview with Pete Fornatale, WNEW-FM, November 1970.

29. Buckley, *Elton*, 86; *Record World*, January 31, 1976.

30. Buckley, *Elton*, 103; Tatham and Jasper, *Elton John*, 62; Rosenthal, *His Song*, 45.

31. *Elton*, vol. 2, no.1, 1975, New York Public Library for the Performing Arts, Elton John clippings file; Peebles, *Elton John Tapes*, 22; Cohn quote and Taupin on "All the Nasties" in Rosenthal, *His Song*, 38.

32. *NME*, March 11, 1972, cited in Buckley, *Elton*, 135.

33. Philip Auslander, *Performing Glam Rock: Gender and Theatricality in Popular Music* (University of Michigan Press, 2006), 228, 6–7, 40, 41, 39.

34. *Melody Maker*, January 1972, cited in Auslander, *Performing Glam Rock*, 134–35, 228; Thomas Geyrhalter, "Effeminacy, Camp and Sexual Subversion in Rock: The Cure and Suede," *Popular Music* 15, no. 2 (1996): 217–25; Gill, *Queer Noises*, 106–13; Robert Duncan, *The Noise: Notes from a Rock 'n' Roll Era* (Ticknor & Fields, 1984), 93.

35. Buckley, *Elton*, 139.

36. Ibid., 211; Alkarim Jivani, *It's Not Unusual: A History of Lesbian and Gay Britain in the Twentieth Century* (Indiana University Press, 1997); Jeffrey Weeks, *The World We Have Won: The Remaking of Erotic and Intimate Life* (Routledge, 2007); Peter Burton, *Amongst the Aliens: Some Aspects of a Gay Life* (Millivres, 1995); Burton, *Parallel Lives*, 50–51.

37. Stephen King, *The Dead Zone* (Viking, 1979), 124; Dodger Stadium concert footage from Russell Harty documentary, untitled, 1975, available at UCLA Film and Television Archive, VA3822.

38. Sklar, *Rocking America*, 150.

39. Gambaccini, *Elton John and Bernie Taupin*, 101; Rosenthal, *His Song*, 55; *Broadcasting*, July 14, 1975; *Record World*, January 31, 1976; *Los Angeles Times*, June 25, 1974.

40. *Radio & Records*, May 25, 1979; Durkee, *American Top 40*, 81-89; *Radio & Records*, February 1, 1974; May 9, 1980; *Broadcasting*, January 29, 1973; James Lull, Lawrence Johnson, and Carol Sweeny, "Audiences for Contemporary Radio Formats," *Journal of Broadcasting* 22, no. 4 (1978): 439-53; *Radio & Records*, August 25, 1978.

41. Greg Shaw, "Elton John: Captain Fantastic and the Brown Dirt Cowboy," *Phonograph Record*, June 1975, available at www.rocksbackpages.com; *Melody Maker*, June 21, 1975; *Record World*, January 31, 1976; Lennon interview with Elsas.

42. *New Yorker*, December 23, 1974; Shaw, "Elton John," 47; Jon Landau, review of *Captain Fantastic and the Brown Dirt Cowboy*, *Rolling Stone*, July 17, 1975.

43. "Last Wall Falls as Top 40 Makes Its Mark on FM Radio," *Broadcasting*, September 24, 1973; Rosenthal, *His Song*, 53; Buckley, *Elton*, 146.

44. Jon Savage, *Teenage: The Creation of Youth Culture* (Viking, 2007); Tatham and Jasper, *Elton John*, 11; *Elton John and Bernie Taupin Say Goodbye Norma Jean and Other Things* (documentary, 1974), cited in Norman, *Sir Elton*, 234-43.

45. *Vogue*, July 1975; *Playboy*, January 1976; Norman, *Sir Elton*, 211; Harty documentary.

46. Barbara Kingsolver, *Pigs in Heaven: A Novel* (HarperTorch, 1999), 30-31; *Elton*, vol. 2, no. 1, 1975, New York Public Library for the Performing Arts, Elton John clippings file; Randi Reisfeld and Danny Fields, *Who's Your Fave Rave? 16 Magazine Teen Idols as You Knew Them . . . and as They Really Were!* (Boulevard Books, 1997), 190.

47. Reisfeld and Fields, *Who's Your Fave Rave?*, 177; *Guardian*, December 1, 2001; *Creem*, February 1975; March 1975.

48. *Classic Albums: Elton John, Goodbye Yellow Brick Road* (VH1, 2001); *Record World*, January 31, 1976; Rosenthal, *His Song*, 114.

49. Stephen Holden, "Elton John Reaches for Artistic Recognition," *New York Times*, December 25, 1977; Norman, *Sir Elton*, 205; *Playboy*, January 1976.

50. *Los Angeles Times*, June 25, 1974; *People*, August 18, 1975; Paula Taylor, *Elton John* (Creative Education, 1975); Jim Morris in Rosenthal, *His Song*, 106.

51. Jahr, "Lonely at the Top"; Phil Sutcliffe, "The Real Elton John Stands Up—Hurrah!" *Sounds*, December 18, 1976; *Rolling Stone*, November 4, 1976, cited in Buckley, *Elton*, 209; Reisfeld and Fields, *Who's Your Fave Rave?*, 190; Rosenthal, *His Song*, 145-47.

52. *Elton John Talking with David Frost* (BBC and PBS, 1991) and *The Barbara Walters Special* (ABC, March 21, 1994), both viewable at UCLA Film and Television Archive.

53. Stuart Hall, "The Great Moving Right Show," *Marxism Today*, January 1979.

54. Fisher, *Something in the Air*, 202; *Radio & Records*, January 29, 1982; February 8, 1980.

55. *Elton John Talking with David Frost*; Buckley, *Elton*, 191; *Freddie Mercury: The Untold Story* (DVD, DoRo, 2000); Edmund White, "Elton John at Fifty: My Life as a Man," *Rolling Stone*, July 10, 1997; *New Yorker*, August 26, 1996.

56. "CHR," *Radio & Records*, December 12, 1980; *The Tonight Show*, November 5, 1980, viewable at Paley Center for Media; *Elton John Live in Central Park New York* (HBO, 1981); *Village Voice*, July 8, 1992.

57. Eric Hobsbawm, *The Age of Extremes: The Short Twentieth Century, 1914–1991* (Michael Joseph, 1994), 304; Jivani, *It's Not Unusual*, 184–94; Weeks, *World We Have Won*, 17–18; John Sweeney, "The Sun and the Star," *Independent*, February 11, 1989, reprinted in Kureishi and Savage, *Faber Book of Pop*, 653–66.

58. Tour details from the fan website Cornflakes & Classics, whizzo.ca/elton; Robert Hilburn, "Moscow: 12 Days That Shook a Rock Critic's World, *Los Angeles Times*, June 10, 1979; *Q*, December 1986.

59. Dave Rimmer, *Like Punk Never Happened: Culture Club and the New Pop* (Faber & Faber, 1986); Napier-Bell, *Black Vinyl, White Powder*, 226–89.

60. *Radio & Records*, October 7, 1983; October 7, 1988; September 14, 1987; August 5, 1983; September 14, 1987.

61. Barnes, "Top 40 Radio"; Simon Frith, "Anglo-America and Its Discontents," *Cultural Studies* 5, no. 3 (1991): 263–69.

62. *Radio & Records*, May 19, 1989; December 8, 1989; January 5, 1990; December 7, 1990.

63. *Radio & Records*, May 10, 1996; September 13, 1991; September 10, 1993; September 9, 1994.

64. Joel Whitburn, *The Billboard Book of Top 40 Hits*, ninth edition (Billboard Books, 2010), 873; Jeremy Tunstall, *The Media Were American: US Mass Media in Decline* (Oxford University Press, 2007); David Hesmondhalgh, *The Cultural Industries*, third edition (Sage, 2013).

65. *Los Angeles Times*, August 30, 1980; Susan Douglas, "Letting the Boys Be Boys: Talk Radio, Male Hysteria, and Political Discourse in the 1980s," in *Radio Reader: Essays in the Cultural History of Radio*, ed. Michelle Hilmes and James Loviglio (Routledge, 2001), 485–504; Gil Troy, *Morning in America: How Ronald Reagan Invented the 1980s* (Princeton University Press, 2005), 267.

66. Rosenthal, *His Song*, 301; *Q*, August 1988.

67. Rosenthal, *His Song*, 456–62; Paul Johnson, "The Menace of Beatlism," *New Statesman*, February 28, 1964, reprinted in Kureishi and Savage, *Faber Book of Pop*, 198; McDonald, "Music Industry."

68. Rosenthal, *His Song*, 456–59; Buckley, *Elton*, 341; *Vanity Fair*, November 1997.

69. Rosenthal, *His Song*, 459; *Barbara Walters Special*, March 21, 1994.

70. *Elton John: Tantrums and Tiaras* (1997; DVD, Echo Bridge, 2008).

71. *Elton John: Live in Barcelona* (DVD, Rhino/WEA, 2002); Buckley, *Elton*, 330; *Chronicle of Philanthropy*, November 9, 2006; *Vanity Fair*, November 1997.

72. Matthew Fraser, *Weapons of Mass Distraction: Soft Power and American Empire* (Thomas Dunne, 2005), 18; Pells, *Not like Us*, 281; Peter Taylor in "Introduction," and Andrew Blake, "Americanisation and Popular Music in Britain," both in *Issues in Americanisation and Culture*, ed. Neil Campbell, Jude Davies, and George McKay (Edinburgh University Press, 2004), 9, 151; Jeremy Tunstall, *The Media Are American: Anglo-American Media in the World* (Columbia, 1977); Tunstall, *Media Were American*, 102; Hesmondhalgh, *Cultural Industries*.

73. Bryan Appleyard, "Popular Culture and Public Affairs," in *Philosophy and Public Affairs*, ed. John Haldane (Cambridge University Press, 2000), 102; Diana West, *The Death of the Grownup: How America's Arrested Development Is Bringing Down Western Civilization* (St. Martin's Press, 2007), 66; Caroline Cass, *Elton John's Flower Fantasies* (Little Brown, 1997), 58; *Vanity Fair*, November 1997.

74. Barry Walters, "Elton John & Rufus Wainwright," *Advocate*, August 15, 2000; *Advocate*, January 31, 2006; *People*, January 16, 1978; January 9, 2006; *New York Times*, December 22, 2005; Terry Goldie, "Liberation," in *English Studies in Canada* 30, no. 4 (2004): 39; *One-on-One with David Frost: Elton John—My Gift Is My Song* (A&E channel program, 1999).

75. Judith Peraino, *Listening to the Sirens: Musical Technologies of Queer Identity from Homer to Hedwig* (University of California Press, 2005); Ivan Raykoff, review of Peraino, *Current Musicology* 82 (Fall 2006), 103–9.

76. Herring, *Another Country,* 14; Tongson, *Relocations,* 103.

77. Durkee, *American Top 40*, 202–10; Fong-Torres, *Hits Just Keep On Coming*, 232; Keith Negus, "Corporate Strategies of the Major Record Labels," in *Global Repertoires: Popular Music within and beyond the Transnational Music Industry*, ed. Andreas Gebesmair and Alfred Smudits (Ashgate, 2002), 21–32; *Radio & Records*, November 22, 1996; December 6, 1996.

78. *Radio & Records*, June 20, 1997; July 4, 1997; March 20, 1998; September 4, 1998.

79. The exhibit © *Murakami*, originally presented at the Museum of Contemporary Art in Los Angeles; Kanye West, interview with MTV, August 18, 2005, at http://www.mtv.com/bands/w/west_kanye/news_feature_081805/index3.html.

80. Roger Blackwell and Tina Stephan, *Brands That Rock: What Business Leaders Can Learn from the World of Rock and Roll* (Wiley, 2003), 62–79.

Chapter Five

1. The recordings were later compiled on Murray Saul, *The Get Downs* (Taurus Gold, 1999).

2. "Murray Saul on Aircheck," WFMU's Beware of the Blog, June 21, 2005, http://blog.wfmu.org/freeform/2005/06/murray_saul_on_.html.

3. Keir Keightley, "Reconsidering Rock," in *The Cambridge Companion to Pop and Rock*, ed. Simon Frith, Will Straw, and John Street (Cambridge University Press, 2001), 109; Alice Echols, "'Shaky Ground': Popular Music in the Disco Years," in *Shaky Ground: The Sixties and Its Aftershocks* (Columbia University Press, 2002), 159–92; Elijah Wald, *How the Beatles Destroyed Rock 'n' Roll: An Alternative History of American Popular Music* (Oxford University Press, 2009), 230–47; Carl Wilson, *Let's Talk about Love: A Journey to the End of Taste* (Continuum, 2007); Kelefa Sanneh, "The Rap against Rockism," *New York Times*, October 31, 2004; Jefferson Cowie, *Stayin' Alive: The 1970s and the Last Days of the Working Class* (New Press, 2010); Steve Waksman, *This Ain't the Summer of Love: Conflict and Crossover in Heavy Metal and Punk* (University of California Press, 2009); Ryan Moore, *Sells like Teen Spirit: Music, Youth Culture, and Social Crisis* (New York University Press, 2009); Michael Kramer, *The Republic of Rock: Music and Citizenship in the Sixties Counterculture* (Oxford University Press, 2013).

4. Susan Krieger, *Hip Capitalism* (Sage, 1979); Sanneh, "Rap against Rockism."

5. Martin Perlich in *Radio Daze: Cleveland's FM Air Wars* (DVD, Harvard 131 Films, 2008); Billy Bass, author interview, July 12, 2010; *Cleveland Plain Dealer*, March 19, 1971. The best overviews are John Gorman with Tom Feran, *The Buzzard: Inside the Glory Days of WMMS and Cleveland Rock Radio—A Memoir* (Gray & Company, 2007); Mike Olszewski, *Radio Daze: Stories from the Front in Cleveland's FM Air Wars* (Kent State University Press, 2003); Deanna R. Adams, *Rock 'n' Roll and the Cleveland Connection* (Kent State University Press, 2002); Adams, *Cleveland's Rock and Roll Roots* (Arcadia, 2010); and Carlo Wolff, *Cleveland Rock & Roll Memories* (Gray & Company, 2006).

6. Tom Donahue, "A Rotting Corpse, Stinking Up the Airways," *Rolling Stone*, November 23, 1967; Keightley, "Reconsidering Rock"; Kramer, *Republic of Rock*; Olszewski, *Radio Daze*, 72; Richard Neer, *FM: The Rise and Fall of Rock Radio* (Villard, 2001), 4.

7. Christopher Sterling and Michael Keith, *Sounds of Change: A History of FM Broadcasting in America* (University of North Carolina Press, 2008), 154; see also Marc Fisher, *Something in the Air: Radio, Rock, and the Revolution That Shaped a Generation* (Random House, 2007); Bass, interview; *Scene*, February 11–17, 2003; Jack Gould, "Around Country, FM Turns to Rock," *New York Times*, May 20, 1970.

8. Michael Keith, *Voices in the Purple Haze: Underground Radio and the Sixties* (Praeger, 1997), 35, 95, 117–23; for segmenting in general, Lizabeth Cohen, *A Consumers' Republic: The Politics of Mass Consumption in Postwar America* (Knopf, 2003).

9. *The AOR Story* (Radio & Records, 1978), available online at http://www.americanradiohistory.com/Archive%20R&R/R&R-AOR-Story.pdf; *Billboard*, April 5, 1969; *Rolling Stone*, April 2, 1970.

10. *The AOR Story*.

11. Ibid.; *Scene*, March 22–28, 1973; Denny Sanders, author interview, July 13, 2010.

12. Bass, interview; Olszewski, *Radio Daze*, 72; *Scene*, March 22–28, 1973.

13. Greil Marcus, "Rock-a Hula Clarified," *Creem*, June 1971; Waksman, *This Ain't the Summer of Love*, 20.

14. Gorman, *The Buzzard*; Susan Douglas, "Why the Shirelles Matter," in *Where the Girls Are: Growing Up Female with the Mass Media* (Times, 1994), 98; John Gorman, author interview, July 18, 2010; *Scene*, February 11–17, 2003; Olszewski, *Radio Daze*, 104–5.

15. Gorman, *The Buzzard*, 23.

16. Cowie, *Stayin' Alive*, 47–48.

17. Adams, *Cleveland Connection*, 121; "It's a Buzzard Birthday," The Buzzard John Gorman blog, April 16, 2008, http://buzzardbook.wordpress.com/2008/04/16/its-a-buzzard-birthday/; *Wall Street Journal*, March 6, 1985; Gorman, *The Buzzard*, 67.

18. Kid Leo interview, *The Album Network*, n.d., in John Gorman personal folders (source of all subsequent Gorman memos), July 1981; *Scene*, tenth anniversary of WMMS supplement, September 1978; *Scene*, February 11–17, 2003.

19. Sanders, interview.

20. Gorman memos, January 8, 1975; June 6, 1974; January 8, 1975; n.d., in Gorman folders, May 1975; *Radio & Records*, May 9, 1975, copy saved in Gorman folders, May 1975.

21. Gorman memos, July 3, 1975; July 11, 1975; *Radio & Records*, January 23, 1976; Gorman, *The Buzzard*, 92–93.

22. Gorman memo, July 15, 1977.

23. *Radio & Records*, February 10, 1978; October 15, 1976.

24. *The AOR Story*.

25. Ibid.

26. *Scene*, April 13, 1978; *Cleveland Plain-Dealer*, February 19, 1978; *Radio & Records*, February 10, 1978; August 8, 1975; August 19, 1977; Mike Harrison, "AOR" column, *Radio & Records*, May 7, 1976.

27. Claude Hall, "Progressive Rock Listeners Do Wash," *Billboard*, July 27, 1968; Murray Saul, author interview, July 15, 2010.

28. *Radio & Records*, February 10, 1978.

29. Gorman, *The Buzzard*, 135; Olszewski, *Radio Daze*, 125; Louis Masur, *Runaway Dream: "Born to Run" and Bruce Springsteen's American Vision* (Bloomsbury, 2009), 48.

30. Daniel Cavicchi, *Tramps like Us: Music and Meaning among Springsteen Fans* (Oxford University Press, 1998).

31. George Lipsitz, "The Class Origins of Rock and Roll," in *Rainbow at Midnight: Labor and Culture in the 1940s* (University of Illinois Press, 1994), 304, 327;

Lawrence Grossberg, "Another Boring Day in Paradise: Rock and Roll and the Empowerment of Daily Life," in *Dancing in Spite of Myself: Essays on Popular Culture* (Duke University Press, 1994), 29–63.

32. Gorman memo, April 8, 1983.

33. *Radio & Records*, May 3, 1985; May 10, 1985.

34. Cowie, *Stayin' Alive*, 296, 324; Keith, *Voices in the Purple Haze*, 193–94.

35. Gorman memos, July 8, 1980; February 24, 1981; November 7, 1980.

36. Gorman memos, April 8, 1980; *Cleveland Plain-Dealer*, February 15, 1981.

37. Gorman memos, April 8, 1983; April 13, 1983; June 1, 1983; July 25, 1983.

38. Wald, *How the Beatles Destroyed Rock 'n' Roll*, 239–40; Echols, "Shaky Ground," 160, 167; Gorman, *The Buzzard*; *Radio & Records*, June 1, 1979.

39. Gorman memo, September 7, 1983; Gorman, *The Buzzard*, 236; Gaye Ramstrom, author interview, July 16, 2010.

40. Gorman memos, September 1, 1983; August 24, 1983; *Radio & Records*, October 7, 1983; *Friday Morning Quarterback*, April 17, 1985.

41. Gorman, *The Buzzard*, 202–36; Ramstrom, interview; *Radio & Records*, April 5, 1985; April 26, 1985; *Crain's Cleveland Business*, March 24, 1986.

42. *Radio & Records*, January 14, 1983; January 21, 1983; April 1, 1983; April 22, 1983; May 6, 1983; October 7, 1983; December 21, 1984; January 11, 1985; *Billboard*, February 5, 1983.

43. *Billboard*, May 28, 1983; October 22, 1983; November 5, 1983; March 17, 1984; April 14, 1984; May 3, 1985; *Radio & Records*, June 7, 1985.

44. Gorman memos, April 27, 1984; October 30, 1984.

45. Sales department brochures, WMMS and Z-100, 1986 and 1987, collection of Gaye Ramstrom; *Radio & Records*, June 10, 1983.

46. Adams, *Cleveland Connection*, 130–31; *Scene*, February 11–17, 2003; Olszewski, *Radio Daze*, 319–20.

47. Gorman memo, May 17, 1985; Jim Marchyshyn memo, April 5, 1985, in Gorman folders, April 1985; *Radio & Records*, June 27, 1986.

48. *Radio & Records*, July 10, 1987; Jeff Kinzbach, *The Best of the Token Jokes of the Morning as Submitted by WMMS Listeners* (Certain Ethnic Publishing, 1985); *The WMMS Morning Zoo Greatest Hits*, vol. 1 (LP, Arista, 1986).

49. *Cleveland Plain-Dealer*, December 8, 1989; *Radio & Records*, November 10, 1989; December 8, 1989.

50. *Radio & Records*, April 15, 1988; March 9, 1990; January 5, 1990.

51. *USA Today*, May 9, 1984; *Radio & Records*, January 11, 1985.

52. Moore, *Sells like Teen Spirit*; Richard Lloyd, *Neo-Bohemia: Art and Commerce in the Postindustrial City*, second edition (Routledge, 2010).

53. *Radio & Records*, September 11, 1992; May 10, 1996; July 5, 1991; August 16, 1991; January 3, 1992.

54. *Radio & Records*, March 13, 1992; October 2, 1992; December 11, 1992.

55. *Radio & Records*, September 11, 1992; November 5, 1993; March 1, 1996.

56. *Radio & Records*, December 2, 1994; Gorman, interview; Olszewski, *Radio Daze*, 434; copies of *Buzzard Bone* at Music Library and Sound Recording Archives, Bowling Green State University; *Radio & Records*, February 24, 1995.

57. *Radio & Records*, March 19, 1993; October 8, 1993; December 15, 1995; September 13, 1996.

58. *Radio Daze* DVD.

59. *Radio & Records*, October 7, 1994; March 14, 1997; February 16, 1996; *Washington Post*, February 25, 1999.

60. *Radio & Records*, October 8, 1993; November 15, 1996; December 13, 1996.

61. *Radio & Records*, July 4, 1997; February 21, 1997; April 24, 1998.

62. *Radio & Records*, March 14, 1997; November 7, 1997.

63. *Radio & Records*, July 17, 1998; February 12, 1999; May 28, 1999; February 11, 2000; August 18, 2000.

64. *Radio & Records*, January 20, 1988; *Cleveland Plain-Dealer*, August 6, 1992.

65. Gorman, interview; *Weekend All Things Considered*, March 15, 2008.

66. Reed Bunzell, *Clear Vision: The Story of Clear Channel Communications* (Bright Sky Press, 2008), 89; Ramstrom, interview; *Forbes*, February 18, 2010.

67. Gorman memo, April 28, 1978.

Chapter Six

1. *Billboard*, January 13, 2001.

2. *Billboard*, January 12, 2002; January 11, 2003; January 10, 2004; January 15, 2005; January 14, 2006; January 13, 2007; January 5, 2008; January 10, 2009; January 16, 2010.

3. Steve Knopper, *Appetite for Self-Destruction: The Spectacular Crash of the Record Industry in the Digital Age* (Free Press, 2009), 250; Keith Caulfield and Geoff Mayfield, "Seeds of Doubt: 15 Years of Nielsen SoundScan Data Reveal Just How Rare Artist Growth Stories Have Become," *Billboard*, September 1, 2007; Chris Anderson *The Long Tail: Why the Future of Business Is Selling Less of More* (Hyperion, 2006); Anita Elberse, "Should You Invest in the Long Tail?," *Harvard Business Review*, July–August, 2008; Elberse, *Blockbusters: Hit-making, Risk-taking, and the Big Business of Entertainment* (Henry Holt, 2013).

4. Eric Harvey, "The Social History of the MP3," *Pitchfork*, August 24, 2009; Jerry Del Colliano cited in Greg Kot, *Ripped: How the Wired Generation Revolutionized Music* (Simon & Schuster, 2009), 23; Steven Levy, *The Perfect Thing: How the iPod Shuffles Commerce, Culture, and Coolness* (Simon & Schuster, 2006), 3; Fred Turner, *From Counterculture to Cyberculture: Stewart Brand, the Whole Earth Network, and the Rise of Digital Utopianism* (University of Chicago Press, 2006); David Kusck and Gerd Leonhard, *The Future of Music: Manifesto for the Digital Revolution* (Berklee Press, 2005), 26.

5. Patrick Burkart and Tom McCourt, *Digital Music Wars: Ownership and Control of the Celestial Jukebox* (Rowman & Littlefield, 2006), 4, 37; Henry Jenkins, *Convergence Culture: Where Old and New Media Collide*, revised edition (New York University Press, 2008), 59–92; Levy, *Perfect Thing*, 2; Jeremy Morris, "Understanding the Digital Music Commodity" (PhD dissertation, McGill University, 2010).

6. Leslie M. Meier, "Promotional Ubiquitous Musics: Recording Artists, Brands, and 'Rendering Authenticity,'" *Popular Music and Society* 34, no. 4 (2011): 399–415; Timothy Taylor, *The Sounds of Capitalism: Advertising, Music, and the Conquest of Culture* (University of Chicago Press, 2012), 214–25.

7. H. Jenkins, *Convergence Culture*; Aram Sinreich, *Mashed Up: Music, Technology, and the Rise of Configurable Culture* (University of Massachusetts Press, 2010).

8. Mark Anthony Neal, "Rhythm & Bullshit? The Slow Decline of R&B," http://www.popmatters.com, June 3, 10, 30, 2005; July 22, 2005.

9. *Airplay Monitor*, February 7, 2003.

10. *Billboard*, September 21, 2002; *Airplay Monitor*, June 20, 2003; *Billboard*, October 18, 2003; *Airplay Monitor*, January 10, 2003; *Billboard*, March 8, 2003; *Airplay Monitor*, July 29, 2005.

11. *Airplay Monitor*, October 24, 2003; October 3, 2003.

12. *Billboard*, February 5, 2005; July 30, 2005; Keith Negus, *Music Genres and Corporate Cultures* (Routledge, 1999); *Airplay Monitor*, October 3, 2003; October 17, 2003; *Billboard*, April 22, 2005; Chris Molanphy, "100 & Single: The R&B/Hip-Hop Factor in the Music Business's Endless Slump," *Village Voice*, July 16, 2012; *Radio & Records*, January 16, 2009.

13. *Radio & Records*, February 8, 2008; October 26, 2007; July 20, 2007; June 22, 2007; Kelefa Sanneh, "In Search of New York at a Hip-Hop Summit," *New York Times*, June 5, 2007.

14. *Billboard*, May 12, 2001; *Airplay Monitor*, October 29, 2004; Wade Jessen, "Country" column, *Radio & Records*, October 27, 2006.

15. *Airplay Monitor*, June 20, 2003; *Billboard*, February 7, 2004; Nadine Hubbs, "'Redneck Woman' and the Gendered Poetics of Class Rebellion," *Southern Cultures* 17, no. 4 (2011): 44–70; *Billboard*, November 19, 2005; April 7, 2007; July 26, 2008.

16. Negus, *Music Genres and Corporate Cultures*, 103–30; *Billboard*, November 17, 2007; June 18, 2005; December 24, 2005; November 1, 2008; October 28, 2006; August 4, 2007.

17. *Billboard*, October 21, 2006; *Radio & Records*, September 7, 2007; *Billboard*, November 11, 2006.

18. *Billboard*, April 21, 2001; Gabriel Rossman, *Climbing the Charts: What Radio Airplay Tells Us about the Diffusion of Innovation* (Princeton University Press, 2012), 59–70; *Airplay Monitor*, February 28, 2003.

19. *Billboard Radio Monitor*, February 6, 2006.

20. *Airplay Monitor*, June 27, 2003; Joshua Clover, *1989: Bob Dylan Didn't Have This to Sing About* (University of California Press, 2009), 73–89.

21. *Airplay Monitor*, March 14, 2003; *Billboard*, March 6, 2004; March 13, 2004; November 5, 2005.

22. *Billboard*, December 21, 2002; *Airplay Monitor*, July 18, 2003; Carter Alan, *Radio Free Boston: The Rise and Fall of WBCN* (Northeastern, 2013).

23. *Airplay Monitor*, March 7, 2003; Clive Davis with Anthony DeCurtis, *The Soundtrack of My Life* (Simon & Schuster, 2012), 489–90.

24. *Airplay Monitor*, August 20, 2004; Samuel Dwinell, "Rock, Enroll: Music and Militarization since 9/11," Gerritt Roessler, "Walking the Great Line: Underoath and Christian Fundamentalism in Punk Rock after 9/11," and Kathryn Wright, "Nine Inch Nails' *Year Zero* and the Biopolitics of Media Convergence," all in *The Politics of Post-9/11 Music: Sound, Trauma, and the Music Industry in the Time of Terror*, ed. Joseph Fisher and Brian Flota (Ashgate, 2011), 13–30, 173–84, 93–106.

25. Richard Lloyd, *Neo-Bohemia: Art and Commerce in the Postindustrial City*, second edition (Routledge, 2010); Kot, *Ripped*; *Radio & Records*, April 18, 2008; Bethany Klein, "The New Radio: Music Licensing as a Response to Industry Woe," *Media, Culture & Society* 30, no. 4 (2008): 463–78; Taylor, *Sounds of Capitalism*; Kiri Miller, *Playing Along: Digital Games, YouTube, and Virtual Performance* (Oxford University Press, 2012).

26. *Airplay Monitor*, December 16, 2005; Deborah Pacini Hernandez, *Oye Como Va! Hybridity and Identity in Latino Popular Music* (Temple University Press, 2010), 142–62.

27. Ricky Martin, *Me* (Celebra, 2010), 80, 125; *Billboard*, June 20, 2009.

28. *Billboard*, May 12, 2001; July 21, 2001; May 10, 2003; George Lipsitz, *Footsteps in the Dark: The Hidden Histories of Popular Music* (University of Minnesota Press, 2007), 54–78; Dolores Inés Casillas, "'¡Puuurrrooo MÉXICO!': Listening to Transnationalism on U.S. Spanish-Language Radio," in *Beyond El Barrio: Everyday Life in Latina/o America*, ed. Gina Pérez, Frank Guridy, and Adrian Burgos (New York University Press, 2010), 44–62.

29. Hernandez, *Oye Como Va!*, 142–62; *Billboard*, February 17, 2001.

30. *Radio & Records*, August 6, 1982; *Airplay Monitor*, November 12, 2004; April 22, 2005; *Billboard*, September 8, 2007.

31. *Billboard*, November 9, 2002; Wayne Marshall, "From Música Negra to Reggaeton Latino: The Cultural Politics of Nation, Migration, and Commercialization," Frances Negrón-Muntaner, "Poetry of Filth," and Tego Calderón, "Black Pride," all in *Reggaeton*, ed. Raquel Rivera, Wayne Marshall, and Deborah Pacini Hernandez (Duke University Press, 2009), 19–76, 324–40; *Billboard*, August 20, 2005; *Billboard Radio Monitor*, September 23, 2005; *Billboard*, September 8, 2007.

32. *Billboard*, July 21, 2001; July 27, 2002; April 25, 2009.

33. *Billboard*, January 24, 2004; January 17, 2009; April 4, 2009; June 21, 2008; April 12, 2008.

34. Mireya Navarro, "Between Gags, a D.J. Rallies Immigrants," *New York Times*, April 30, 2006; *New Yorker*, October 23, 2006; *Billboard*, May 13, 2006; October 11, 2008; Adrián Félix, Carmen González, and Ricardo Ramírez, "Political Protest, Ethnic Media, and Latino Naturalization," *American Behavioral Scientist* 52, no. 4 (2008): 618–34.

35. *Radio & Records*, CHR special package, May 1, 2009.

36. *Billboard*, April 26, 2008; *Radio & Records*, January 1, 2008; *Billboard*, February 7, 2009.

37. *Billboard*, May 12, 2001; October 20, 2004.

38. *Radio & Records*, October 13, 2006; June 27, 2008; July 4, 2008.

39. Sasha Frere-Jones, "1 + 1 + 1 = 1," *New Yorker*, January 10, 2005; Karen Tongson, "The Grain of Glee," *In Media Res*, April 5, 2010; *Airplay Monitor*, June 13, 2003.

40. *Billboard*, January 17, 2004; *Airplay Monitor*, October 21, 2005.

41 Sean Ross, "Just How Standardized Are Today's Radio Stations?," *Billboard*, August 2, 2003; Rossman, *Climbing the Charts*, 11–43; Richard Peterson, "Why 1955? Explaining the Advent of Rock Music," *Popular Music* 9, no. 1 (1990): 97–116.

42. Rossman, *Climbing the Charts*; Hua Hsu, "A Song So Awful It Hurts the Mind," *Slate*, December 6, 2005.

43. *Rolling Stone*, February 21, 2008; Joshua Gamson, *Freaks Talk Back: Tabloid Talk Shows and Sexual Nonconformity* (University of Chicago Press, 1999).

44. Rachel Devitt, "Lost in Translation: Filipino Diaspora(s), Postcolonial Hip Hop, and the Problems of Keeping It Real for the 'Contentless' Black Eyed Peas," *Asian Music* 39, no. 1 (2008): 108–34; Christine Bacareza Balance, "Hooligans in Wondaland, Gibson Amphitheatre, Universal City, June 21, 2011," *Journal of Popular Music Studies* 23, no. 4 (2011): 489–94; Jon Caramanica, "Bruno Mars in Ascension," *New York Times*, October 5, 2010.

45. Davis, *Soundtrack of My Life*; Clive Davis with James Willwerth, *Clive: Inside the Record Business* (William Morrow, 1975).

46. Gary Trust, "Why Isn't R&B Radio Shopping at the 'Thrift Shop'?," *Billboard*, January 26, 2013.

47. Karl Hagstrom Miller, *Segregating Sound: Inventing Folk and Pop Music in the Age of Jim Crow* (Duke University Press, 2010).

48. Jean-Christophe Agnew, *Worlds Apart: The Market and the Theater in Anglo-American Thought, 1550–1750* (Cambridge University Press, 1986); Peter Fornatale and Joshua Mills, *Radio in the Television Age* (Overlook Press, 1980), xv–xxv.

49. James Gregory, *The Southern Diaspora: How the Great Migrations of Black and White Southerners Transformed America* (University of North Carolina Press,

2005); Elaine Tyler May, *Homeward Bound: American Families in the Cold War Era* (Basic Books, 1988); for Robert Christgau's notion of monoculture, see Devon Powers, *Writing the Record: The Village Voice and the Birth of Rock Criticism* (University of Massachusetts Press, 2013).

50. Bruce Schulman, *The Seventies: The Great Shift in American Culture, Society, and Politics* (Free Press, 2001); Eric Schlosser, *Fast Food Nation: The Dark Side of the All-American Meal* (Houghton Mifflin, 2001).

Index

Page numbers followed by *f* indicate a figure.

movement and, 23–24, 30–31, 47–54; on contemporary hit radio (CHR), 222; in country music venues, 79, 87; disco and, 19, 32, 62–64; funk of, 14, 16, 48–50, 57, 197, 219–20; gospel roots of, 33–36, 41, 61, 277n15; hip-hop of, 64–67, 263; racial packaging of, 16; in Top 40 format, 15–16, 30, 40–41, 46–47, 66, 243; in the 2000s, 242–45; urban contemporary sound of, 13, 30–31, 53, 69, 242–45; vaudeville circuit of, 31–32; versatility and eclecticism of, 33, 35, 38, 40, 42; white backlash and, 59–64. *See also* race; rhythm and blues format; soul genre
black nationalism, 23–24, 30–31, 47–54
Black Rock Coalition, 30–31
Blackwell, Chris, 129, 147
Blair, Tony, 24, 159, 186
Blake, Andrew, 188
Blauel, Renate, 180
blaxploitation, 54, 61
BLF Bash, 219
bluegrass, 79, 102
Bluesology, 160, 165
Boehme, Gerry, 224
Bogart, Neal, 61–63
Bolan, Marc, 169–70
Born in the U.S.A., 198, 226
"Born to Run," 198, 214–15, 236
Bortnick, Chuck, 225, 228
Bouvard, Pierre, 226
Bowie, David, 159, 178; AOR and, 202–4, 217; on black music, 64; fluid sexuality of, 170–71, 180, 190
boy bands, 191
Boy George, 183, 196
Bradford, Perry, 31
Branson, Missouri, 105
Brass Are Comin', The, 121–23
"Break It to Me Gently," 19
Brenner, Becky, 246
Brill Building writers, 7, 42–43, 95–96, 132
British invasions, 22; by the Beatles and pop, 6, 11, 44, 124, 162–65, 174; by New Pop, 183–84; by Pop Art, 156f, 160–63, 176f; by punk, 146, 181
Brooks, Garth, 15, 26, 72–73, 107, 238, 245
Brother, Brother, Brother, 52
Brother Rice High School, 28
The Brothers: Isley, 51

Brothers Johnson, 132, 138, 140, 144
Brown, Amos, 32
Brown, Chris, 241
Brown, James, 19, 33, 42, 48, 69, 256–57; funk of, 219; at the Grand Ole Opry, 79; identity pride of, 31, 44, 49–50, 86; on the Isley Brothers, 46; on Nixon, 49
Brown Skin Models, 34, 263
Bruce, Denny, 131
Bruce, Larry, 226
bubblegum pop, 61
Buddah Records, 61
Burkart, Patrick, 240
Burkhart, Kent, 183, 210
Burnstein, Cliff, 204
Burton, Dewey, 204–5
Burton, Jolene, 133
Burton, Peter, 160
Butler, Jay, 179

Cafaro, Al, 239
Café Society cabaret, 9–10, 50
Calderón, Tego, 255
Calderone, Tom, 229
Calloway, Cab, 36
Campbell, Olive Dean, 75
"Candle in the Wind," 24, 159, 175, 179, 186, 191
Captain Fantastic and the Brown Dirt Cowboy, 160, 161f
Captain & Tennille, 115, 138, 141
Caramanica, Jon, 262, 264
Carey, Mariah, 15, 152
Carmichael, Stokely, 47–48
Carpenter, Karen, 26, 133–36
Carpenter, Richard, 133–36
Carpenters, the, 22, 112, 114–16, 128, 133–36, 138, 153
Carr, Vikki, 137
Carson, Johnny, 3, 21, 70, 73, 95–97, 101, 105
Carson, Tom, 96
Carter, Dan, 84–85
Carter, Jimmy, 70, 90, 92–94, 103, 144
Carter Family, 72, 75
Cash, Johnny, 26, 81, 83, 84, 86, 99–100, 111
Casillas, Dolores Inés, 253
CBS FM, 201
Cecil, Malcolm, 53, 68
Cedric the Entertainer, 55
Chambers, Iain, 162–64